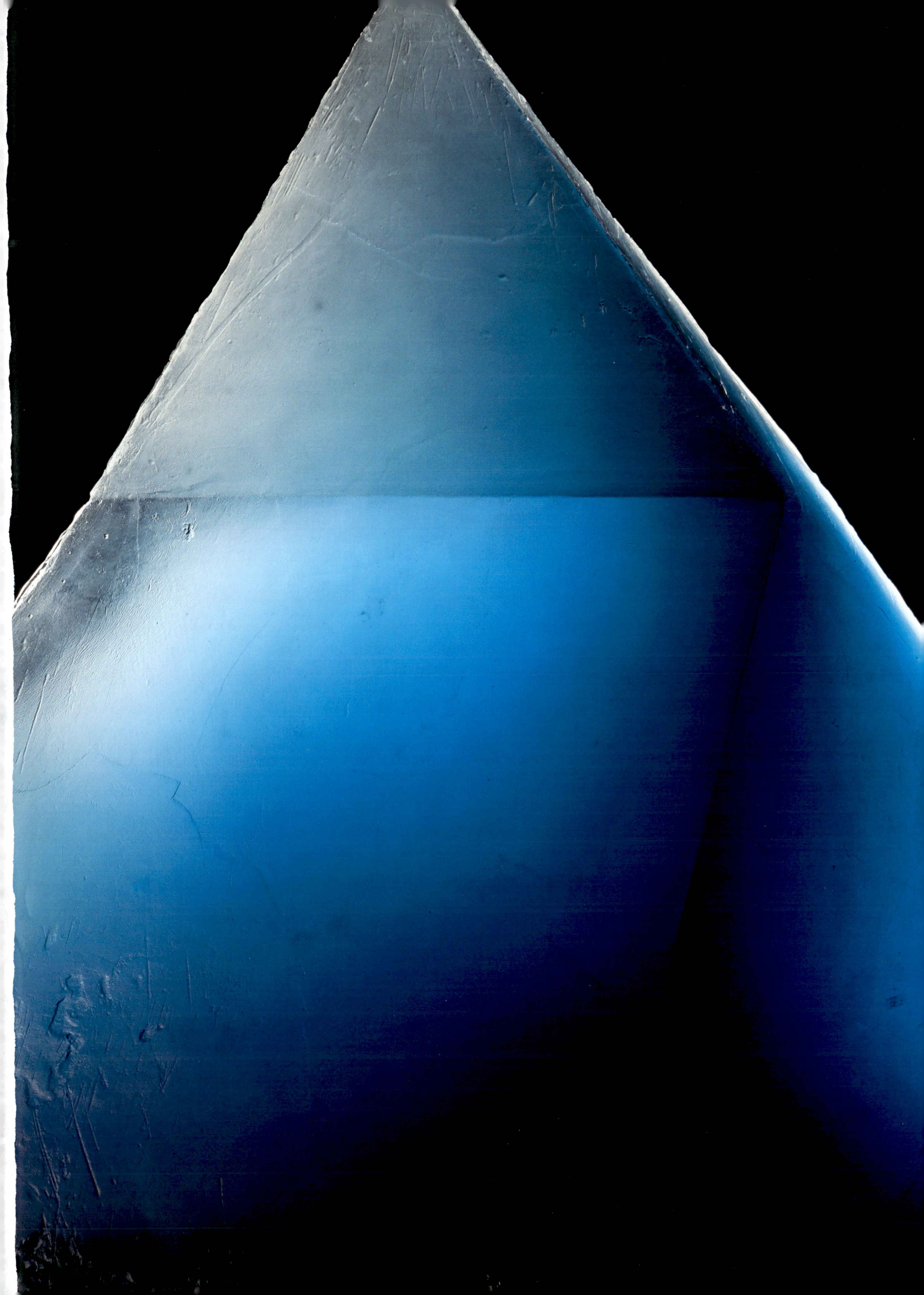

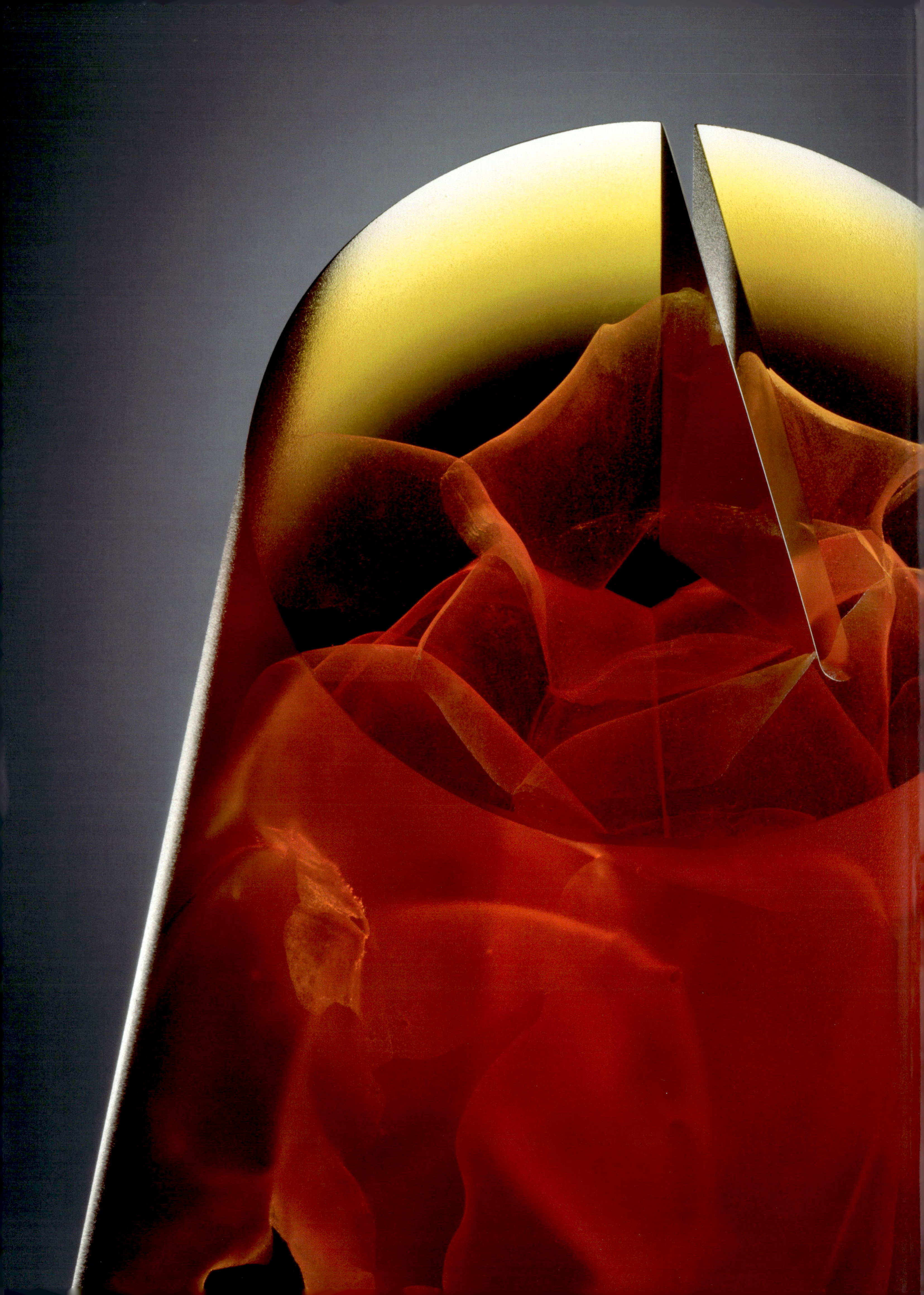

THE GLASS COLLECTION

Flint Institute of Arts, Flint, Michigan

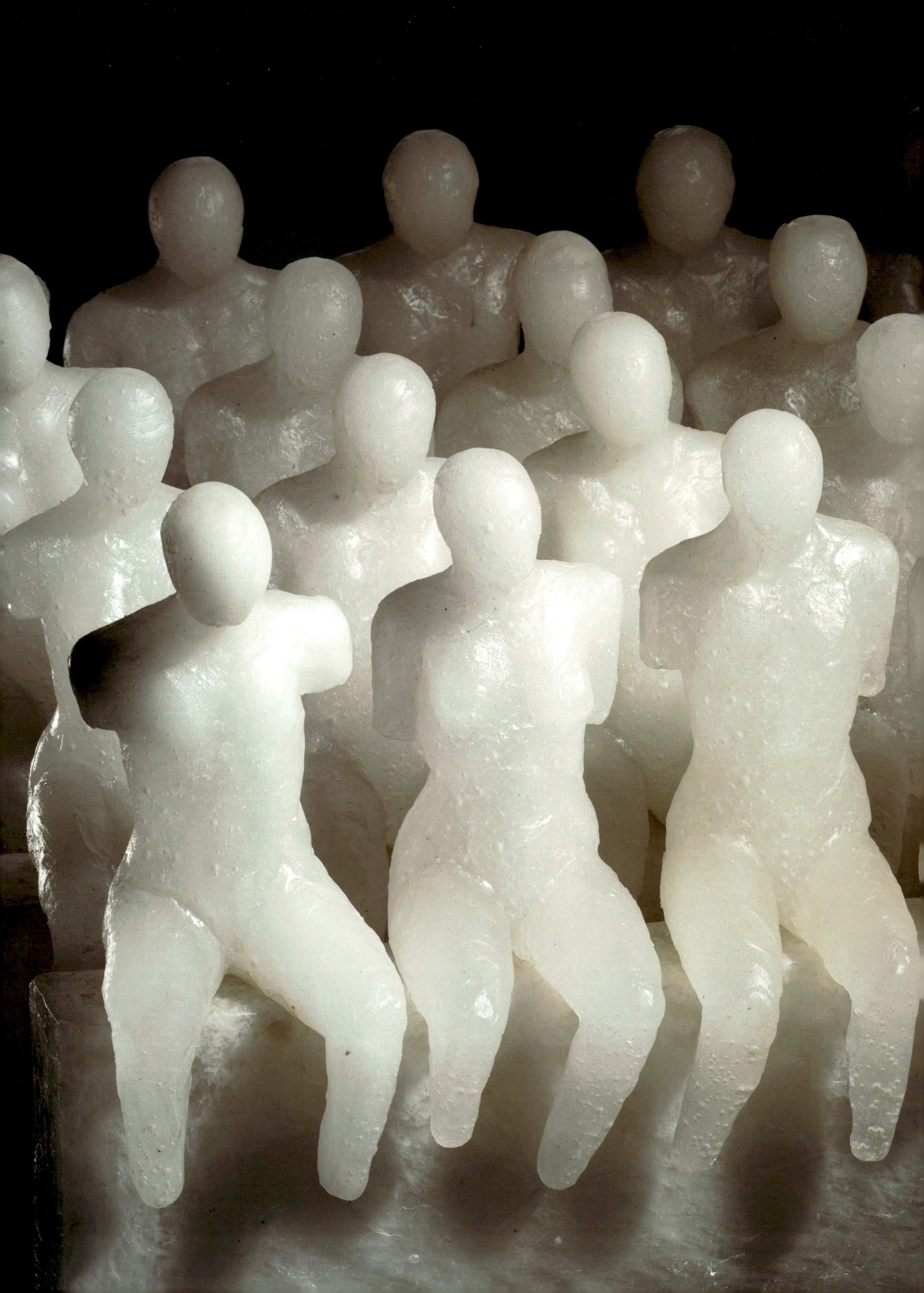

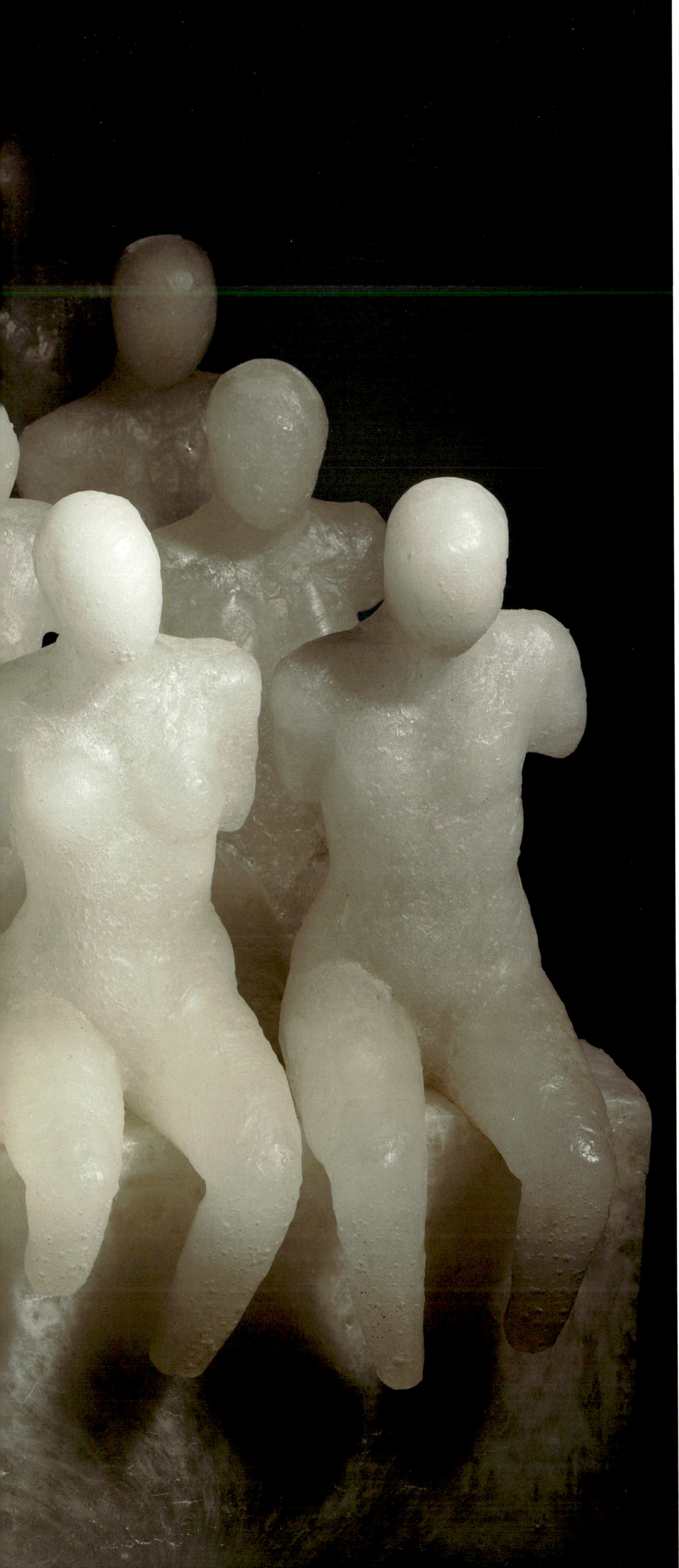

Contents

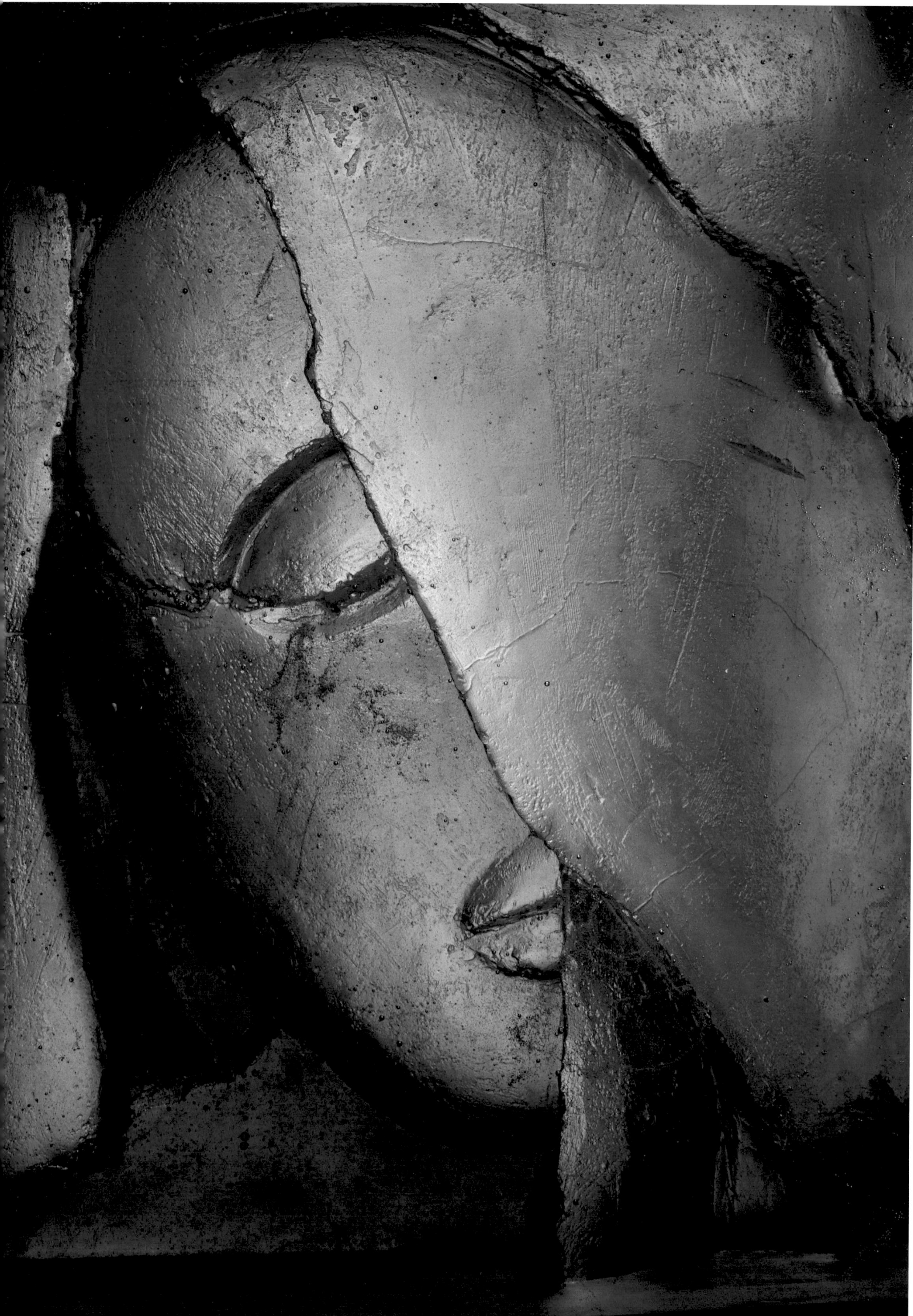

Contemporary Craft in Flint

JOHN B. HENRY,
EXECUTIVE DIRECTOR,
FLINT INSTITUTE OF ARTS

Since its founding in the 1800s, Flint, known first for carriages, then later cars, has been a community of makers. About 1910, the city entered a period of radical change that led to the tremendous growth of the automobile industry. Figures like William (Billy) Durant, J. Dallas Dort, Walter P. Chrysler, Charles W. Nash, and Charles Stewart Mott established what would become General Motors. Of these captains of industry, some chose to lead from Flint and, in the process, contributed to the long and distinguished history of the Flint Institute of Arts (FIA; fig. 1). Generations of mechanical and skilled trades workers who innovate, create, invent, and embrace new technology made Flint the ideal city in which to have both an Art School and a Museum. Additionally, many of the city's great leaders had the vision and courage, through good times and bad, to sustain the service, creativity, and commitment to excellence that have become the hallmarks of the FIA. This legacy continues today with individuals, businesses, and foundations supporting the vision of an expanded Art School and Museum that focus on lifelong learning opportunities that are a natural extension of the interests, skills, and abilities of its community.

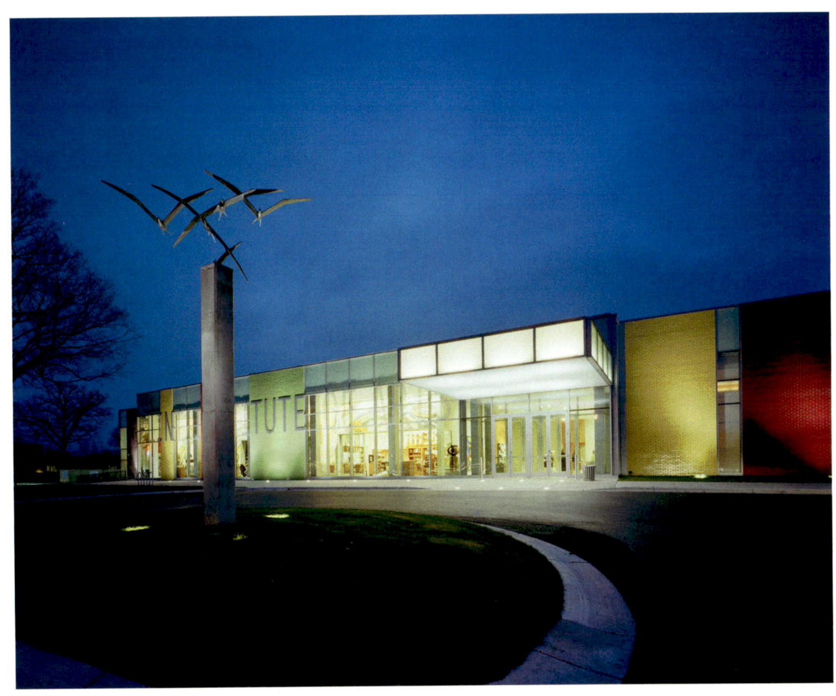

FIGURE 1. Flint Institute of Arts (FIA) in the Flint Cultural Center

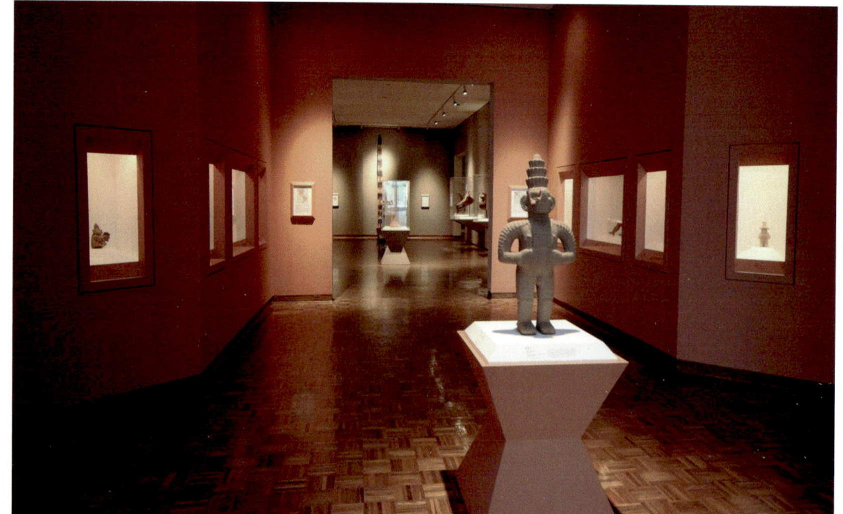

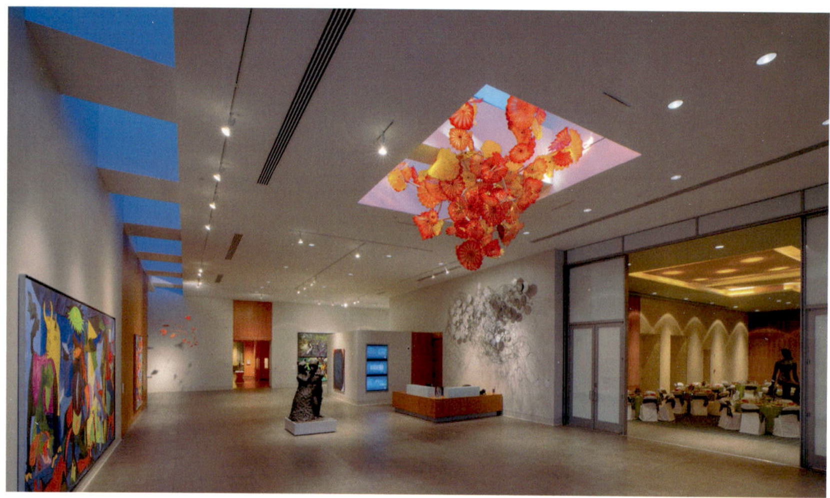

For almost ninety years, the Flint Institute of Arts, the second largest art museum in the state of Michigan, has been a part of Flint's industrial history by fusing the sometimes disparate experiences of art-making and art-viewing with an Art School and Museum. Established in 1928 as an Art School, it still functions today as a teaching institution dedicated to visual arts education. Today, the collection, which began in 1929 with the first work purchased by public subscription and now numbers more than 8,000 objects—from ancient to contemporary (figs. 2–3), is our most enduring legacy, one that reveals the tastes, intellects, and interests of a community that had such an impressive and lasting influence on American industry and design. With the addition of a new wing focusing on Contemporary Craft, as well as a glassmaking space in the Art School, the FIA builds upon and highlights the long tradition of craft in Flint. The Contemporary Craft wing features the long-term loan of twenty-first-century glass from the Isabel Foundation of the Sherwin and Shirley Glass collection as well as gifts of ceramics from Dr. Robert and Deanna Harris Burger of the same period, roughly the mid-1960s to the present.

WHAT IS CRAFT?

"Contemporary craft is about making things," according to Laurie Britton-Newell, curator at the Victoria & Albert Museum, London, "It is an intellectual and physical activity where the maker explores the infinite possibilities of materials and processes to produce unique objects." Throughout history, the boundaries between fine art and craft have often been blurred—in the Middle Ages, for example, mediums such as painting and sculpture were considered "craft" but today they would be classified as fine art. In the nineteenth century, shortly after the Industrial Revolution, English and American artists began the Arts and Crafts Movement that challenged these boundaries, with artists simultaneously working in furniture, textiles, and ceramics, as well as painting and sculpture. In the twentieth century in the United States, artists once again explored and deconstructed the boundaries between fine and applied arts. The most significant areas of experimentation and innovation were in the field of ceramics and glass.

MAKING CRAFT AT THE FIA

There is a long history of teaching fine and applied arts at the FIA Art School. Ceramics, in particular, is the largest and most popular department, and enrollment continues to grow. In 1930, the FIA introduced a clay modeling class under the direction of J. Emmet Shultz, a ceramic modeler at the Flint Faience & Tile Company, a subsidiary of AC Spark Plug and one of the best Arts and Crafts tile companies in the United States in the 1920s and 1930s. According to the September 28, 1930, *Flint Daily Journal*, the class embraced "not only the making of pottery for personal enjoyment but [provided] an understanding of the modeling requirements of the industrial world." In addition, several FIA Art School instructors worked at the tile company.

The educational value of connecting works in the permanent collection created by masters in the field to the studio hands-on experience has always been central to our mission (fig. 4). With the addition of a comprehensive glassmaking program in the Art School to an already successful ceramics program, visitors explore for themselves the parallel stories and similar approaches that exist between glass and ceramics. Currently, the Art School offers instruction in three glassmaking techniques—slumping, fusing, and mosaic—and a new flamework studio has just been completed. Hot glassmaking at the FIA enables the Institute to continue the tradition of craft in our community and provide a new visual component to the general visitor that includes not only the museum experience, but also the opportunity to witness the process of art being made.

To accomplish this, the Art School courtyard, which is adjacent to the Claire Mott White Art School wing, has been converted into a more functional and utilitarian art-making space to present live glass- and ceramic-making demonstrations. This provides a unique context for understanding

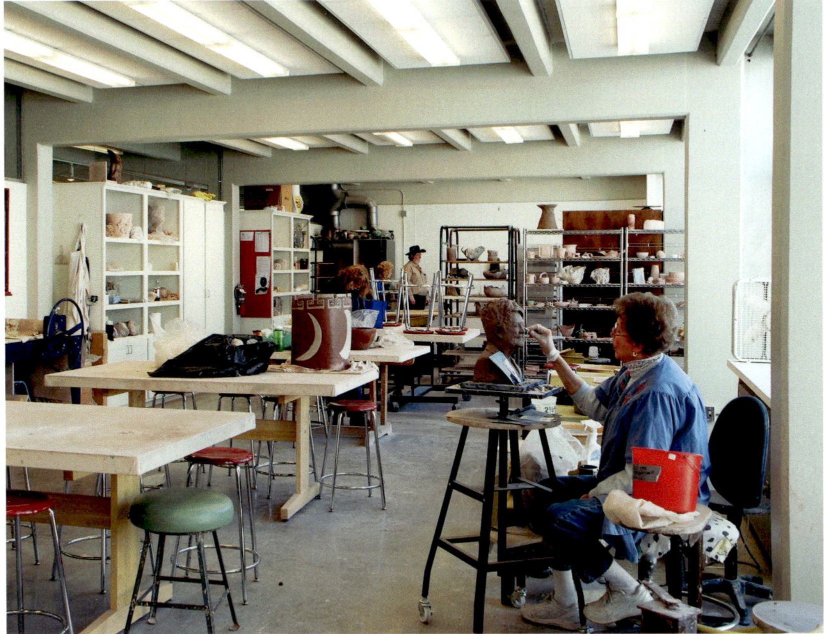

FIGURE 4. Kathryn Sharbaugh Ceramics Studio in the FIA Art School

the works on view, with visitors watching something made and then seeing in the galleries similar artistic expressions. By offering the excitement of the live process and the satisfaction of the finished product, we answer the frequently heard question: "How did they do that?"

HISTORY OF GLASS AND ITS CONNECTION TO CERAMICS

Though artisans have been exploring the characteristics of glass (from vessels to jewelry to ornamentation) for thousands of years, the artistic potential of glass has only been explored in earnest in the last fifty to sixty years. In the nineteenth and early twentieth centuries, glass objects (such as paperweights or vases) were made in factories or studio workshops, and though seen as artful they were not an expression of an individual artist. Glass as a medium of the fine arts, and thus an individual expression of the artist, emerged in the 1960s during the Studio Glass Movement, which took place mainly in the United States.

In 1962, Harvey Littleton organized an eight-day glassblowing workshop at the Toledo Museum of Art. This event, held at an established museum, helped create an acceptance for glass as a medium for fine art, especially among universities teaching art. Littleton, credited with liberating glass from the factory setting, pioneered the development of small furnaces that allowed artists (mostly potters) to work with the material in their studios.

The studio glass field continued to expand in the 1960s and 1970s, with artists' skills improving and a greater number of universities establishing programs specifically devoted to glassmaking. During the 1980s, American studio glass became a global movement, with exhibitions devoted to glass held around the world. New techniques, such as casting, fusing, and flameworking, were embraced by artists. Several technical improvements affected works of this period, including an increase in colors available and the growth in production of large-scale sculpture. By the 1990s, artists began to produce objects in workshops because of the many technical demands of the process. It was also during this time that access to glass-making was greatly increased through public studios across the United States.

In the last decade and a half, glass artists have continued to build on the technological and aesthetic developments of those who came before, moving design and contemporary art into new directions. These artists continue to demonstrate that glass is the ultimate contemporary material: singular in its ability to change color and texture and offering a surprising capacity for variety in shape, size, and subject matter.

GLASS TRANSCENDS THE ORDINARY

"Glass is light," according to glass artist Jaroslava Brychtová, "We introduce the light dynamic into the center of the glass mass. That is the definition of the fourth dimension, which cannot be achieved in any other material." While glass seems to be an ordinary material (we use it every day and it surrounds us), its property of transparency lends it an otherworldly presence, because it can be looked through, yet remain solid. It's this paradoxical quality (fragile and strong, colored and colorless, light-reflecting and light-absorbing) that fascinates viewers.

It is also a medium that is less threatening to most viewers in contrast to an abstract painting, for example. Viewers marvel at the abstract shapes of Dale Chihuly's *Flint Institute of Arts Persian Chandelier* in the FIA Lobby (see fig. 3), never once questioning its reason for being or the intentions of the artist. An abstract painting or sculpture of a different material, on

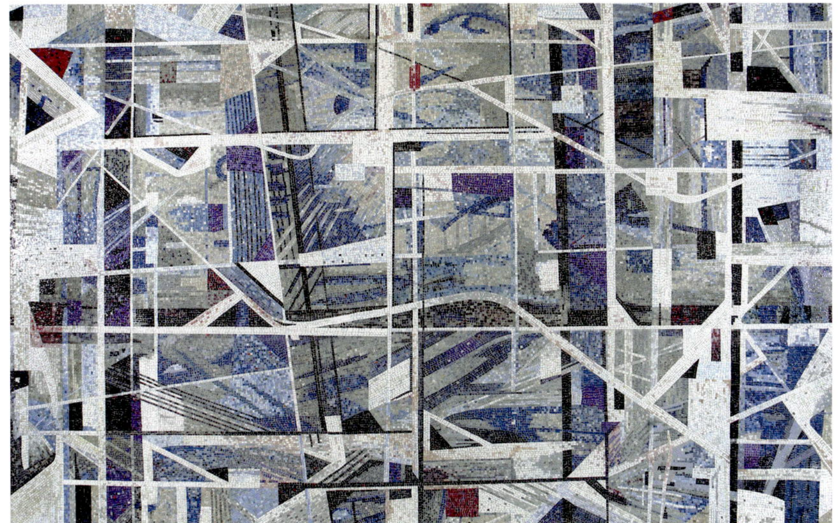

the other hand, often leaves visitors scratching their heads wondering how they should react.

POPULARITY OF GLASS AT THE FIA

Over the years, as public demand for expanded offerings increased, the FIA relocated to more accommodating facilities. At the same time, a tradition was established of presenting loan exhibitions of the highest quality art borrowed from collectors, dealers, and museums. As a result, the public developed an ever-increasing appetite for larger and more impressive offerings. From the modest space it occupied in 1928 in the Brownson-Fisher Building on East Third Street, the FIA moved to two other addresses downtown before moving to its present location in the Flint Cultural Center. Progressively bigger, each space provided more and larger galleries and studio classrooms.

When the FIA moved into its current location in 1958, two commissions were installed on permanent public display. These works included a stained glass window titled *Dove of Peace* (12' × 7') by Abraham Rattner and two glass mosaic murals titled *Industrialization of Flint* (10' × 18') and *Spirit of Cultural Development* (10' × 16') by Edmund Lewandowski (fig. 5). These works began the FIA's history of collecting and exhibiting glass. In the late 1960s, the heirs of Mrs. Viola E. Bray (known also for her important gift of the Viola E. Bray Renaissance Gallery and its masterworks of tapestries and decorative arts; fig. 6) donated her collection of important eighteenth-century etched crystal goblets and nineteenth-century paperweights. Since

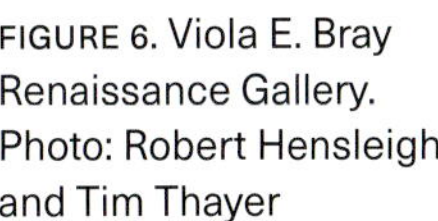

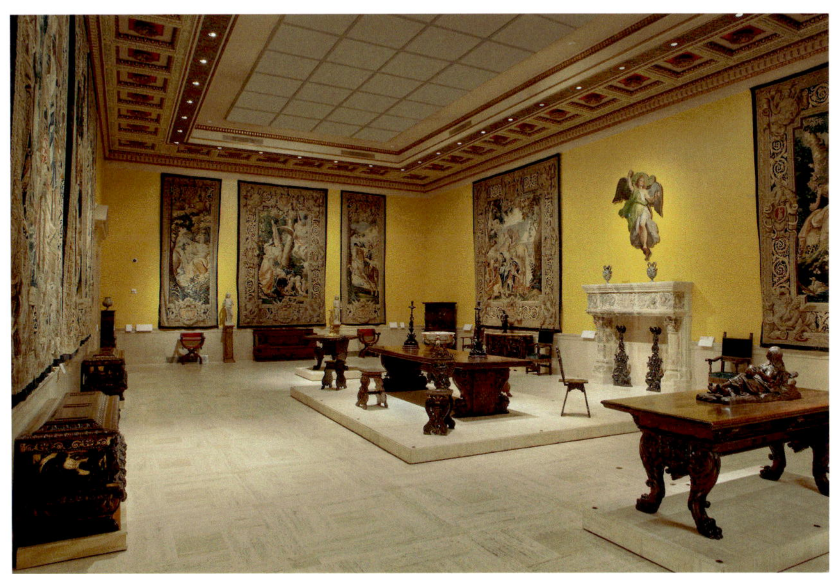

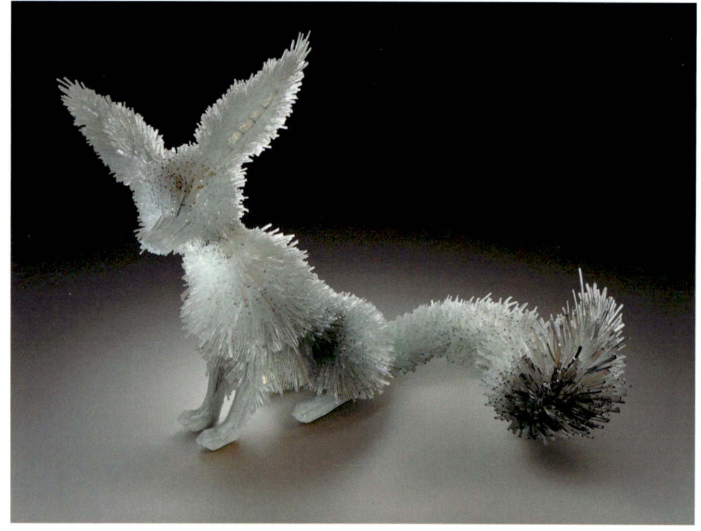

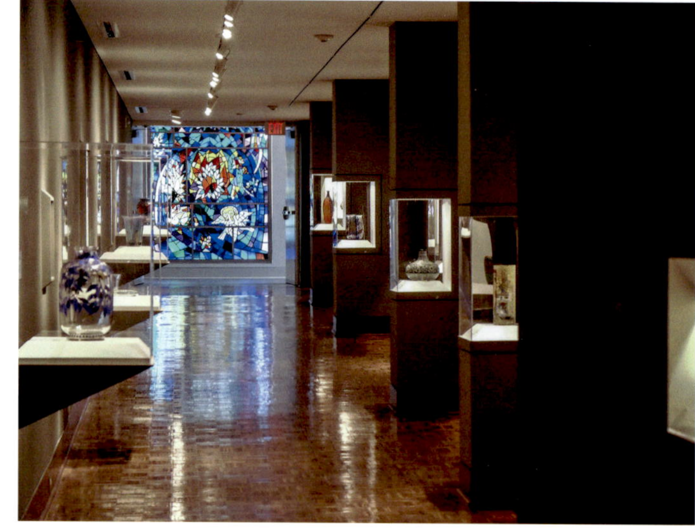

then, the FIA glass collection has grown through gifts of works by contemporary artists, including Dale Chihuly, Harvey Littleton, Kari Russell-Pool, Pawel Borowski, Marvin Lipofsky, Ann Wolff, and Marta Klonowska, to name a few (fig. 7).

In 2009, the FIA welcomed the largest number of visitors in its history with two blockbuster exhibitions: *Blown Away: International Glass of the 21st Century* and *Dale Chihuly: Seaforms*. Also in 2009, the FIA commissioned Chihuly with funds donated by Claire and William S. White, the Charles Stewart Mott Foundation, and the Isabel Foundation to create the *Flint Institute of Arts Persian Chandelier* installed in the FIA Lobby. This was followed by near record attendance for a retrospective exhibition of the esteemed Italian glass master Lino Tagliapietra in 2010. In 2012, the FIA opened a new decorative arts gallery (now named the Ann K. Walch-Chan Decorative Arts Gallery; fig. 8) with the popular exhibition, *Captured in Glass*, featuring a survey of more than 200 glass paperweights from the nineteenth century to present day, followed by an exhibition of French Art Deco glass from the Ed and Karen Ogul Collection. And most recently, the FIA unveiled a stained-glass window by Louis Comfort Tiffany, the first work by this artist to enter the collection, given to the FIA by the Bishop-Miner Family (fig. 9).

It is clear from visitor reactions (and museum shop sales—the highest during the glass exhibitions) that most people share a fascination with the beauty of glass. So pervasive in our daily experience, this medium resonates in a specific and personal way and nearly everyone can admire the artists' skillful manipulation of the materials and appreciate the imagination of artists who create glass works as art.

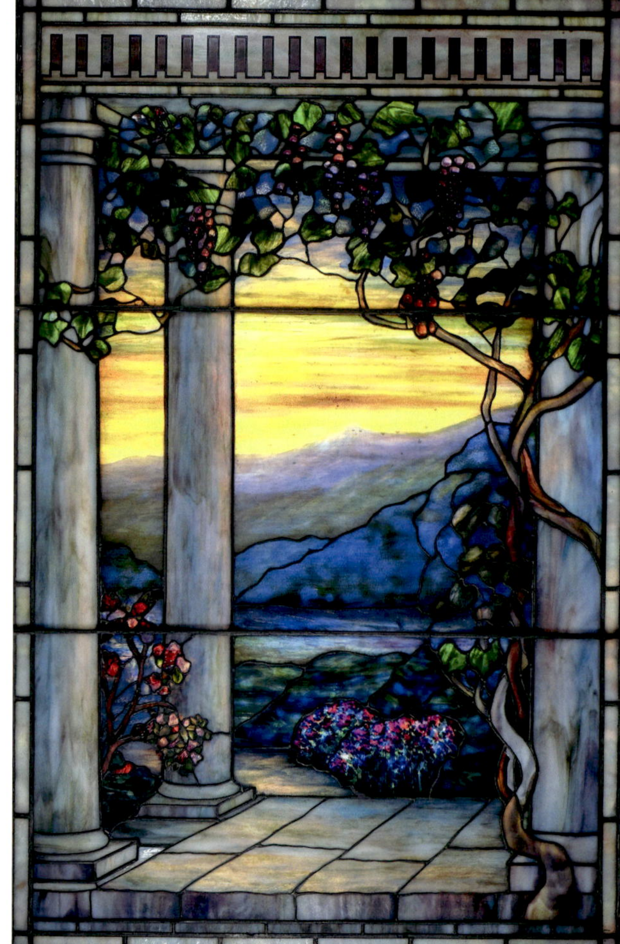

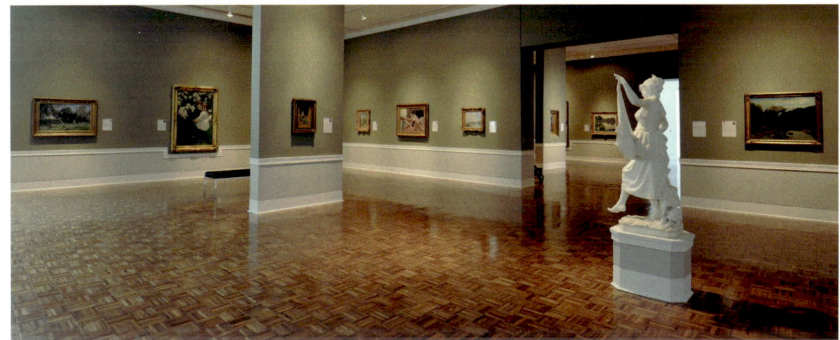

FIGURE 10. Johnson and Rabiah Galleries, featuring nineteenth- and early twentieth-century art

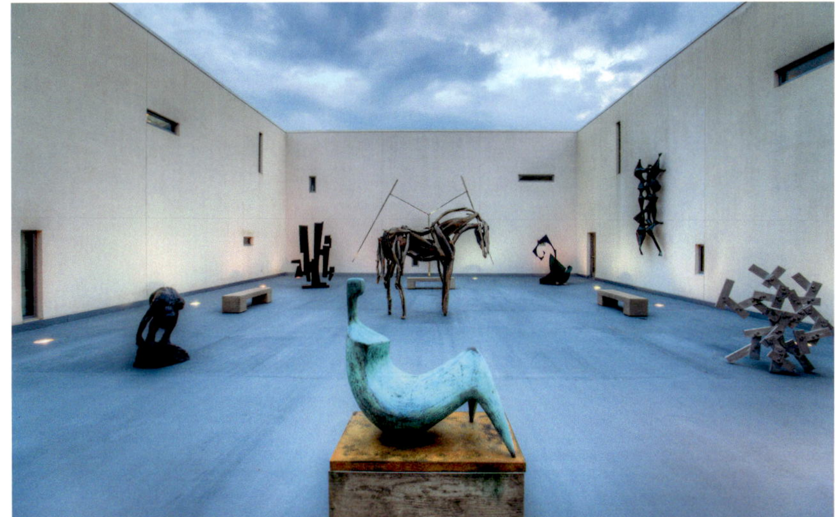

FIGURE 11. Hurand Sculpture Courtyard, featuring contemporary sculpture

LOOKING TOWARD THE FUTURE

Since its founding in the late 1920s, the FIA's mandate to care for and exhibit the permanent collection, as well as provide lifelong learning opportunities in the studio arts, has been supported by the generosity of donors in the community. Early visionaries such as George Crapo Willson, the first president of the FIA's Board of Trustees; his daughter Frances Willson Thompson and her son Jack; Charles Stewart Mott and his wife Ruth; Enos and Sarah DeWaters; Viola E. Bray and her daughter Bertha and son-in-law William Richards; Donald E. and Alice D. Johnson; Dr. Fouad A. Rabiah (fig. 10); and Art and Bess Hurand (fig. 11), all made significant financial contributions to ensure a bright future for the FIA. The loan of the Sherwin and Shirley Glass Glass Collection from the Isabel Foundation continues the legacy of Flint's leaders and philanthropists who have made the FIA what it is today.

ACKNOWLEDGMENTS

The new wing in the Museum and art-making space in the Art School would not have been possible without the generosity and vision of the Charles Stewart Mott Foundation's Trustees, including William S. White, Chairman and CEO, and Ridgway H. White, President. The C. S. Mott Foundation's continuing investment into the growth of the FIA and other Flint Cultural Center organizations demonstrates its commitment to arts and culture as a critical force for positive change in our community. I would also like to recognize the Isabel Foundation, named after the mother of Claire M. White, late wife of William S. White, and their children, Tiffany Lovett and Ridgway White. The Isabel Foundation purchased the Sherwin and Shirley Glass Glass Collection with the intention of placing the works on long-term loan to the FIA and provided funds to make this catalogue possible. This generosity demonstrates the passion and deep commitment of the White family to art and art education in Flint, as well as honoring the intentions of the Glasses, who desired that their collection be shared with the public.

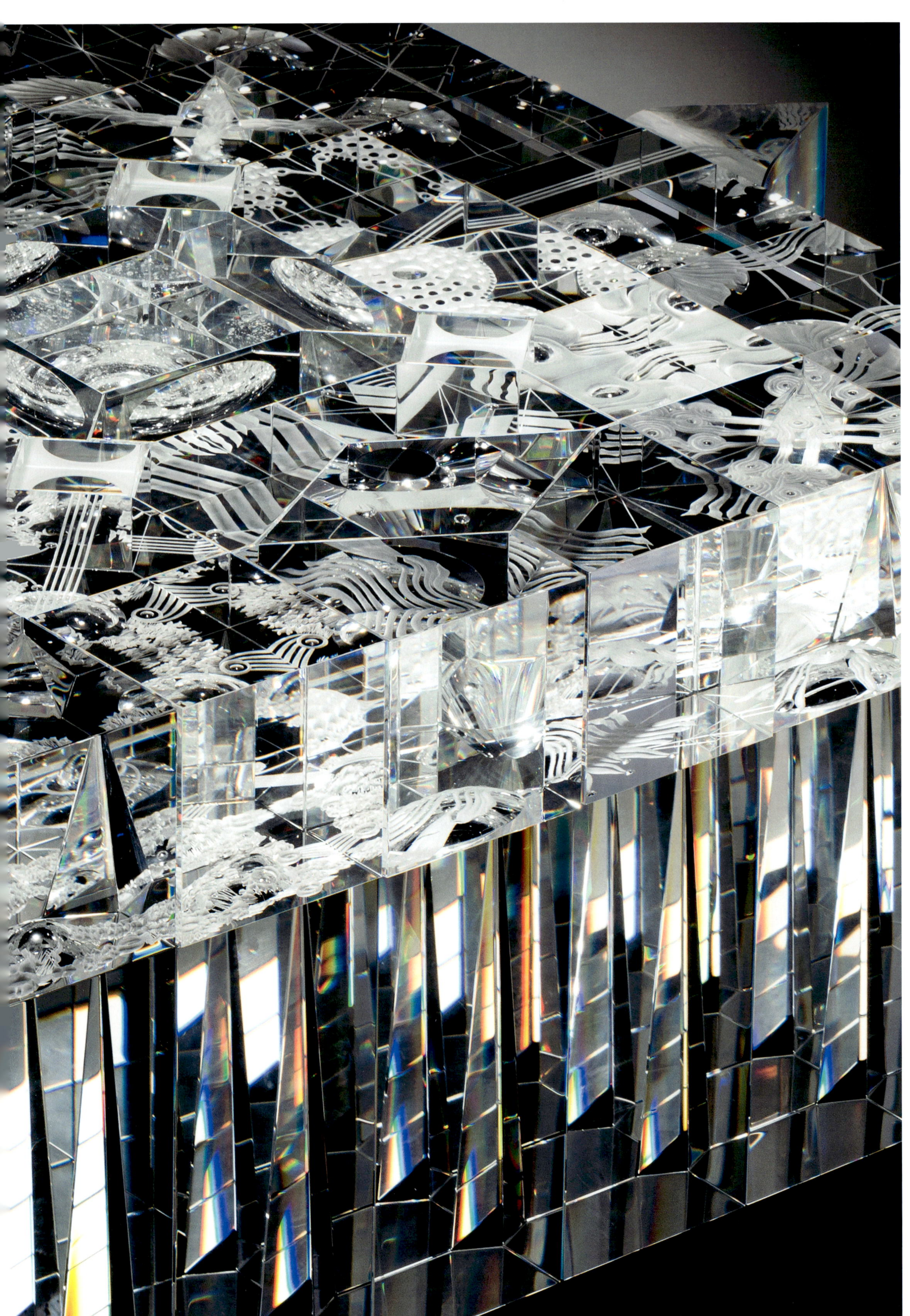

A Quest for the Best
The Sherwin and Shirley Glass Story

FERDINAND HAMPSON,

FOUNDER, HABATAT GALLERIES

It was in late April of 2000 when I received a call at Habatat Galleries, just north of Detroit. The woman on the line told me she was interested in learning about studio glass and was calling on the suggestion of the noted Atlanta collector Dr. Stanley Cohen. Judging by her sweet southern accent I assumed she was from the same region. We were at the end of our 28th Annual International Exhibition so I suggested that she come see it. To my surprise, she told me that she would see me tomorrow!

This was the beginning of what ultimately resulted in the greatest single-decade collection of studio glass ever assembled.

The following day, Shirley Applebaum, soon to be Shirley Glass, arrived at Habatat. She was in her late fifties, looked forty, and had an unassuming charm and wit that was contagious. After she distributed fruit from Georgia to the staff, we started discussing art while walking through the exhibition. She had borrowed a catalogue of the exhibition from Dr. Cohen and to my surprise had not only memorized the names of artists but seemed to have committed the full text to memory. She had left the catalogue with her fiancé Sherwin Glass and called him three times that day to tell him about certain sculptures. Shirley had a strong interest in why the works were made—not as much how. By the end of the day they had selected three pieces, each having a depth beyond the natural beauty of glass. One of these was Clifford Rainey's *Counting* (cat. 107). This female torso was filled with social commentary and addressed current issues in a variety of ways. Not all art relies on traditional beauty and that the Glasses acquired this compelling sculpture to begin their collection signaled to me how important this relationship could be. As an art dealer this is the client that you live for—it makes your career meaningful.

SHERWIN GLASS 1927–2005

That summer Shirley invited us to their home in the Atlanta suburb of Suwanee, where we met Sherwin for the first time. He was in the final stages of a divorce and as part of the settlement the 30,000 sq. ft. mansion nestled in the 750-acre estate was to be sold. My wife Kathy asked them to turn on every light so we could look at it outside as evening approached. They obliged, and after a half hour of flicking switches, we all went out to admire what I was told was the largest mansion in Atlanta.

Sherwin, who came from a humble background, was perhaps even more unassuming than Shirley. I remember a story that John Neubert, Sherwin's house manager and right-hand man since 1991, told me, that

OPPOSITE: FIGURE 1. Eric Hilton, *The Source of the Infinite* (detail, cat. 58)

gave an insight as to his personality: During the construction of the Suwanee mansion, Sherwin enjoyed wandering around the site, sometimes carrying a rake. One afternoon a smiling foreman came up to Sherwin and told him that a worker had spotted this old man who wasn't doing a lick of work and was just leaning on a rake. The worker suggested that he be fired. Sherwin told the foreman to send him this man. An hour later a trembling young man entered Sherwin's office, cap in hand and regret on his face. Sherwin asked if he said this and the distraught worker told him it was true. Sherwin told him that he was getting a raise because he was obviously looking out for the owner's welfare—and thanked him!

In 1949 Sherwin started Farmers Home Furniture, a single store in south Georgia. By 2001, the *Atlanta Journal* estimated his worth at $300 million. Farmers Home Furniture is the largest by-number furniture store chain in the United States.

He was legendary for his generosity to charities, especially in the Jewish community. He really enjoyed people, and part of his collecting interest was in meeting artists and other collectors. His wife Shirley became a huge part of his life. They had a great love and devotion to each other. I always will remember Sherwin telling me while shaking his head, "That Shirley, she is so damn smart!"

In 2003 Sherwin became ill. He passed away in 2005.

SHIRLEY GLASS 1943–2009

Shirley Glass was born into a middle-class family in Miami, Florida. She moved to Atlanta in 1963. Two previous marriages resulted in two adult children. When she married Sherwin, he had two adult children from his first marriage and two preteen sons from his second. Shirley was not college educated but started several businesses. At the time of her death she served on the board of directors for Farmers Home Furniture. She had an active interest in art and confided to me that she had always been drawn to glass. After the sale of the Suwanee mansion, the newly married couple combined two condos (two floors above Elton John) in downtown Atlanta, with an eye toward displaying the collection that they were intending to acquire. Shirley shared Sherwin's passion for philanthropy.

When Sherwin became ill, Shirley was not only by his side but learned all that she could about his condition, medications, and nutrition, and she virtually coordinated every aspect of his health care. She seemed to sense what would keep him engaged in life and collecting was one of several things that seemed to hold his interest.

THE COLLECTION 2000–2009

After Shirley's first visit to Habatat Galleries, we traveled to see a glass exhibit at the Dennos Museum in Traverse City, Michigan, along with other glass activities that I had coordinated. We hit it off as couples. Sherwin and I came from similar backgrounds and we were all married for a relatively short period. This was not the last trip we did together and my wife, Kathy, and I found ourselves traveling to Atlanta quite often. They had their own opinions concerning art but always discussed them with me—even if they were acquiring a work from another gallery. I loved introducing them to artists. So many times I heard, "I like that sculpture but can you make it larger?" This is music to the ears of any sculptor! As an added bonus, they loved the idea that they were supporting the artists with their purchases.

Shirley wanted the best, the finest, and the most significant work that each artist could create. If it wasn't available she and Sherwin would commission it. As with all collectors, living with the art is the best learning experience. Their collecting as a survey of studio glass continued but now artists like Howard Ben Tré, Clifford Rainey, Janusz Walentynowicz, Martin Blank, Mary Shaffer, William Morris, Steve Linn, and Stanislav Libenský and Jaroslava Brychtová became favorites and were rewarded with multiple purchases. In a way their choices were shaping what was important in studio glass. Sherwin was a little slower accepting more conceptual work. Shirley would tell me go talk to Sherwin about this or that piece so he would understand it better. Usually this worked, however I do remember him defending his point of view so well that he convinced me to tell Shirley it would be better to hold off on that purchase!

Sometimes they would give me a mission such as, "Can you find me that nine-foot-long *Green Eye of the Pyramid* by Libenský?" (cat. 79). It was an edition of five and all had been sold many years prior. After a year of searching and negotiating, I found this sculpture in Japan. Another time they told me that they loved a Pavel Hlava in the Four Seasons in Prague. The artist had passed away several years before but they asked, "Can you get me an even better one?" After a good deal of searching, I found a sculpture (*Flower*; cat. 59) in the archives of his son-in-law, Tomas Hlavicka.

On another occasion I arranged for them to visit Ben Heineman, a legendary businessman in Chicago. Ben had an amazing collection and was fascinated by early works of the most successful artists who worked with glass. Three years earlier, Ben asked if I could arrange a commission from the artist Eric Hilton. He had seen a "Masterwork" on display at the Corning Museum of Glass called *Innerland*, so complex a work of art that the museum published a book on this single piece. Ben told me he would like a sculpture similar to this but bigger and after nearly two years the sculpture was complete and prominently displayed in his living room. After an enjoyable visit, I left with Sherwin and Shirley, who told me after the condo door closed that they really liked that Eric Hilton, and in classic fashion asked, "Do you think he could make it bigger?" After another two years, the largest Hilton of this series (*The Source of the Infinite*; fig. 1) weighing over 800 pounds and comprised of nearly 100 glass elements was prominently displayed in the Glasses' living room!

After only two short years of marriage, Sherwin's illness became a large part of their daily existence. However, with Shirley's energy and nursing, they still traveled, planned, and collected. Shirley knew that Sherwin missed the country life that he had at Suwanee. He missed having exotic birds that had roamed his previous property and their shared interest in nature and the outdoors. In November of 2004, they acquired 1,150 acres about two hours north of Atlanta. They began making plans for an extraordinary country home that unfortunately Sherwin would never see. While under construction, they lived in a small home on the property and resumed the exotic bird collection. The mountain home was designed to display art. While under construction, Shirley invited the famed sculptor noted for large-scale works in glass Howard Ben Tré and his wife, Wendy, to discuss a possible commission. It was Howard's first visit and of course he was expecting an impressive home. We arrived at the small farmhouse and Howard looked a bit startled. After greetings, Shirley asked Howard where he would like to see this commission. It was the first time that I saw Howard look bewildered! After a very good laugh we proceeded to the construction site where he ultimately created two majestic sculptures (*Glass Towers*; cat. 8).

Shirley's knowledge of art and artists who work with glass kept growing. She would ask questions until she drained me of all knowledge of a particular artist or concept. She really did not need me to consult on

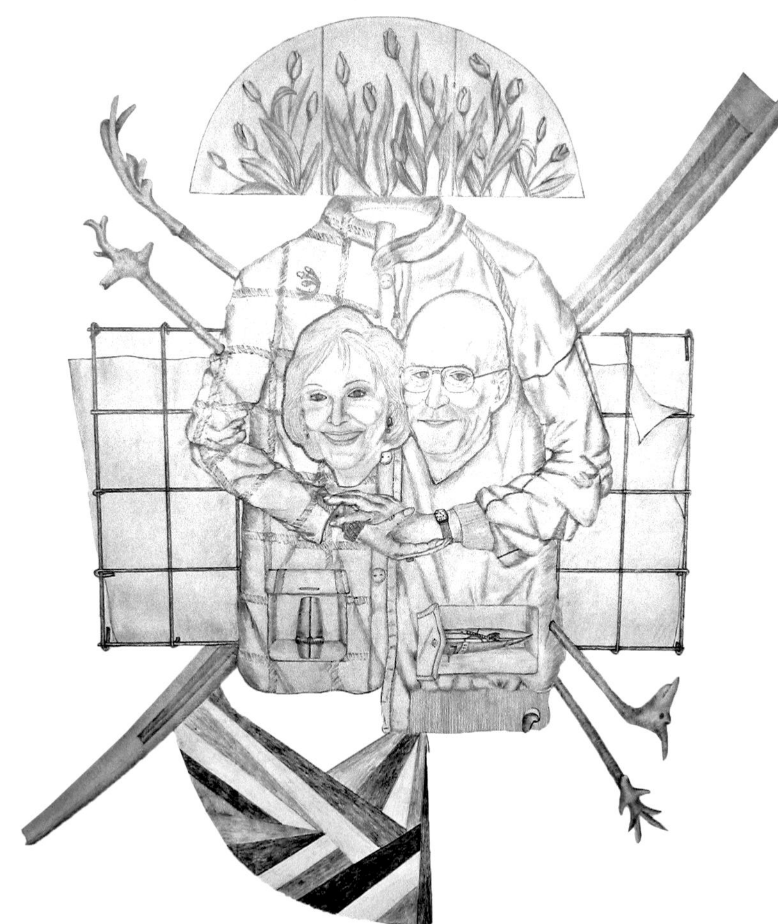

acquisitions but she had promised Sherwin that she would always talk to me before making any glass purchase. To honor his wishes, she would call me from other galleries or drag me over to look at a sculpture that she was interested in at one of the art fairs that she frequented.

Shirley was doing pretty well. The mountain home was completed in 2008 and my wife and I spent Thanksgiving with her celebrating this spectacular home and setting. Shortly after this, the inconceivable happened. In late January of 2009 Shirley, at age sixty-seven, was diagnosed with a terminal illness.

I remember the last time I saw her. It was late April of 2009, and after much deliberation she decided to come to our Annual International Exhibition at Habatat Galleries in Royal Oak, Michigan. She had so many friends who were collectors and artists that it made her temporarily forget her problems. She told me how wonderful it was being there, enjoying the art and the people. Shirley acquired her last works and it was the last time I would see her. She passed away in November of that year.

AWAITING A HOME

Shirley remained optimistic till the end but we did have a discussion of what she would like to see happen with the collection. Earlier, I had a similar conversation with both Sherwin and Shirley. They both hoped that the collection would eventually be donated to a museum. They wanted to have a major publication and some type of name recognition. They also wanted at least part of the collection to always be on display. They commissioned the artist Steve Linn to create a wall sculpture that presented images of Shirley and Sherwin surrounded by works in their collection (fig. 2). They confided to Steve and me that they hoped that this work would be an entrance piece to their collection in a museum.

At Shirley's funeral, a discussion occurred concerning the wishes for the collection of both Shirley and Sherwin. It was my understanding that the CEO of Farmers Home Furniture who would be involved in the estate also understood their wishes. For the next six months, I worked with my wife and staff members of Habatat Galleries to find a suitable home and fulfill their wishes. Of the 140 museums that we contacted, five appeared to have the interest and ability to meet the criteria. However, plans changed in the interim and communications between the estate and me would break down. Apparently, the estate was not interested in donating but now wanted to sell the collection.

One of my initial contacts for a possible donation was the Flint Institute of Arts. I knew and respected the director, John Henry, and years prior, Shirley, Sherwin, my wife, and I stopped by the FIA while traveling to Traverse City in northern Michigan. They were impressed by the friendliness of the folks there and the presentation of the museum itself. Shirley had a warm spot for Michigan, having traveled there many times for one of her businesses. Her best friend and former business partner lived in Royal Oak, where Habatat Galleries is headquartered. I stayed in contact with John Henry but to bring the collection to Flint was a monumental task, especially during a severe recession. Meanwhile, it appeared the collection would be acquired by investors or be sold a piece at a time to a number of collectors.

It took six years, but thanks to the efforts of John Henry and his staff, and the vision and tenacity of William S. White, CEO of the Charles Stewart Mott Foundation, the wishes of Shirley and Sherwin were realized. It required a complex negotiation involving the acquisition of the Glass Glass Collection by the Michigan-based Isabel Foundation, who in turn made an arrangement for a loan to the Flint Institute of Arts. The C. S. Mott Foundation has given $8.5 million as part of a $17.5 million capital campaign and endowment to create an 11,000 sq. ft. space for a new wing. Additionally, a 3,620 sq. ft. makerspace was built that includes a state-of-the-art glass studio with stadium seating.

For my part in all of this I am deeply grateful. Sherwin and Shirley's wishes have been completely fulfilled.

I have had a long and, by most standards, a very successful career, but for my small part in executing my friends' wishes I am profoundly proud. This has been the highlight of my career.

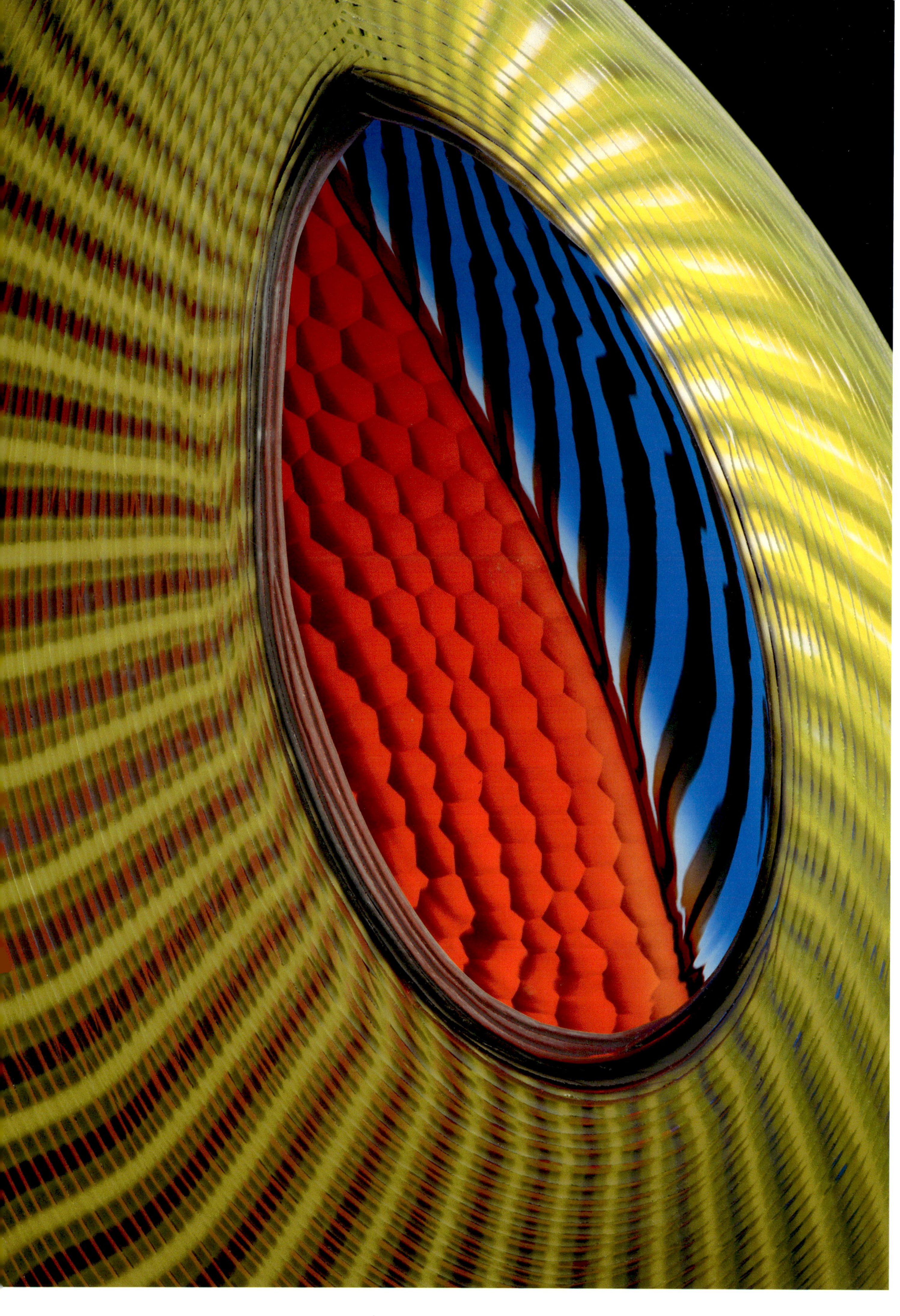

Tradition, Innovation, and Meaning
The Sherwin and Shirley Glass Glass Collection

PATRICIA GRIEVE WATKINSON

From Bohemia to the New World, from Murano's fiery furnaces to the damp of the Pacific Northwest, the Sherwin and Shirley Glass Glass Collection recognizes the long roots that glass has as a means of artistic expression, and, at the same time, celebrates the broad and spectacular flowering of the medium at the opening of the twenty-first century. Sixteen countries and eighty-eight artists are represented in this collection. The artists are diverse in every way: from **Klaus Moje** in Australia, who combines ancient fusing techniques with contemporary use of color, to Germany's **Josepha Gasch-Muche**, who uses LCD screens broken into innumerable shards of glass.

The tradition of using glass to create objects of beauty, utility, inspiration, and prestige can be traced back for centuries. Among these sixteen countries, the Czech Republic and Italy have the longest traditions of glassmaking. By contrast, the United States and Australia are glass newcomers.

While most of these works of art were created in the twenty-first century, several remind us of the historical traditions of glassmaking. Take, for example, the work of the Italian artists represented here. Venetian glassmaking traces its origins to the thirteenth century with the long tradition of craftsmen on the island of Murano. In 1291, the Venetian Republic, fearing that the fires used to melt glass might ignite the city, ordered all glassmakers sequestered on Murano. Over the centuries the fame of Venetian glass has become worldwide. Its factories are well-known brands—Barovier & Toso, Gabbiani, Salviati, Seguso, and Venini. Its hallmark style of intricate, decorative, colorful creations from chandeliers to goblets is widely recognized.

Most Venetian glass is "mouth- blown"—a highly skilled activity. A small amount of molten glass is gathered from a furnace on the end of a hollow pipe and with human breath is gently formed into a bubble. The bubble, while still hot, can be shaped, stretched, and added to. These additions are often hot-sculpted, as heated, malleable glass is turned into flowers, figures, or flourishes. Once cold, the glass can be further embellished by carving into its solid surface. The importance of these age-old techniques in the twenty-first century is evidenced by the continued use of Italian words for techniques used by today's artists, no matter their nationality— *murrine, millefiore, battuto, filigrano, reticello, incalmo.*

It is noteworthy that all the Italians—all major artists—in the Sherwin and Shirley Glass Glass Collection have intimate association with Venetian manufacturing traditions. Each was born on Murano. **Livio Seguso** is part

OPPOSITE: FIGURE 1. Lino Tagliapietra, *Bilbao* (detail, cat. 121) Note: Catalogue numbers are given when artists' works are mentioned by title. All works by artists can be found alphabetically listed by last name in the catalogue section, pp. 34–199.

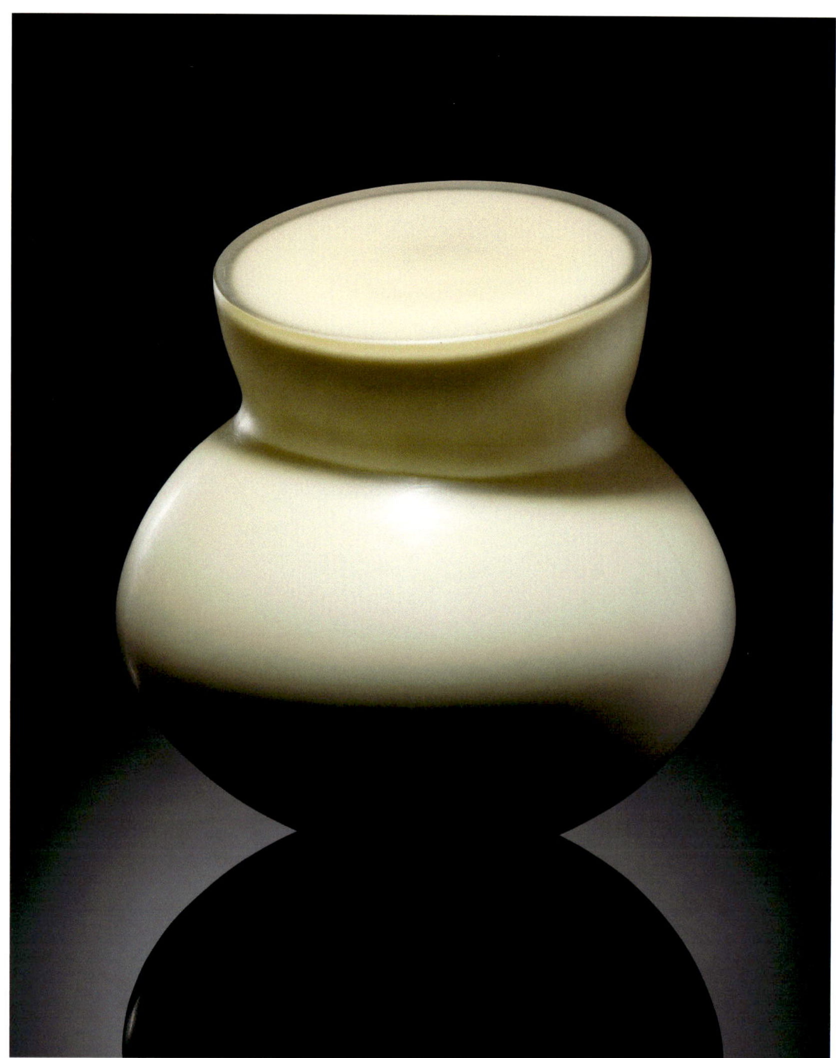

of the Seguso glass dynasty of over six centuries. **Laura de Santillana**'s grandfather founded the Venini Company where she worked as a designer. **Davide Salvadore** is descended from a family of glassworkers and was employed in several workshops. **Lucio Bubacco**, son of a glass *Maestro*, began making tiny glass animals as a boy and continues with lampworked extravaganzas today. **Lino Tagliapietra**, the only one of this group with no direct glassmaking heritage, nevertheless became enamored with glass at the tender age of ten and soon began in the lowliest of positions in the workshops. By twenty-two, he was recognized as a *Maestro*, the highest possible level of skill.

Each has moved beyond the narrow expectations of the factory floor to find a singular, personal voice as an artist. Tagliapietra's *Bilbao* and *Stromboli* are magnificent and colorful blown vessels that showcase the artist's consummate skill and the unique expressiveness he has found in his later years. Tagliapietra is one of the most respected and admired of living glassblowers today. Using a variety of techniques, *Bilbao*, part of a series inspired by the forms of Frank Gehry's Guggenheim Museum, combines different rhythmic patterns like different sounds in a musical composition (fig. 1). It is further overlaid with long, parallel incisions that impose yet another rhythm on Tagliapietra's creation. Salvadore's imaginative take on a dramatic stringed instrument, *Springarpa 1*, also combines a mix of patterns and colors, in this case inspired by traditional African textiles (cat. 114). Like Tagliapietra, he has a complex use of *murrine* and canework and adds to the rhythmic patterning with areas of carving (*battuto*).

After the colorful exuberance of Tagliapietra and Salvadore, both de Santillana and Seguso present calmer, more contemplative pieces. Both still use mouth-blown glass. Seguso's choice of colorless, crystal glass emphasizes sculptural form, light, and space over surface. De Santillana's milky-colored closed vessel has a sensuous surface and a mirrored interior that implies a sense of meditative mystery. Her piece can be more fully understood when we know that its title, *Bodhi*, is Sanskrit for the Buddhist concept of "enlightenment" or "awakening" (fig. 2).

Italian artists are not alone in claiming a centuries-long involvement with glass. Bohemia, now incorporated into the Czech Republic, can trace its artistic use of glass back to the Renaissance. Bohemian decorative glassware—blown, cut, and engraved—has ranged from elegant vases and costume jewelry to chandeliers. Bohemia has been Austrian, German, and Czechoslovakian, but none of the vagaries of politics or war has halted the region's production of glass. From the mid-nineteenth century on, specialized technical schools have taught traditional glassmaking skills, encouraged innovation, and fed the industry's need for employees. The towns of Kamenický Šenov, Nový Bor, and Železný Brod each have important schools with close connections to major glass factories. In addition, Prague's Academy of Applied Arts, established in 1885, also has a long history teaching design in glass, especially for architectural purposes.

Schools and factories play an important role in the development of contemporary glass sculpture in the Czech Republic. Of the major Czech artists represented in this collection, many were students or teachers in the schools, while some were involved in the factories. In addition, the factories and smaller glassmaking facilities were where many of the glass sculptures were fabricated—some still are today. Czech artists are used to relying on highly skilled technicians to execute their work. Indeed, not until later in the twentieth century were Czech glass artists free to have their own private studios. During the long years of Communism (1948–1989), artists' creativity was directed to commissions made in official glassmaking facilities. The resulting works of art were owned and exhibited by the state. Under the Communist regime, there could be no such thing as a private art owner or commercial art market.

Ironically, Communism brought some benefits to artists working in glass: they were permitted to work in this medium that was considered "safe," without the dangerous potential for ideological insurrection that painting and sculpture might possess. It is worth remembering that, in 1974, in Communist Russia, an unsanctioned art exhibition was actually bulldozed by the authorities, so great was the fear of freedom of expression. Glass, however, was seen as part of Czechoslovakia's proud history, a tribute to Communism. Czech glass was winning prizes abroad. It was not understood that artists were using glass as a powerful vehicle for self-expression.

The most rightfully lauded of contemporary Czech artists, whose work still stands head and shoulders above their peers, is the couple **Stanislav Libenský** and his wife **Jaroslava Brychtová**. Well-represented by six pieces in the Sherwin and Shirley Glass Glass Collection, they are certainly among its star artists. A famed teacher as well as a prolific artist, Libenksý first taught in Nový Bor, then directed the Železný Brod school, and finally was an inspirational Professor at Prague's prestigious Academy of Applied Arts for almost twenty-five years.

Libenský and Brychtová established a new tradition for sculptural glass—monumental cast glass—using a process where chunks of glass are melted in a mold. As artists, they were fully cognizant of twentieth-century developments in European art, especially Cubism and Constructivism. They had traveled widely and seen at first hand works by Abstract artists in

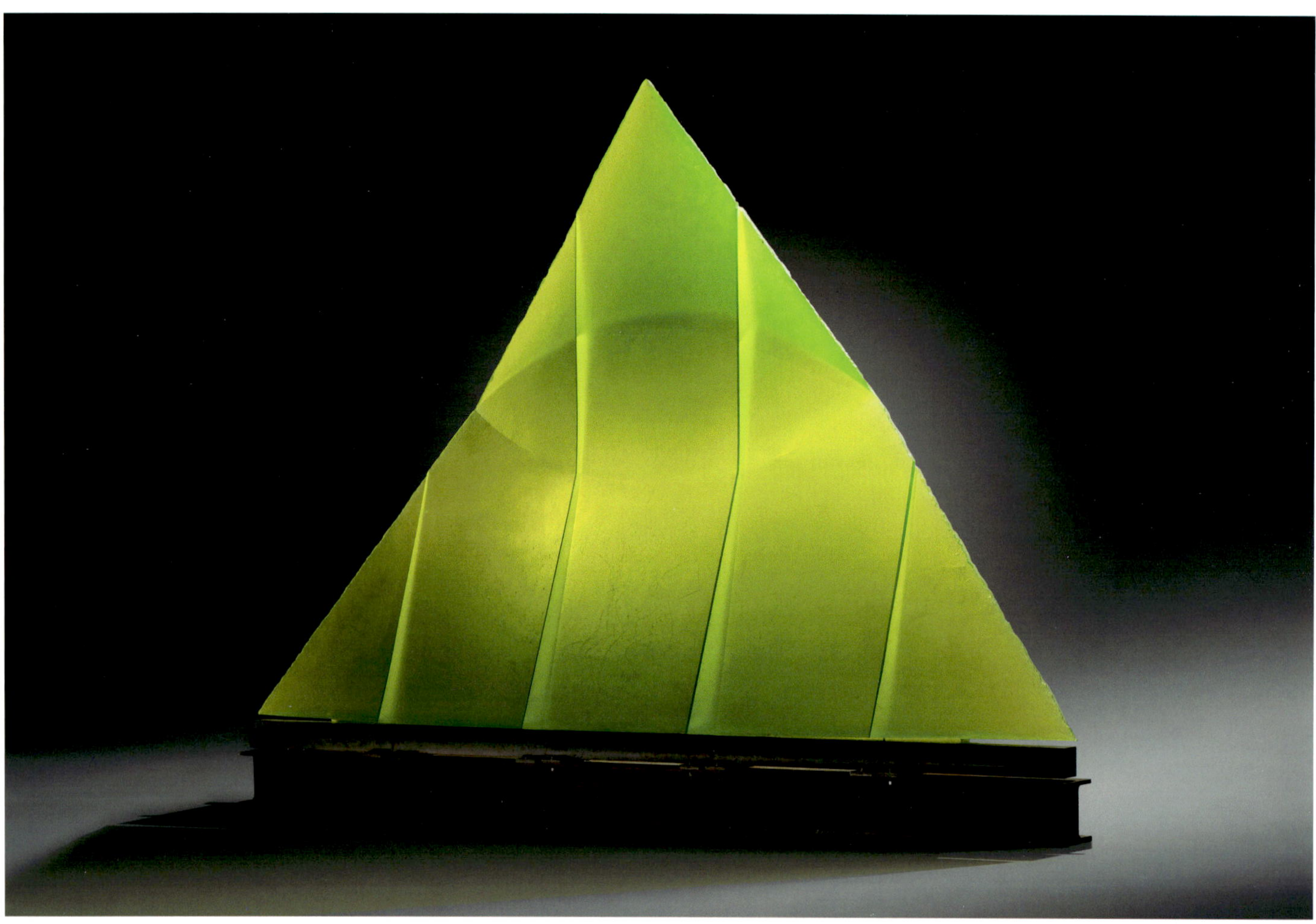

many countries. All this informed their work. Used to creating glass for architectural settings, Libenský and Brychtová often made their free-standing sculptures on a monumental scale. Almost seven feet tall, their magnificent *Green Eye of the Pyramid* is among the largest pieces in this collection (fig. 3). In this work, as in all of their sculptures, simple, translu-cent shapes shift and become more complex as the viewer moves or as the daylight changes. Color, too, alters as the density of the glass varies. Angled planes suggest and reveal mysterious interior voids. Above all, the work is a poem to light itself, a search for the transcendent.

Important contemporaries of Libenský and Brychtová are René Roubíček, Václav Cigler, and **František Vízner**. Vízner is represented by a simple cast-glass, nonfunctional, bowl-shaped work, its center a glowing red. It is a small but telling example of the artist's exquisite craftsmanship and his creation of singular, numinous objects. **Petr Hora**, another Libenský contemporary, continues his colleague's investigations into abstraction and the spatial relationships of color and light in cast glass (*Neptune, Hadros*, cats. 61–62), while **Pavel Hlava** takes a different path, using blown then precision-cut glass in a more decorative fashion (*Flower, Untitled Kiss*, cats. 59–60).

Many gifted students of Stanislav Libenský continued their teacher's exploration of cast glass: **Latchezar Boyadjiev, Stanislava Grebeníčková, Vladimira Klumpar, Ivan Mareš**, and **Yan Zoritchak**. Each is represented in the collection. Klumpar's sculptures, especially, are a fascinating develop-ment from Libenský and Brychtová's with the introduction of precise sur-face patterns, use of complex faceting that increases optical complexity, and often specific reference to the natural world, as in *After Rain* (cat. 69). A contemporary of Klumpar's, Slovakian artist **Zora Palová**, was a student of Václav Cigler. She, too, works abstractly with cast glass and yet makes reference to nature: her gray *North Sea Waves* evokes the chill of Northern waters (cat. 104). In Hungary, the noted artist **Maria Lugossy** shares many of the Czechs' concerns in her humanistic work, *Double Form*, made, however, not from cast glass but from laminated glass sheets (cat. 87).

In 1962, a year before Libenský started teaching at Prague's Academy of Applied Arts, halfway around the world, an event happened that could not have contrasted more with the sophistication of Czech glass production. In Toledo, Ohio, Harvey Littleton, a ceramic artist, and Dominick Labino, a research scientist from one of the town's glass manufacturing plants, conducted an experimental workshop. Littleton wanted to see if glass melted in his small homemade furnace could be used to blow a bubble.

Unbeknownst to Littleton and Labino, their experiment would herald what came to be called the Studio Glass Movement. "Studio" is the key word here. Littleton's hope was that any artist might be able to use glass in the seclusion of his or her own studio, working independently, and not under the thumb of industry. His thinking reflected a desire, certainly characteristic of the 1960s, for art to be a direct expression of the individual, made by hand and emblematic of a simple, authentic lifestyle. He wanted glass to be as readily available to the artist as other mediums such as painting, pottery, jewelry, or weaving.

Bubbles were indeed blown in Toledo, and the workshop's success inspired a second workshop three months later. Excitement grew about the discovery of this "newly" available and mysterious material—glass. Littleton already taught ceramics at the nearby University of Wisconsin–Madison and was allowed to add glass to his course offerings. Curious students registered, among them, Dale Chihuly, Fritz Dreisbach, and **Marvin Lipofsky** (fig. 4). With a speed that can only happen in the United States, the enthusiasm for glass caught on and other universities started glass programs. Littleton's students soon found themselves graduating, starting

FIGURE 4. Marvin Lipofsky, *IGS VI #8* (cat. 85)

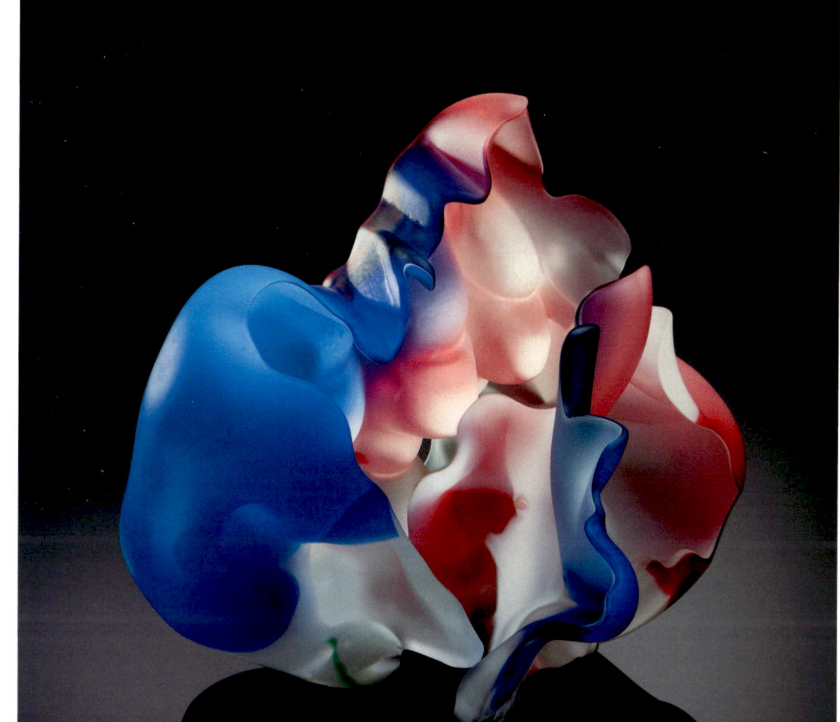

their own university glass programs, and teaching yet other students the mysteries of glass, albeit, when compared to their contemporaries in Italy and the Czech Republic, at a decidedly unsophisticated and experimental level.

Surely no one in 1962 in Toledo, Murano, or Prague, could possibly have dreamt of the widely diverse ways glass would be used some fifty years later, nor the equally diverse reasons for using this material that takes so much mastery and enthralls so many artists. The Sherwin and Shirley Glass Glass Collection showcases this diversity with eighty-eight well-established, yet greatly different, artists—half are American—whose work ranges from naturalistic to abstract, whimsical to tragic, intimate to grand.

By the mid-1970s more than one hundred art schools across the United States had decided to offer glass. One of those programs, at the Rhode Island School of Design, was expanded and transformed by Dale Chihuly, who also taught summers at Haystack Mountain School of Crafts in Maine. These two teaching experiences got Chihuly dreaming about creating a summer glass program in his native Washington State—and so, in 1971, Pilchuck Glass School was born. Located in the foothills of the Cascade Mountains, Pilchuck was then just fields, forest, and fog. There was no infrastructure, no amenities, nowhere to live. This, however, meshed nicely with the prevalent "hippie" philosophy of going "back to the land" and "dropping out" of society. The intent was to learn to make glass objects, and within a few days of finishing their makeshift dwellings and building a furnace with scrap materials, those gathered at Pilchuck had acquired propane, melted glass, blown bubbles with much excitement, and created a wide array of globular, expressionistic vessels.

Although their glassblowing abilities developed swiftly, it became pretty clear that American artists could benefit from those for whom glass was a more honored tradition. Already, in 1968, Chihuly had worked at Venini in Murano. In 1969, he had visited Libenský and Brychtová. In 1979, Tagliapietra was invited to teach at Pilchuck for the first of many summers. His skills, disciplined work ethic, and willingness to share began to raise the standards of the American Studio Glass Movement—and to change the attitudes of the artists involved. In 1982, Libenský and Brychtová obtained government permission to attend Pilchuck as artists-in-residence—the first of many visits. They brought an intellectual and philosophical focus that found fertile ground. These are just some examples of the pattern of exchange—and friendship—that began to characterize the Studio Glass Movement. Artists from around the world came, and still come, to schools and universities throughout the United States. American artists, in turn, travel the world to study, to give workshops, to work with foreign colleagues, and to collaborate on teams making art together. As a result, the world of glass is a wide and collegial one where the sharing of ideas, techniques, and muscle has become expected behavior, to a degree rarely found with other art mediums.

Chihuly's creation of Pilchuck Glass School and his own astounding decades-long work as an artist have led the avant-garde in the development of blown glass as fine art. In 1986, Chihuly was only the third American ever to have a solo exhibition at the Louvre in Paris. His influence is inestimable. Many artists have collaborated with Chihuly, lending their skills to augment his. Several are represented in this collection. **Joey Kirkpatrick** and **Flora C. Mace** share a diverse range of interests and materials, often choosing subject matter that celebrates nature. Their *trompe l'oeil* oversized apples from 2005 are exquisitely pigmented—an effect created by artfully sifting crushed glass onto the heated bubble's skin

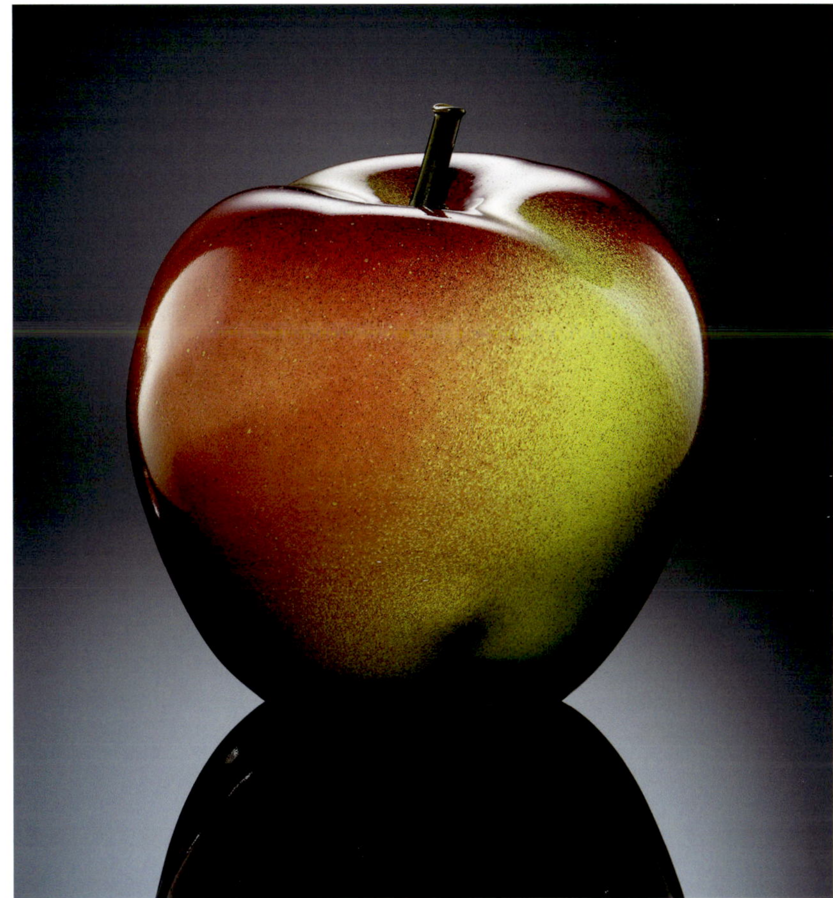

(fig. 5). **William Morris**, whose memorable work is also blown and hot-sculpted, likewise uses a fascinating range of methods to "trick the eye" into believing that glass may actually be horn or bone, wood or ceramic. His haunting sculptures take us to a world of his imagining where we might uncover the remains of ancient cultures or encounter indigenous peoples of great dignity (*Zande Man*; cat. 100).

Glassblower **Martin Blank**, who worked for Chihuly for years, is widely known for his figurative and abstract sculpture that captures the fluidity of molten glass and "freezes" it, like a dance in mid-air. **Sabrina Knowles** and **Jenny Pohlman**, who met while working at Pilchuck, together created *Aryades*, a blown vessel that divides into two stylized heads at the top of an elegant long neck, encased with metal bands (cat. 71). Like all their work, *Aryades*, with its curves, beads, and innate female strength, is an homage to the women of Africa and to a country which the artists know well. Two other women working with blown glass are each inspired by nature and have taught at Pilchuck. **Debora Moore**'s passion is orchids. She has traveled the world in search of these exotic flowers and her art presents exquisite orchids with daring hues, often on a scale unknown in nature. **Karen Willenbrink-Johnsen** loves plants, animals, and birds, frequently with a touch of humor. Her five splendid falcons in the Sherwin and Shirley Glass Glass Collection are decorated with and named after blossoms—wisteria, rhododendron, dogwood, quince, and plum—as if she had discovered several new species of bird.

Nature is the inspiration for several artists in this collection, as it has been for visual artists for generations. It is possible that the qualities of glass—its intense color, translucency, and inherent vitality—are unusually effective at mimicking aspects of nature in three dimensions, especially the characteristics of plants and flowers. **Paul Stankard**'s creations are unbelievably realistic miniature worlds where flowers, tendrils, roots, insects, and the occasional tiny figure are encapsulated in a block of clear glass. They are every child's dream of a magical realm. Based on the tradition of paperweights, Stankard's works nevertheless take the conventional format to new heights. Japanese artist **Kimiake Higuchi** also reveres the beauty of flowers, creating highly lifelike blooms in *pâte de verre*, while Italy's **Miriam Silvia di Fiore** considers nature on a larger scale. Her realistic landscapes are meticulously constructed as she draws with glass powders and wires on layer after layer of glass, heating the glass in the furnace after each additional layer.

Ginny Ruffner's work *Inventing Flowers* stems from a different purpose—from an intellectual questioning of the meaning of nature and a study of contemporary scientific efforts of bio-engineers to restructure our natural world (fig. 6). From her *Aesthetic Engineering Series*, this is a bouquet of joyful, yet strangely altered flowers—multicolored foxgloves and unidentifiable blooms with marbled petals. **Steffen Dam** from Denmark also creates plants that do not exist in nature. He, too, looks to science for his inspiration. But Dam looks back in time—to early naturalists and their understanding of the world through the collection of specimens. His glass panel *The Secret Life of Plants* displays thin, luminous cross-sections of plantlike shapes that have the diaphanous beauty of old scientific glass slides but are nevertheless fictional creations (cat. 32).

The human figure, a longstanding subject in Western art, concerns many artists in this collection. **Mary Van Cline**, **Irene Frolic**, **Clifford Rainey**, and **Karen LaMonte** focus on female beauty. Van Cline emphasizes the sensuous back of an elegantly draped model. The smoothness of the skin

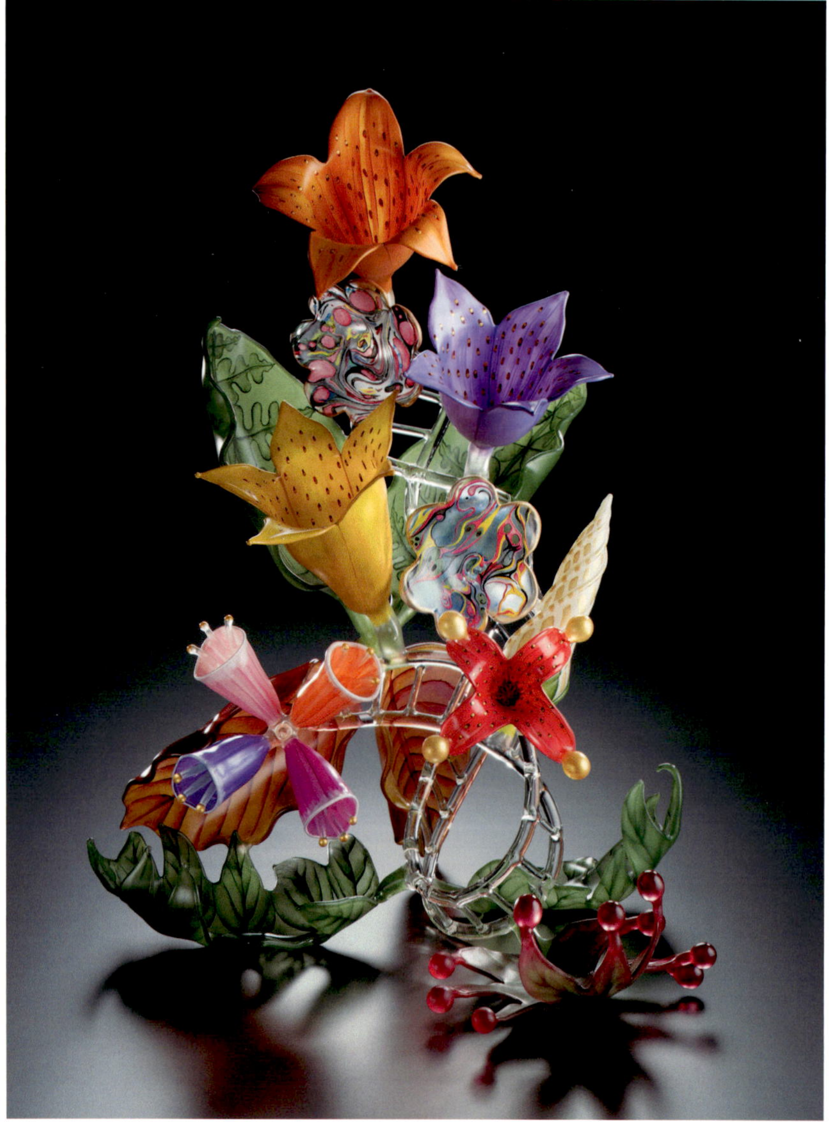

FIGURE 6. Ginny Ruffner, *Aesthetic Engineering Series: Inventing Flowers* (cat. 112)

and the contrasting crystalline quality of the drapery show a masterful use of cast *pâte de verre*. Frolic sculpts a noble, yet tragic, woman's profile on the elongated sweep of a powerful neck. Rainey's female torso, in opaque dark blue glass with surface hatch marks and only one breast, suggests that the body has suffered and needs the metal support the artist provides. LaMonte's "figure" is actually a void within a spectacular, flowing crystal dress, where the form of the body is only hinted at and the dress exudes a powerful presence of its own.

Other artists move beyond the physical beauty of the human face to suggest an underlying psychology. **Ann Wolff** is from Germany and her sculpture *Blues* denotes not only the color of the cast glass she uses but also the mood of a partly concealed, introspective face. The work provides alternating views as the face is veiled, then exposed, as if we are witnessing changing thought patterns (cat. 138). The idea of the human head as a container for the spirit is also a focus for Swedish artist **Bertil Vallien**. In his *Janus*, one face looks boldly forward and another more delicate, half-hidden face looks backwards, encased in a wedge of clear glass. As the viewer moves, that face is mirrored in the glass, so it becomes multiplied and changes character as different personalities seem to emerge (cat. 124).

Moving from the seriousness of Vallien's vision to the lightheartedness of other works, there is no loss in skill, only change in intention. Polish artist **Stanislaw Borowski** counts on whimsy and humor in his fanciful *Chaise Longue*, its back an etching of the debaucheries that might have taken place on its accommodating surface (cat. 19). **Hank Murta Adams**'s roughly cast heads come from a lifetime of crazy characters. His crude, expressive use of glass seems to thumb its nose at the "finish-fetish" of his colleagues. Almost three decades older than Adams, German artist **Erwin Eisch** also creates expressive heads that have a special place in this collection. Born into a glassmaking family, Eisch trained as a painter and sculptor and grew fascinated with the freedom with which American artists used glass as an expressive material. Meeting, and befriending, Harvey Littleton in 1962 further inspired Eisch and he became a recognized, central figure in the development of the Studio Glass Movement in Europe. Eisch's large heads are kindly caricatures of individuals he knows well in the world of contemporary glass, with a stylistic debt to not only German Expressionism but also to American Pop and Funk art.

Roughly speaking, the Sherwin and Shirley Glass Glass Collection is equally balanced between representational and nonobjective or abstract works of art. One glass blower who devoted a lifetime to abstract work is **Marvin Lipofsky**. He takes a glass bubble, created in glorious color, and extends, shapes, and manipulates it. Then, once cold, the bubble is cut into, revealing its mysterious interior and seeming to expose the human breath that brought it into being. Lipofsky's shapes are so organic, so related to the original bubble, which is after all a form of nature, that they seem to manifest nature itself.

There is no greater contrast to Lipofsky's organic shapes than the hard-edged geometries and optical effects used by **Eric Hilton**, **Steven Weinberg**, **David Huchthausen**, **John Kuhn,** and **Tom Patti**. Both Hilton's and Weinberg's work depends on the absolute purity of colorless, highly polished, cast crystal glass. With great precision, each cuts into or molds the glass, creating internal shapes that assume a life of their own: with endless reflection, refraction, mirroring, and shifting, the insides of these sculptures become puzzling, intricate environments where the mind and eye can wander endlessly. Huchthausen uses techniques to similar effect, with the addition of color. His small piece *Mirage* is just that—an optical

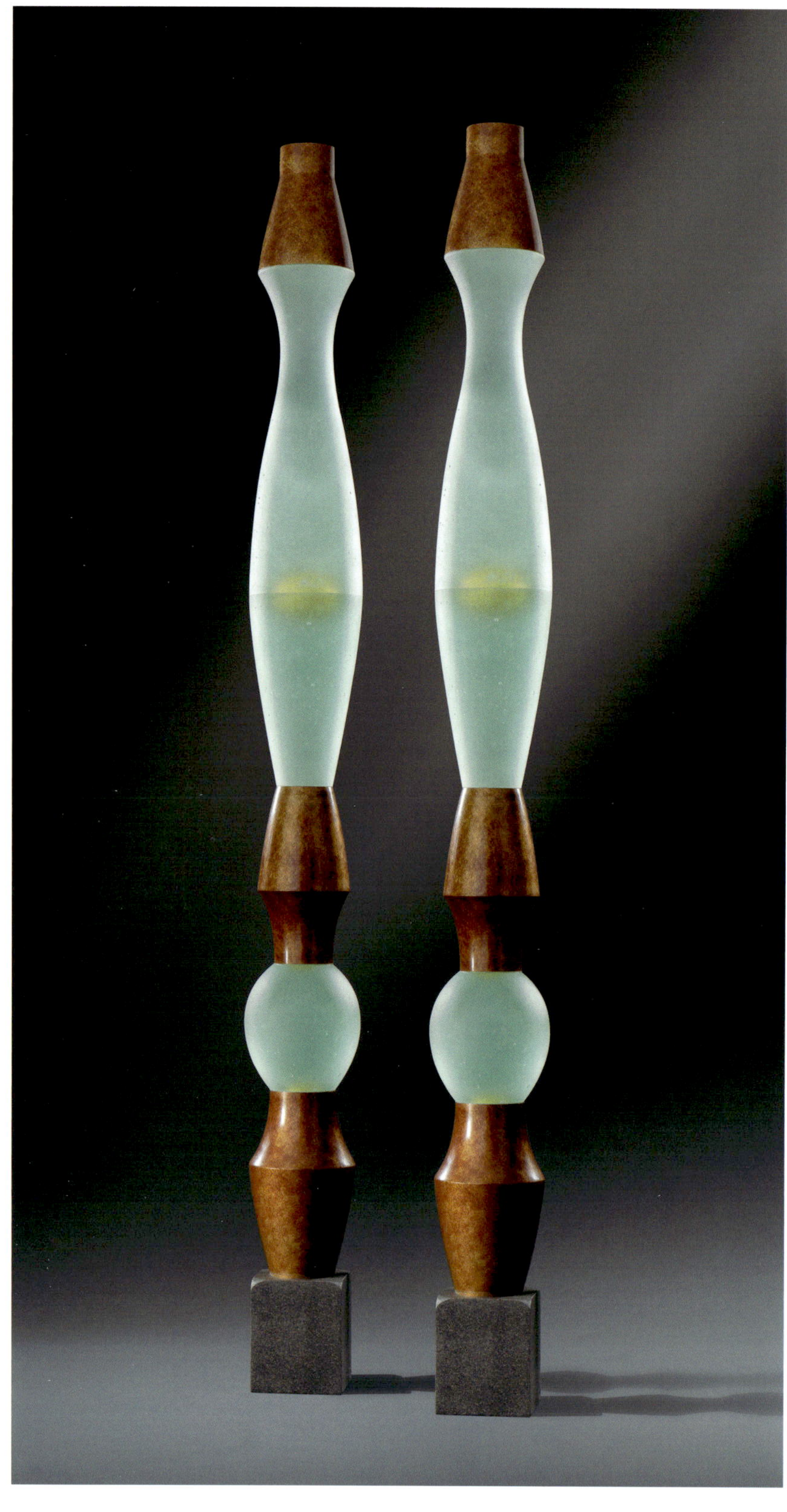

illusion of form and color that changes dramatically with every change in viewpoint (cat. 63). Kuhn precision-cuts his crystal glass into small, faceted segments before laminating them together, creating the lively, light-scattering effects of sparkling jewels. Patti, however, works differently. His characteristically small, clean-cut work is built by fusing differently formed layer upon layer of industrial sheet glass that eventually creates a central, symmetrical shape. The clearly visible layers play with the optics of the simple shape, making for an intriguing visual complexity.

Glass looks stunningly different in the hands of **Howard Ben Tré** and **Daniel Clayman**, who choose to use the material in a minimalist fashion, eschewing its propensity for shine, sparkle, and pizzazz. Both use mostly monochrome glass, where the subtlety of light is suggested by a quiet luminosity and where form, not color, is the primary interest. Both work on a large, sometimes monumental, scale with cast glass. Ben Tré's *Glass Towers*, measuring over nine feet, have a powerful presence and allude to stelae or columns of antiquity—an intentional reference of their creator (fig. 7). Clayman's *Juncture* has a serene simplicity as it enfolds space and activates an internal play of light (cat. 28).

Both Ben Tré and Clayman have used metals—even gold—along with glass. Other artists in this collection also use metal in different ways as an intrinsic part of their work with glass: **David Bennett, Bella Feldman, Ginny Ruffner, and Albert Young,** among others. For years **Dan Dailey** has been creating vessels in a style reminiscent of Art Deco, where the "handles" are stylized and whimsical metal figures that dance and cavort with abandon (*Trance*; cat. 31). The appeal of combining glass and metal has much to do with contrasts in texture and form, in juxtapositions between apparent strength and fragility, and in two distinct materials each formed by fire. The artist who has probably understood this the longest is **Mary Shaffer**. For almost fifty years, as an early participant in the Studio Glass Movement, Shaffer has paired slumped glass with metal structures and found objects, capturing or creating an interaction between the two, at once sensuous and dynamic. In *Wall Wave*, a magnificent smooth ribbon of glass is squeezed out of a metal box high on a wall and frozen in mid-air (cat. 119). Shaffer's work is the "freeze frame" of action in a movie: the action might well continue, had she not stopped it.

Albert Paley's *Half Twist* also combines glass and steel, although Paley has come to this use somewhat differently, albeit for similar effect, after a long career as a celebrated metal sculptor (cat. 103). This piece is a collaboration with glass artist Martin Blank, but it is an indication of just how far glass has begun to spread into a wider sphere of sculptors and painters. Many artists who would not be categorized as "glass artists" now use the medium when their vision or their subject matter calls for it. Numbered among these—and there are plenty—are practitioners as diverse as Kiki Smith, known for her female imagery and experimental sculpture; Maya Lin, sculptor and land-artist; and Fred Wilson, installation artist and political activist.

None of these artists would see themselves as part of the Studio Glass Movement, although they have clearly benefitted from it. Undoubtedly the Studio Glass Movement itself has changed radically since its idealistic early days, to the point where the name may indeed be a misnomer. The simplicity of an isolated studio is now often traded for the individual artist establishing a costly small-scale industrial operation—necessitated by increasingly sophisticated methodologies. And the separation of artists from the glass industry itself was never that absolute: Vallien is a lifelong celebrated designer for Sweden's Kosta Boda; Dailey has designed for Cristallerie Daum in France and for other companies. Yet other artists call on industry to assist them in the completion of their own work: LaMonte's glass dresses are cast in a workshop in the Czech Republic. It all adds to a rich tapestry as glass threads its way into the ever-changing history of art in the twenty-first century. It remains to be seen what the future holds for the medium of glass, what role today's many up-and-coming younger artists will play, and how this collection amassed by Sherwin and Shirley with such enthusiasm and love will resonate with artists and audiences in the years to come.

PATRICIA GRIEVE WATKINSON is an essayist on the art and artists of the Pacific Northwest. She is the former director of the Museum of Art at Washington State University, the Fort Wayne Museum of Art in Indiana, and Pilchuck Glass School in Washington State.

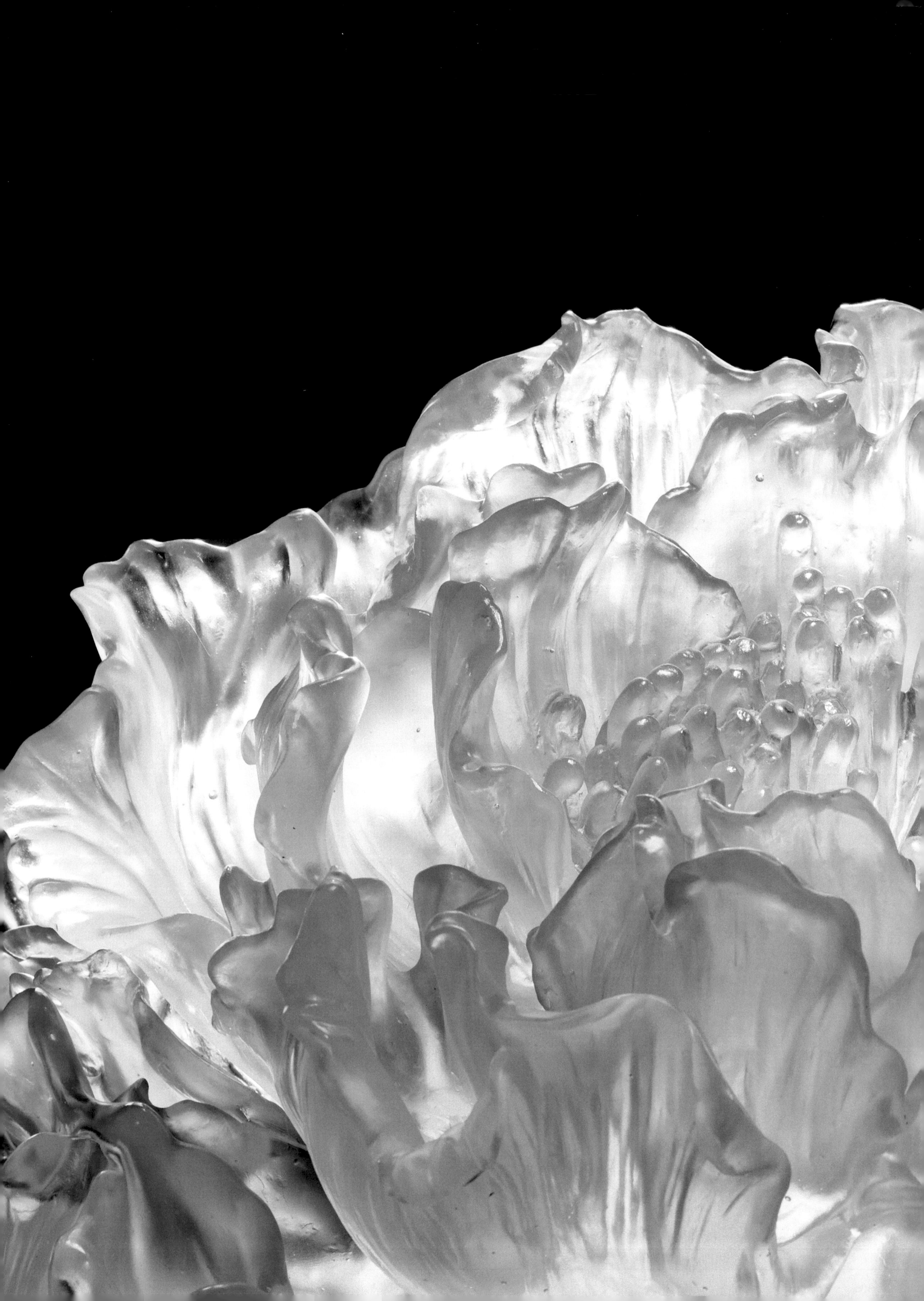

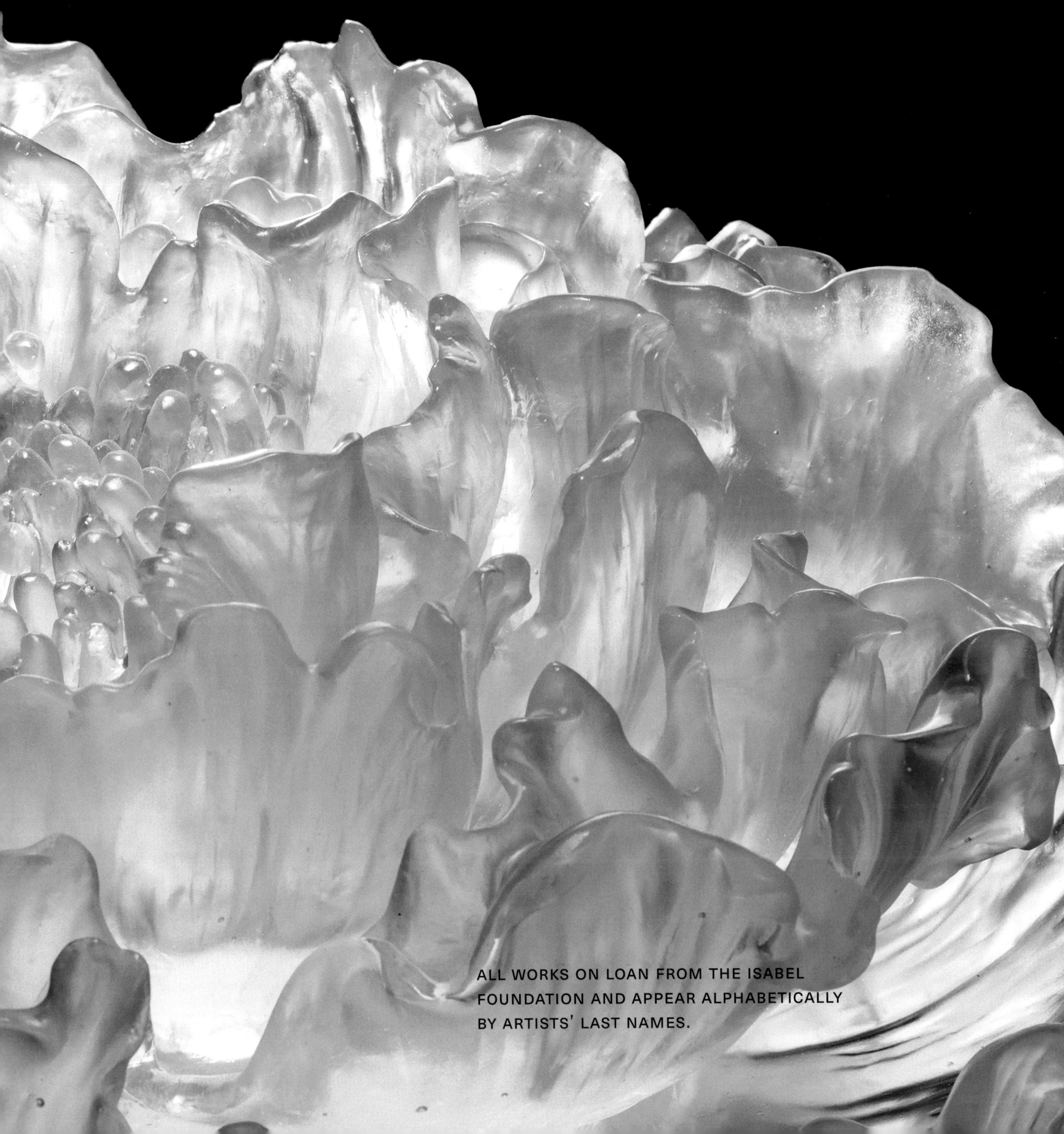

CATALOGUE

ALL WORKS ON LOAN FROM THE ISABEL
FOUNDATION AND APPEAR ALPHABETICALLY
BY ARTISTS' LAST NAMES.

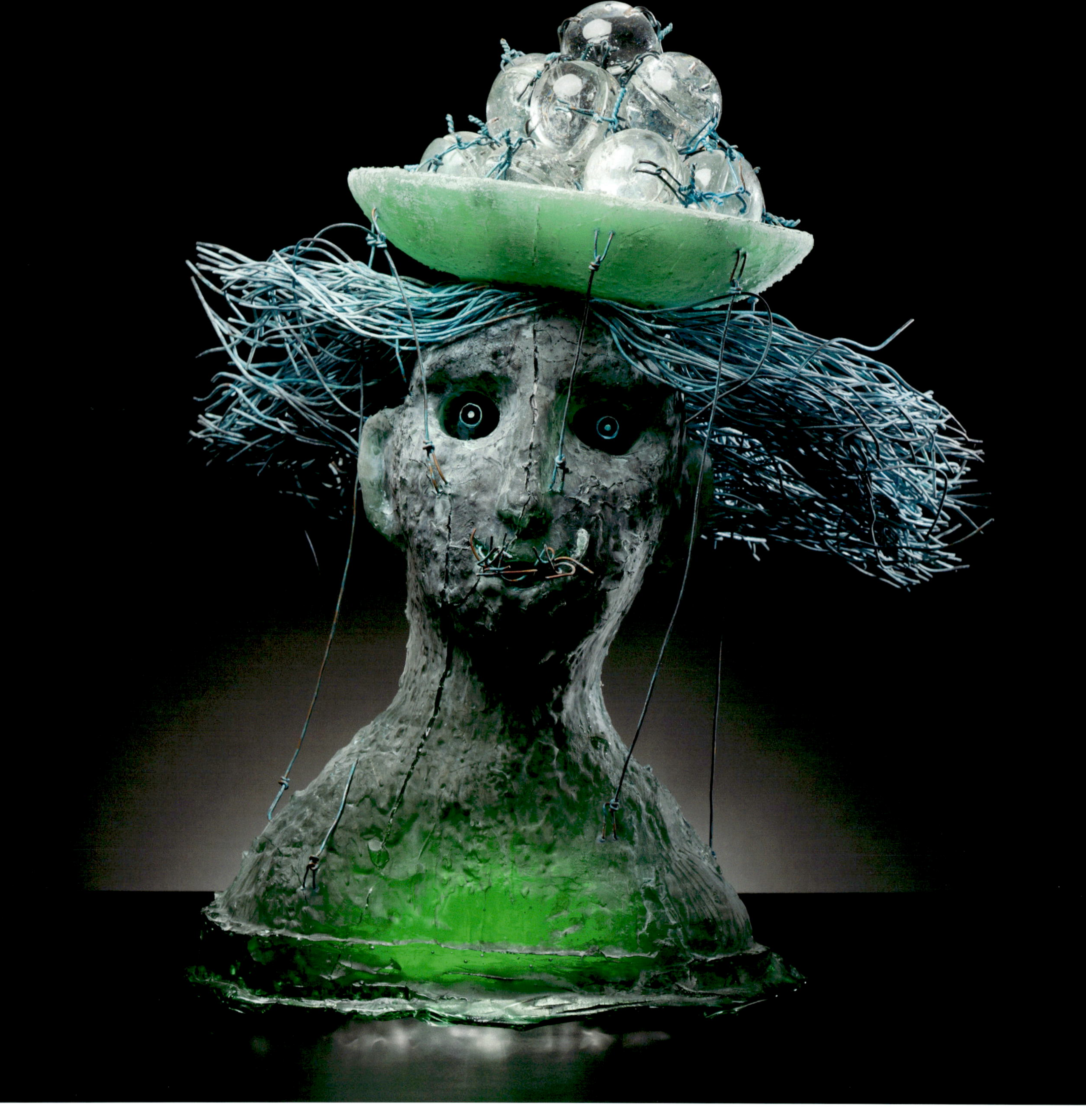

1   Hank Murta Adams   AMERICAN, BORN 1956   *Icee*   2006
CAST GLASS, COPPER   29 × 26½ × 22 INCHES   L2017.4

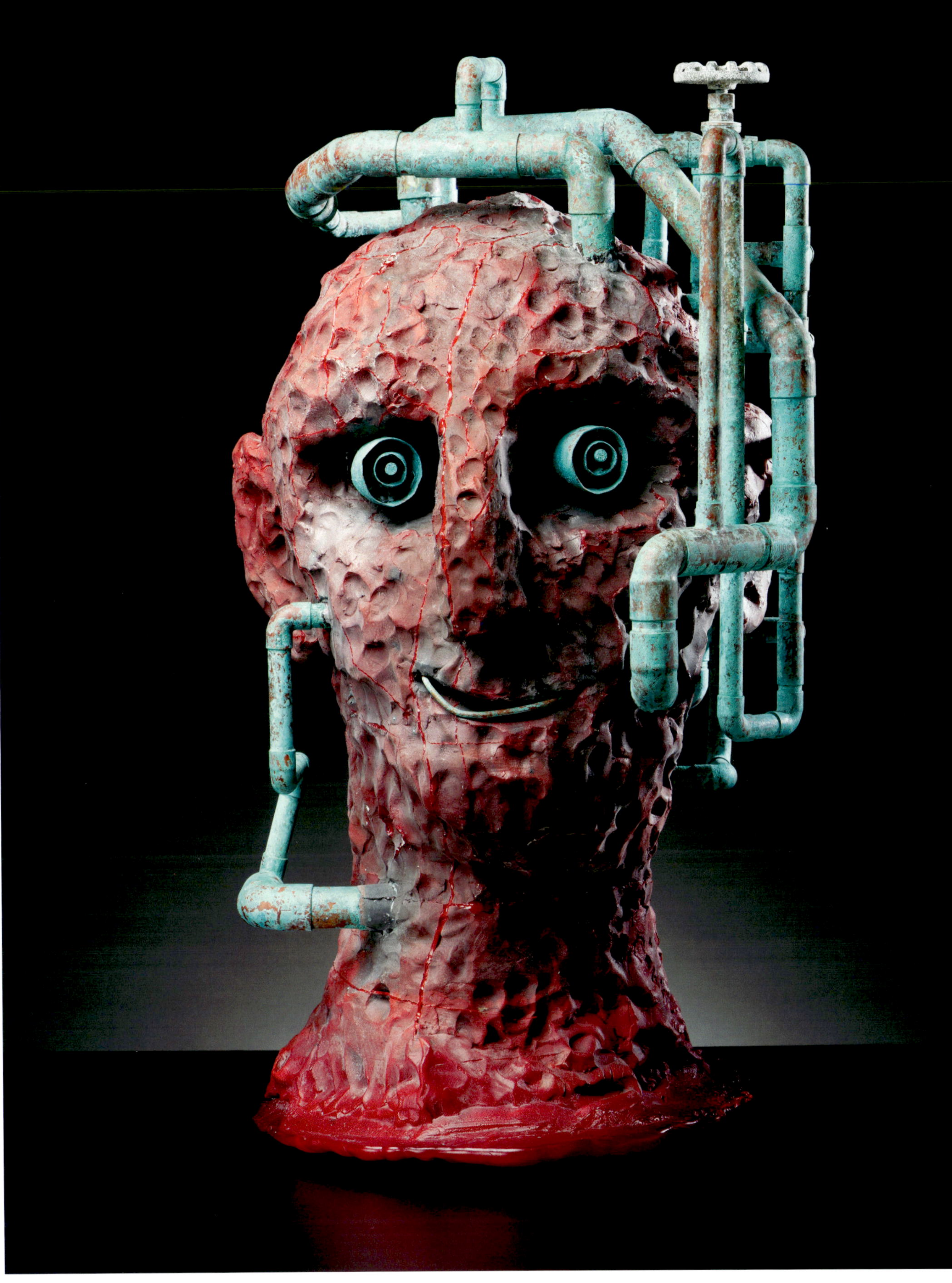

2   Hank Murta Adams   AMERICAN, BORN 1956   *Roto*   2004
CAST GLASS, COPPER   28½ × 15 × 13¾ INCHES   L2017.142

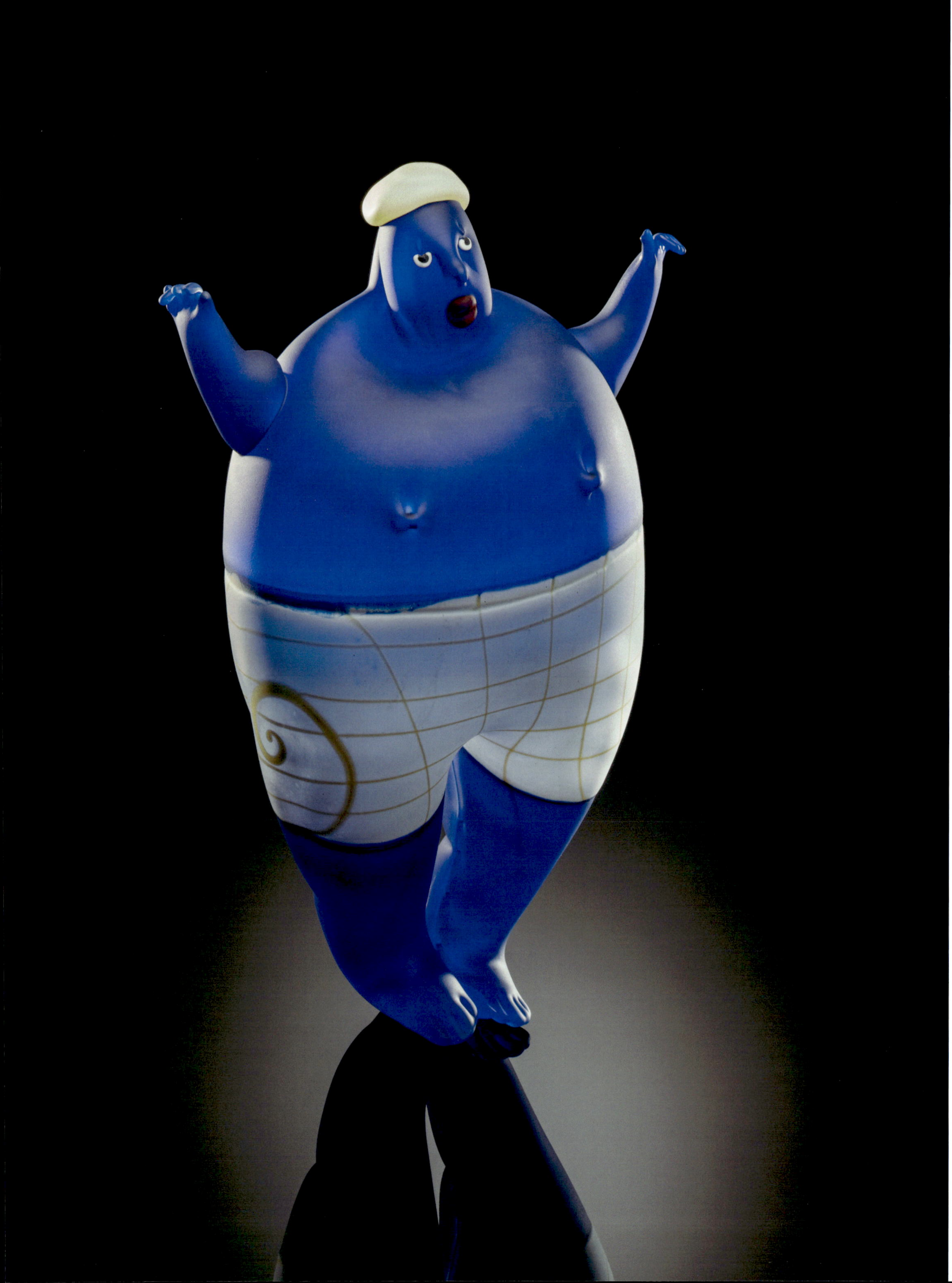

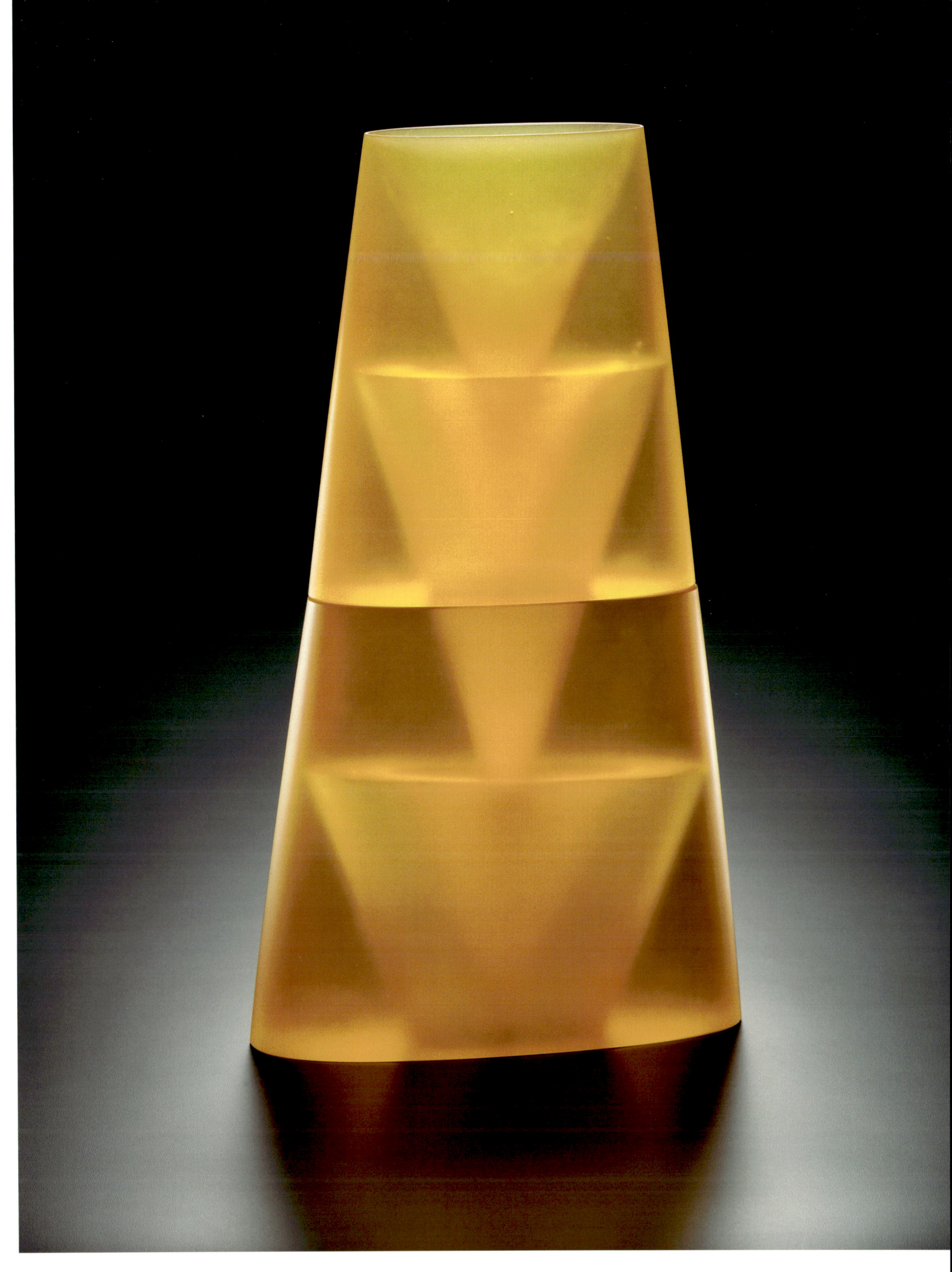

4 Vladimír Bachorík CZECH, BORN 1963 *Escallation* 2005
CAST GLASS 23½ × 13¹⁄₁₂ × 4 INCHES L2017.13

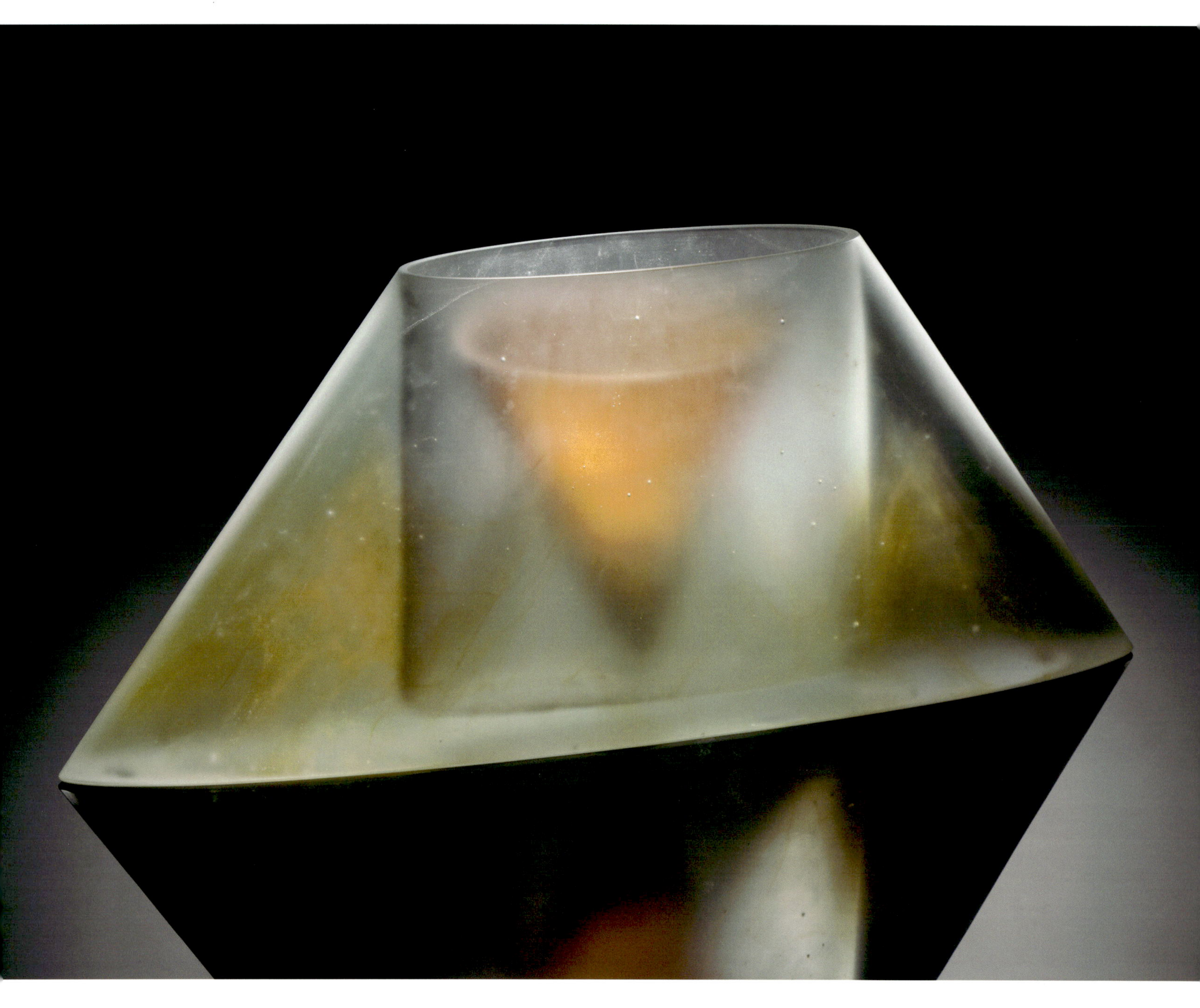

5 Vladimír Bachorík CZECH, BORN 1963 *Admittance* 2000
CAST GLASS   10⅜ × 26⅝ × 4⅞ INCHES   L2017.12

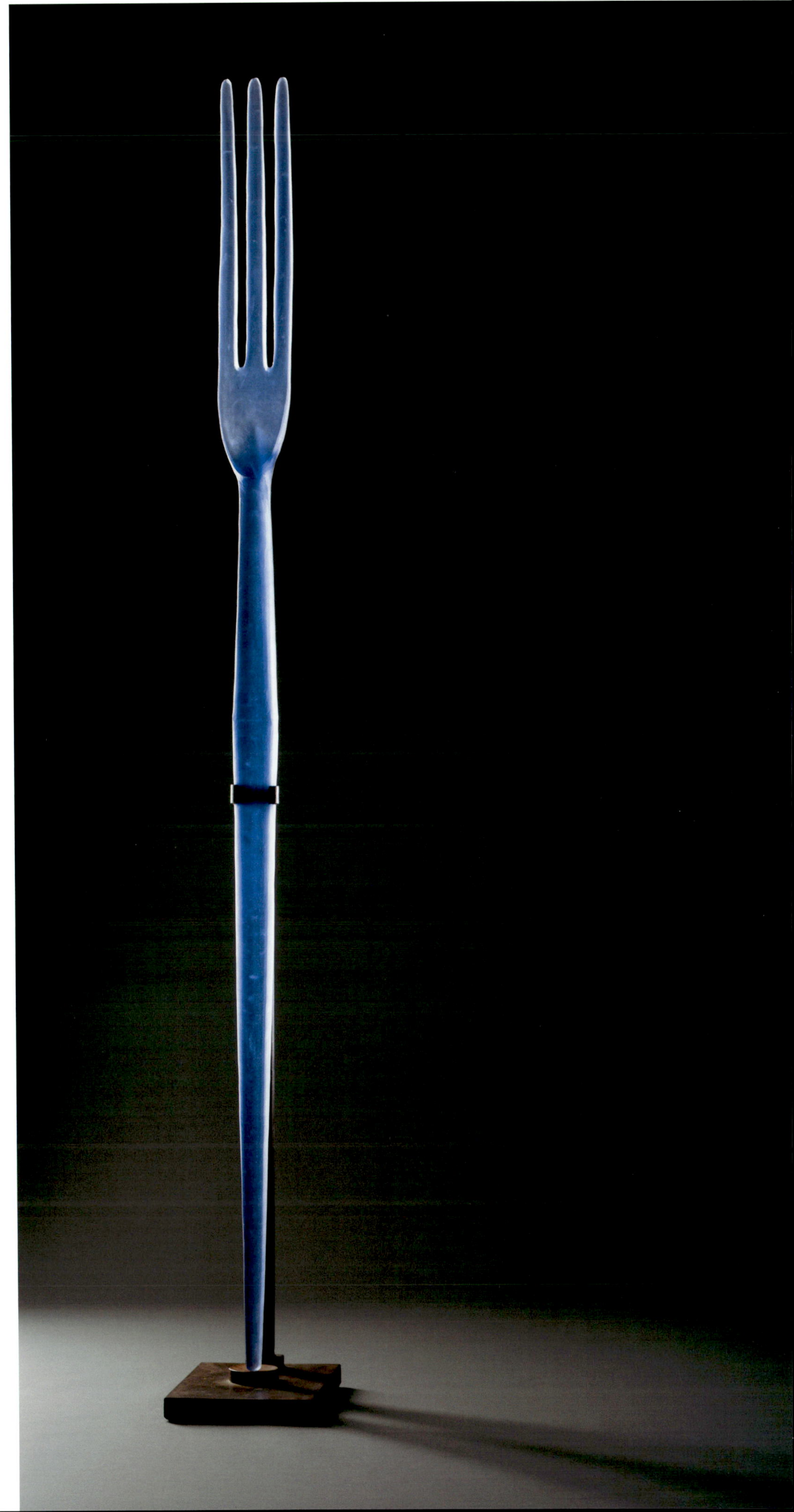

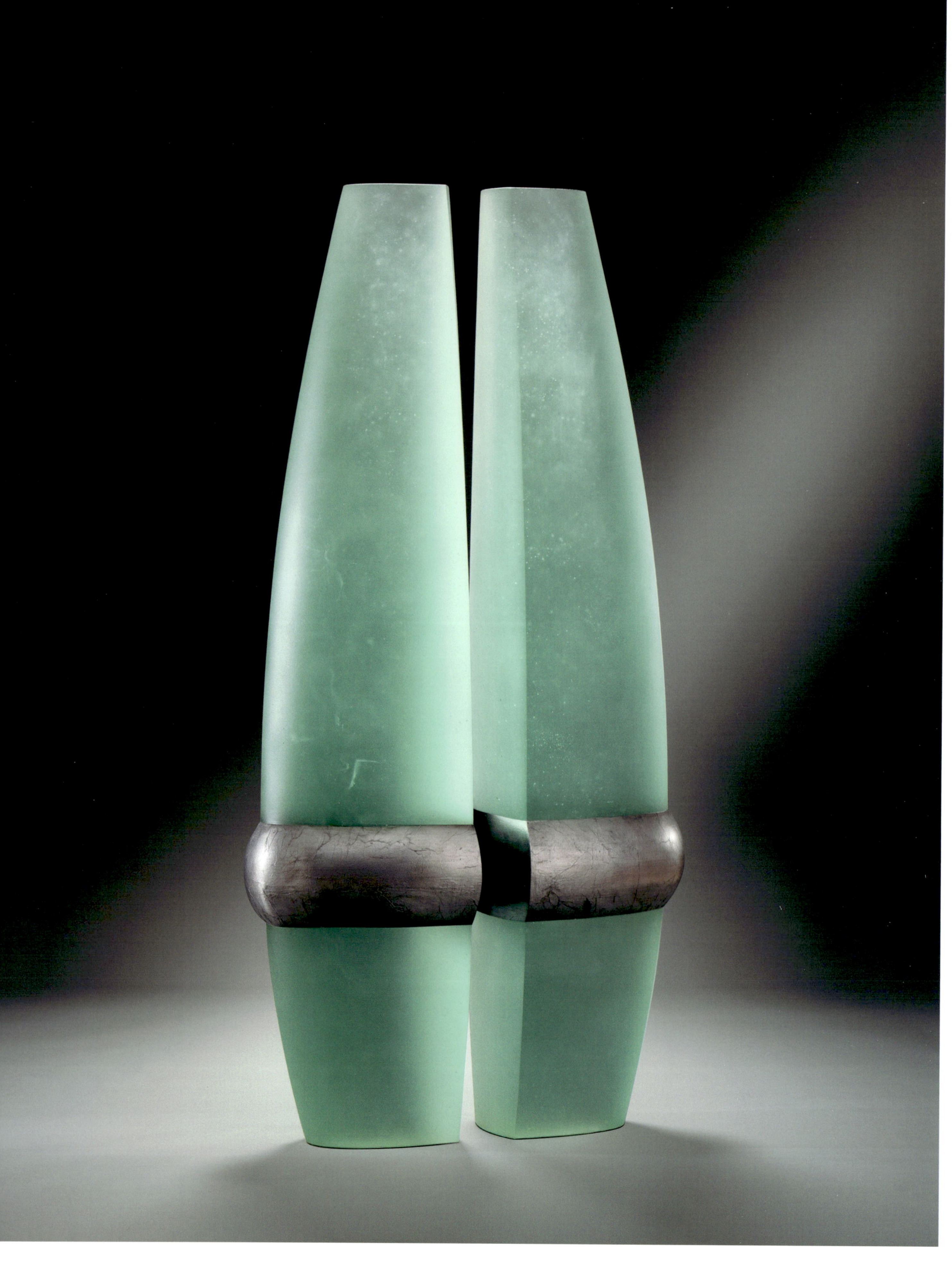

7   Howard Ben Tré   AMERICAN, BORN 1949   *Two*   2002
CAST GLASS, LEAD, PIGMENTED WAXES   60 × 29½ × 15½ INCHES (OVERALL)   L2017.15

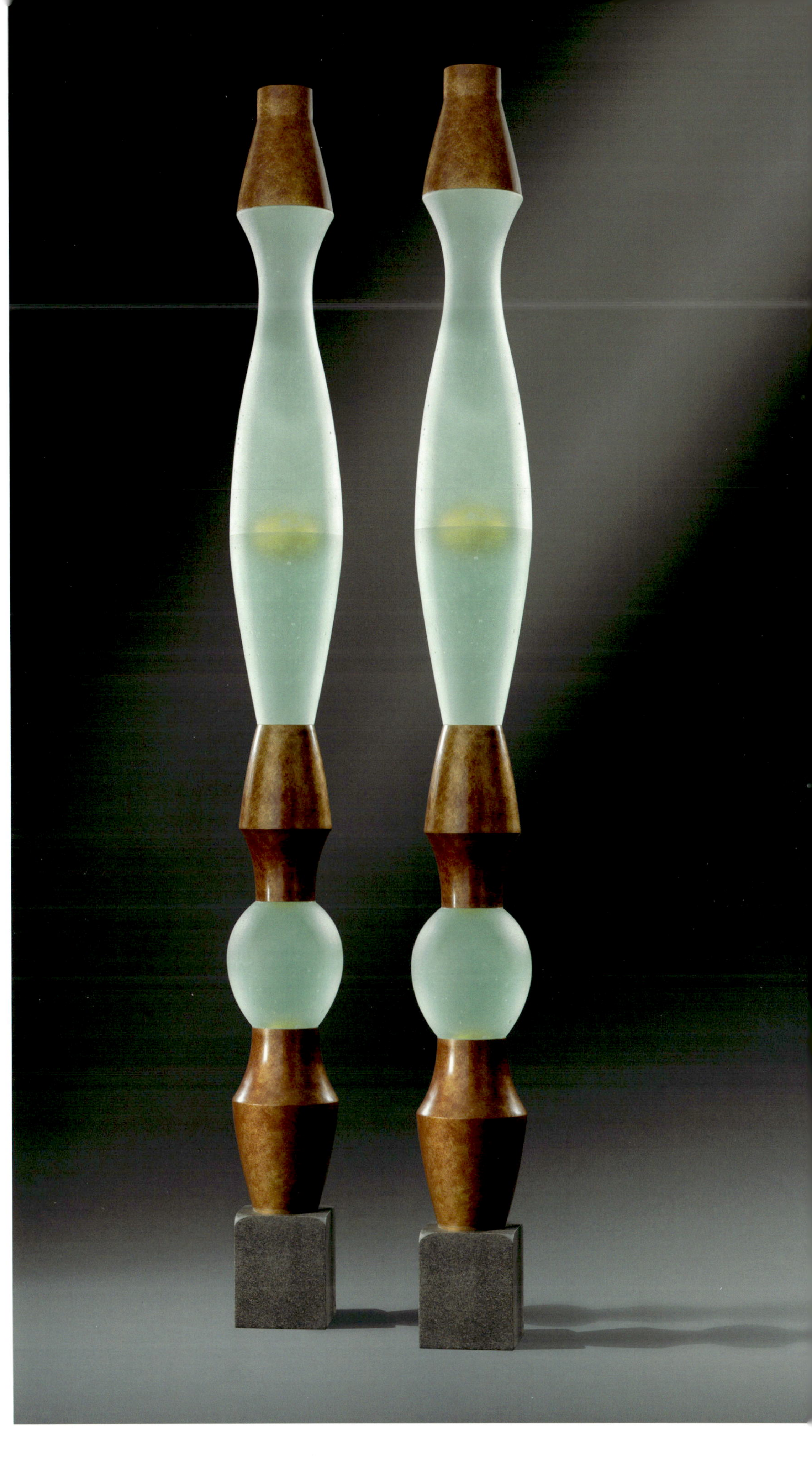

8 Howard Ben Tré   AMERICAN, BORN 1949   *Glass Towers*   2006
CAST GLASS, CAST BRONZE, GOLD LEAF, PATINA, GRANITE BASE
EACH: 118 × 10 × 10 INCHES   L2017.16

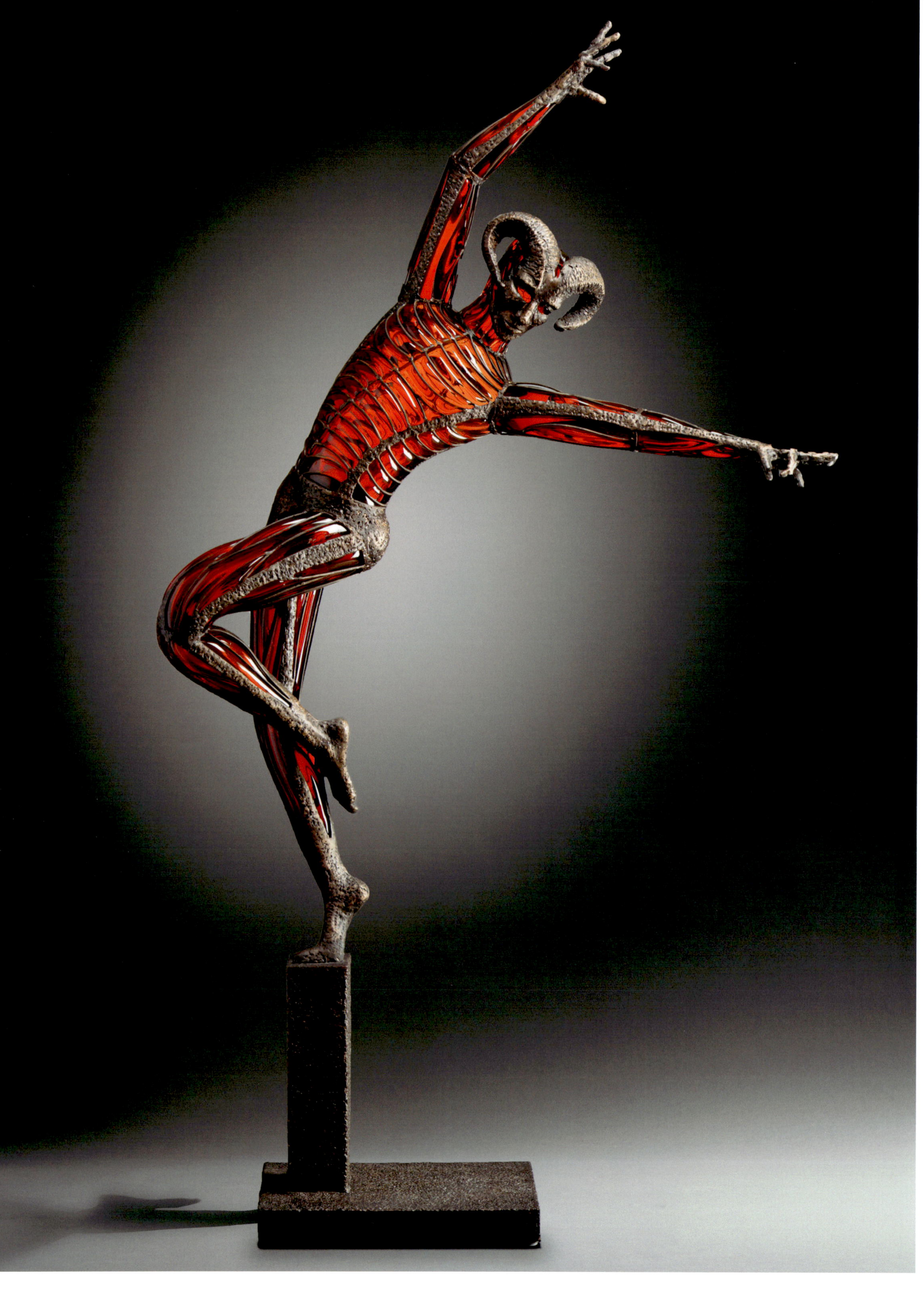

9 David Bennett AMERICAN, BORN 1941 *Twisting Aries Dancer* 2004
BLOWN GLASS, BRONZE   86 × 48 × 25 INCHES   L2017.29

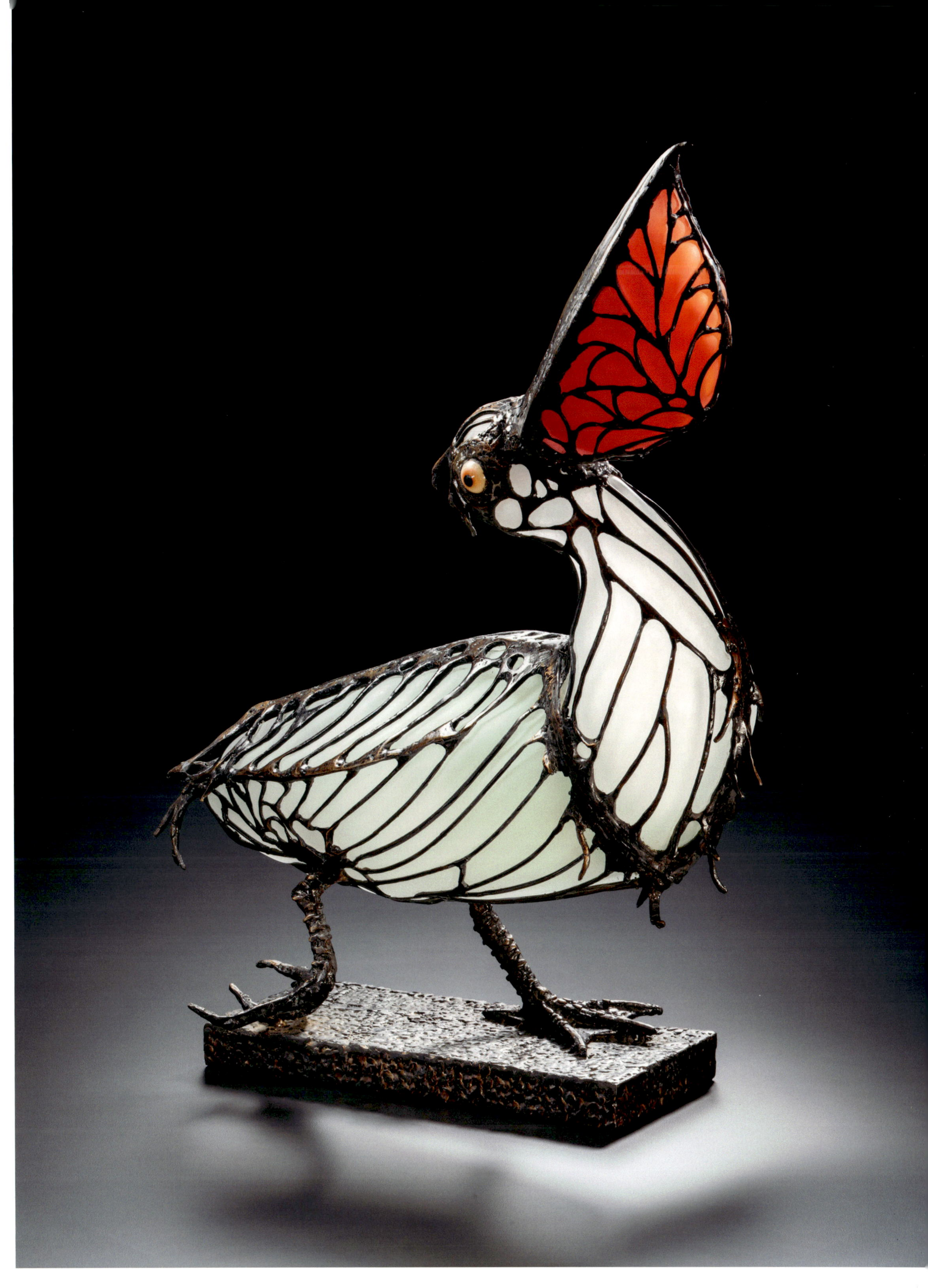

10   Drew Bennett   AMERICAN, BORN 1970   *Pelican*   2004
BLOWN GLASS, BRONZE   24 × 20¼ × 8 INCHES   L2017.30

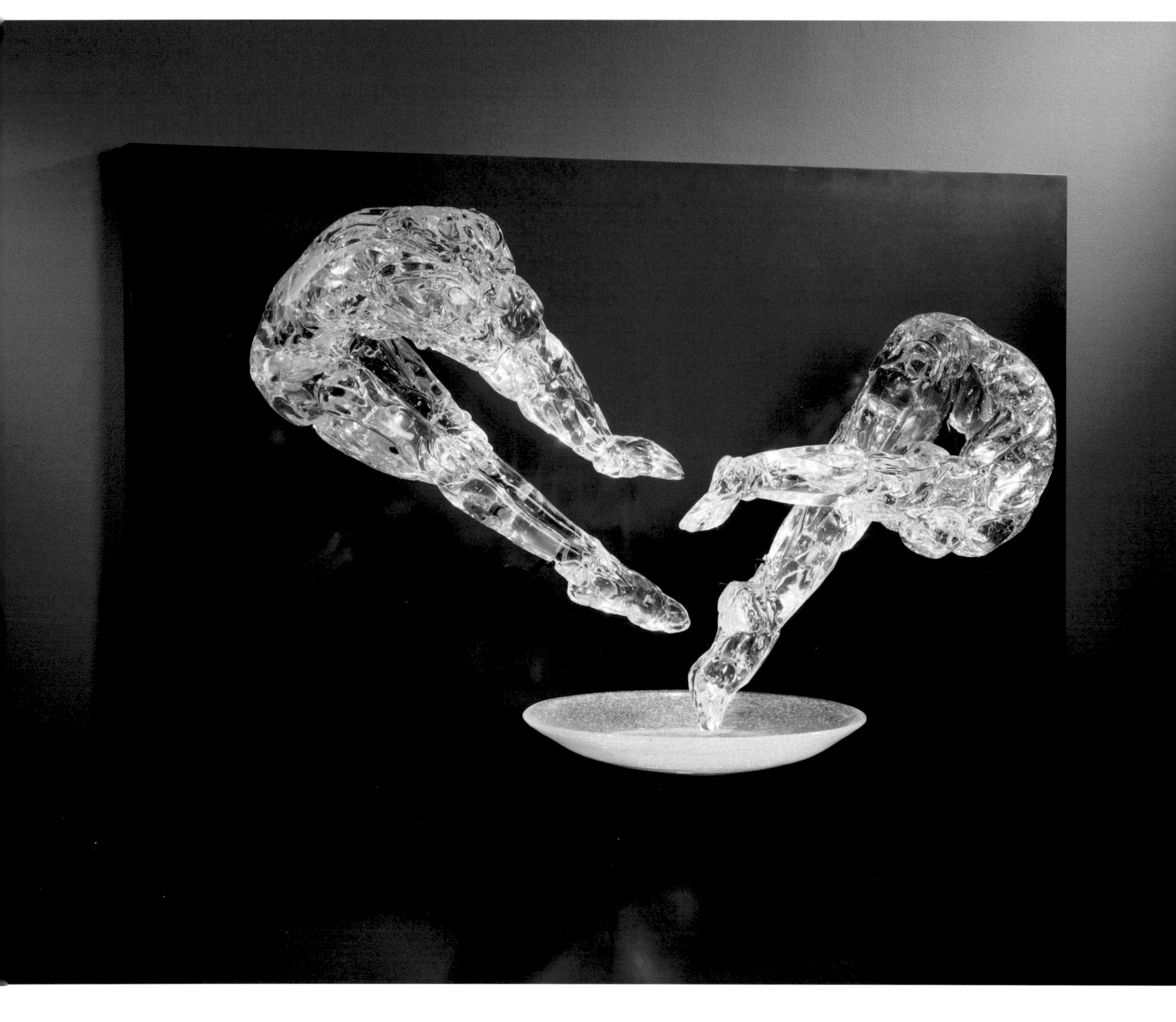

11   Martin Blank   AMERICAN, BORN 1962   *Drink from the Cup*   2000
HOT-SCULPTED GLASS, STEEL FRAME   40 × 64 × 24 INCHES   L2017.17

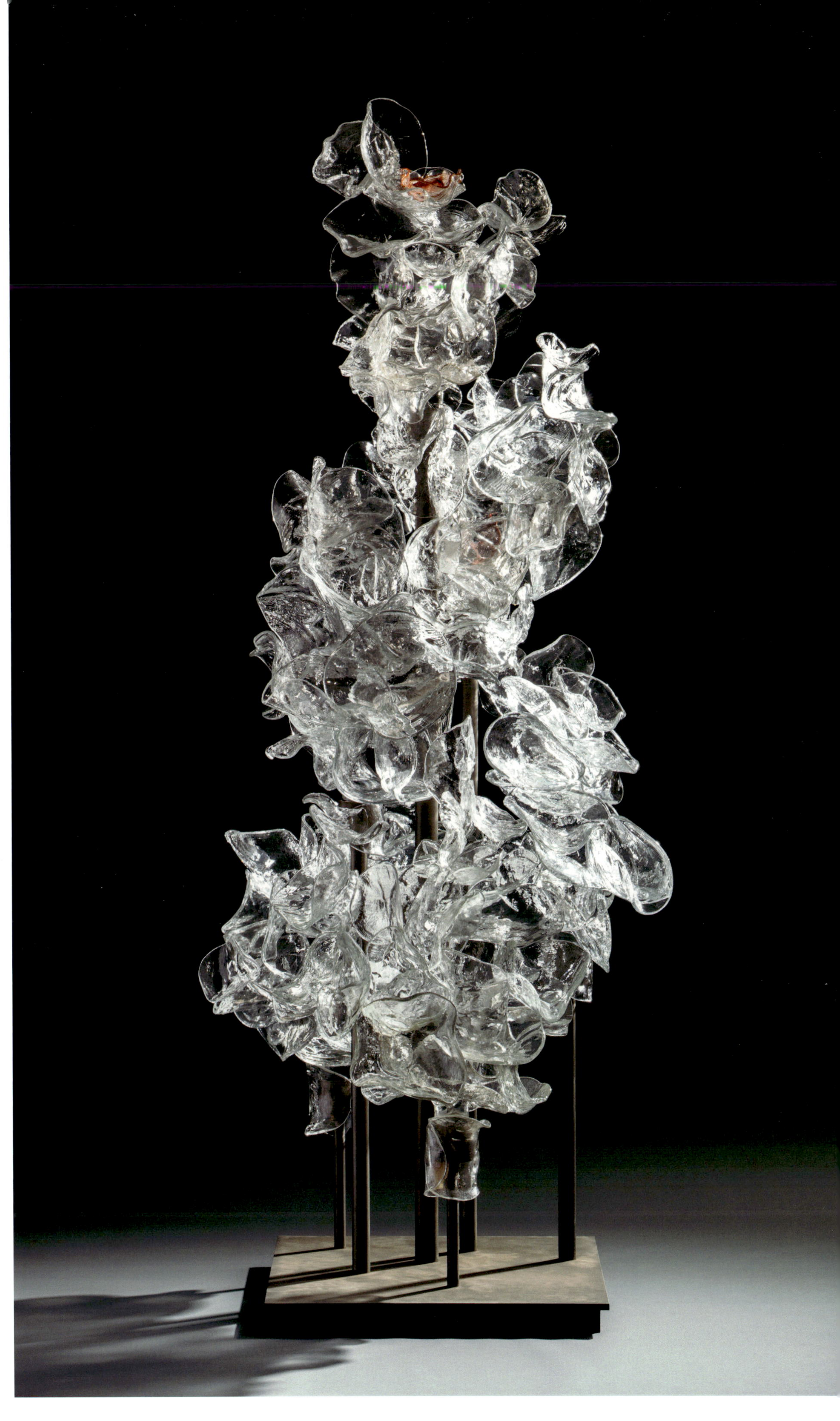

12   Martin Blank   AMERICAN, BORN 1962   *Steam Portrait*   2007
HOT-SCULPTED GLASS, STAINLESS STEEL STAND   98 × 36 × 30 INCHES   L2017.20

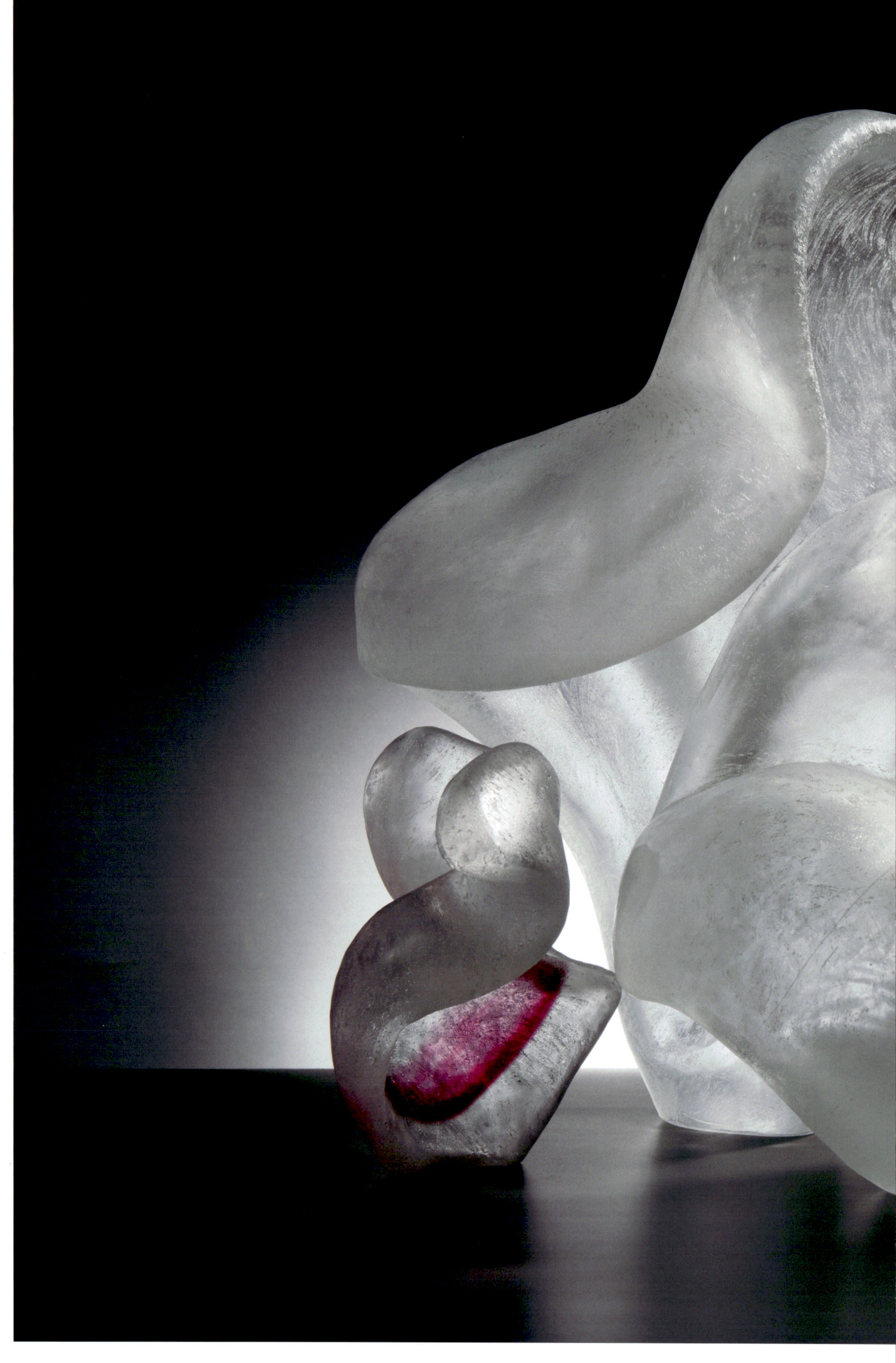

13   Martin Blank   AMERICAN, BORN 1962   *Via*   2002
HOT-WORKED GLASS   28½ × 36 × 15 INCHES   L2017.18

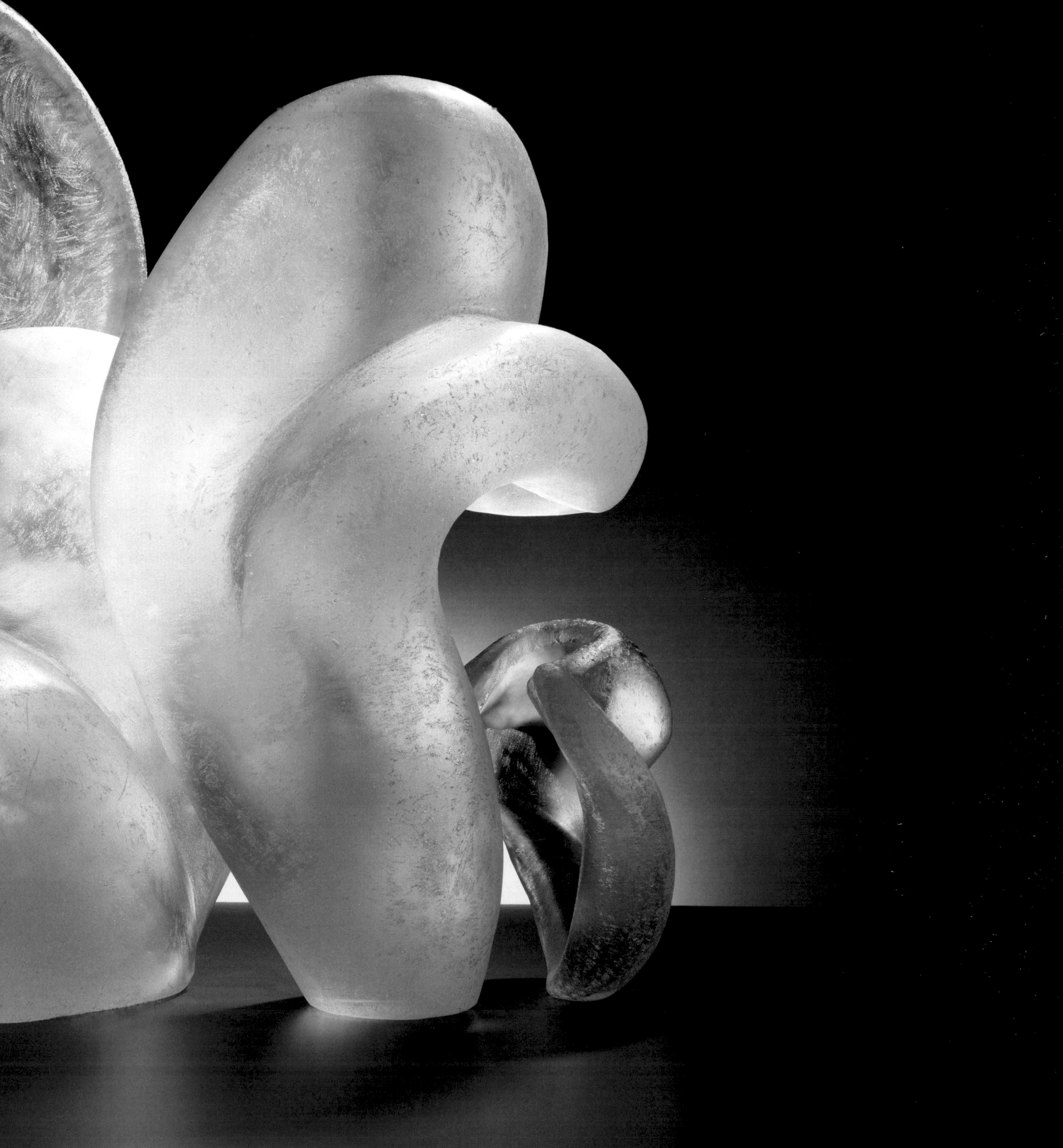

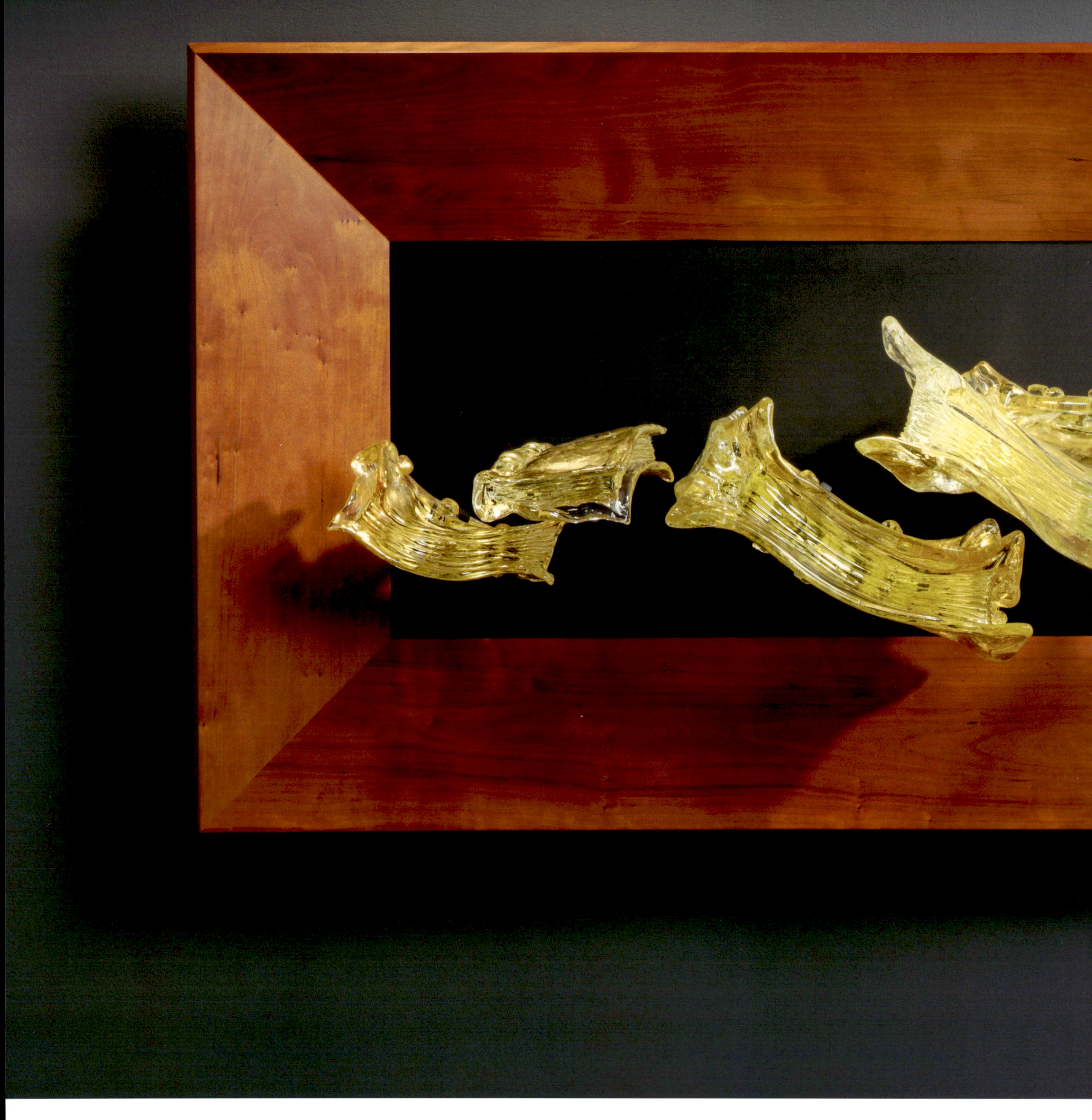

14   Martin Blank   AMERICAN, BORN 1962   *Whispering Tales*   2005
HOT-SCULPTED GLASS, STEEL AND WOOD FRAME   31 × 75 × 19 INCHES   L2017.19

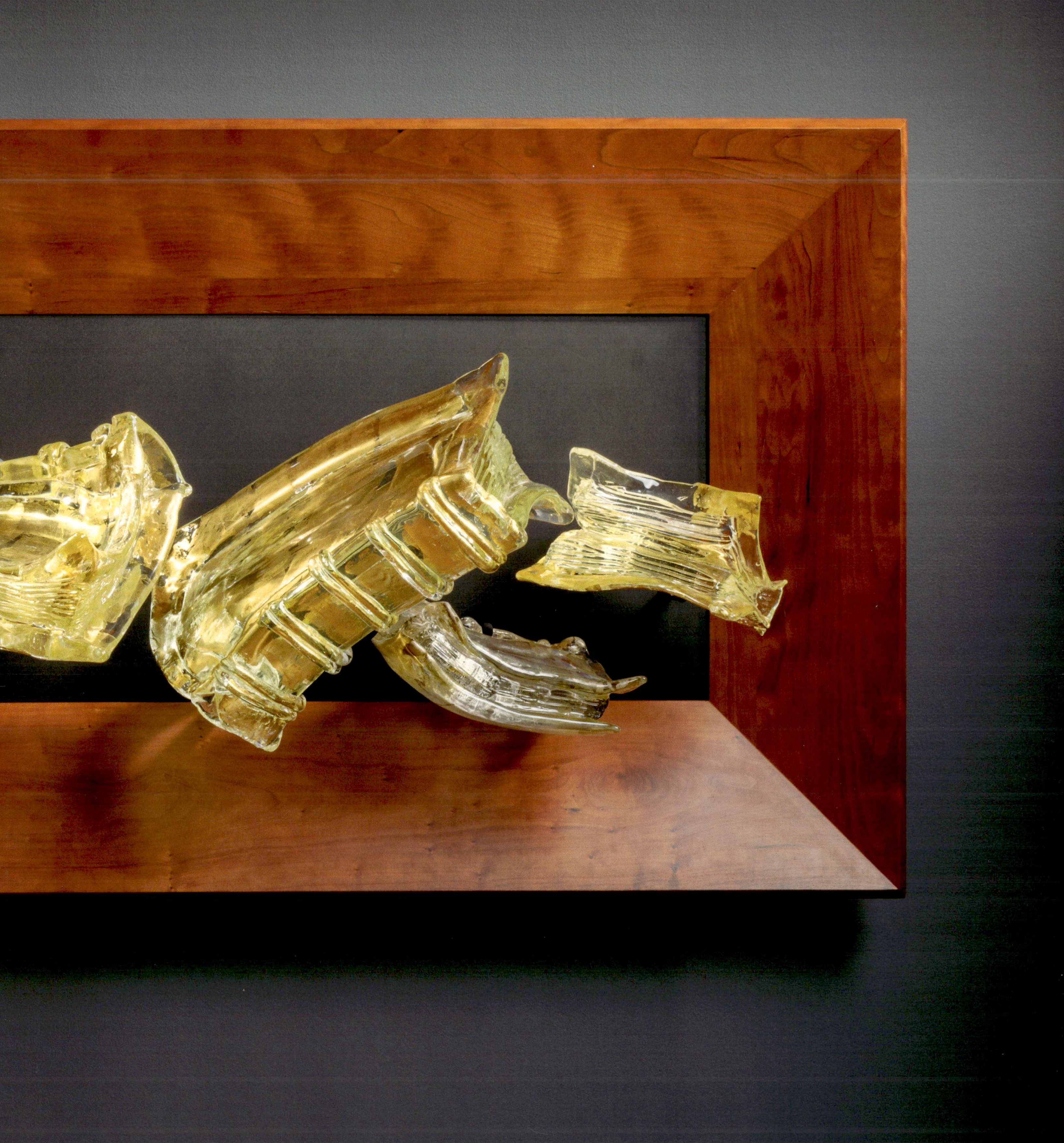

15   DESIGNED BY Pawel Borowski for Studio Borowski   POLISH, BORN 1969   *Frog*   2006
BLOWN GLASS WITH LIGHT, STEEL FEET   22½ × 23½ × 21¼ INCHES   L2017.94

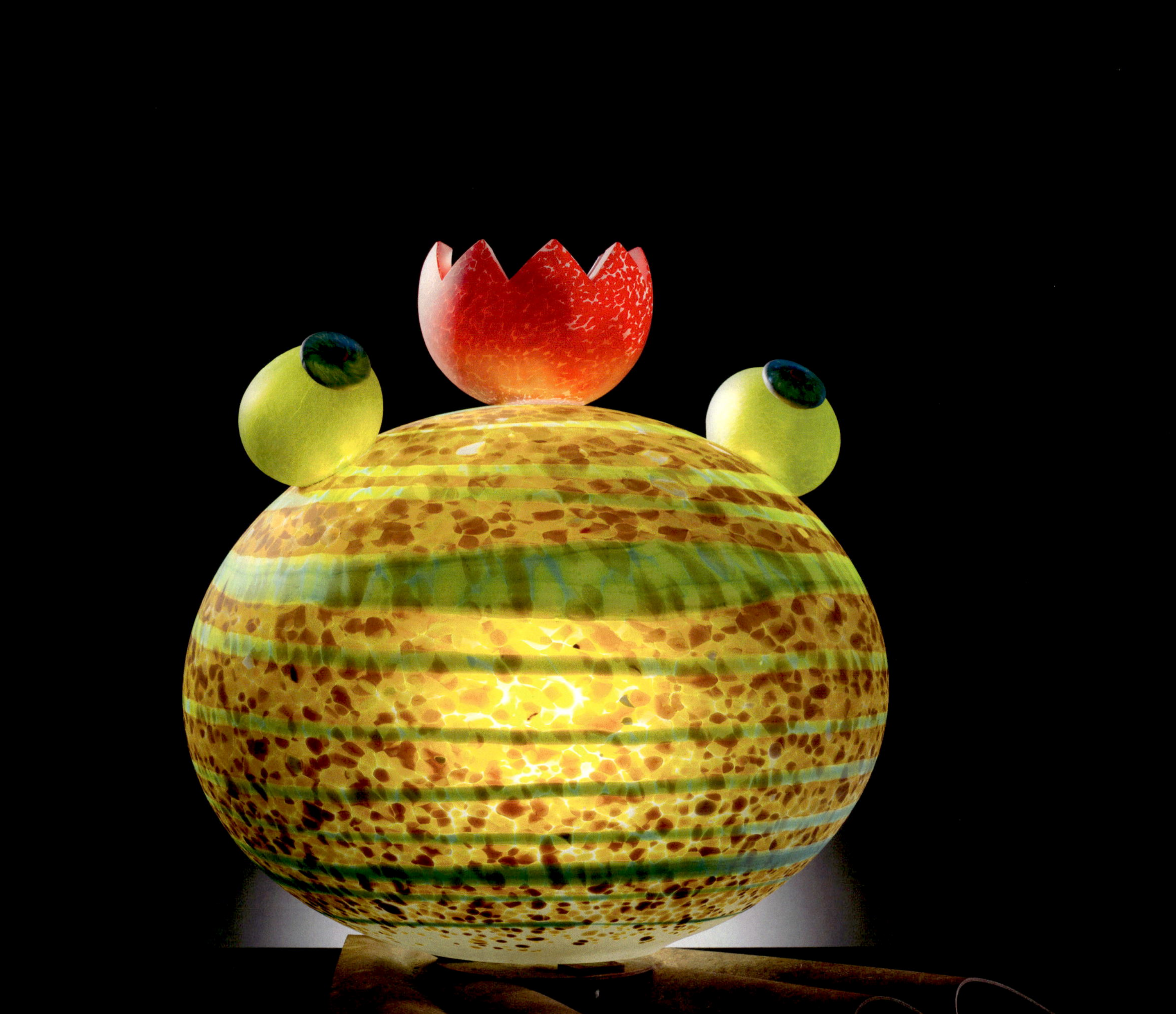

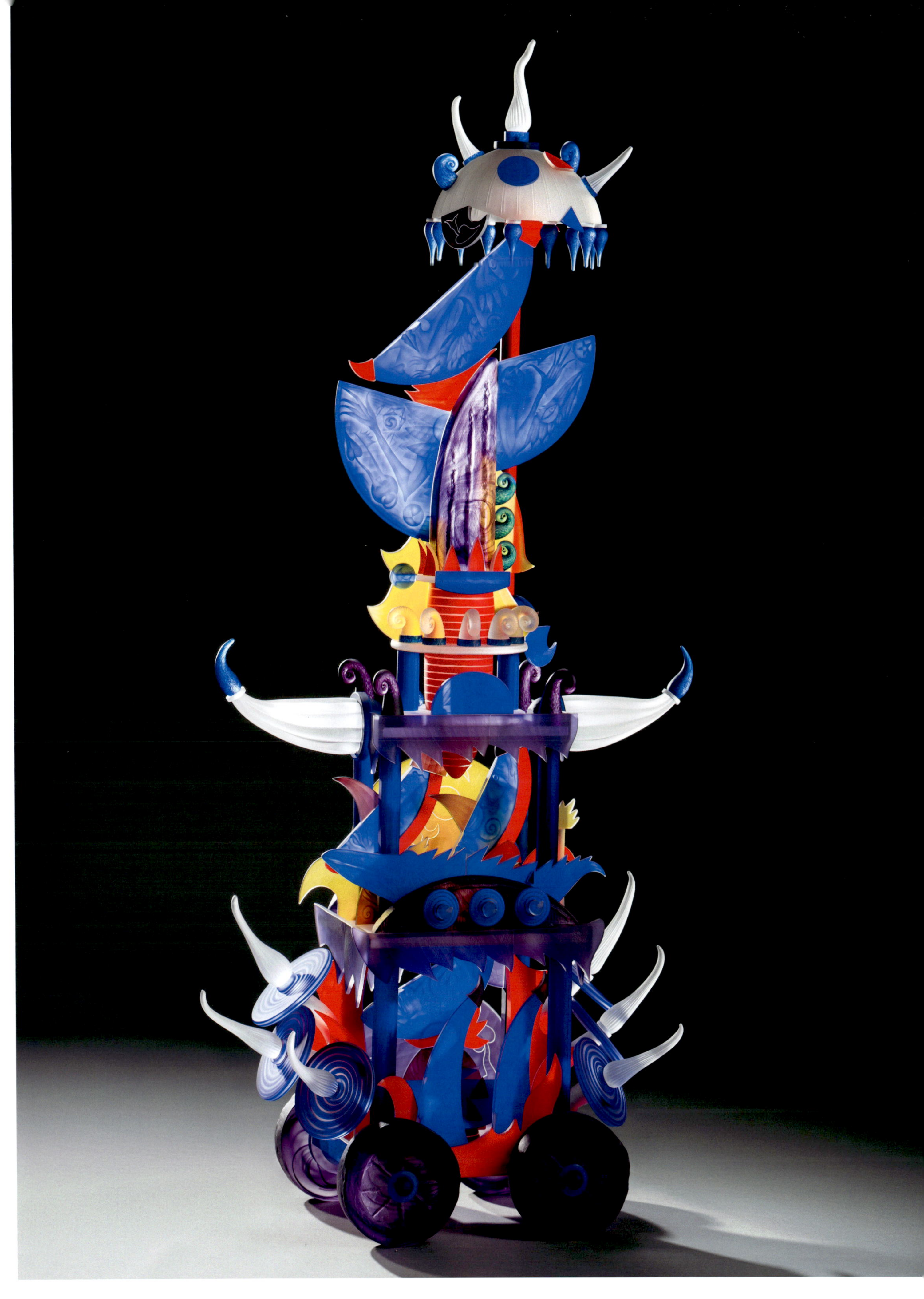

16   Pawel Borowski   POLISH, BORN 1969   *Circus*   2004   51
BLOWN, SANDBLASTED, AND ENGRAVED GLASS   78 × 34 × 19¼ INCHES   L2017.93

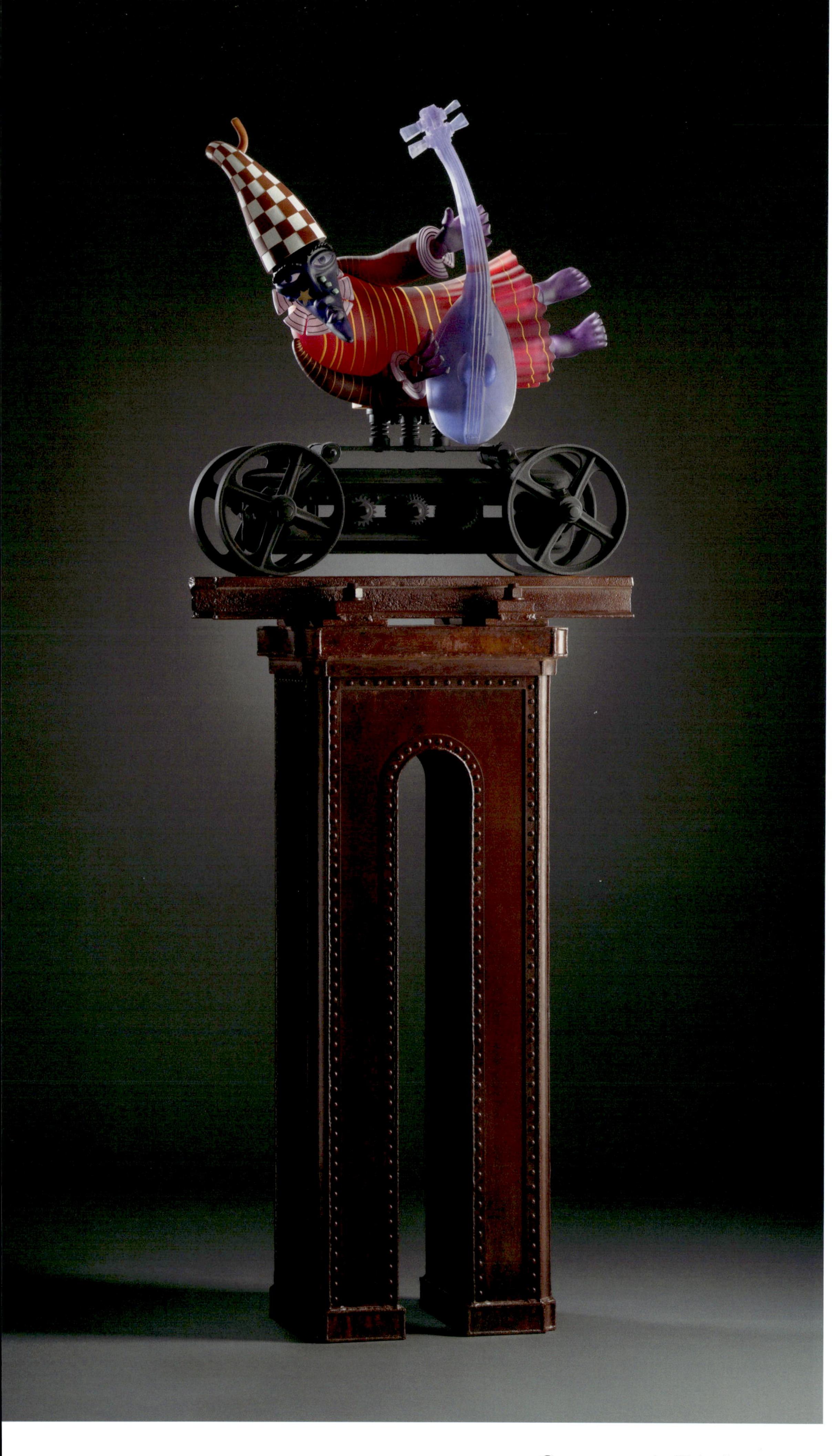

17 Stani Jan Borowski POLISH, BORN 1981 *Summoner's Tale II* 2008
HOT-WORKED GLASS WITH MIXED MEDIA 78½ × 28½ × 14 INCHES L2017.61

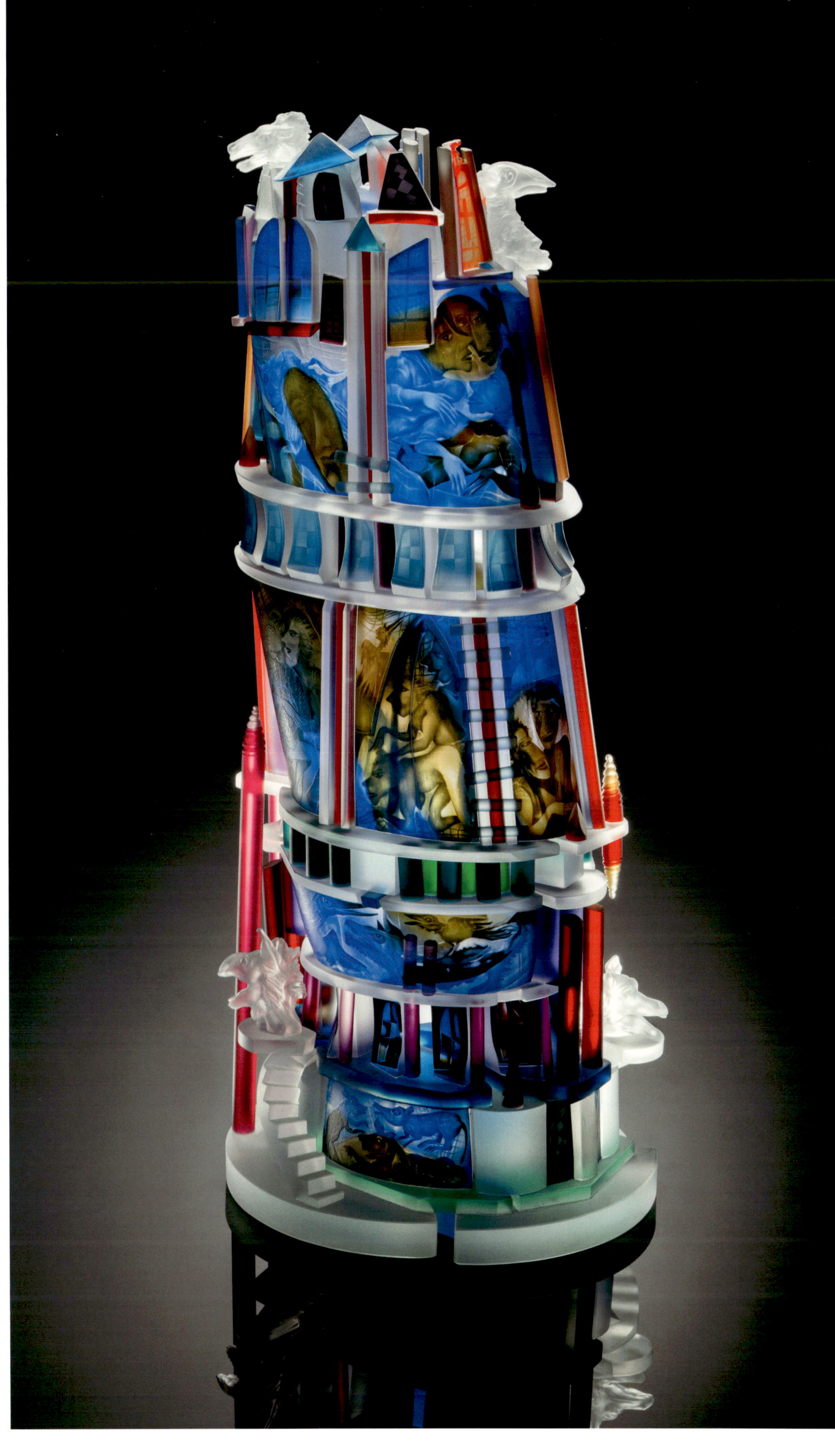

18   Stanislaw Borowski   POLISH, BORN FRANCE, 1944   *Tower of Desires II*   1999

BLOWN, COPPERWHEEL ENGRAVED, COLORED, AND ASSEMBLED GLASS   18½ × 7½ × 6½ INCHES   L2017.107

19 Stanislaw Borowski POLISH, BORN FRANCE, 1944

Chaise Longue 2001
BLOWN, COPPERWHEEL ENGRAVED, COLORED,
AND ASSEMBLED GLASS
9½ × 13¾ × 6¾ INCHES L2017.108

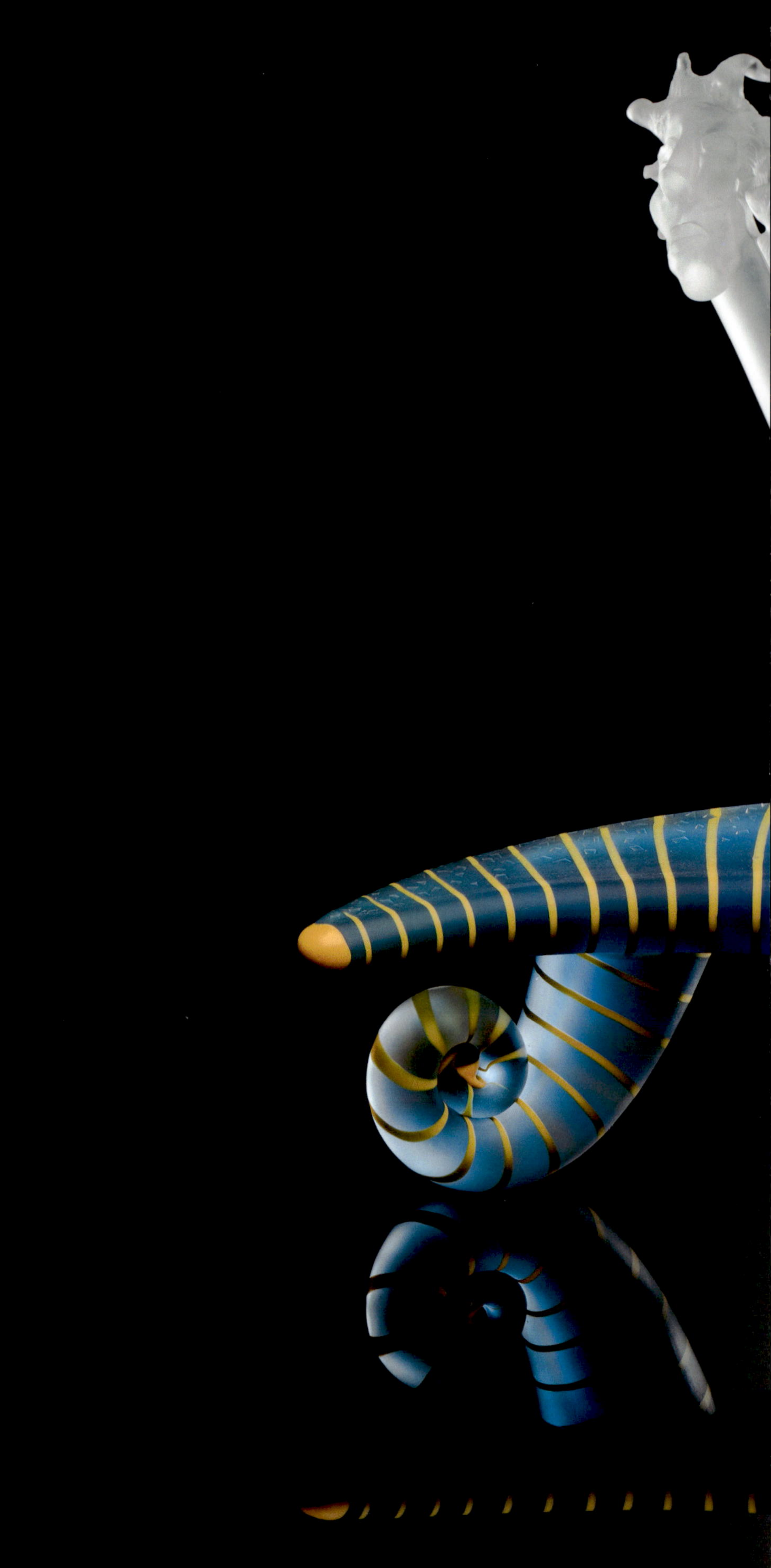

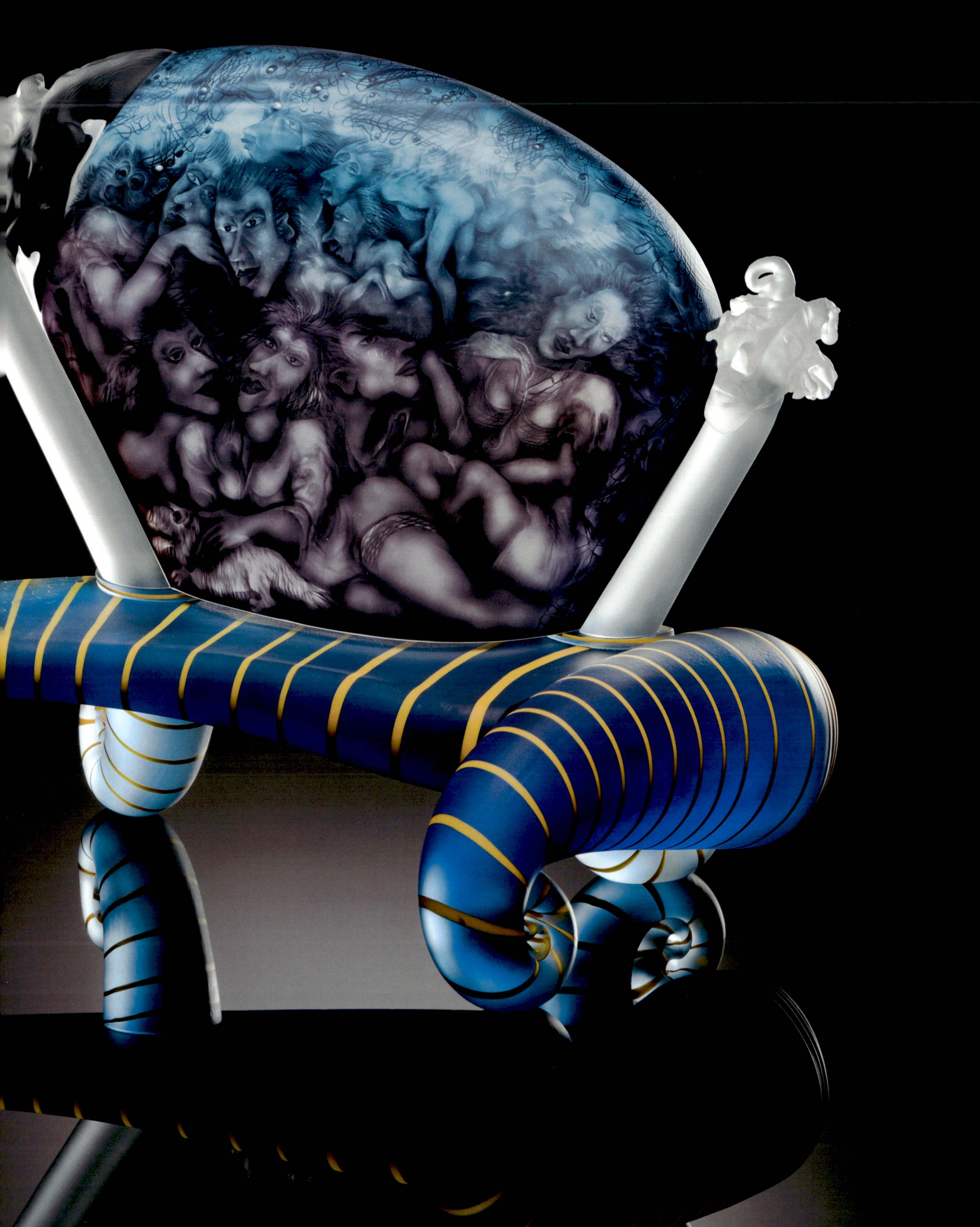

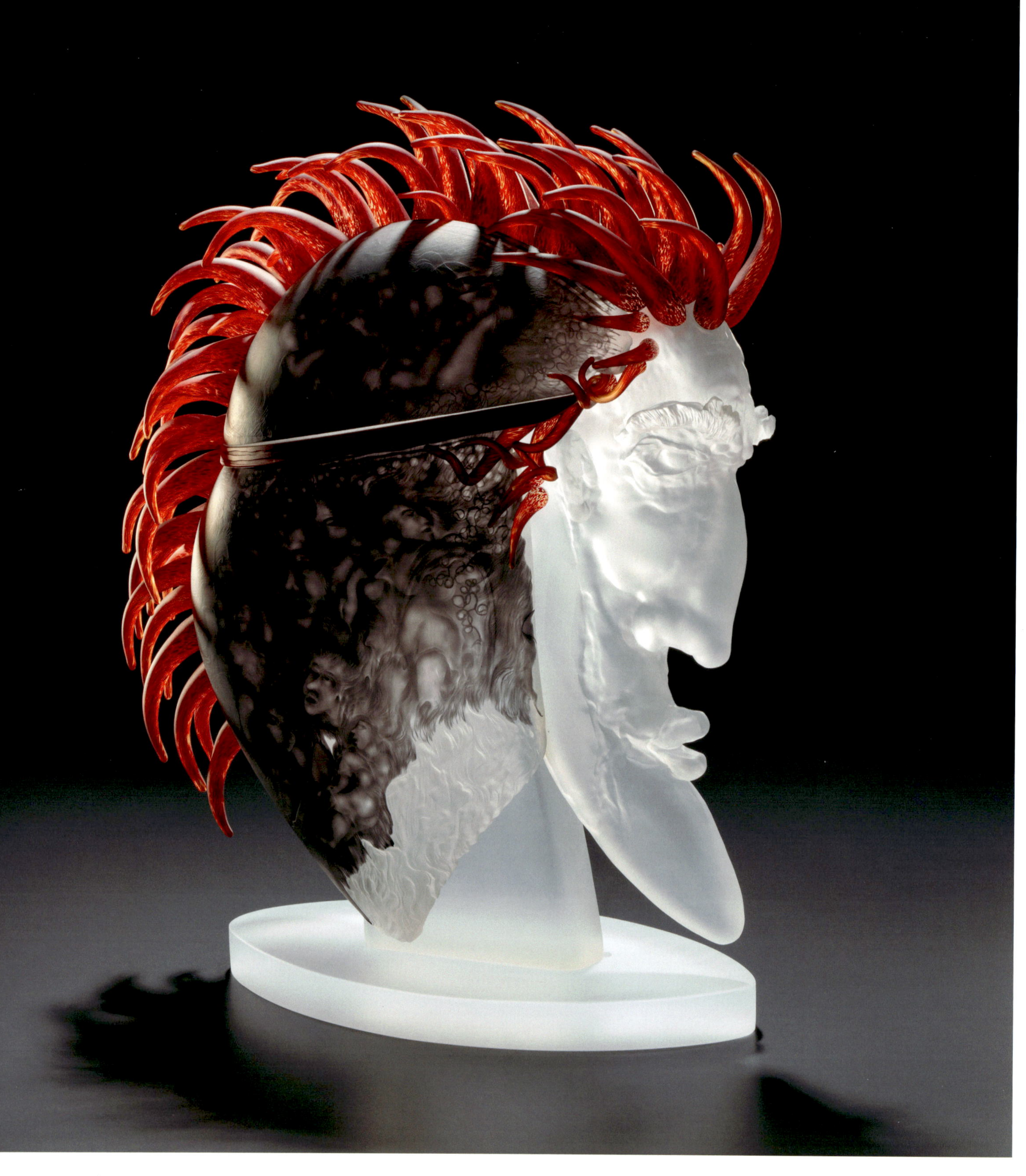

20   Stanislaw Borowski   POLISH, BORN FRANCE, 1944   *Grande Valentino I*   2005
BLOWN, COPPERWHEEL ENGRAVED, COLORED, AND ASSEMBLED GLASS   23¼ × 18¾ × 7¼ INCHES   L2017.109

21   Latchezar Boyadjiev   BULGARIAN, BORN 1959   *Figure*   2000
CAST AND ACID-POLISHED GLASS   28¼ × 27½ × 3½ INCHES   L2017.1

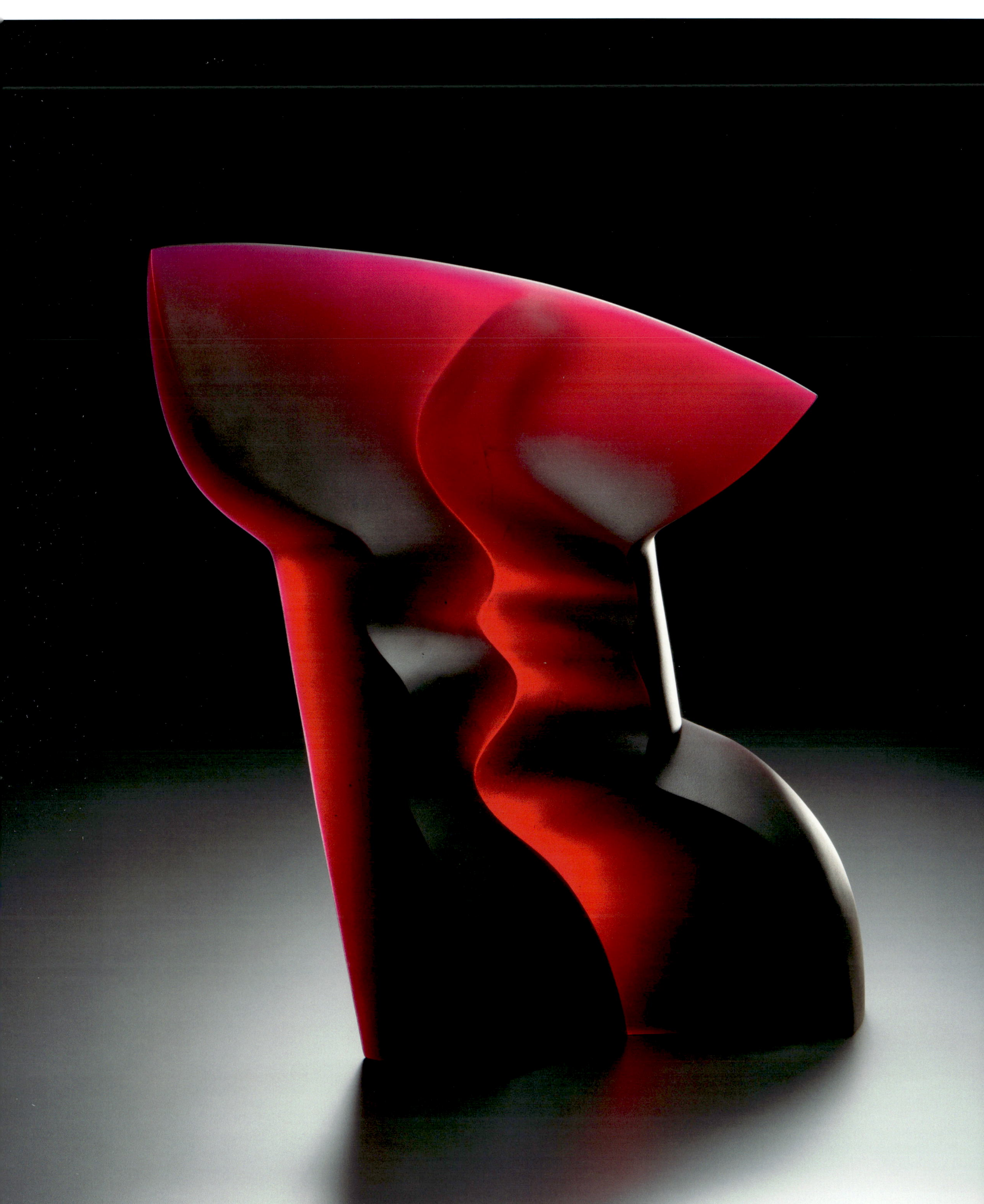

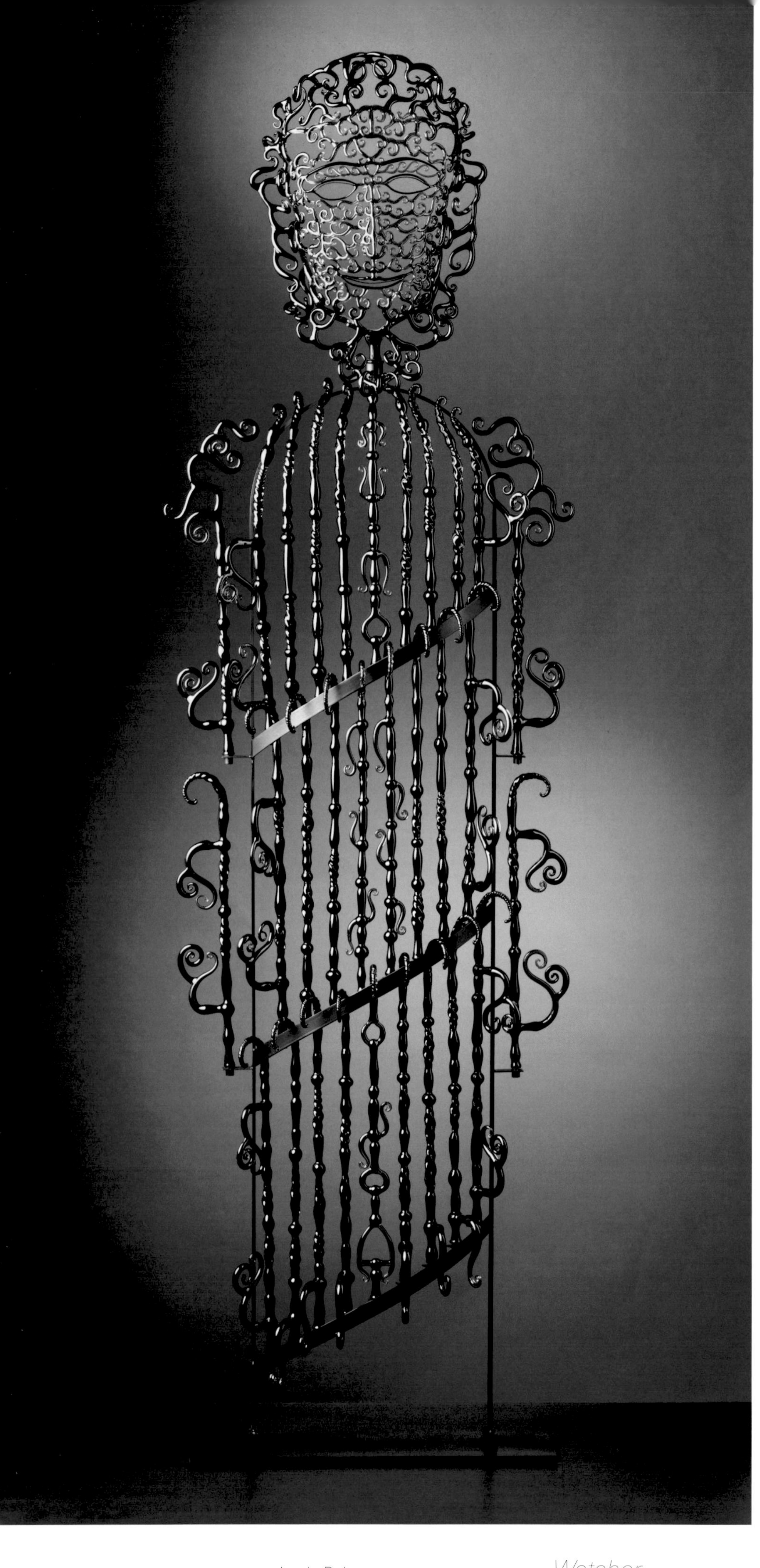

22 Lucio Bubacco ITALIAN, BORN 1957 *Watcher* 2009
LAMPWORKED GLASS, STEEL STAND   86½ × 21¾ × 9¾ INCHES   L2017.140

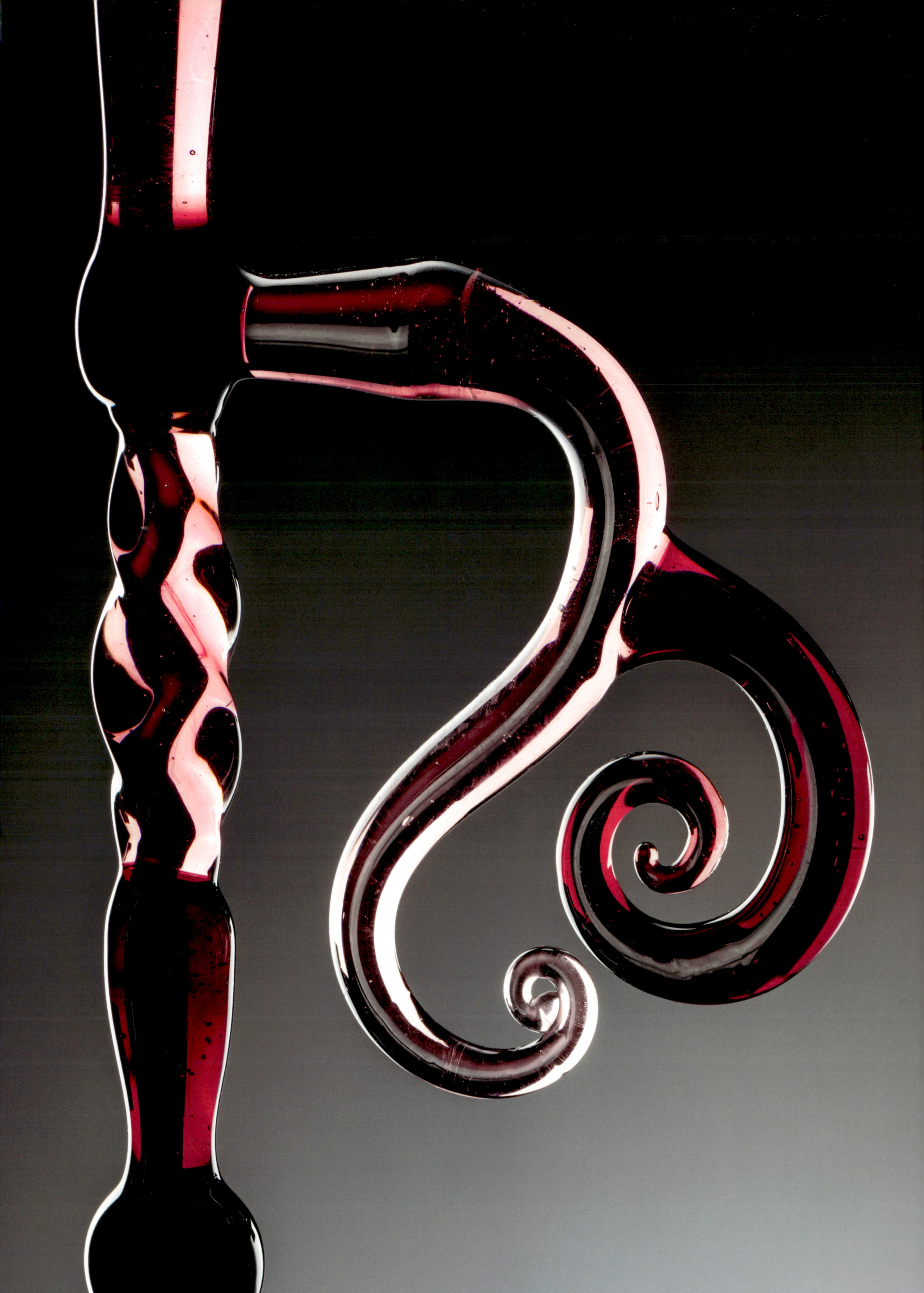

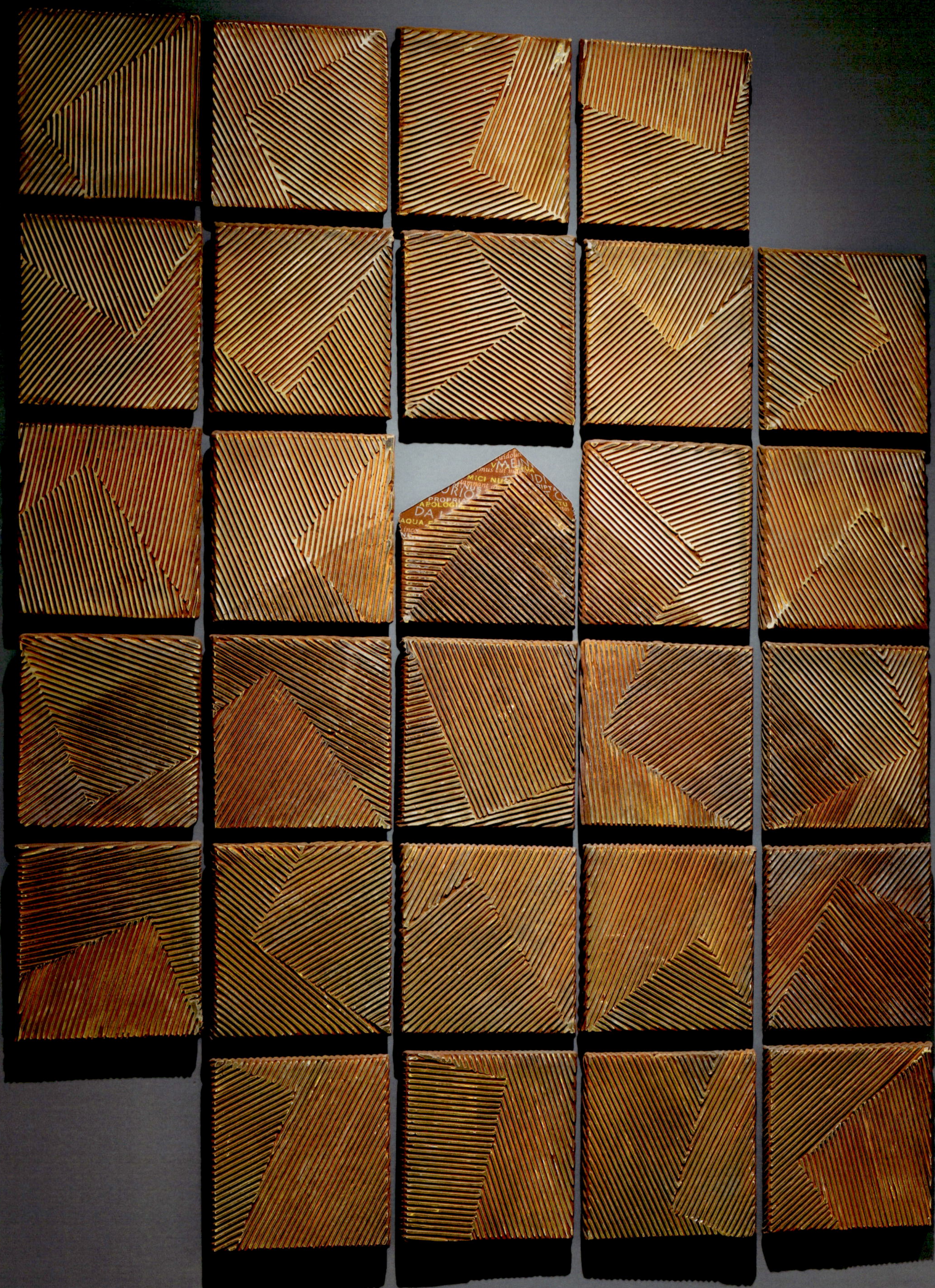
VMEIN
MICI NVT
PROPRIA
APOLOGI
DA
AQVA E

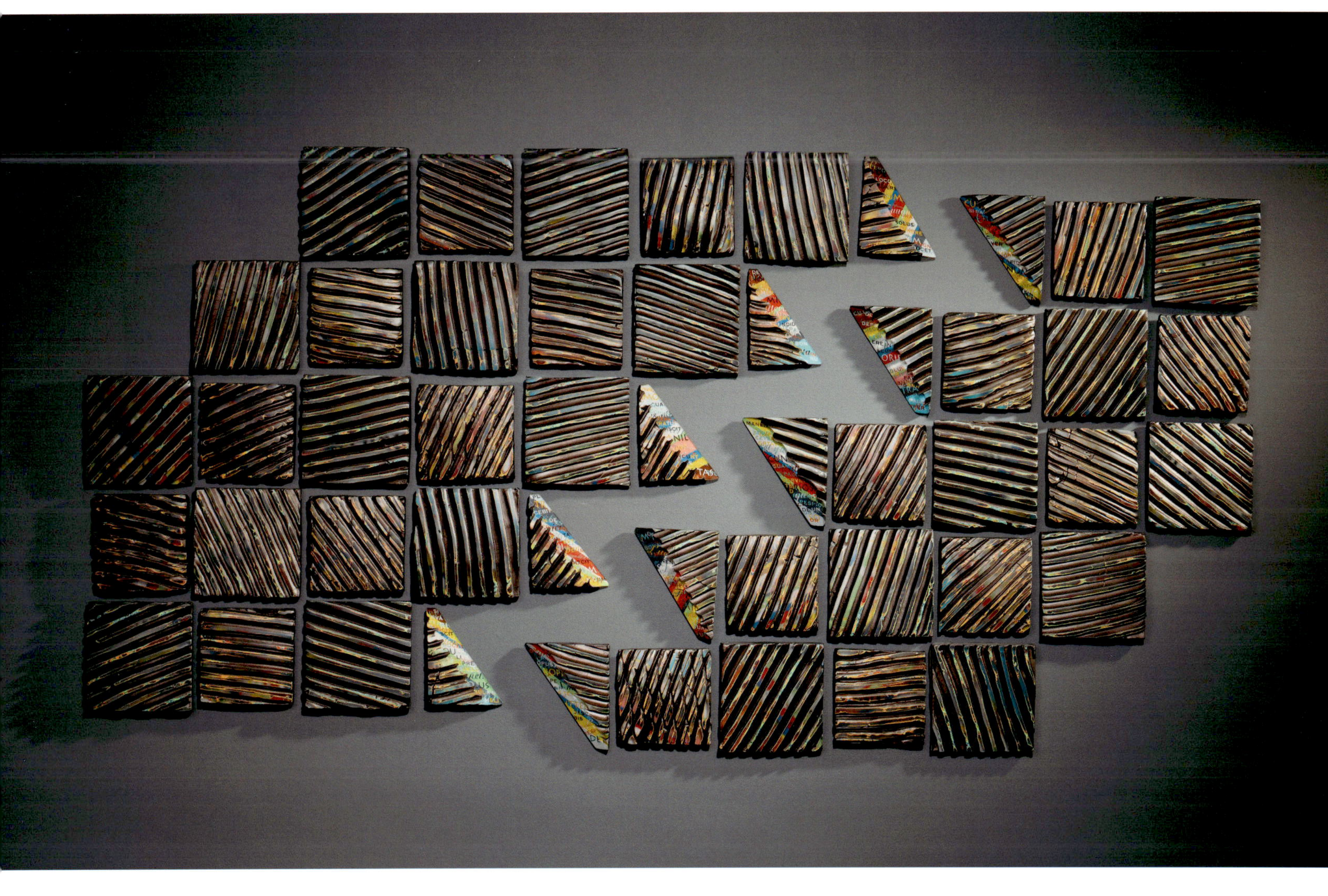

24   William Carlson   AMERICAN, BORN 1950   *Incitamentum*   2000
GLASS, PIGMENT   50 × 101 × 1¾ INCHES (OVERALL)   L2017.126

23   William Carlson   AMERICAN, BORN 1950   *Prenso*   2006
GLASS, PIGMENT   72 × 59 × 1½ INCHES (OVERALL)   L2017.125

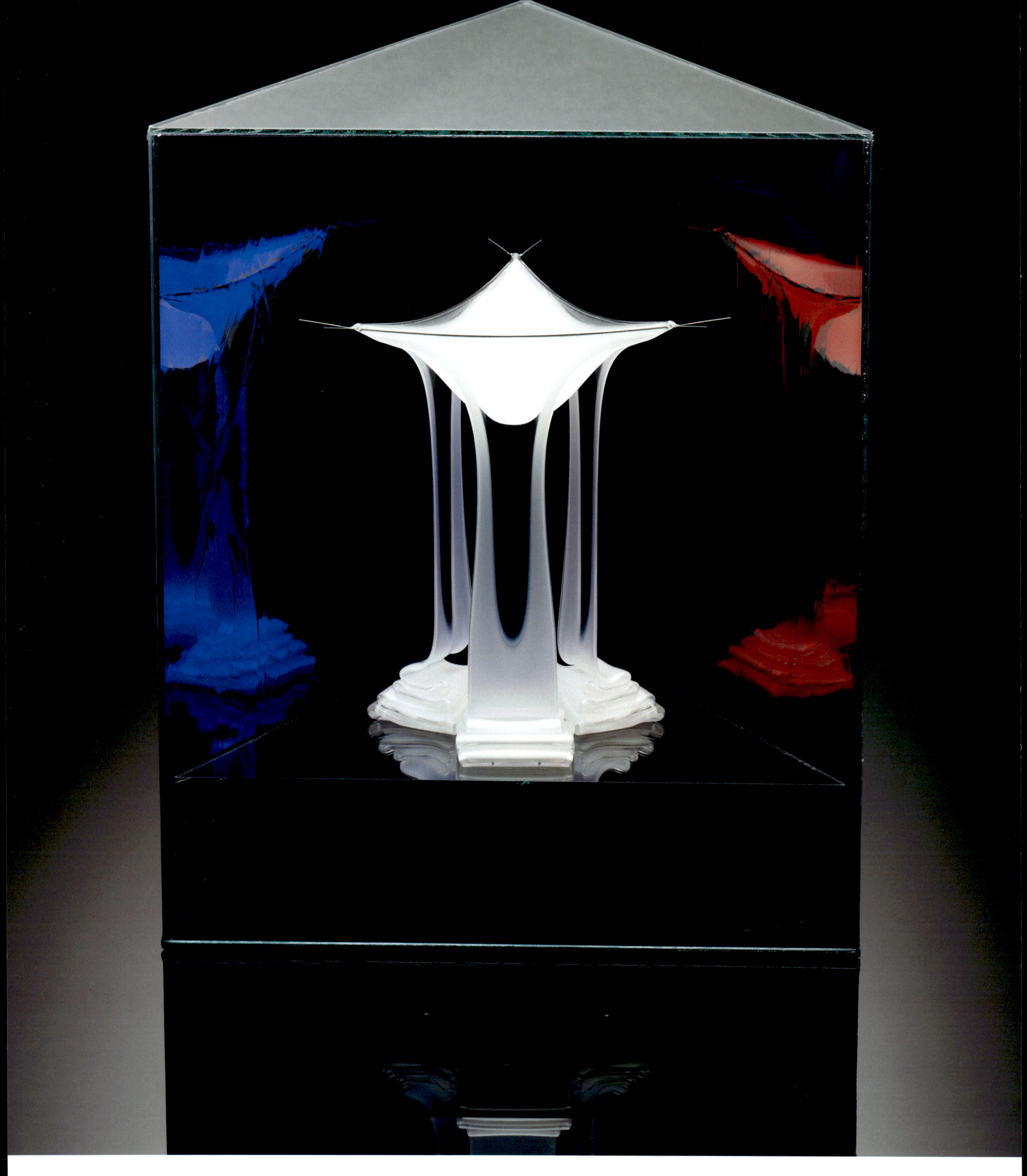

25   Sydney Cash   AMERICAN, BORN 1941   *White Trifold*   1993
SLUMPED GLASS   11½ × 10 × 8½ INCHES   L2017.21

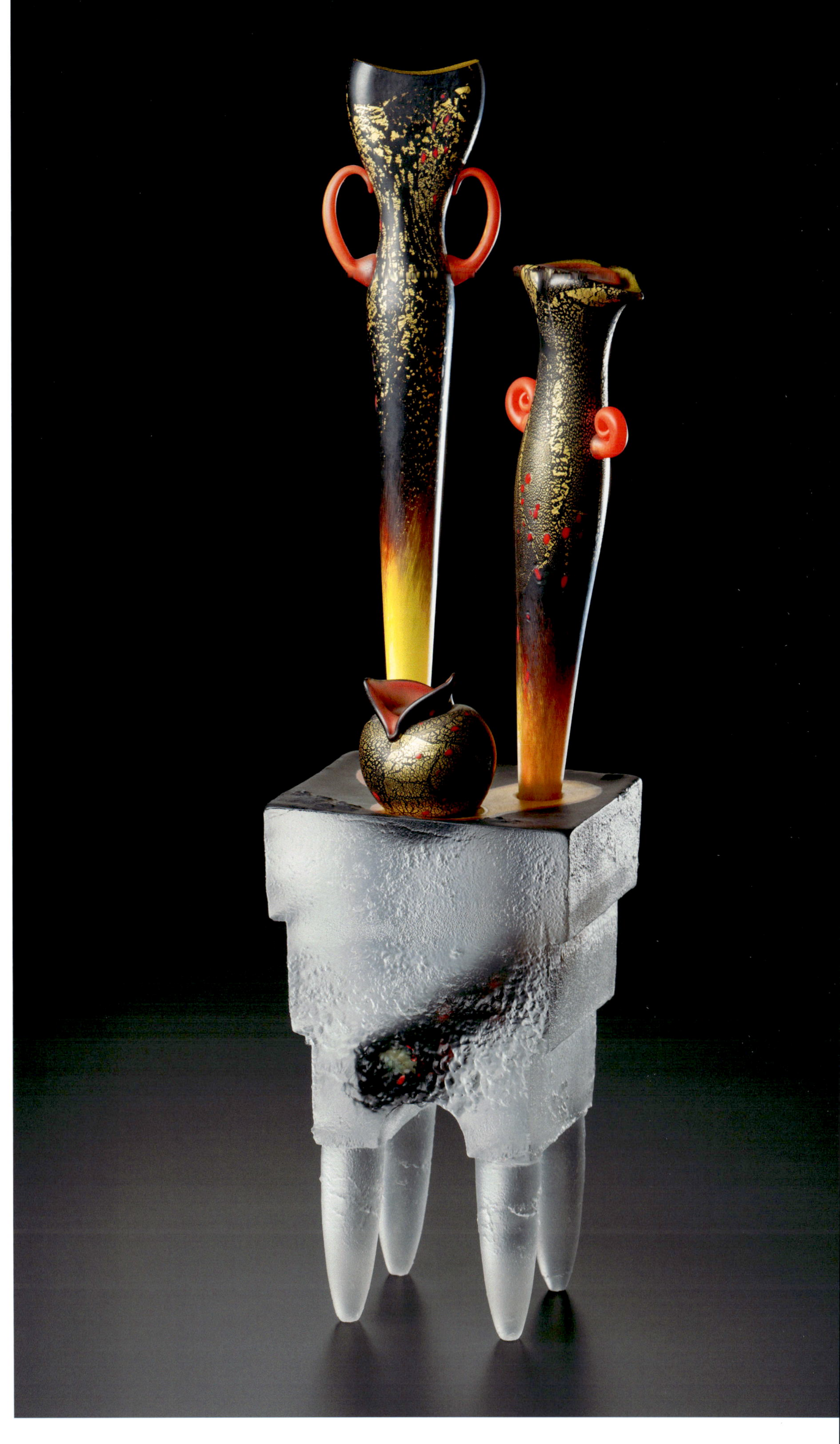

26 José Chardiet   AMERICAN, BORN CUBA, 1956   *Kanazu*   2002
BLOWN AND SANDCAST GLASS   29½ × 9 × 6½ INCHES   L2017.22

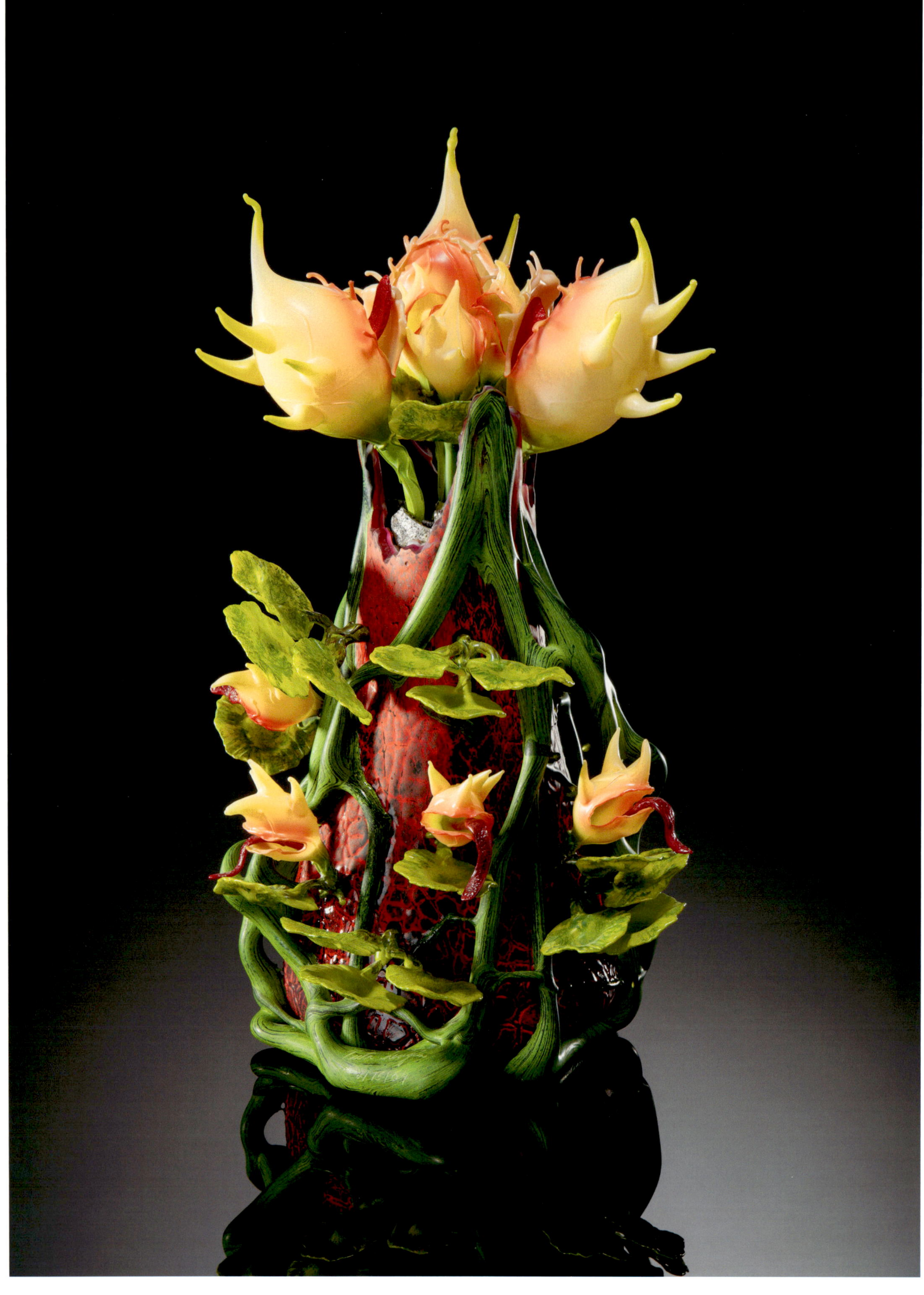

27 Victor Chiarizia AMERICAN, BORN 1957 *Enigma of Fulfillment* 2004
BLOWN AND LAMPWORKED GLASS 15½ × 9¼ × 8¾ INCHES L2017.23

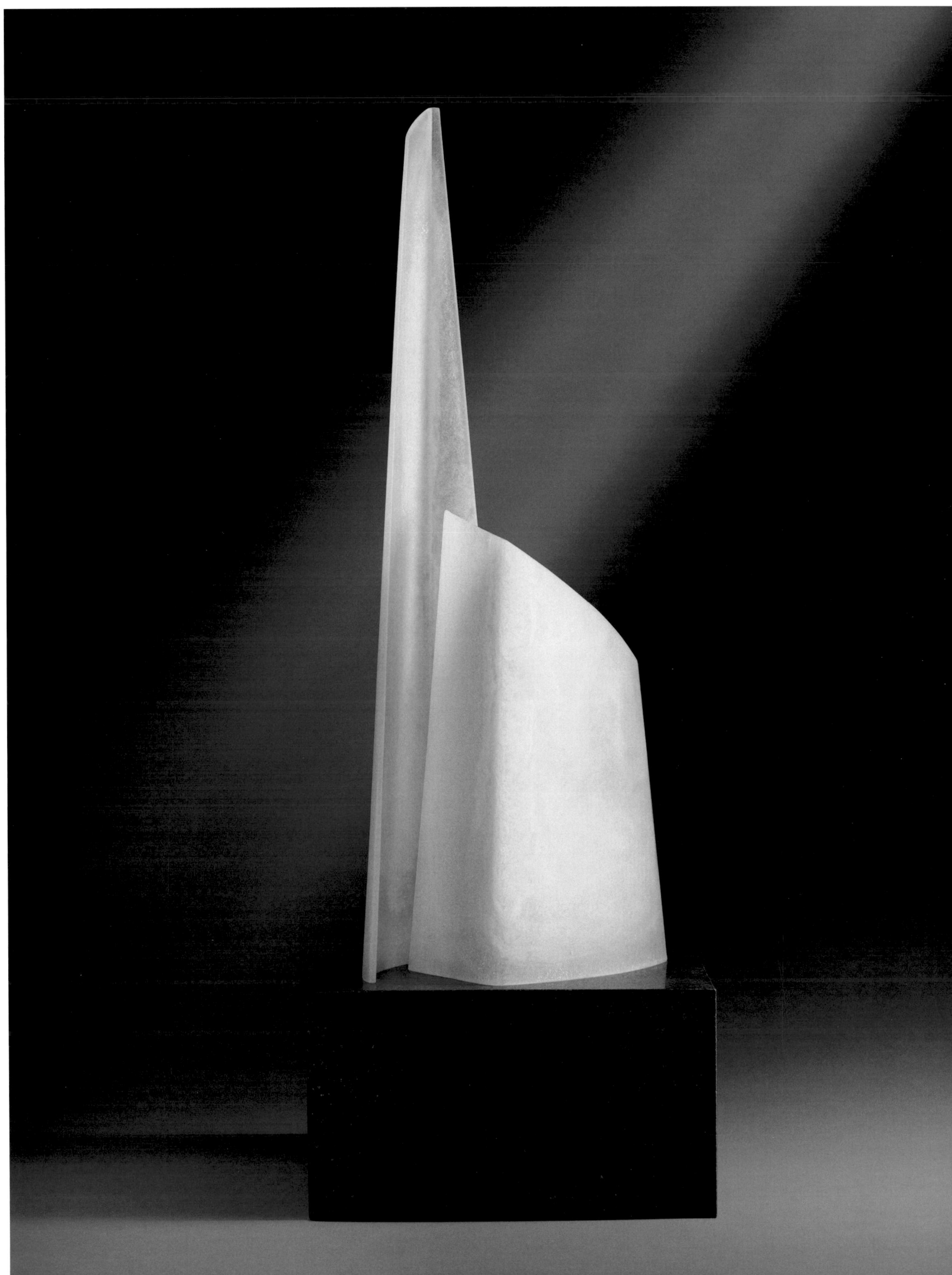

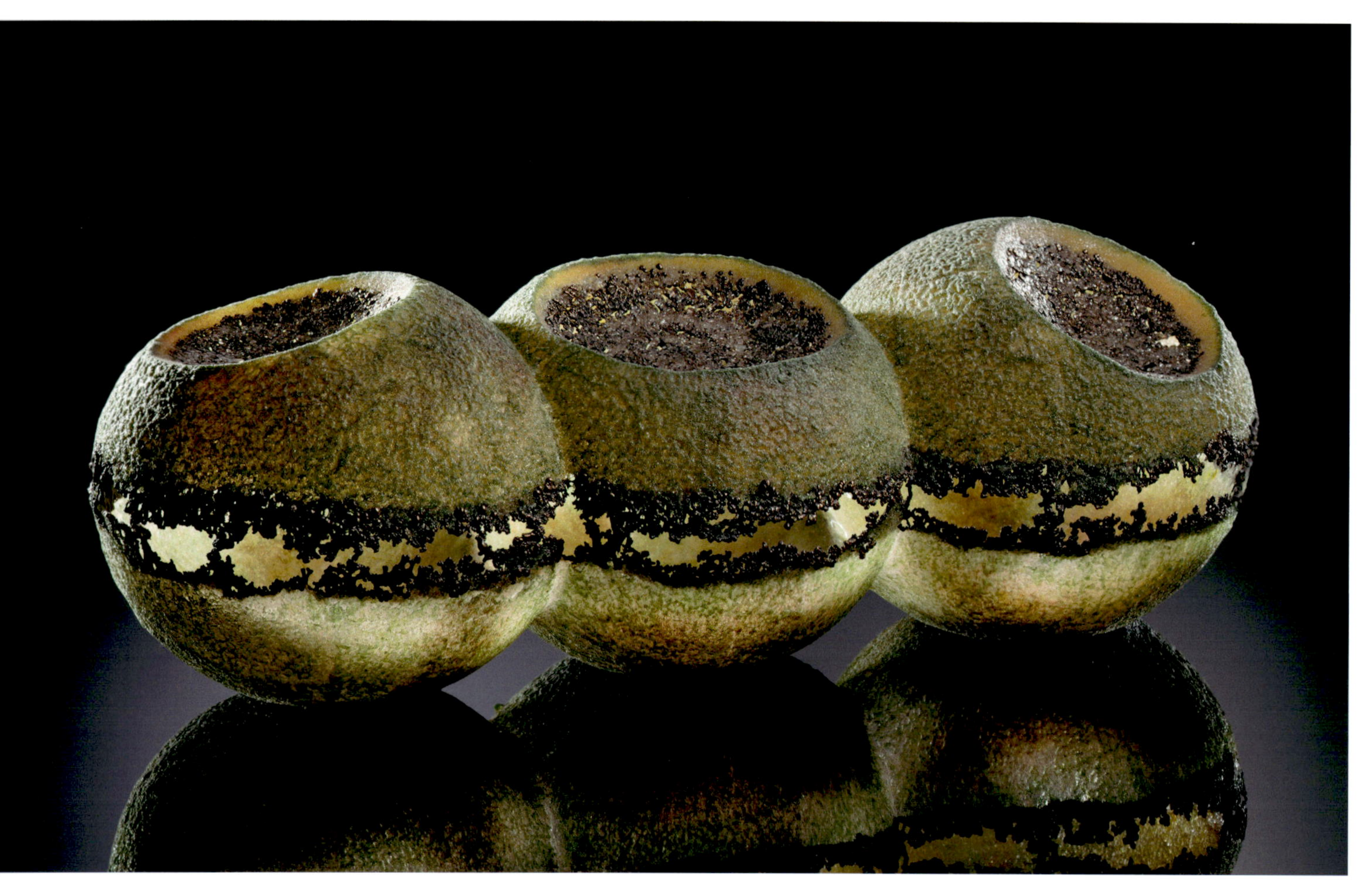

29 Deanna Clayton AMERICAN, BORN 1968 *Namaste* 2009

PÂTE DE VERRE, ELECTROPLATED COPPER WIRE   9¾ × 30 × 12 INCHES (OVERALL)   L2017.25

30   Steve Clements AMERICAN, BORN 1948, Leah Wingfield, AMERICAN, BORN 1957
Mechanics of Optimism   2005
CAST GLASS, WOOD, METAL, OIL PAINT   18¾ × 26 × 8½ INCHES   L2017.136

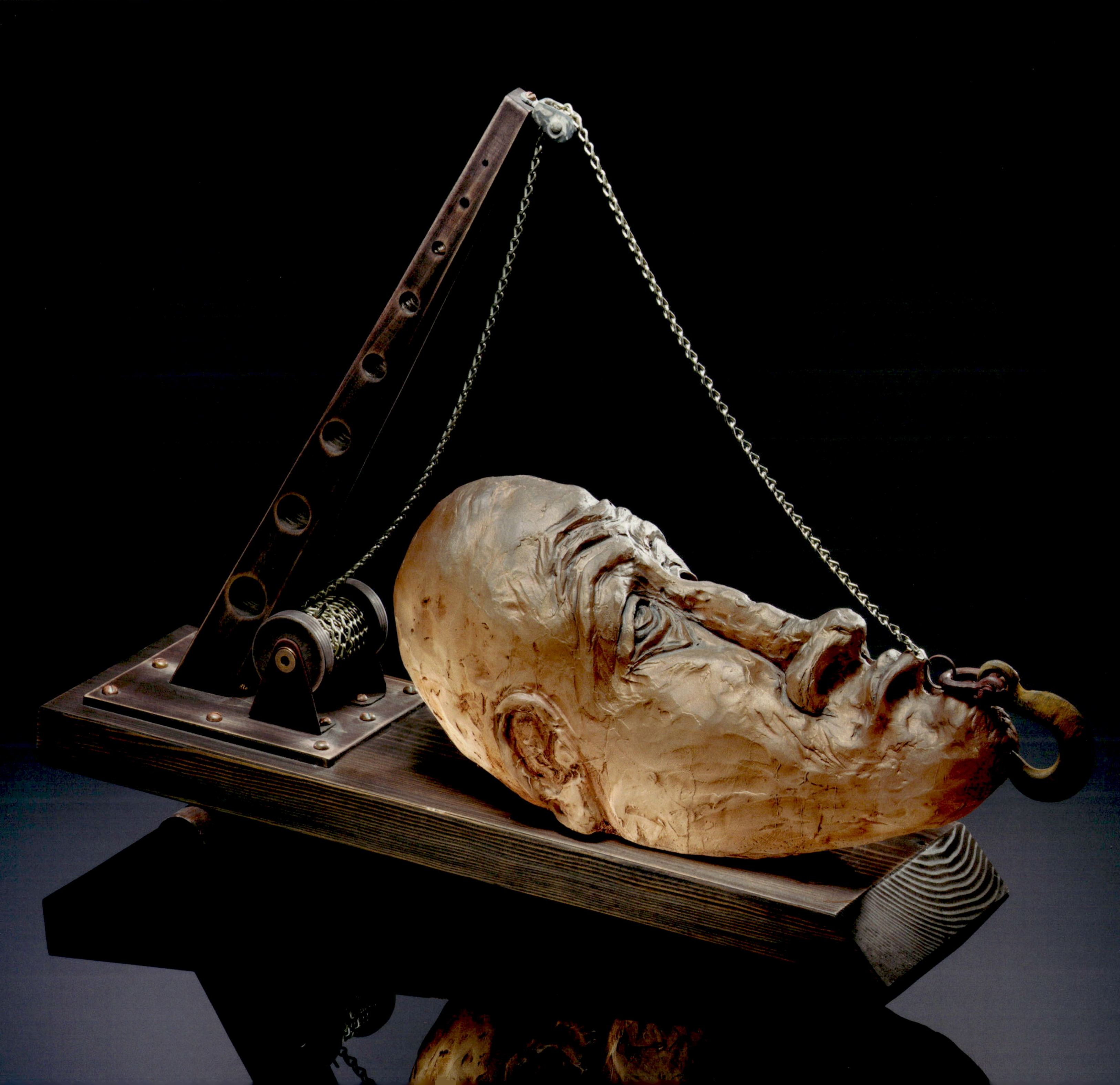

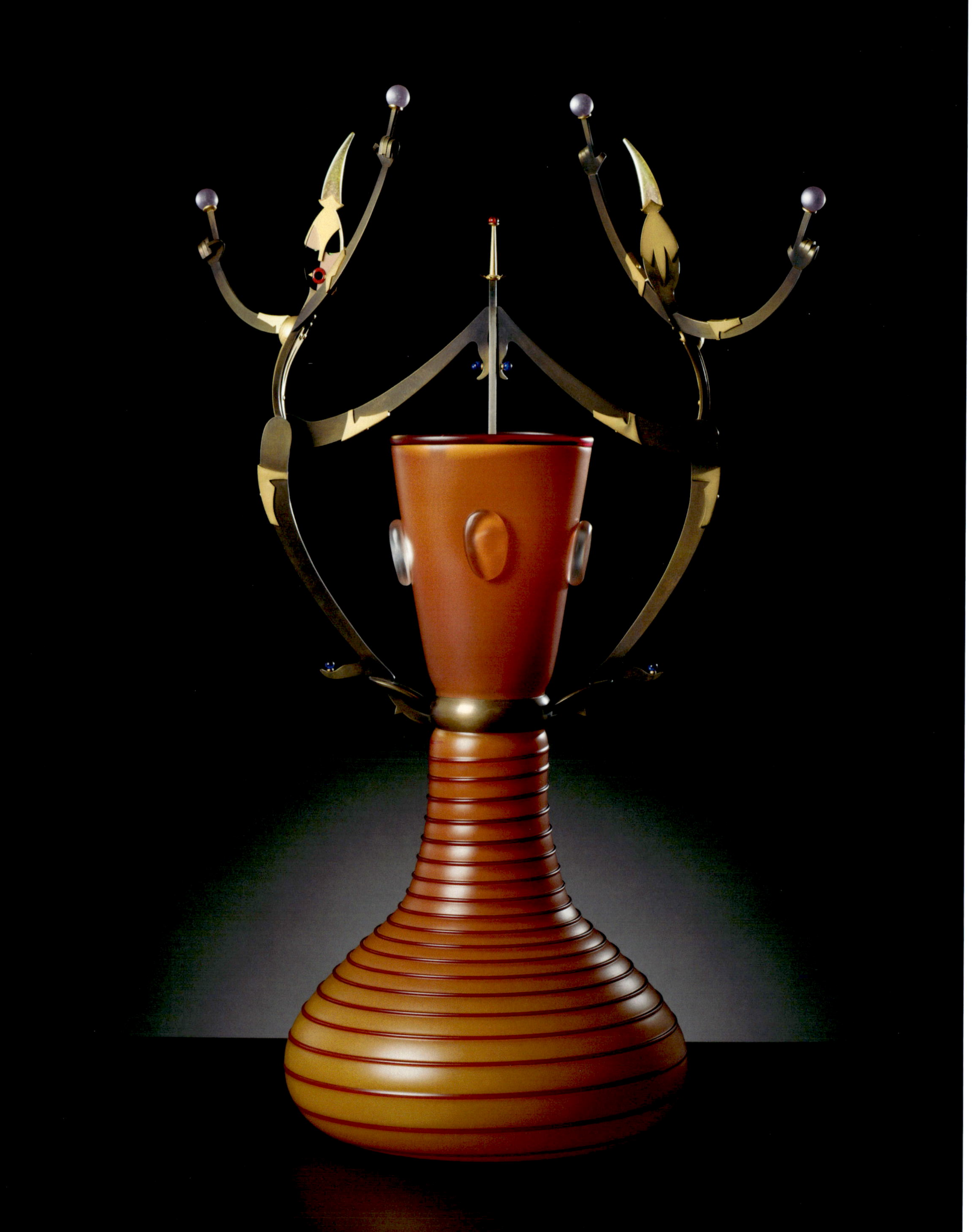

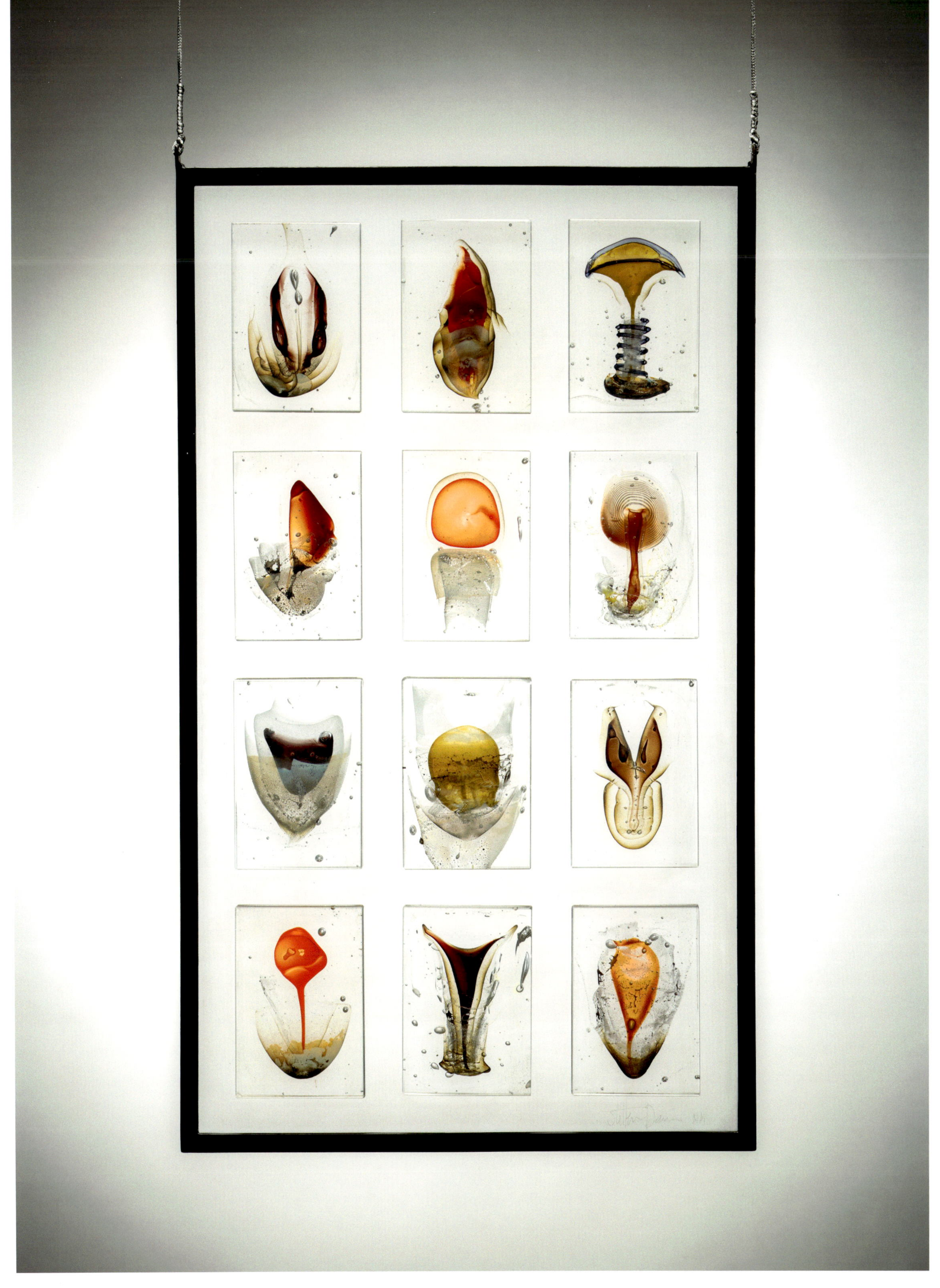

32   Steffen Dam   DANISH, BORN 1961   *The Secret Life of Plants*   2001
BLOWN, CUT, AND POLISHED GLASS, STEEL FRAME   31¼ × 18½ × 1½ INCHES   L2017.28

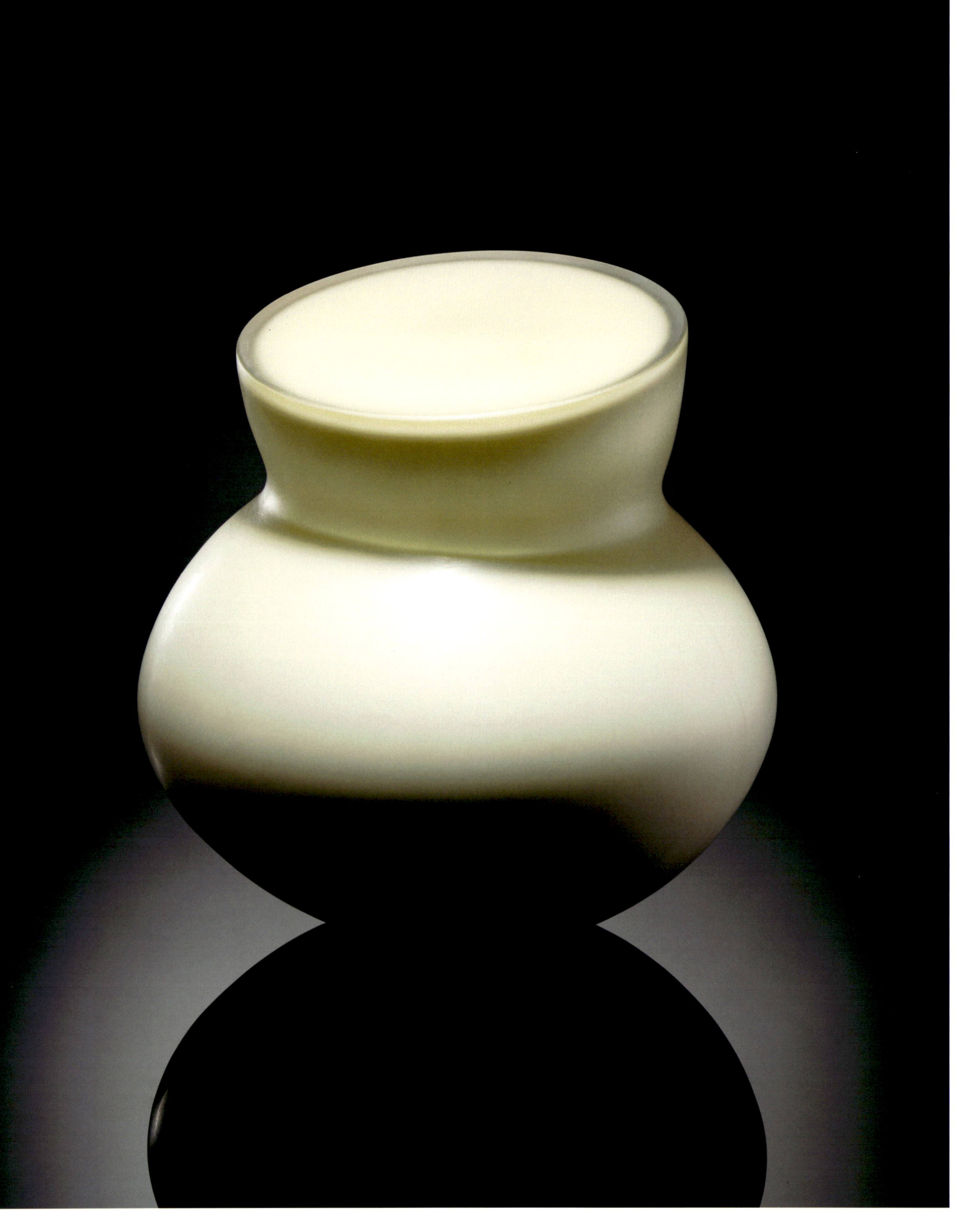

33   Laura de Santillana   ITALIAN, BORN 1955   *Bodhi (Ivory)*   2006
BLOWN GLASS, HAND GROUND WITH MIRRORED INTERIOR   16 × 16 × 16 INCHES   L2017.31

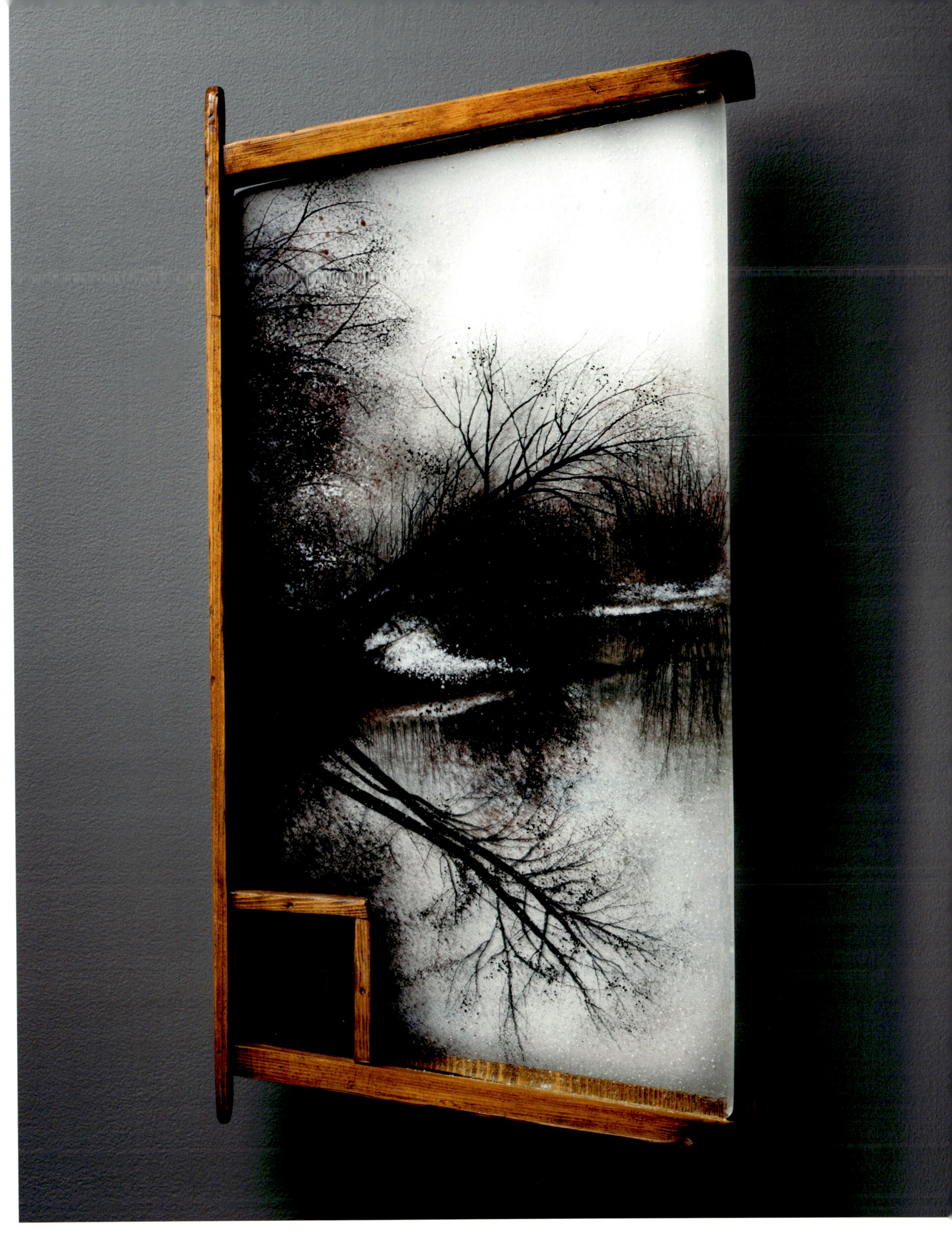

34   Miriam Silvia di Fiore   ITALIAN, BORN ARGENTINA, 1959   *Washing Board*   2009
FLAMEWORKED AND KILN-WORKED GLASS, FOUND OBJECT   30¾ × 16 × 5¾ INCHES   L2017.32

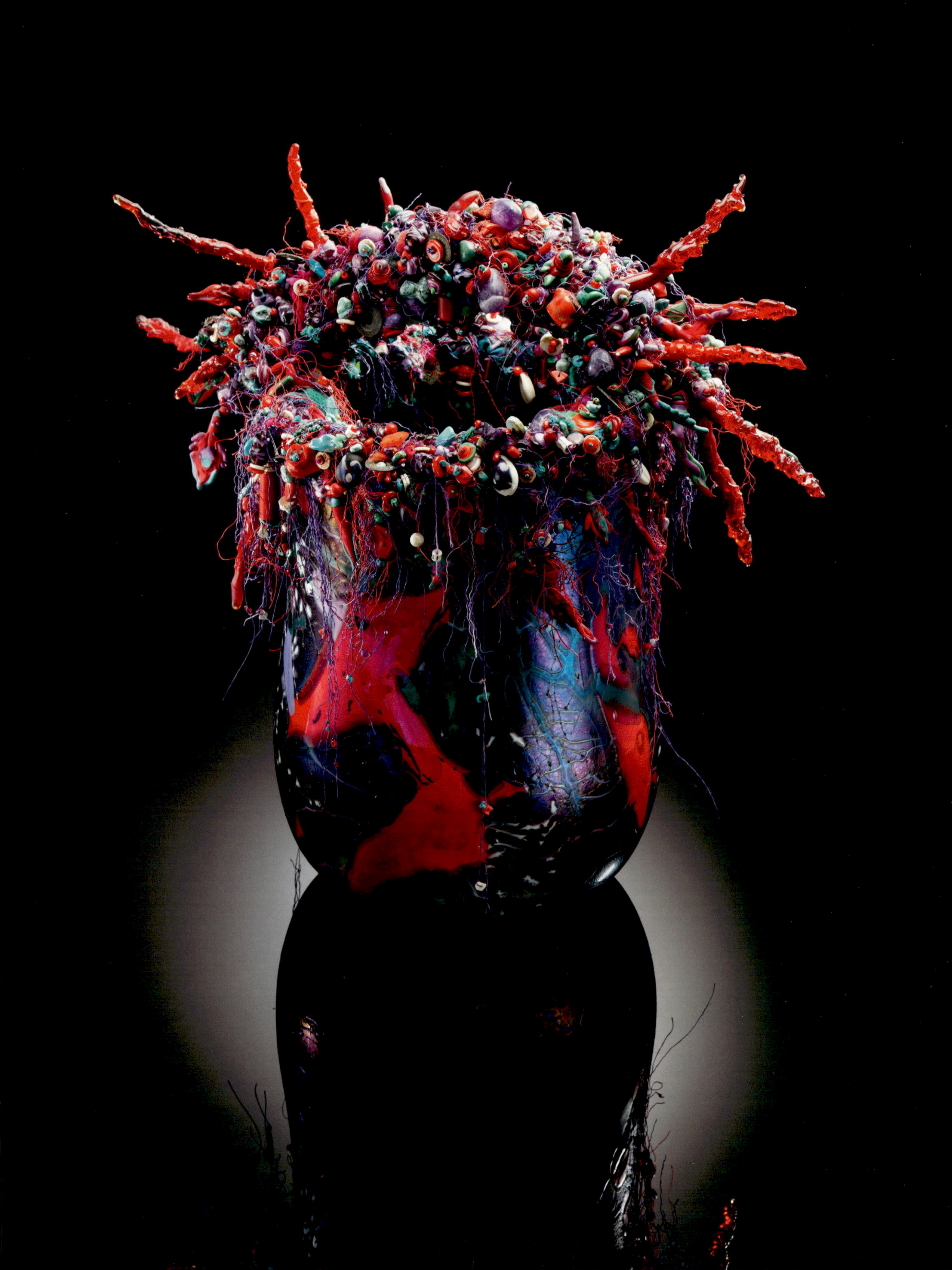

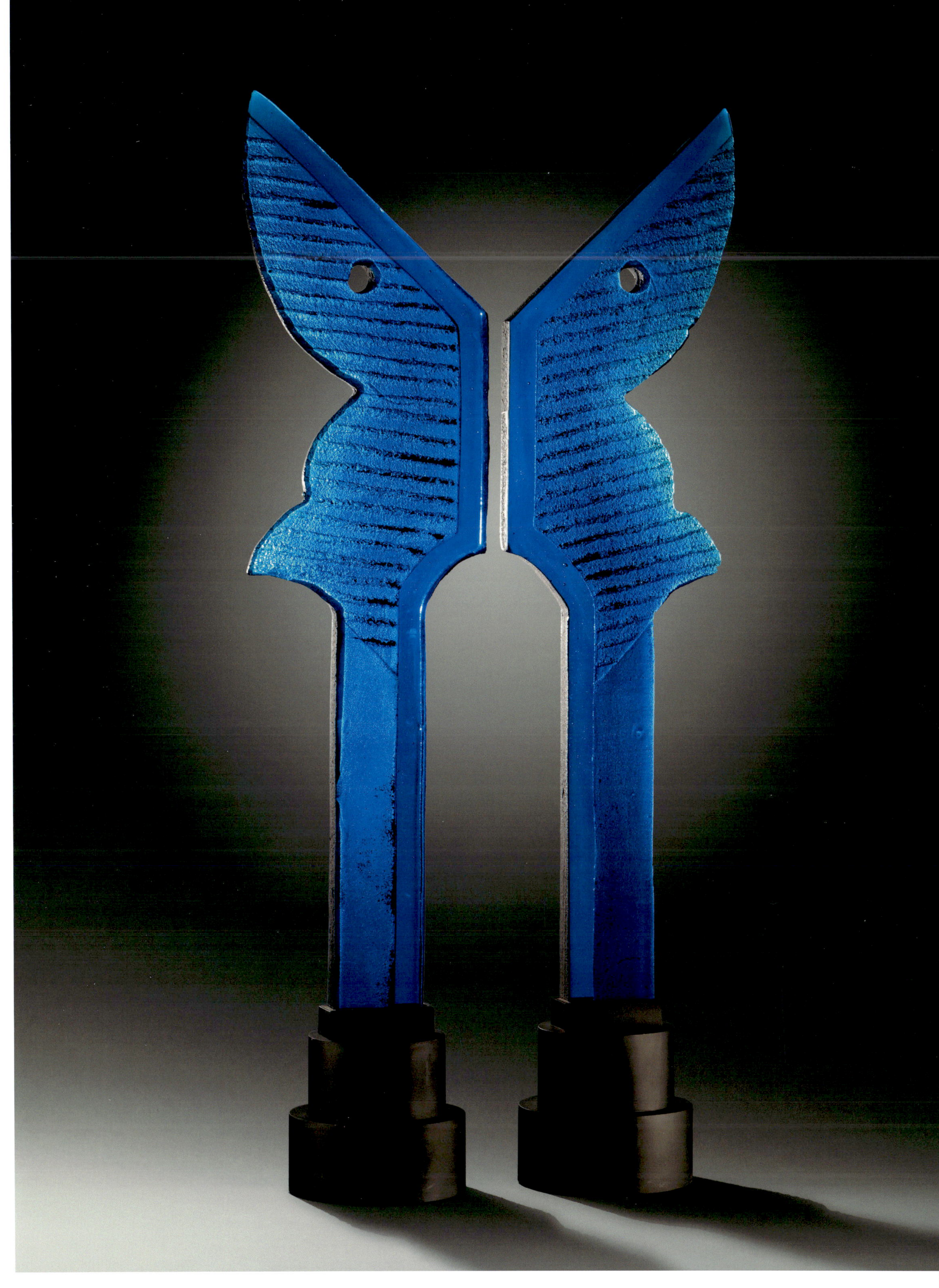

36 Stephen Dee Edwards AMERICAN, BORN 1954 *Blue Swallow Tail* 2002
SANDCAST GLASS, STEEL BASE   87¼ × 40 × 14½ INCHES (OVERALL)   L2017.34

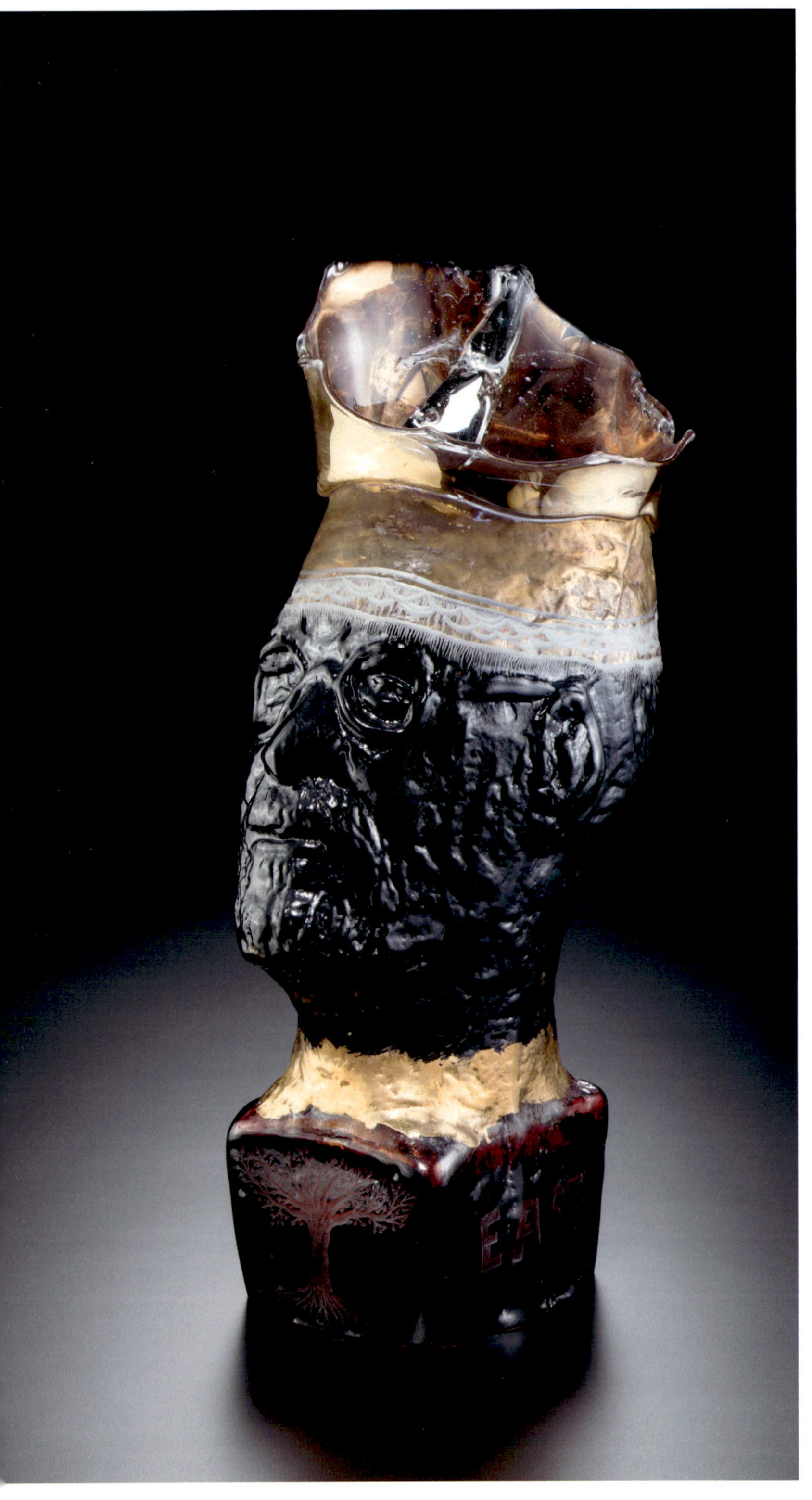

37   Erwin Eisch   GERMAN, BORN 1927
East and West: Harvey Littleton   2002
MOLD-BLOWN GLASS   23¾ × 8¾ × 11½ INCHES   L2017.36

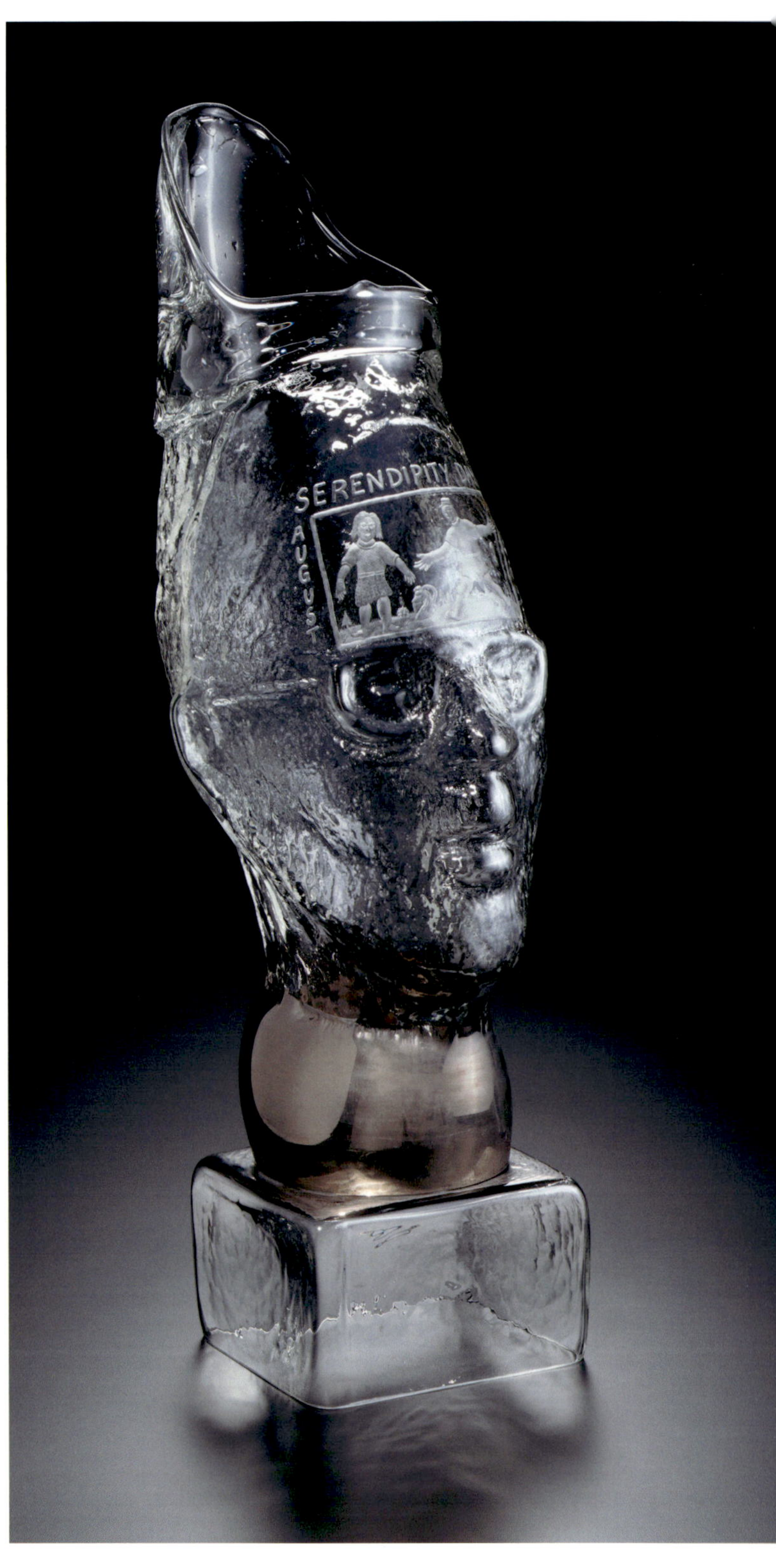

38   Erwin Eisch   GERMAN, BORN 1927
Serendipity: Harvey Littleton   2004
MOLD-BLOWN GLASS   27¼ × 7½ × 11 INCHES   L2017.37

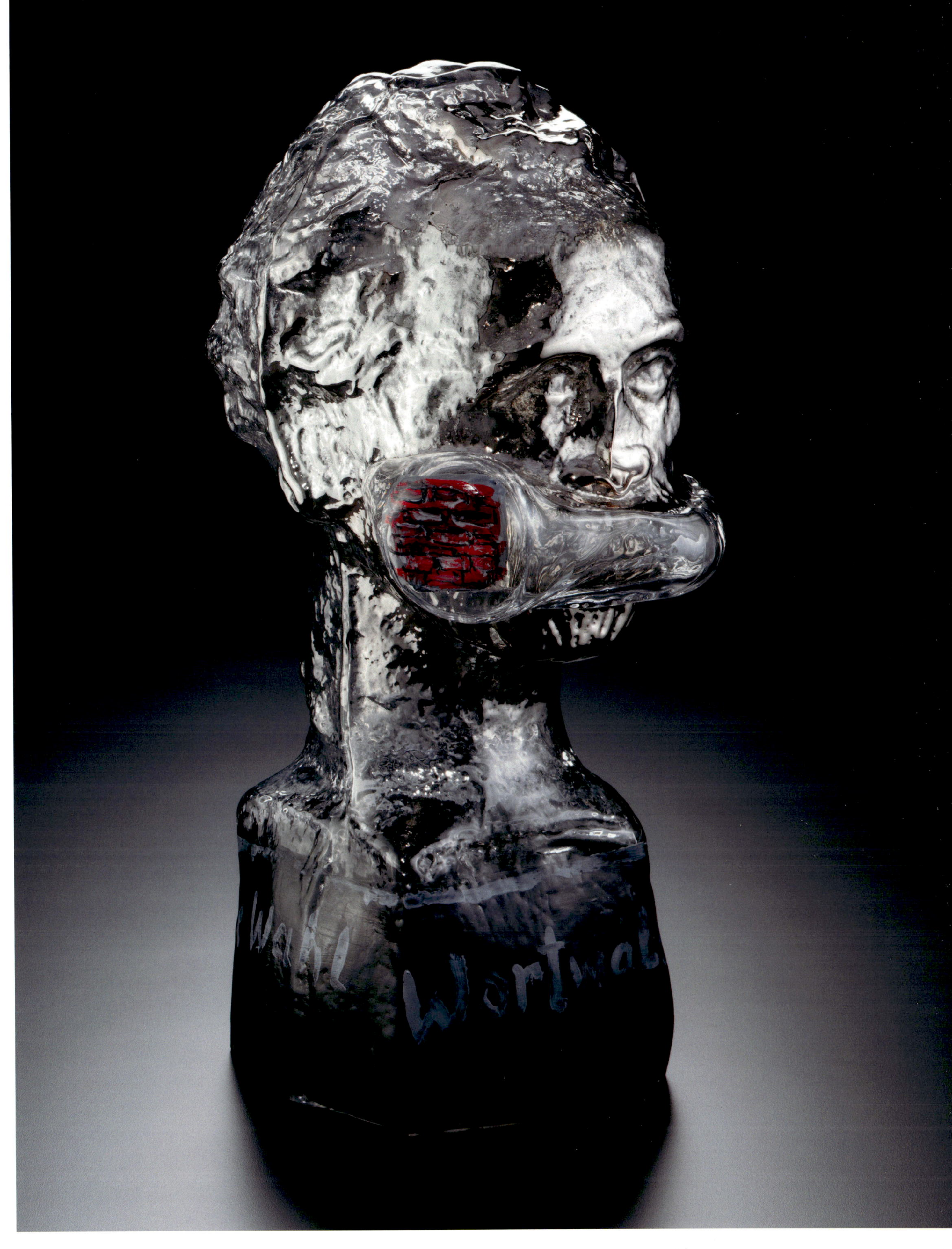

39   Erwin Eisch   GERMAN, BORN 1927   *Wortwall: Self-Portrait*   2002
MOLD-BLOWN GLASS   20 × 9½ × 11½ INCHES   L2017.35

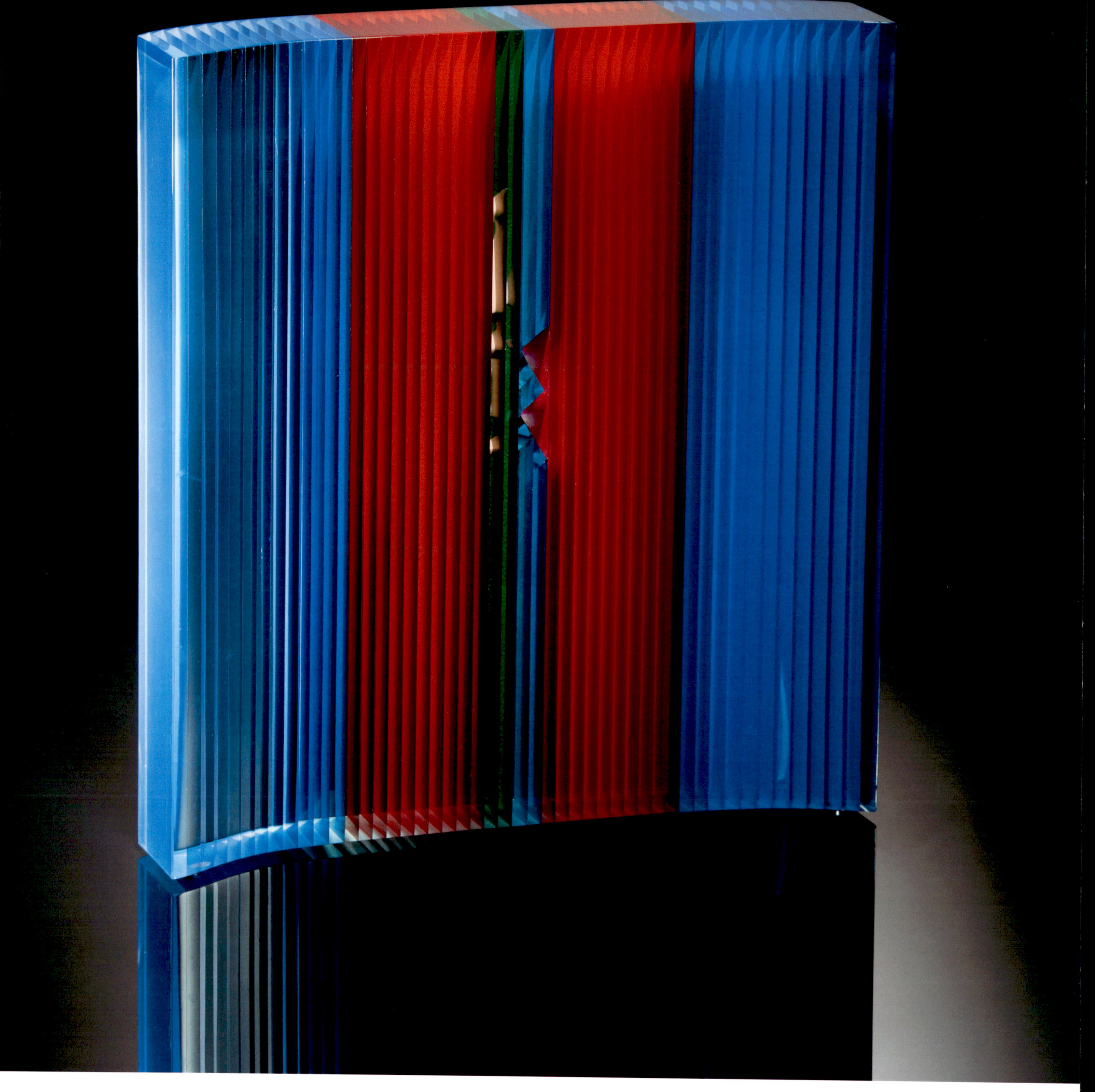

40 Bohumil Eliáš, Sr. CZECH, 1937–2005 *Silent Inhabitant* 2003
CAST AND LAMINATED GLASS 15½ × 14¾ × 3¾ INCHES L2017.38

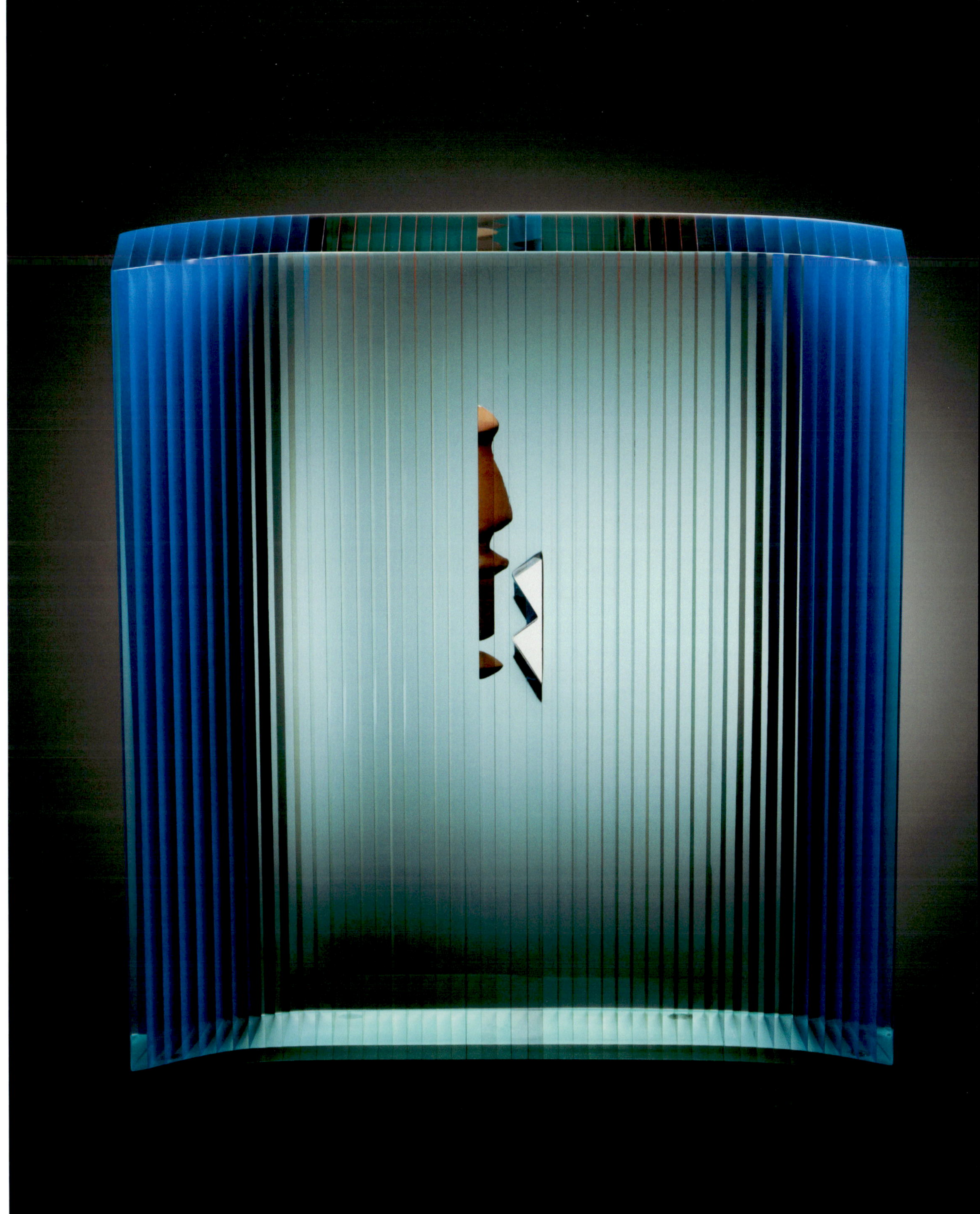

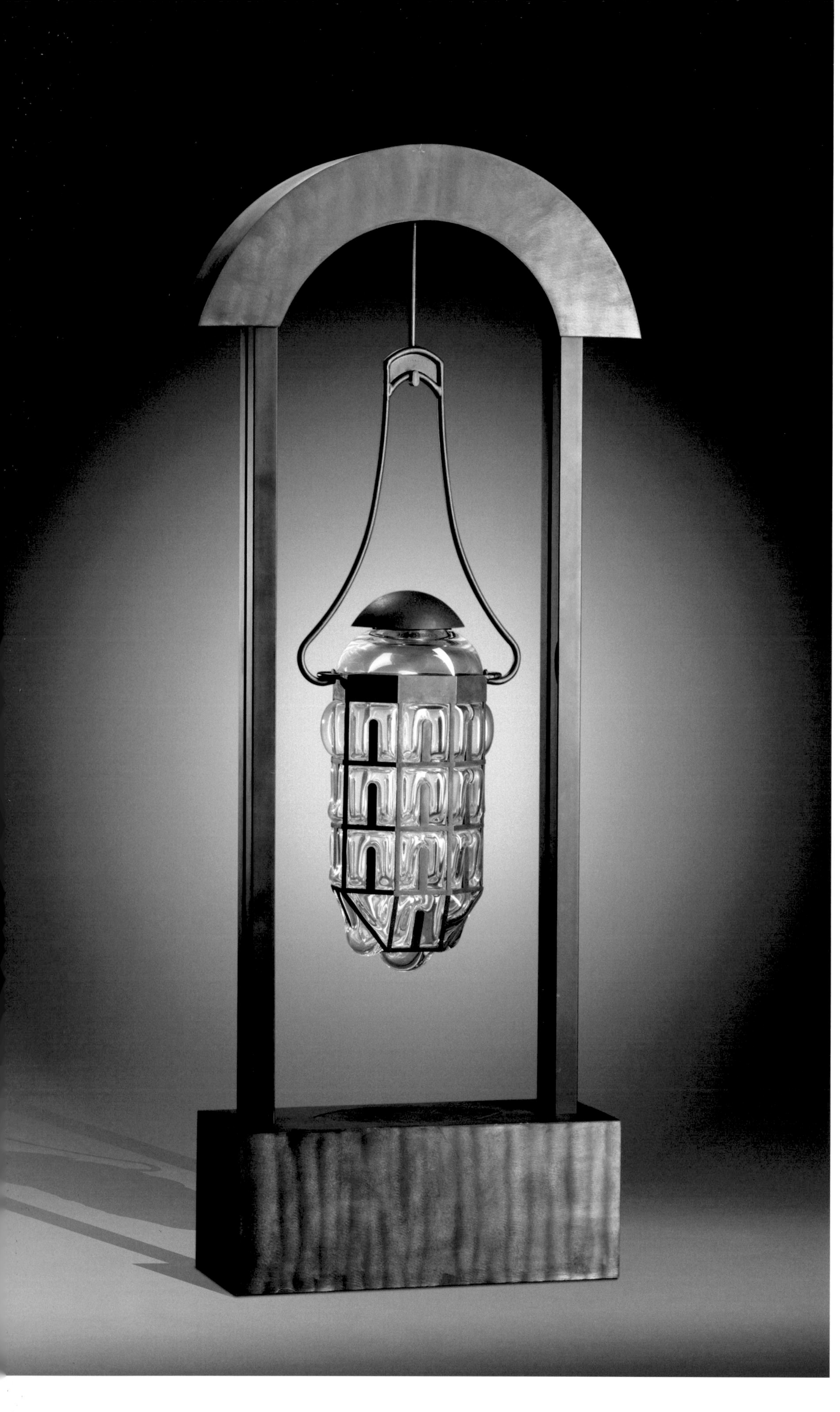

41 Bella Feldman AMERICAN, BORN 1930 *He* 2004
BLOWN GLASS, BRONZE, STEEL   87¼ × 36½ × 12¾ INCHES   L2017.40

  Irene Frolic   CANADIAN, BORN POLAND, 1941   *Fierce Beauty V*   2006
CAST GLASS   20½ × 11 × 9 INCHES   L2017.42

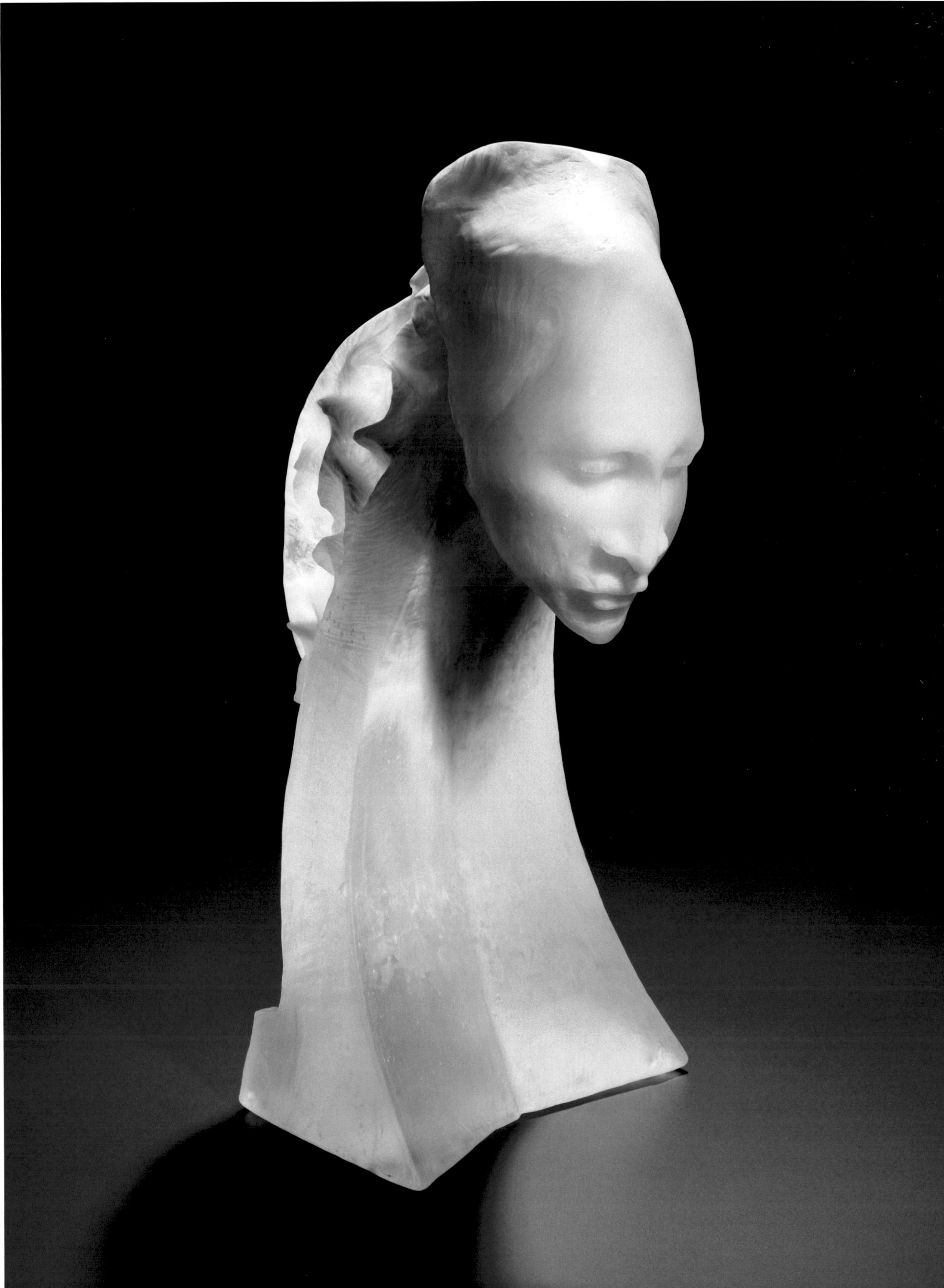

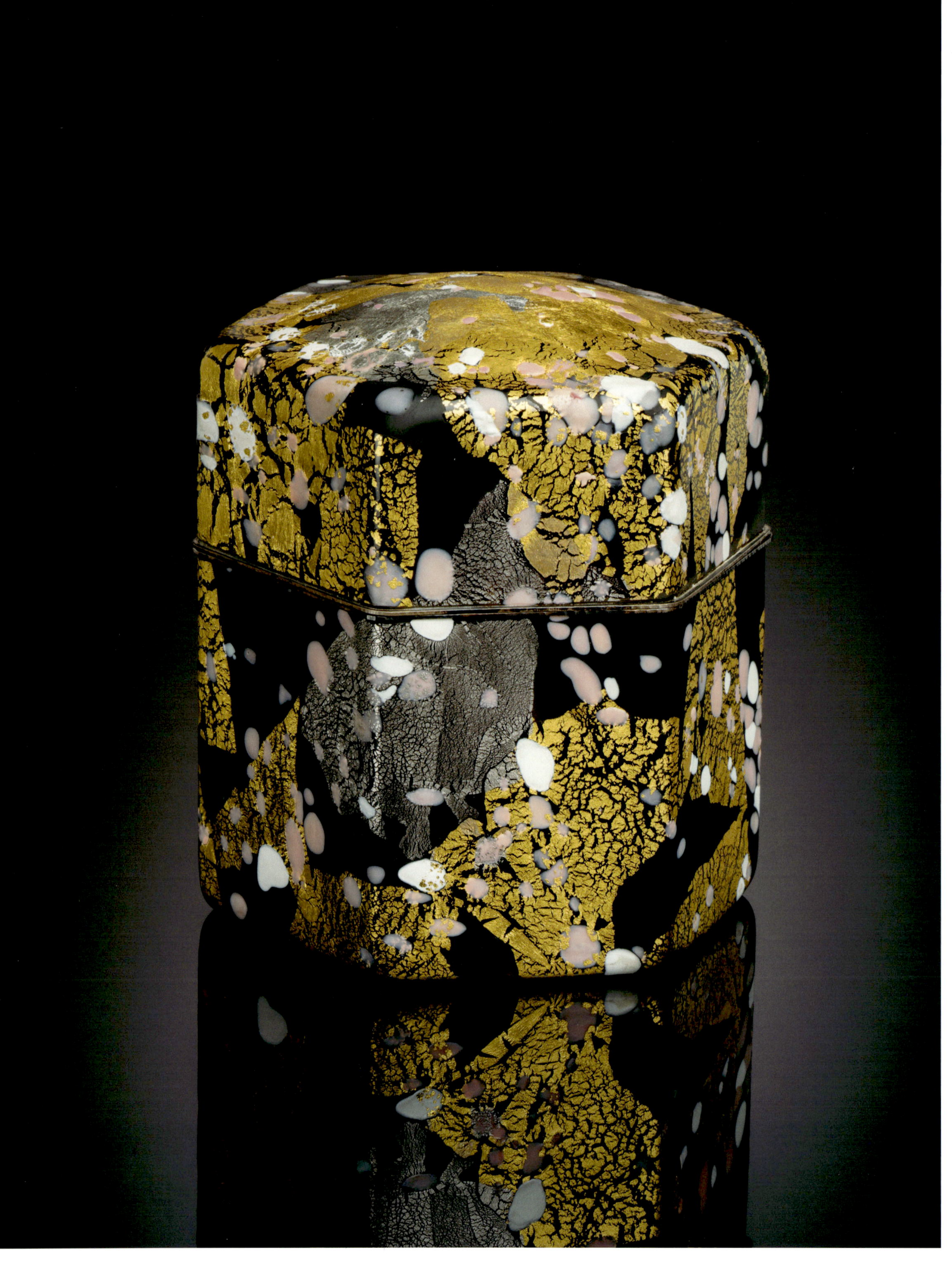

43   Kyohei Fujita   JAPANESE, 1921–2004   *Tatsuta*   N.D.
MOLD-BLOWN GLASS WITH GOLD AND SILVER LEAF   6¼ × 5¾ × 5 INCHES   L2017.48

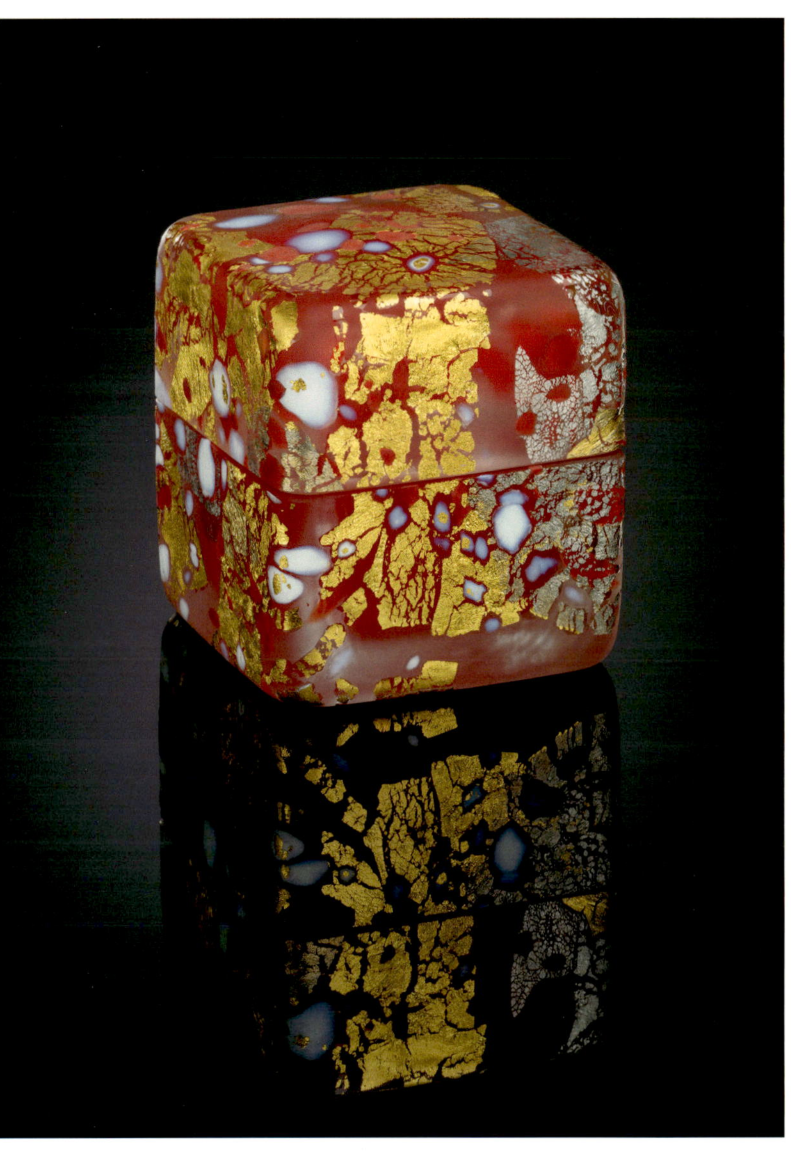

44   Kyohei Fujita   JAPANESE, 1921–2004
Untitled   1987
MOLD-BLOWN GLASS WITH GOLD AND SILVER LEAF
3½ × 3 × 3 INCHES   L2017.43

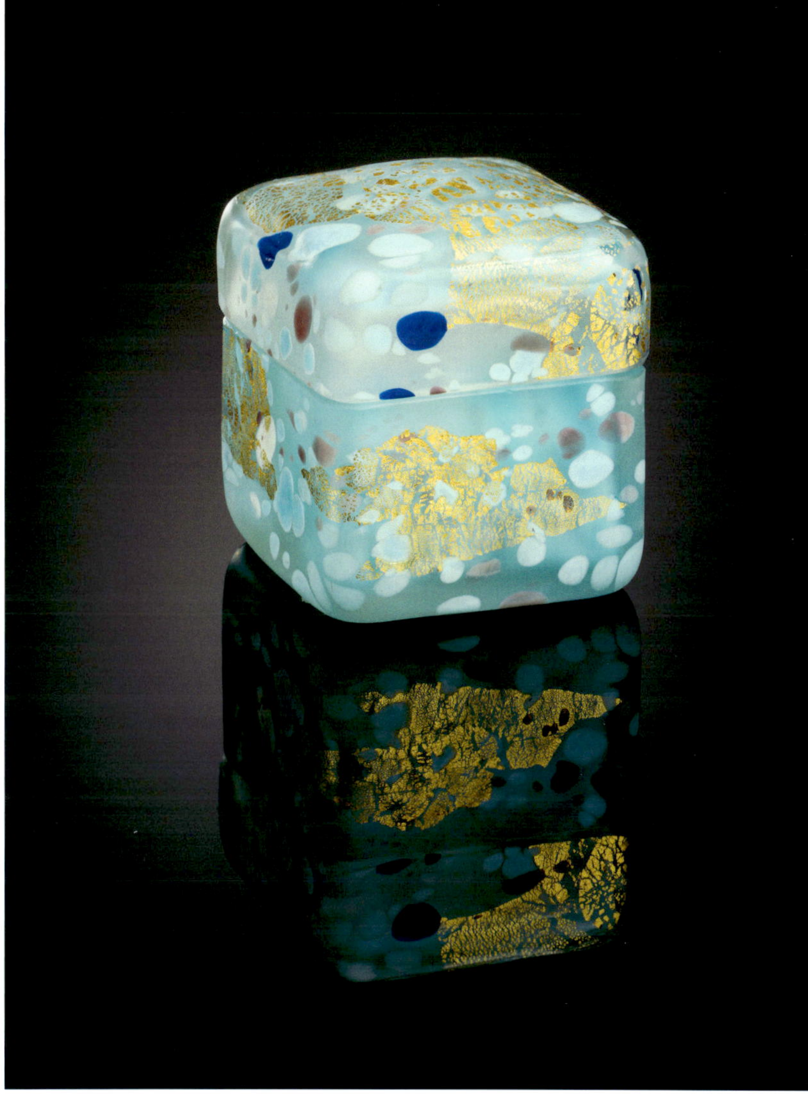

45   Kyohei Fujita   JAPANESE, 1921–2004
Cherry Blossoms at Night   1998
MOLD-BLOWN GLASS WITH GOLD AND SILVER LEAF
3¾ × 3⅛ × 3⅛ INCHES   L2017.44

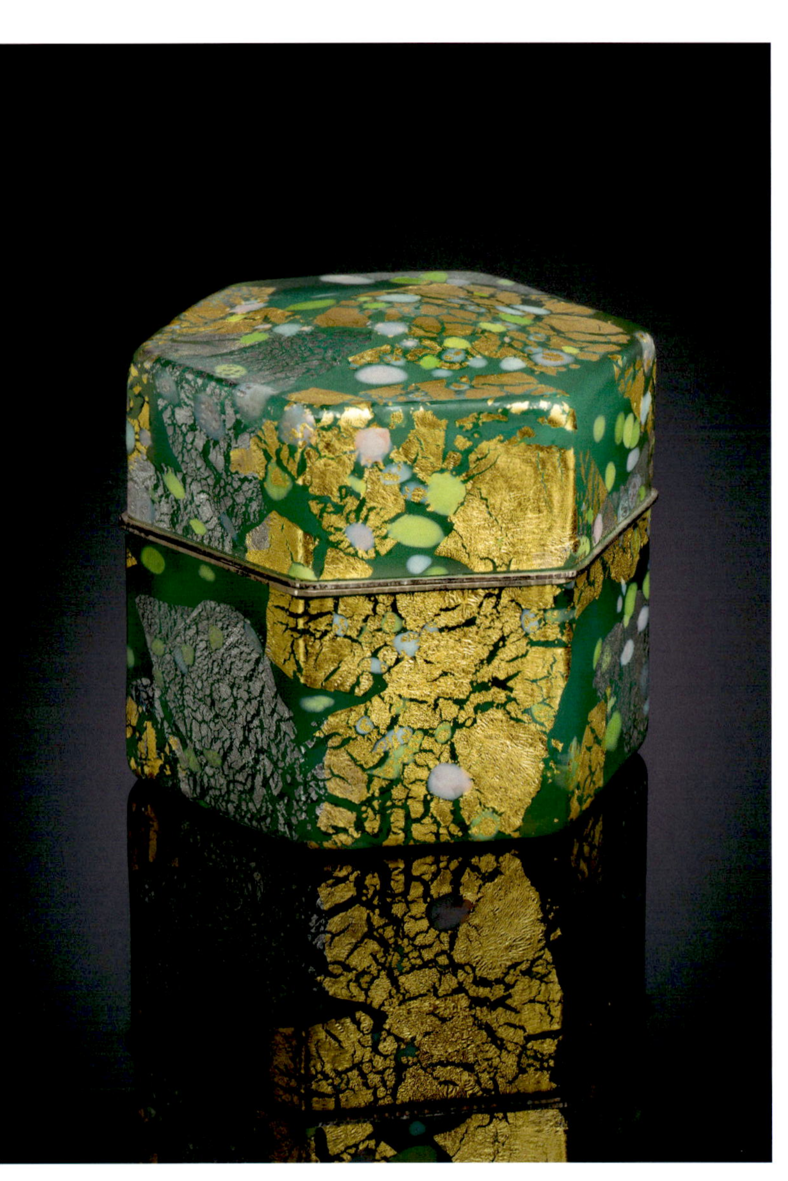

46   Kyohei Fujita   JAPANESE, 1921–2004
Fujimusume   N.D.
MOLD-BLOWN GLASS WITH GOLD AND PLATINUM LEAF
3½ × 3½ × 3 INCHES   L2017.46

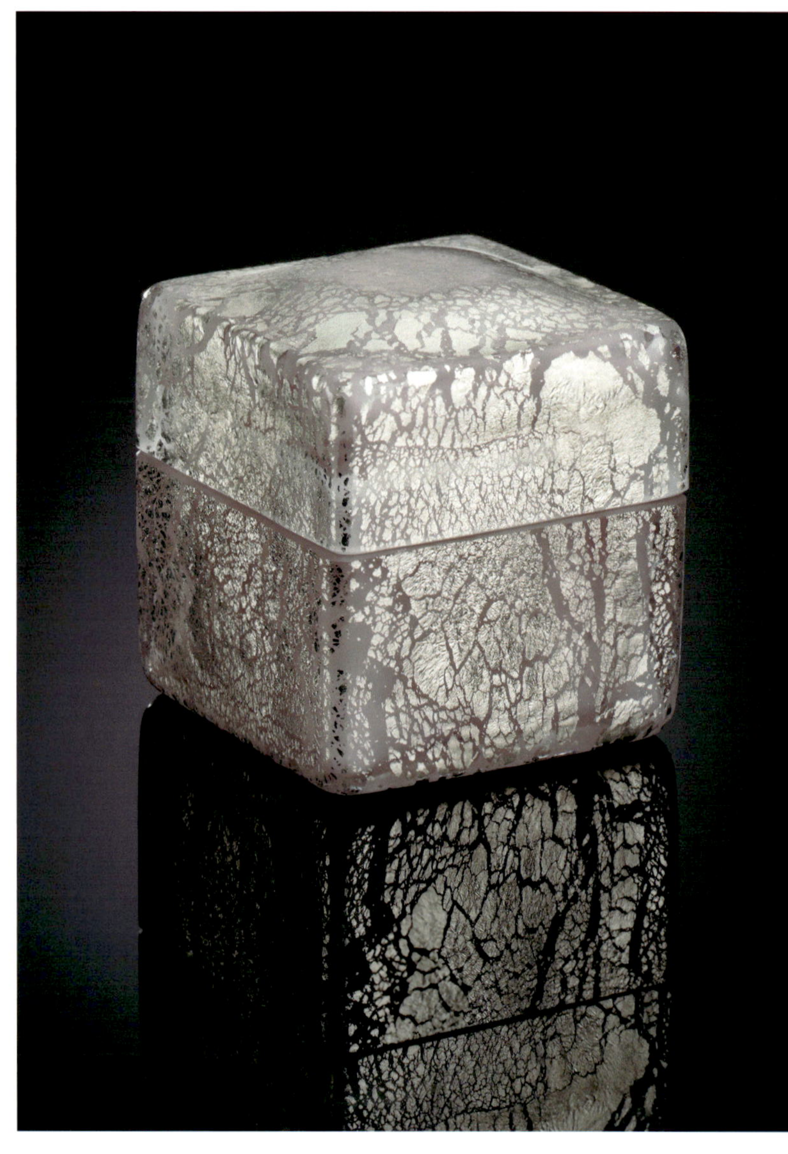

47   Kyohei Fujita   JAPANESE, 1921–2004
Muromachi   N.D.
MOLD-BLOWN GLASS WITH PLATINUM LEAF
3½ × 3 × 3 INCHES   L2017.45

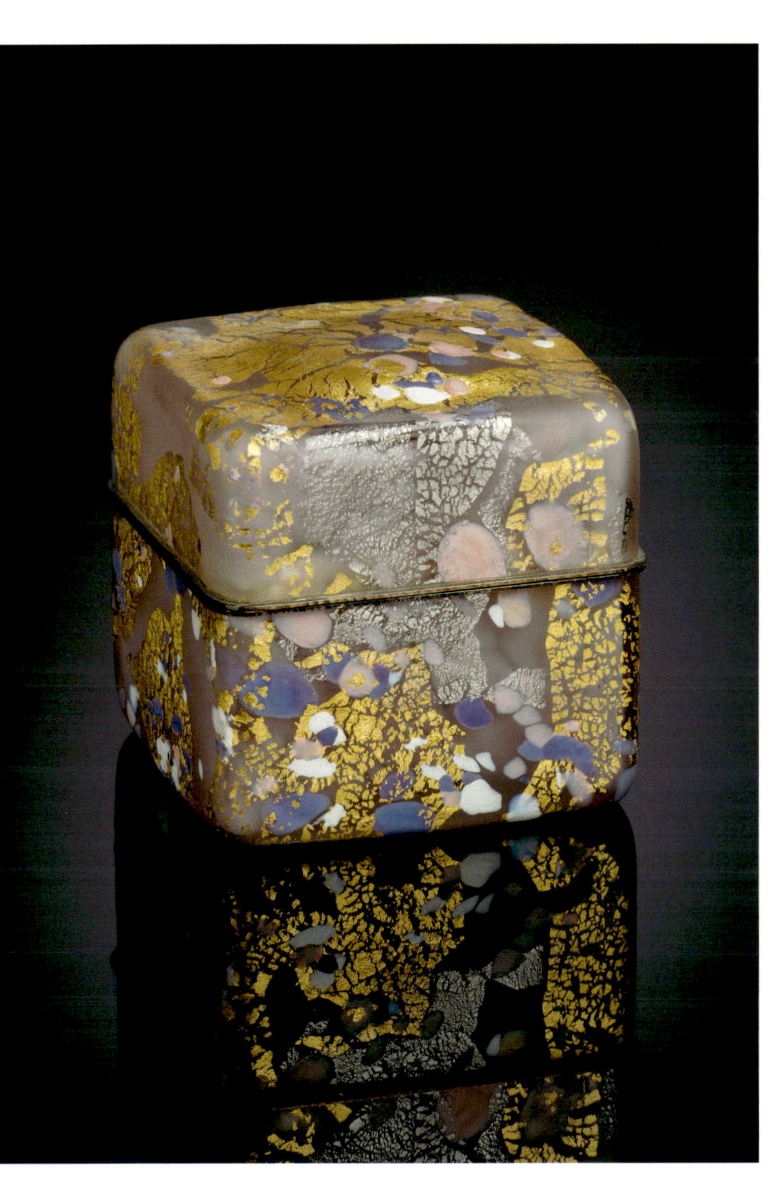

48   Kyohei Fujita   JAPANESE, 1921–2004
Taketori Tale   N.D.
MOLD-BLOWN GLASS WITH GOLD AND SILVER LEAF
4 × 4 × 4 INCHES   L2017.47

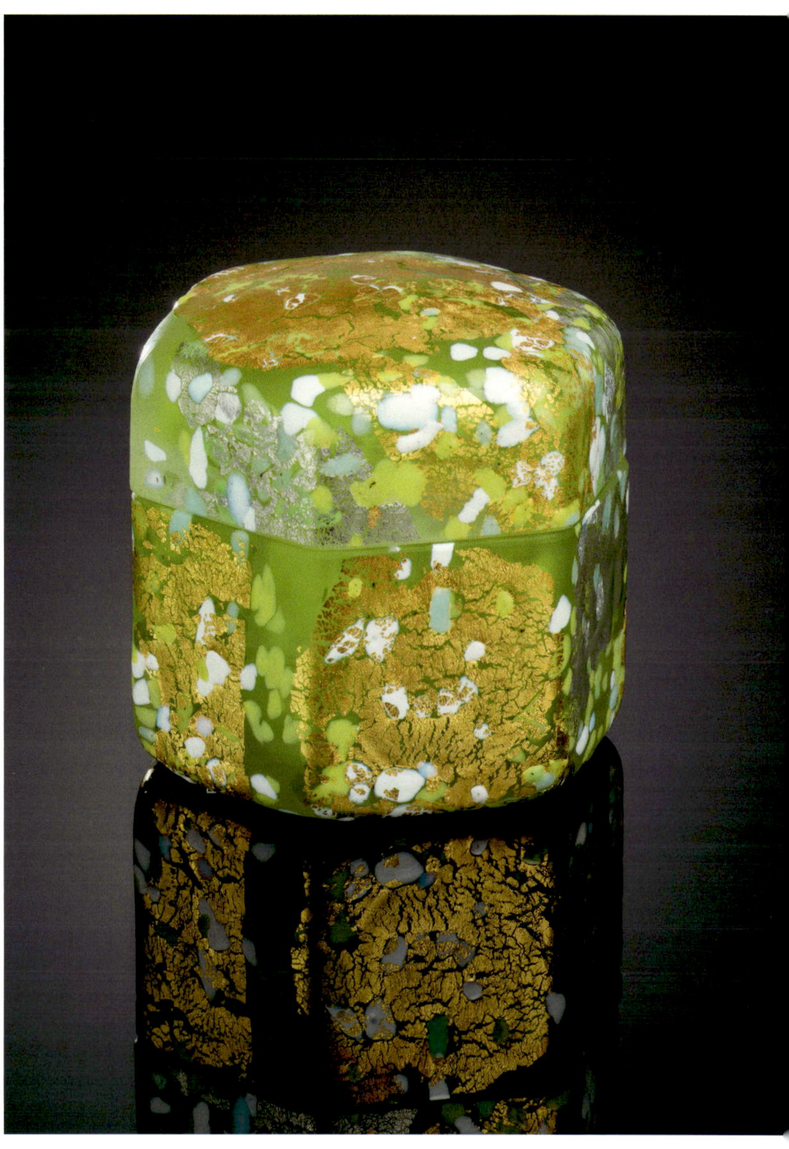

49   Kyohei Fujita   JAPANESE, 1921–2004
Untitled   CA. 1984
MOLD-BLOWN GLASS WITH GOLD AND SILVER LEAF
4 × 4½ × 4 INCHES   L2017.49

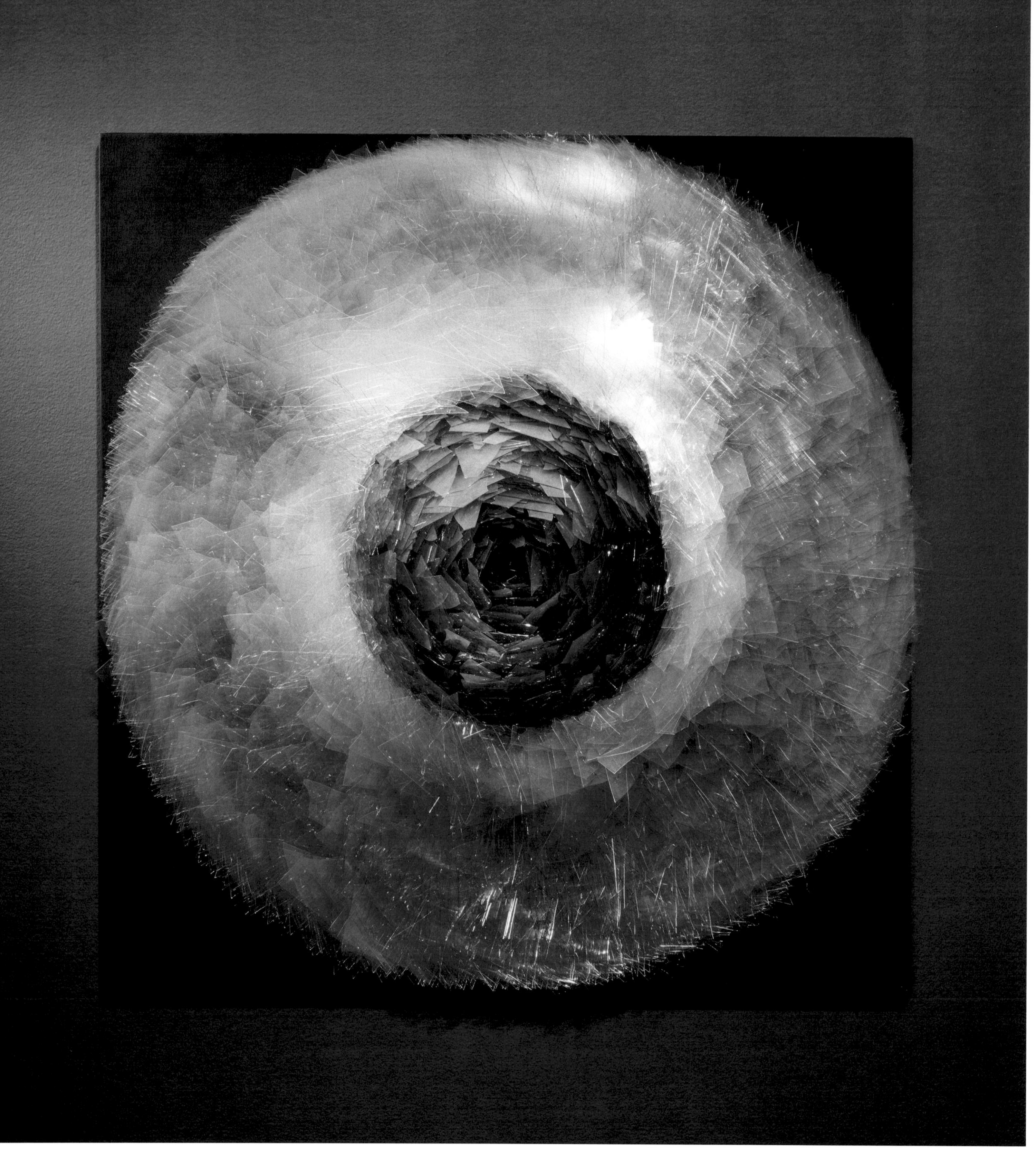

50   Josepha Gasch-Muche   GERMAN, BORN 1944   *Black*   2009
ASSEMBLED GLASS ON WOOD BACKING   25½ × 25½ × 8 INCHES   L2017.52

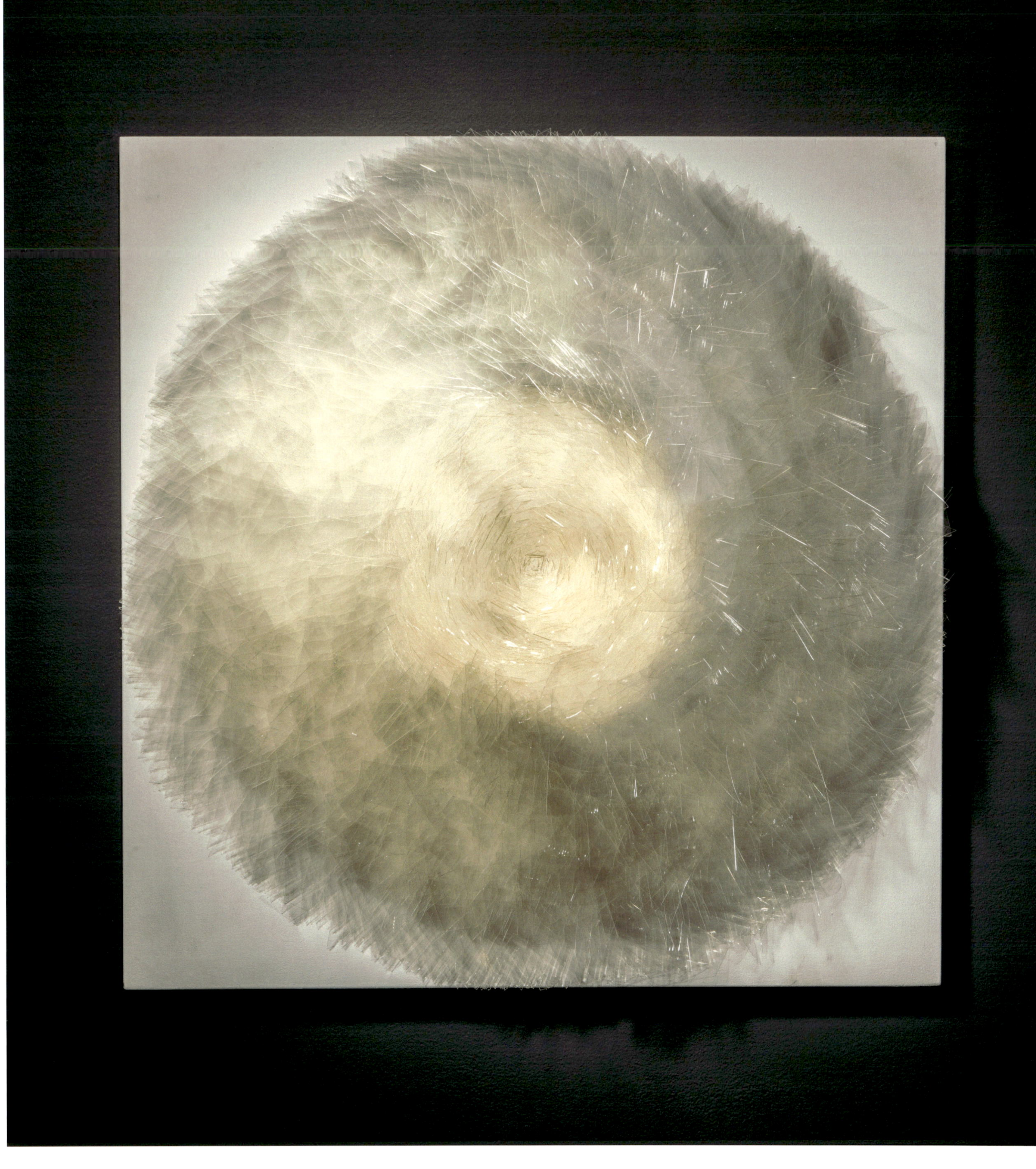

51   Josepha Gasch-Muche   GERMAN, BORN 1944   *White Trifold*   2009
ASSEMBLED GLASS ON WOOD BACKING   25½ × 25½ × 5 INCHES   L2017.51

 Michael Glancy   AMERICAN, BORN 1950

Sterling Convergence   2002

ENGRAVED BLOWN GLASS, ENGRAVED

INDUSTRIAL PLATE GLASS, COPPER, SILVER

8½ × 12 × 12 INCHES   L2017.53

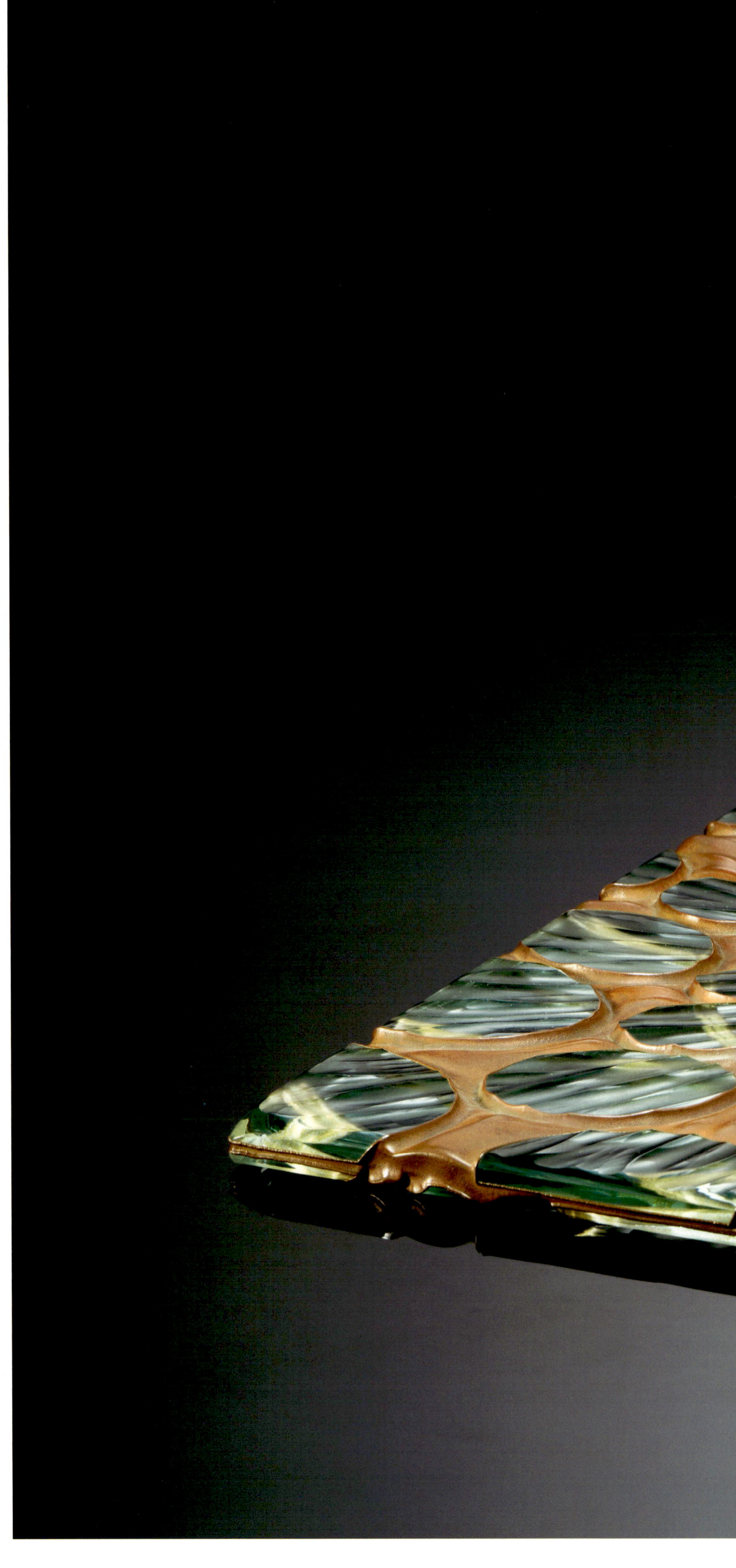

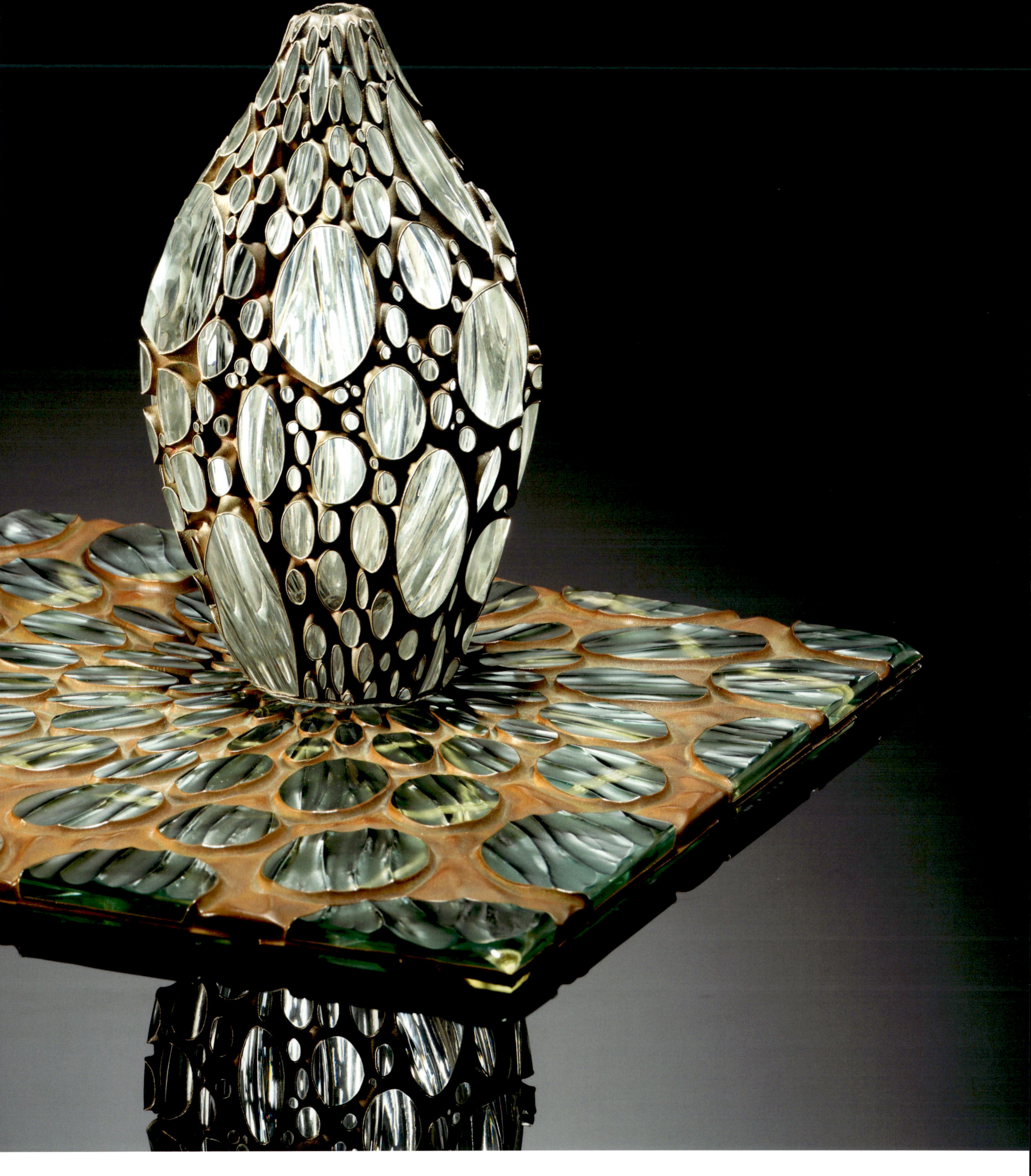

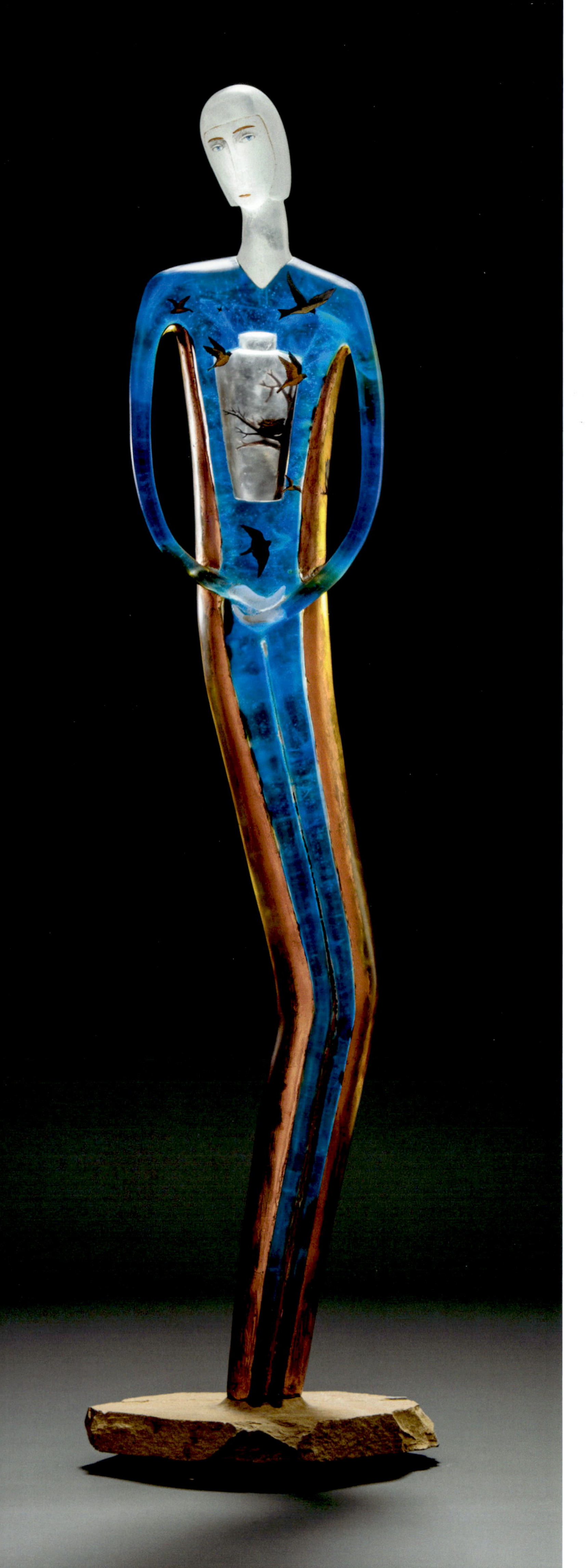

53   Robin Grebe   AMERICAN, BORN 1957   *Arboretum*   2004
GLASS, STONE, WOOD   67 × 17½ × 14½ INCHES   L2017.54

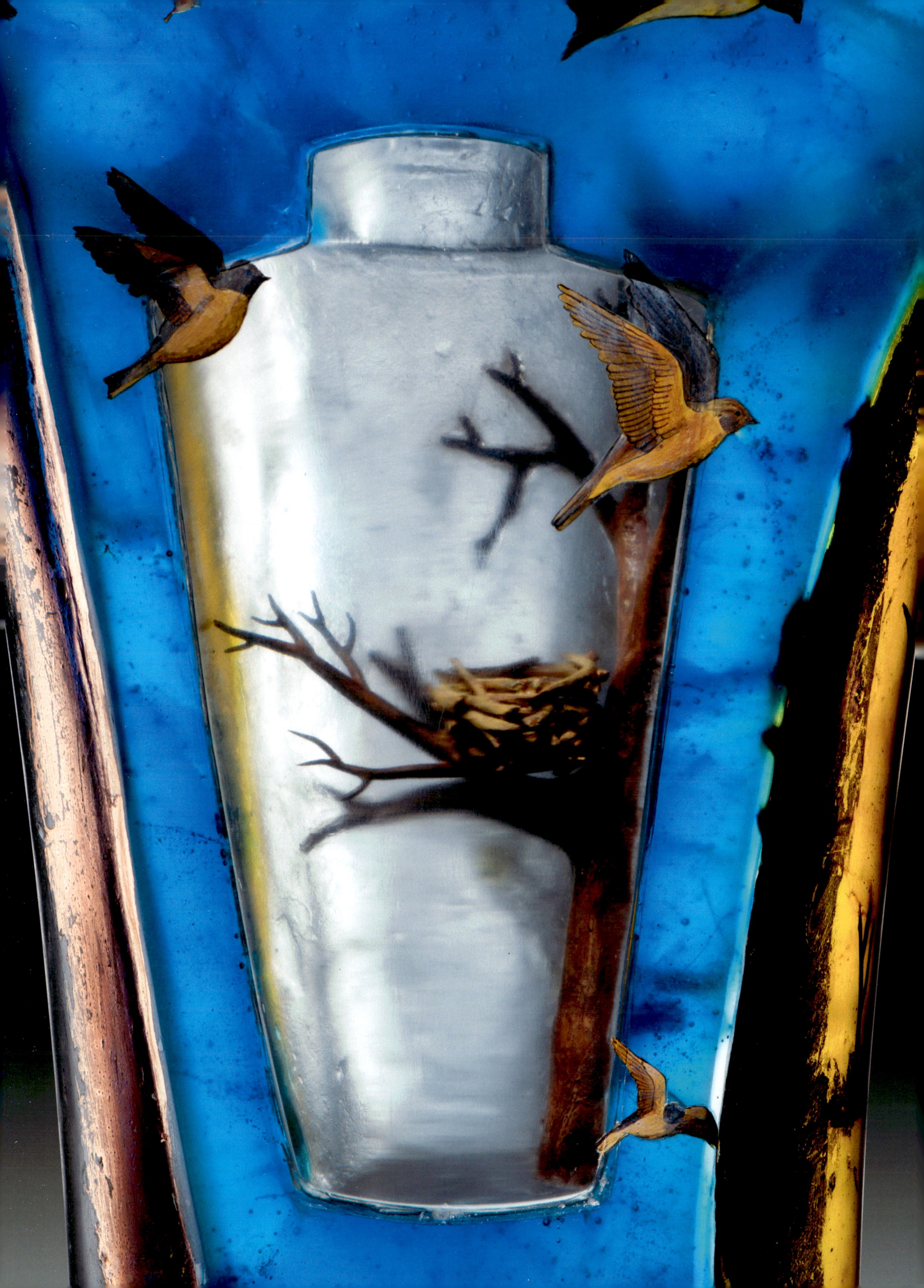

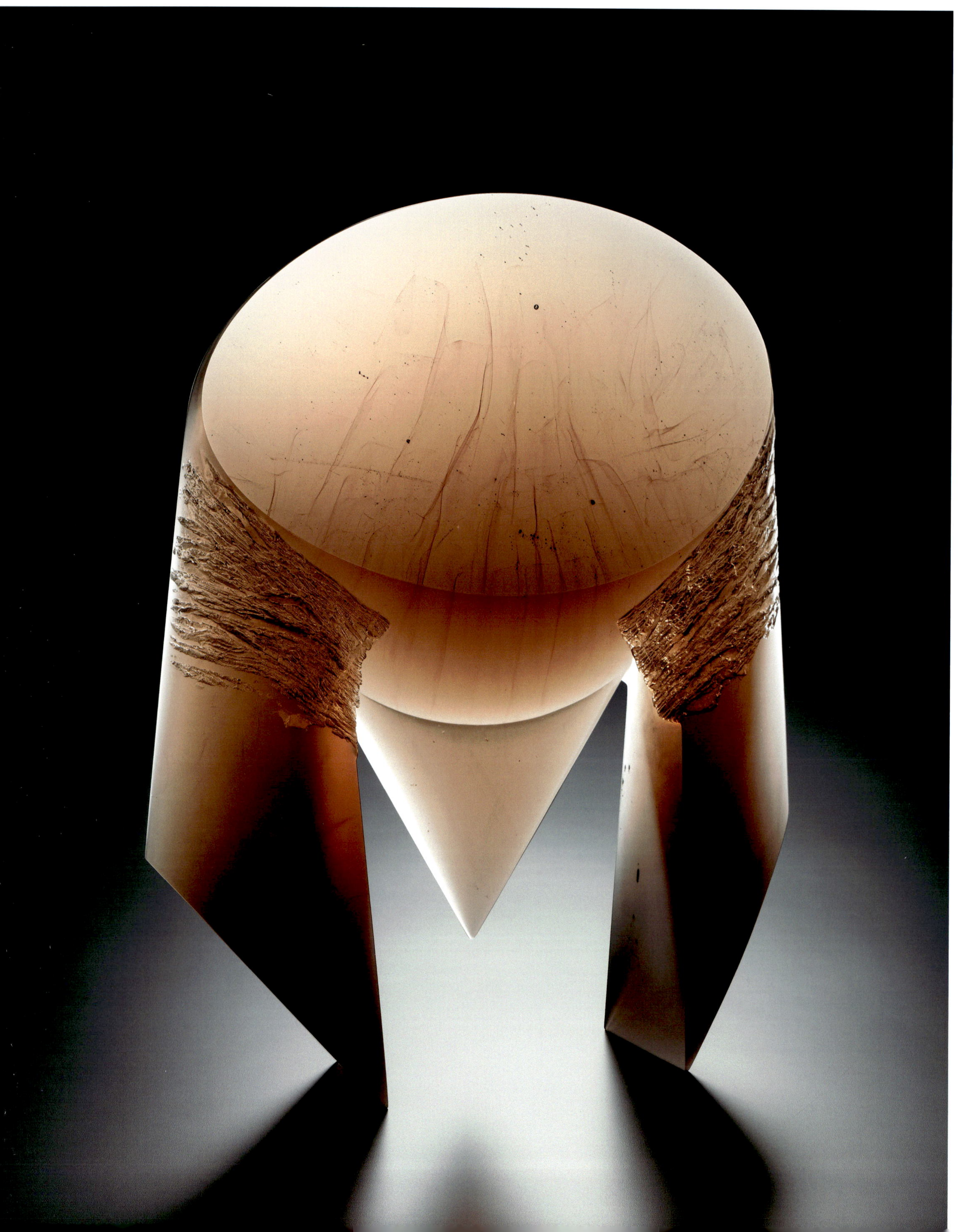

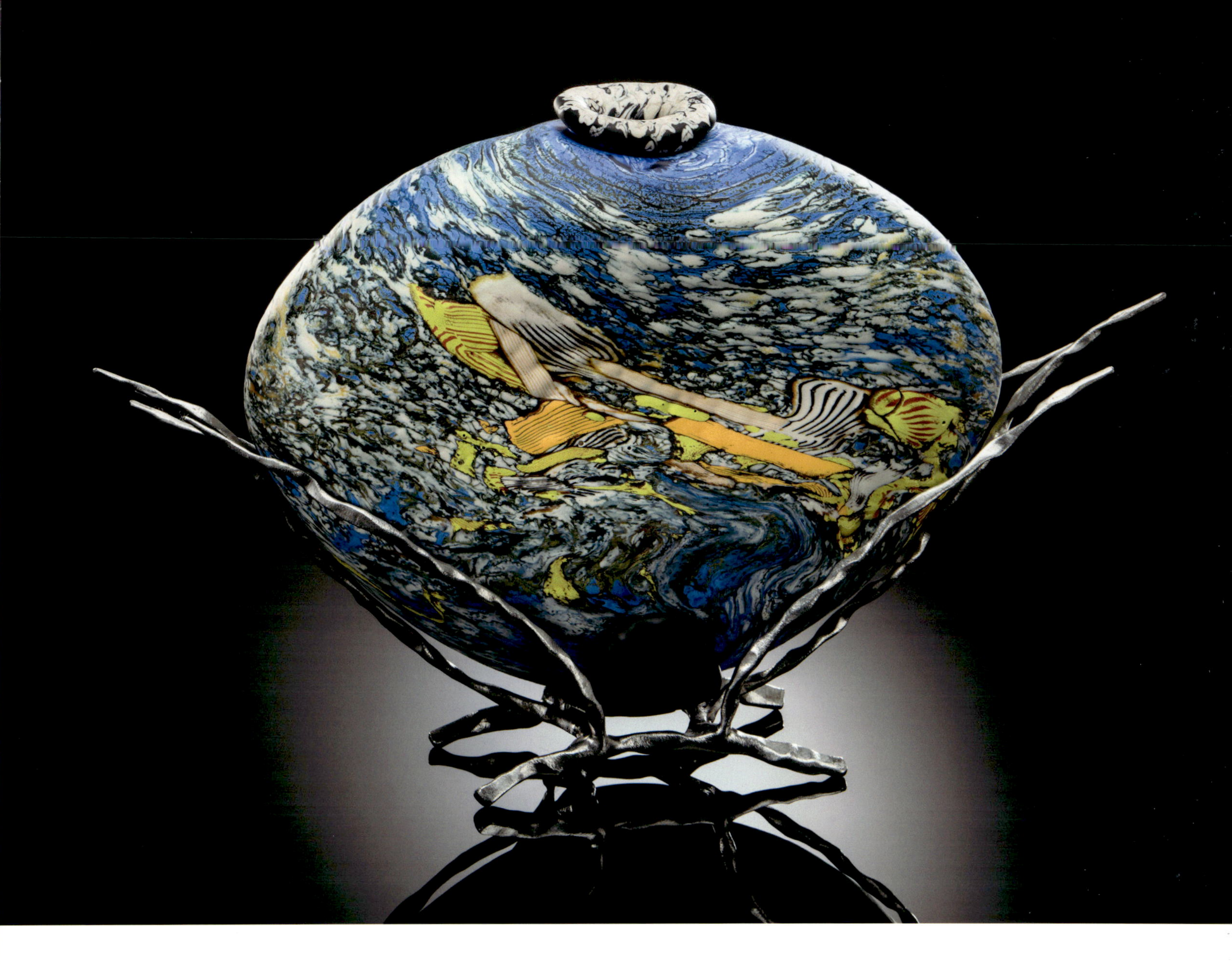

55   Colin Heaney   AUSTRALIAN, BORN 1948   *Canefield Phasmid*   2004

BLOWN AND COLD-WORKED GLASS, STAINLESS STEEL   13¾ × 22⅞ × 4¼ INCHES   L2017.56

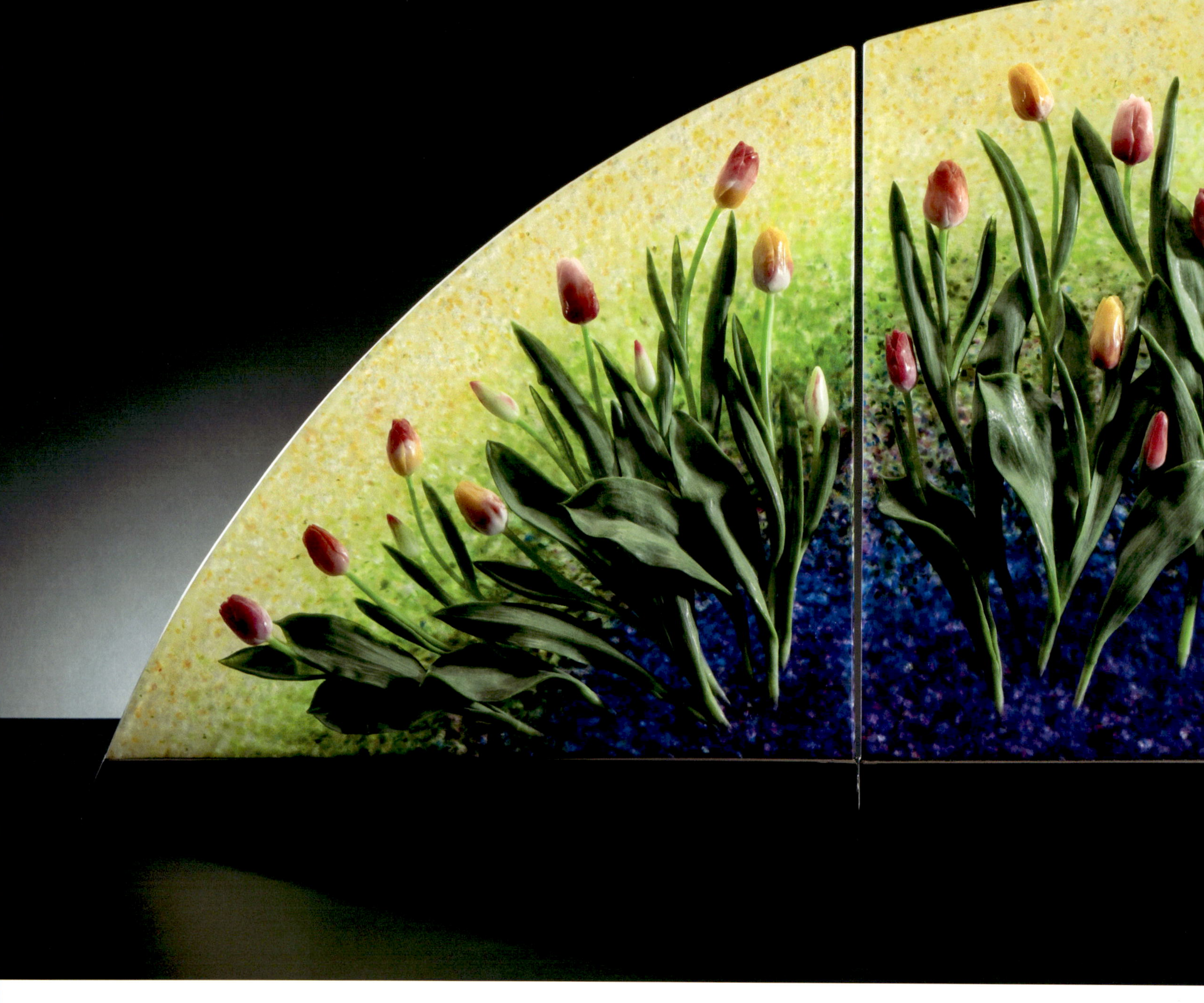

56   Kimiake Higuchi   JAPANESE, BORN 1948   *Tulip Panel*   2003
PÂTE DE VERRE, STEEL STAND   23½ × 65 × 8 INCHES   L2017.65

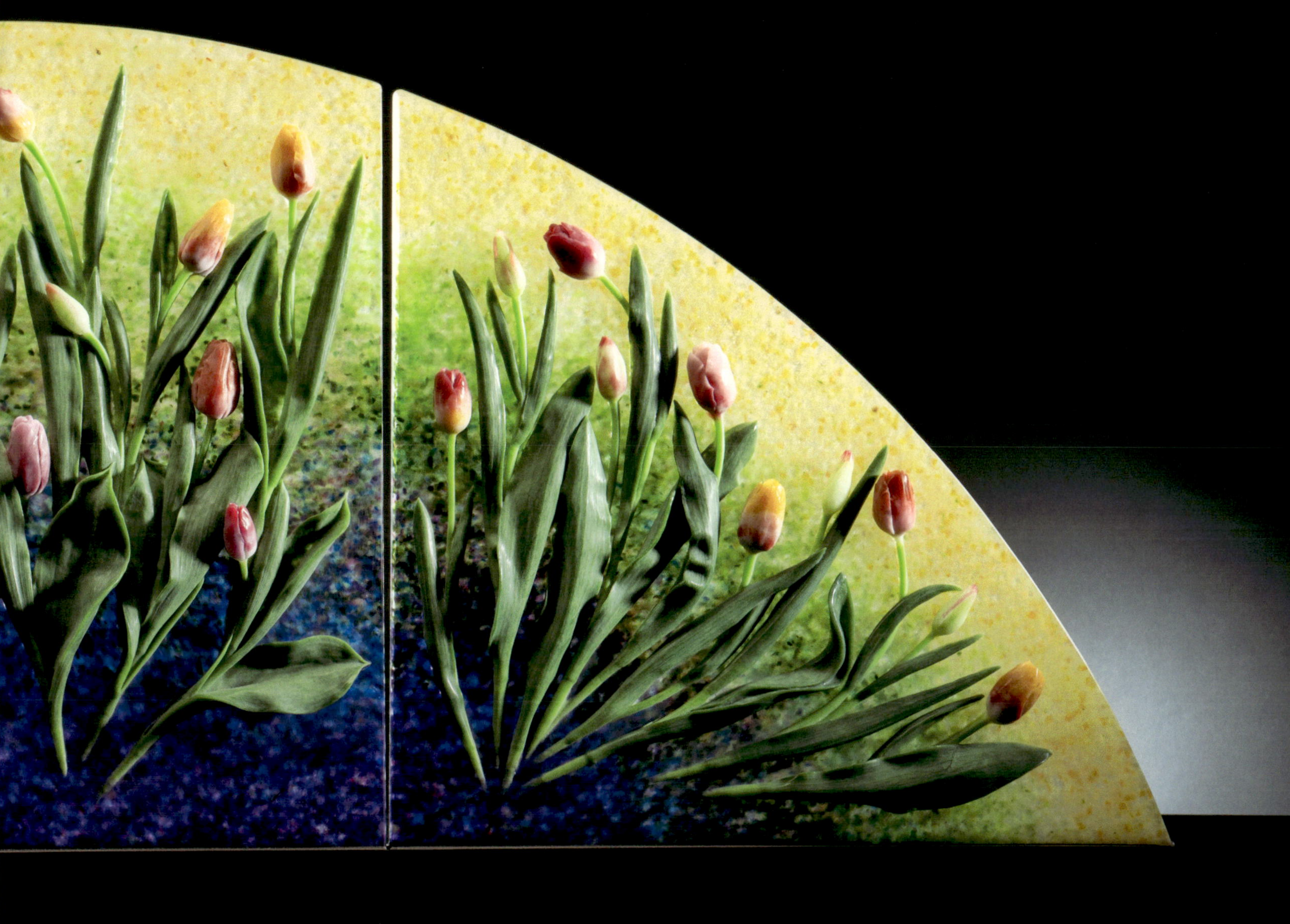

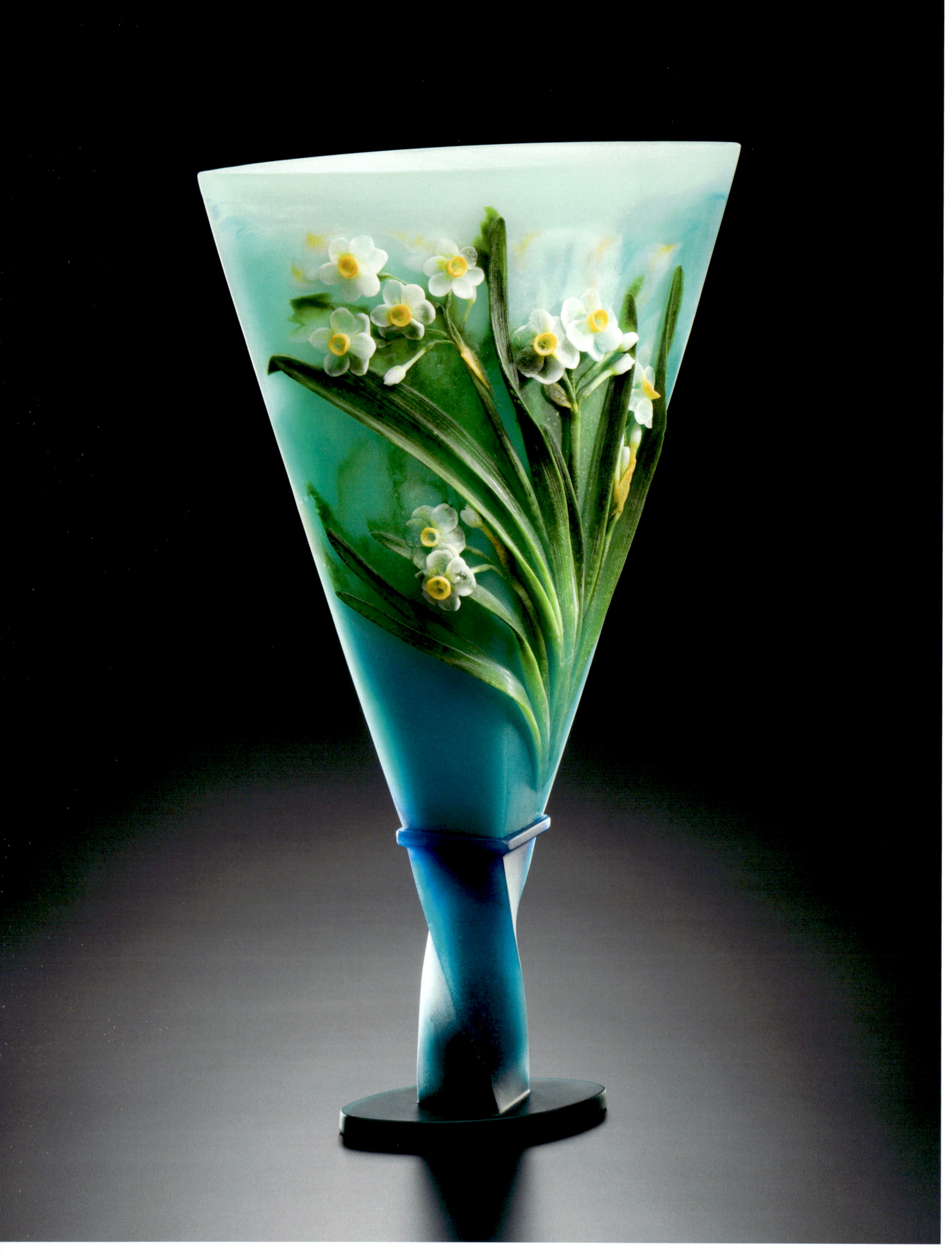

57   Kimiake Higuchi   JAPANESE, BORN 1948   *Daffodil Vase*   N.D.
PÂTE DE VERRE   23 × 14⅛ × 5¾ INCHES   L2017.64

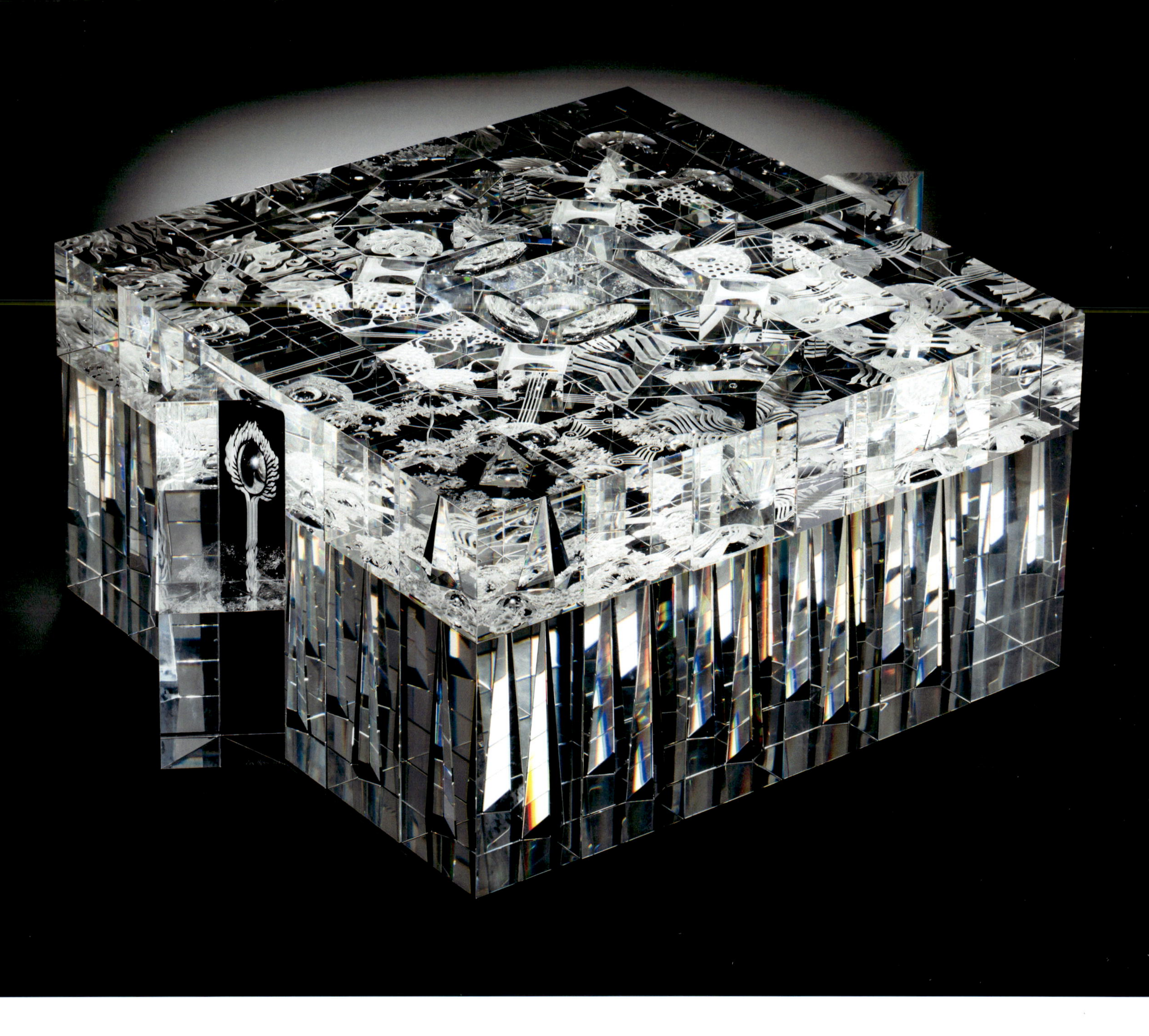

58   Eric Hilton   BRITISH, BORN 1937   *The Source of the Infinite*   2003–04
ENGRAVED, CUT, AND POLISHED LEAD CRYSTAL   12½ × 24 × 31 INCHES (OVERALL)   L2017.57

59   Pavel Hlava   CZECH, 1924–2003   *Flower*   2001
BLOWN, CUT, AND ASSEMBLED GLASS   16¾ × 21¼ × 3 INCHES   L2017.58

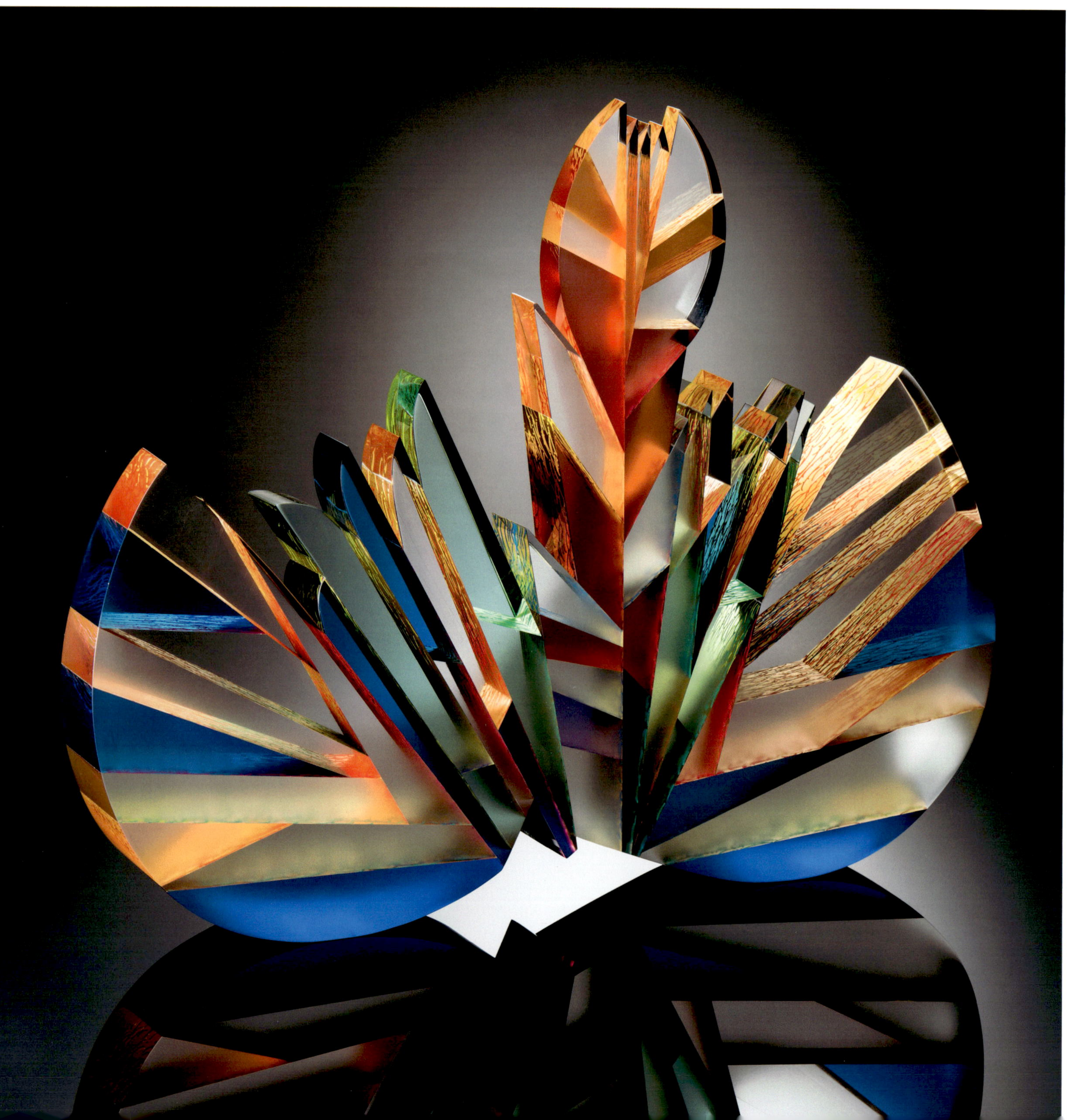

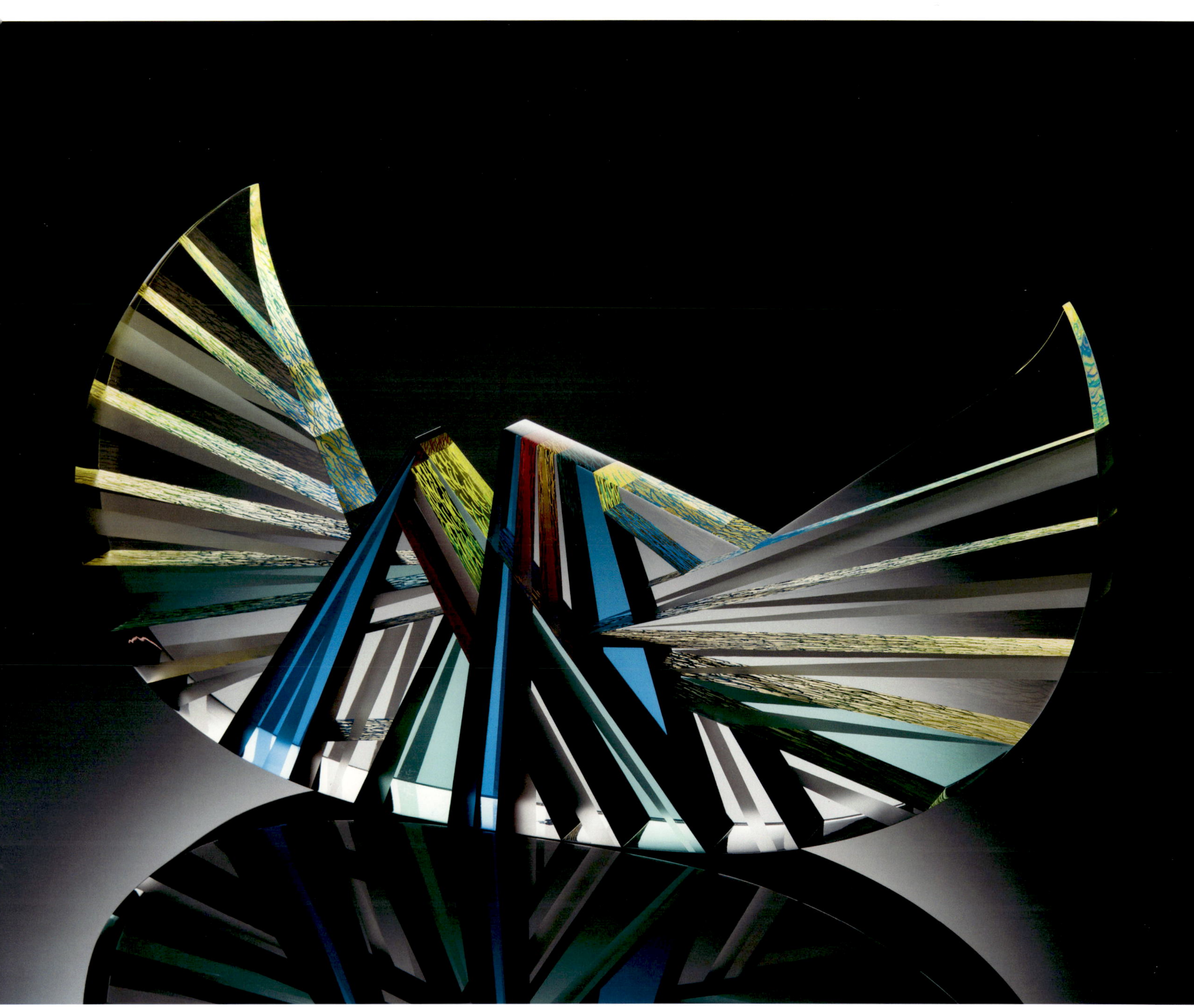

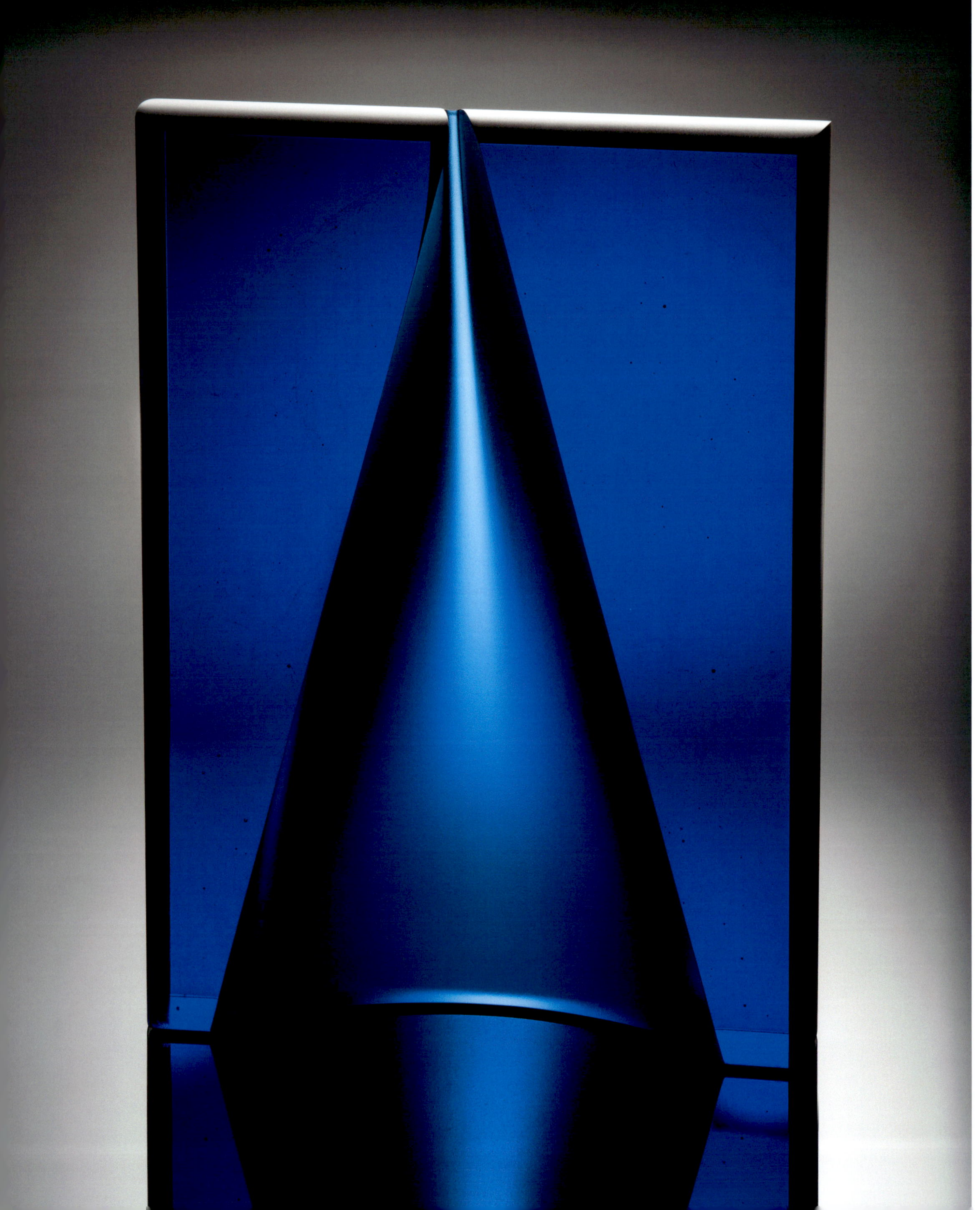

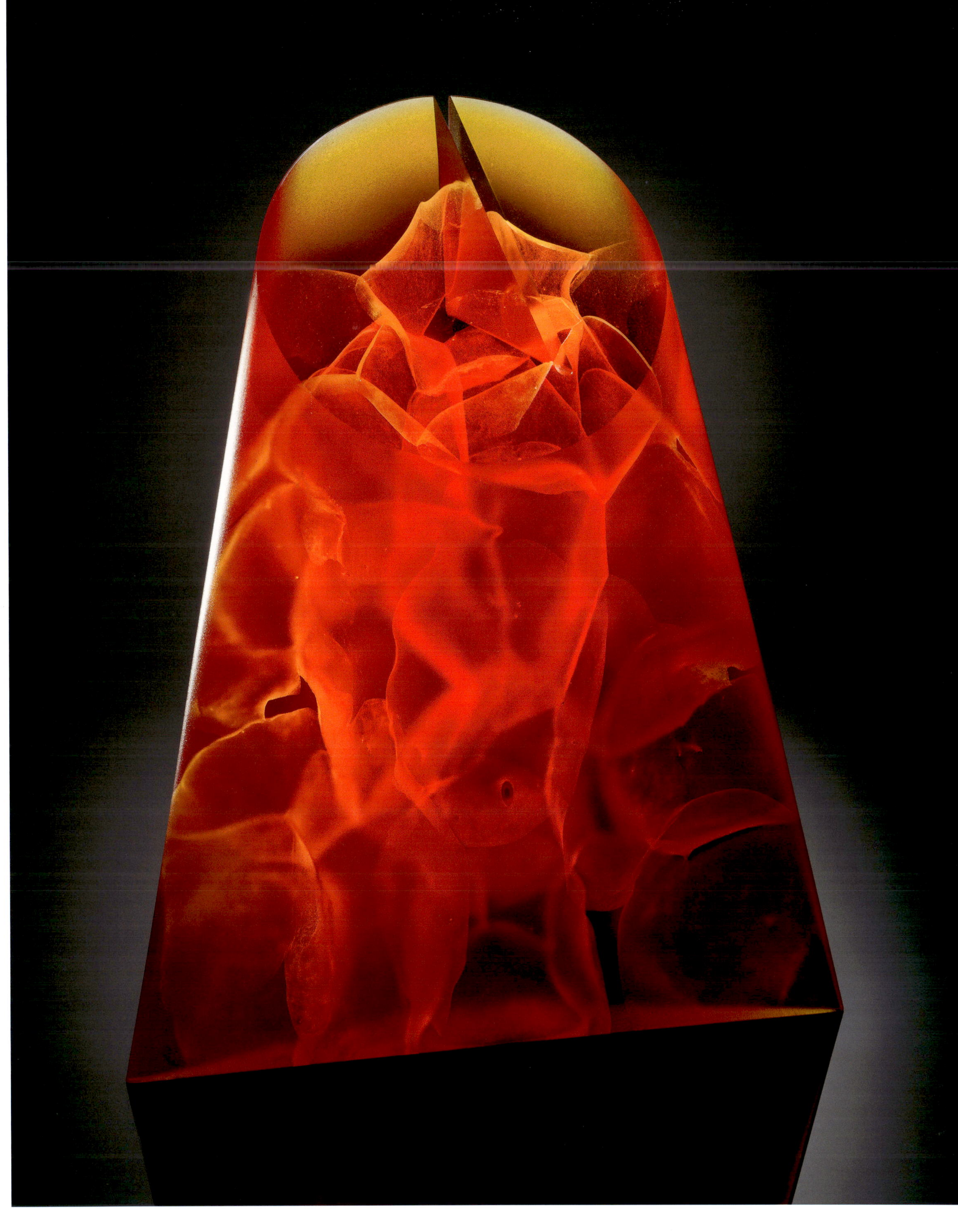

62   Petr Hora   CZECH, BORN 1924   *Hadros*   2006
CAST AND ACID-POLISHED GLASS   18¾ × 15½ × 4¾ INCHES   L2017.59

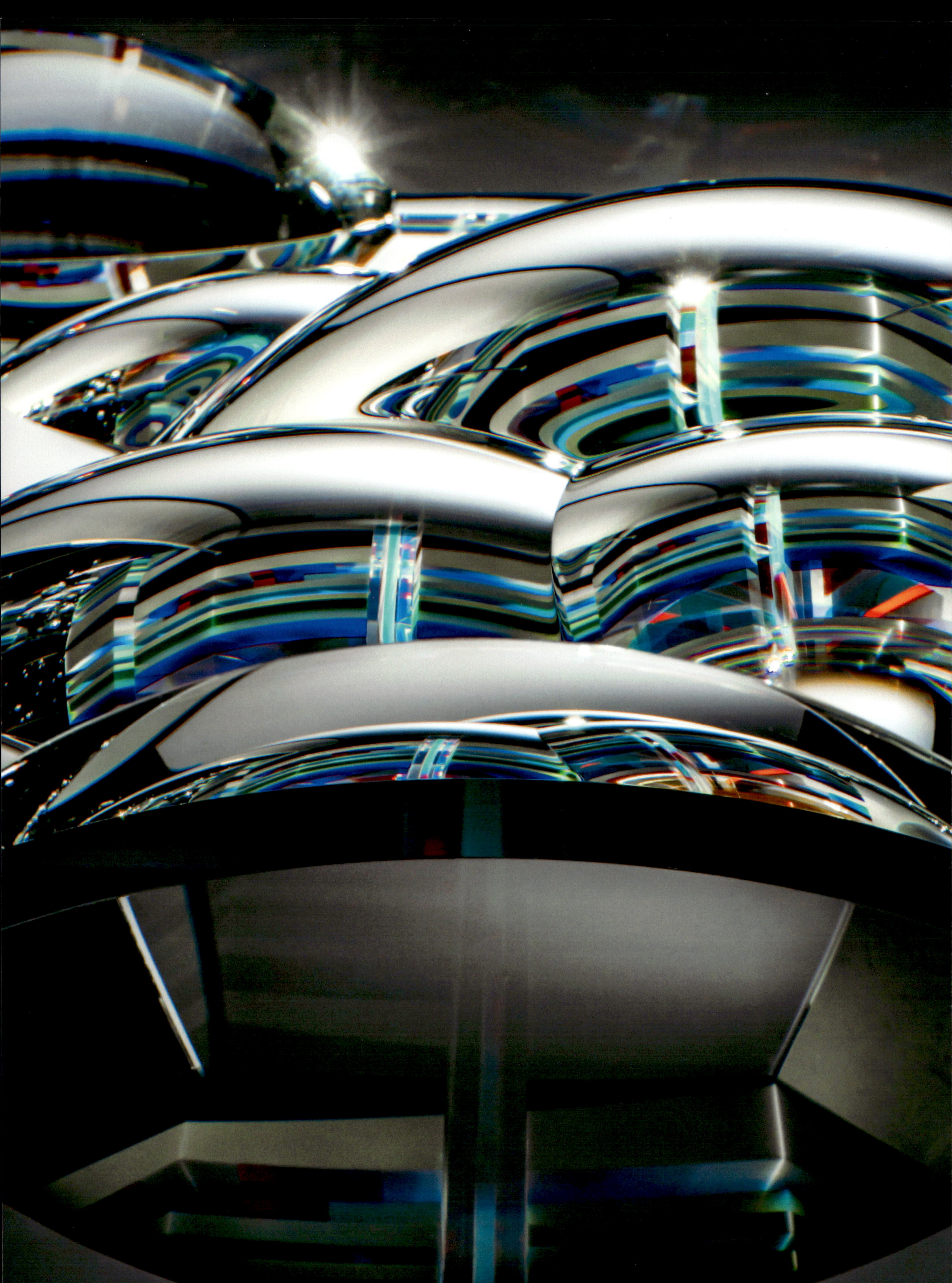

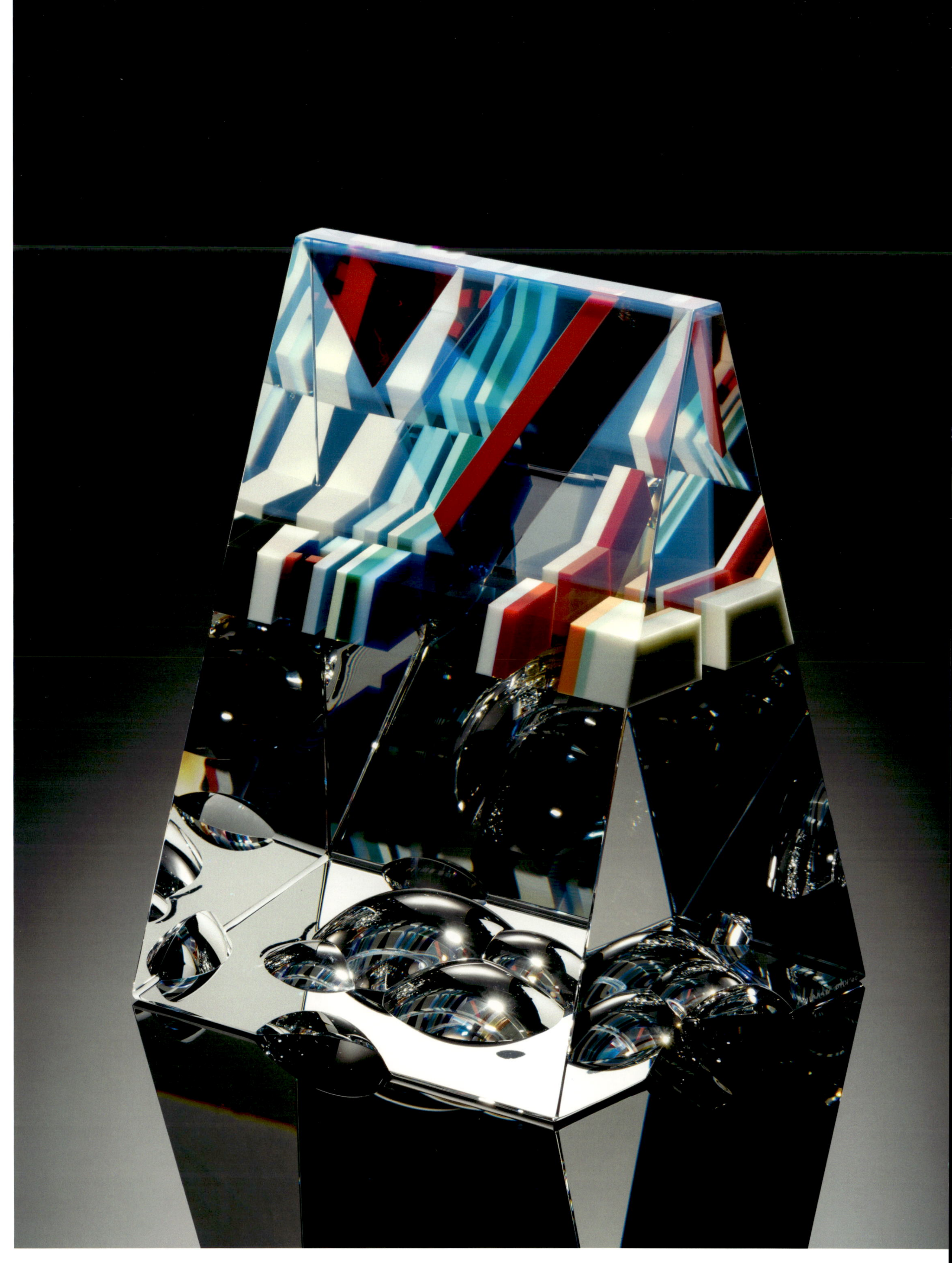

63   David Huchthausen   AMERICAN, BORN 1951   *Mirage*   2000
CAST AND LAMINATED GLASS   12½ × 8¾ × 9¼ INCHES   L2017.60

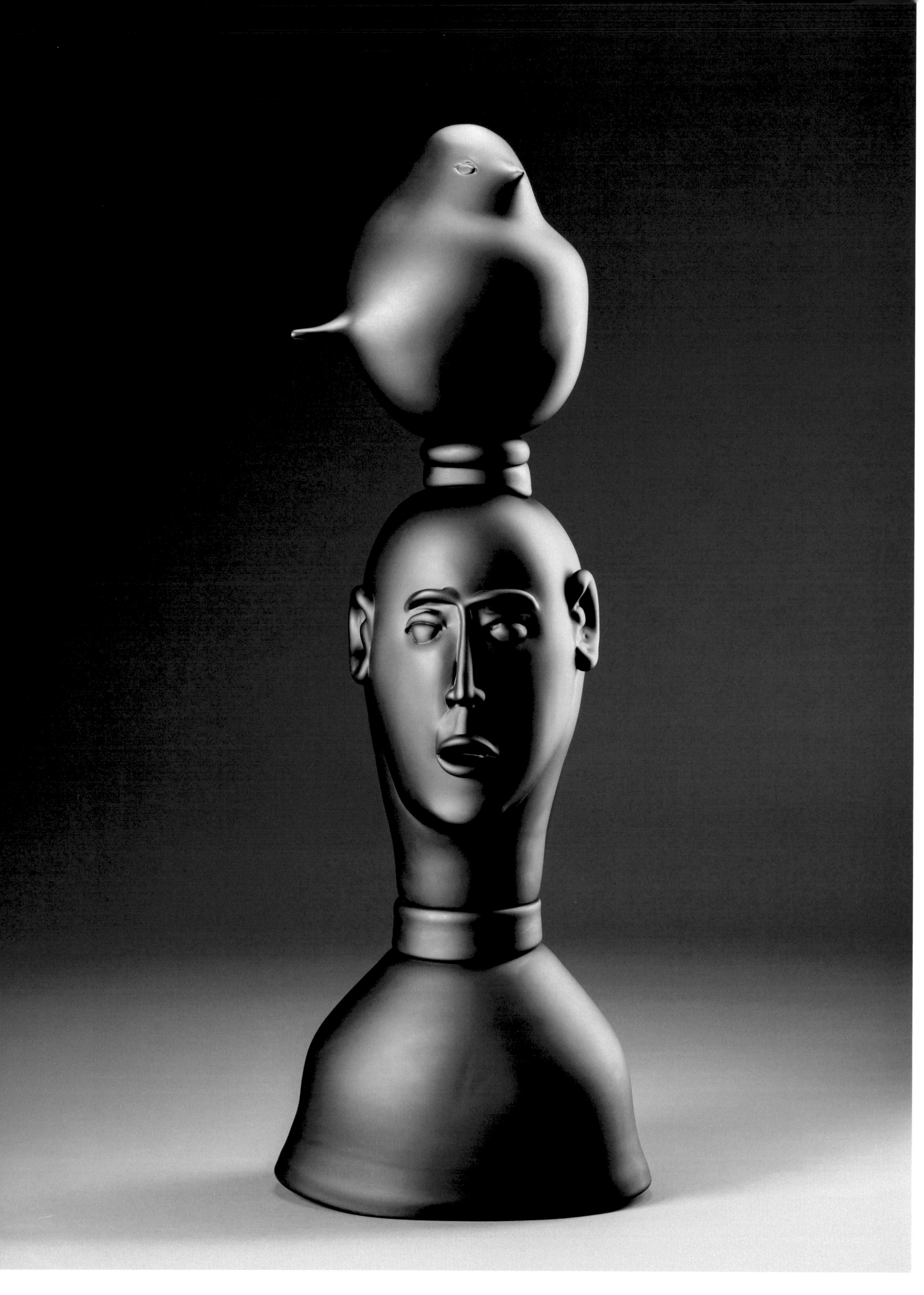

64 Richard Jolley AMERICAN, BORN 1952 *Featherhead #6* 2008
HOT-FORMED GLASS FABRICATED 49 × 18½ × 16 INCHES L2017.63

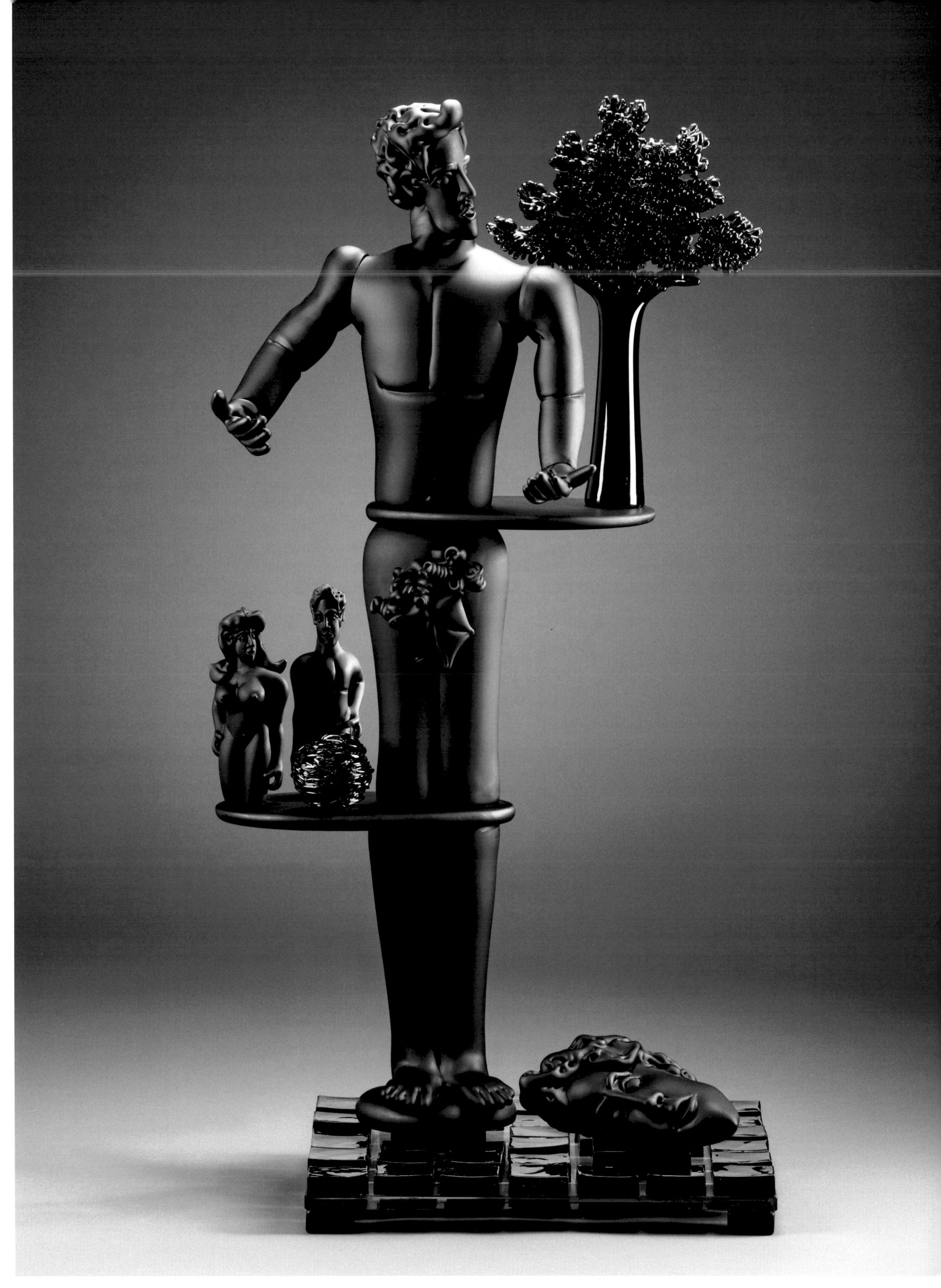

65 Richard Jolley AMERICAN, BORN 1952 *Translating Substance #26* 2006
HOT-FORMED GLASS FABRICATED   54 × 29 × 20½ INCHES   L2017.62

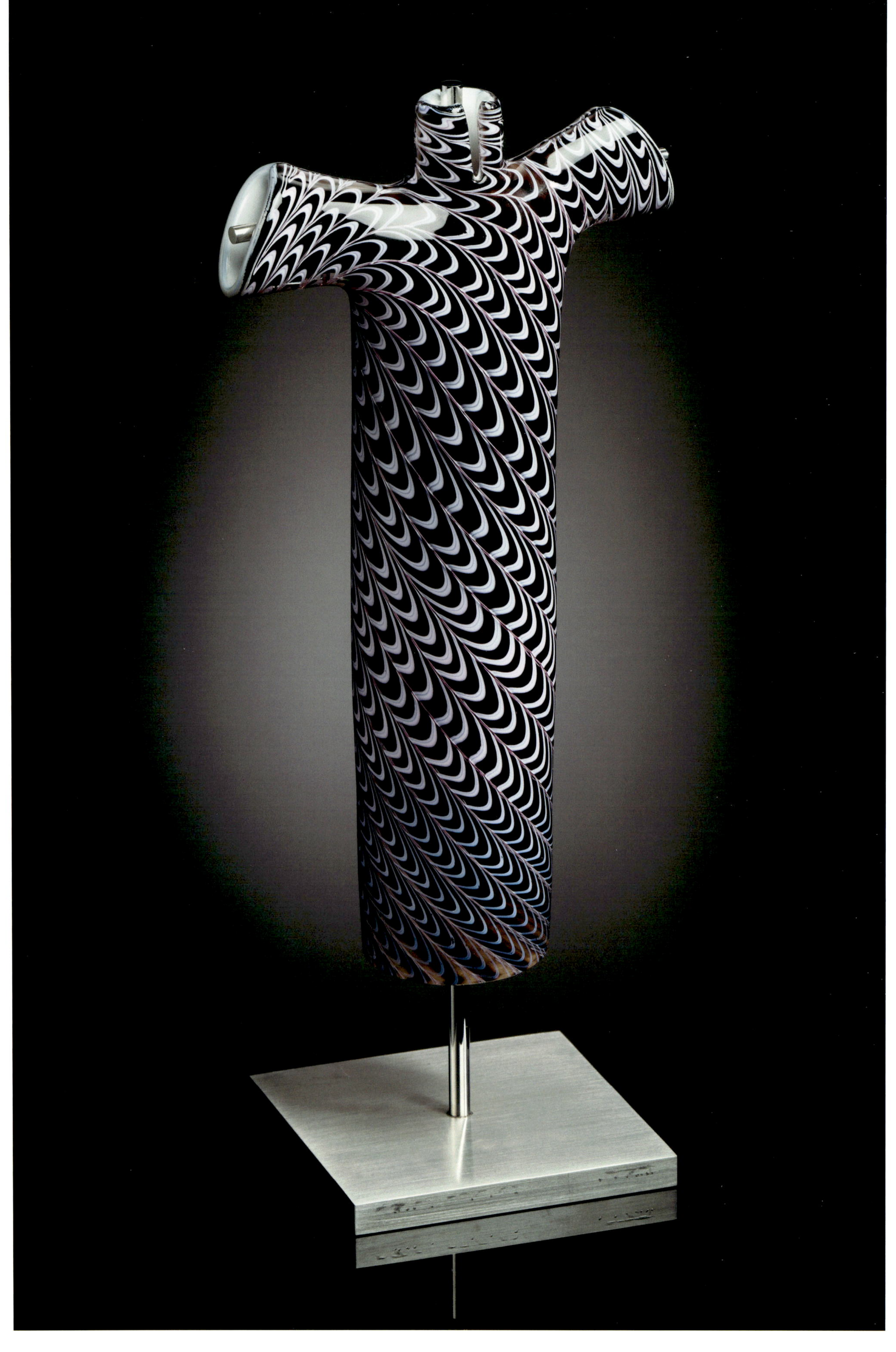

66   Gerry King   AUSTRALIAN, BORN 1945   *Semblance #02*   2002
BLOWN GLASS, STAINLESS STEEL STAND   15½ × 6¾ × 5 INCHES   L2017.50

67   Joey Kirkpatrick AMERICAN, BORN 1952,
     Flora C. Mace AMERICAN, BORN 1949
     Red Apple   2005
     BLOWN GLASS   16 × 18 × 16 INCHES   L2017.85

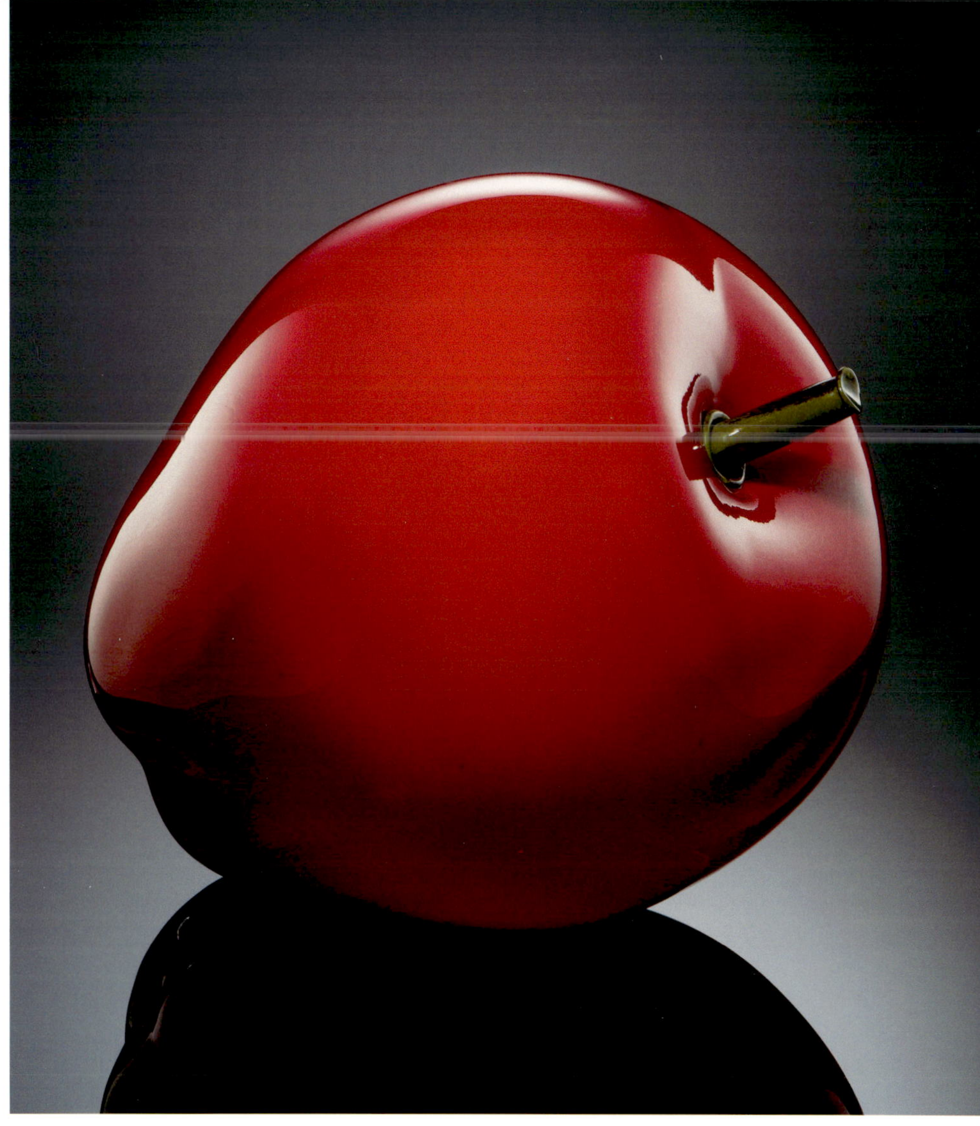

68   Joey Kirkpatrick AMERICAN, BORN 1952,
     Flora C. Mace AMERICAN, BORN 1949
     Red/Green Apple   2005
     BLOWN GLASS   17 × 15 × 16 INCHES   L2017.86

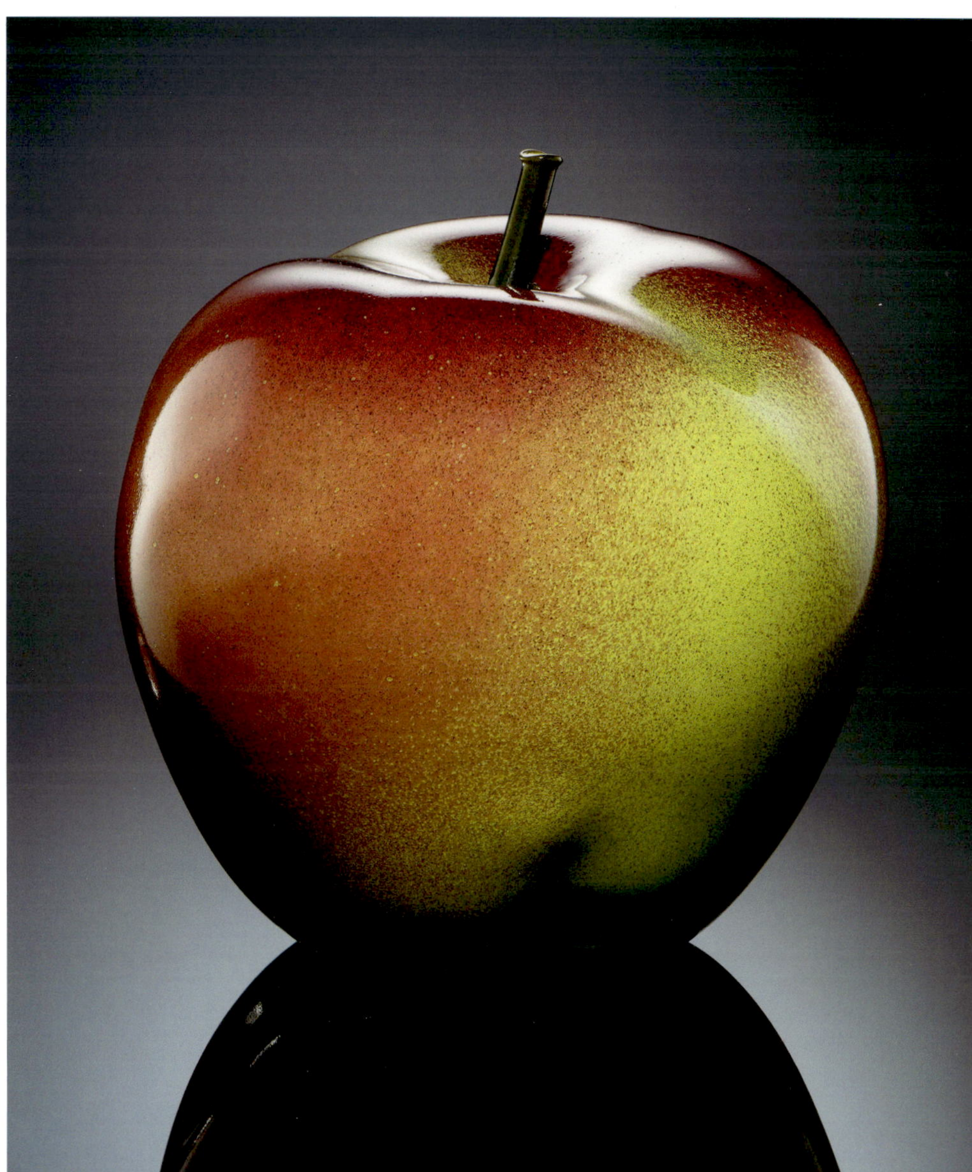

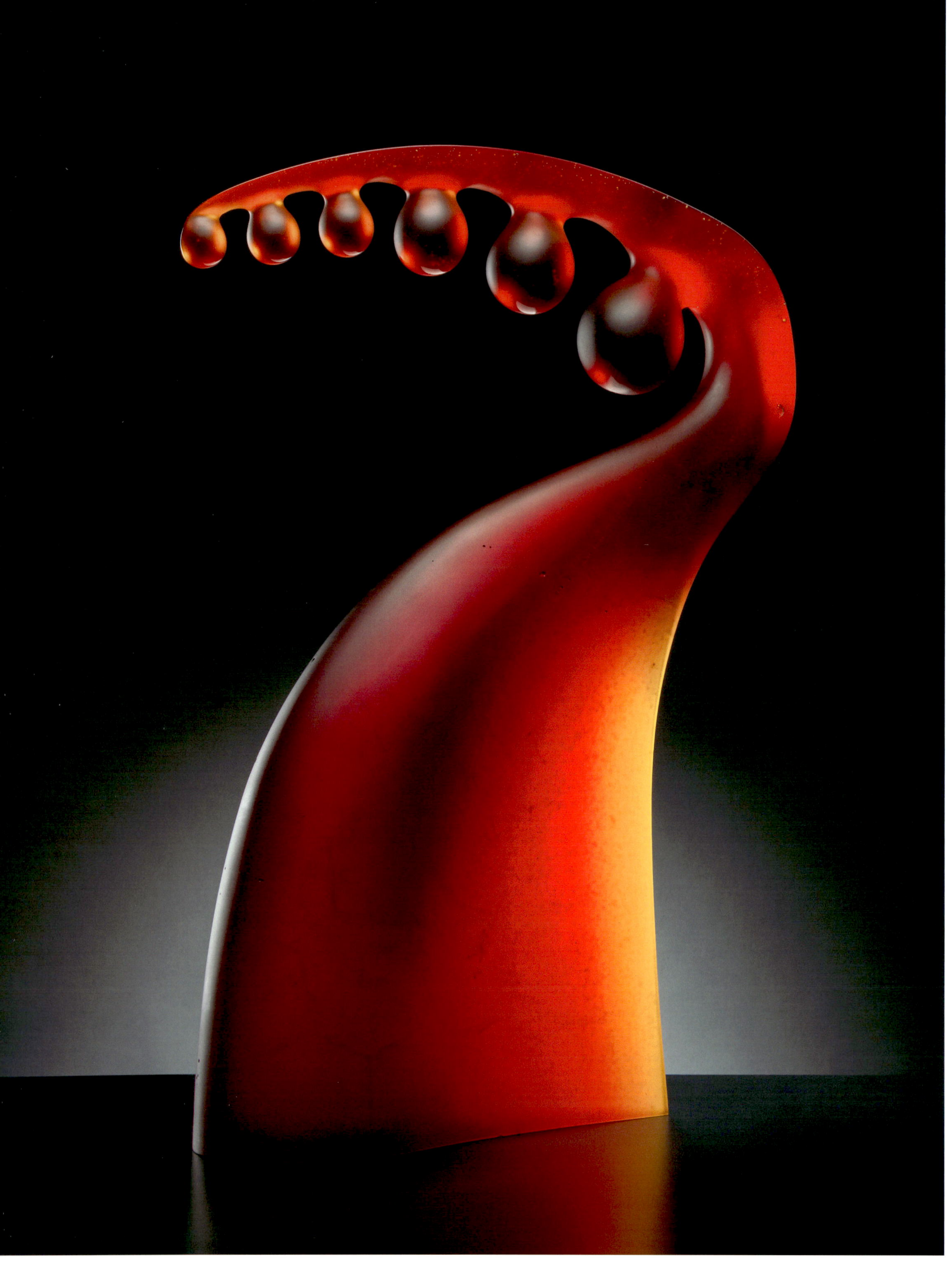

69   Vladimira Klumpar   CZECH, BORN 1954   *After Rain*   2007
CAST GLASS   33¾ × 23½ × 8¾ INCHES   L2017.67

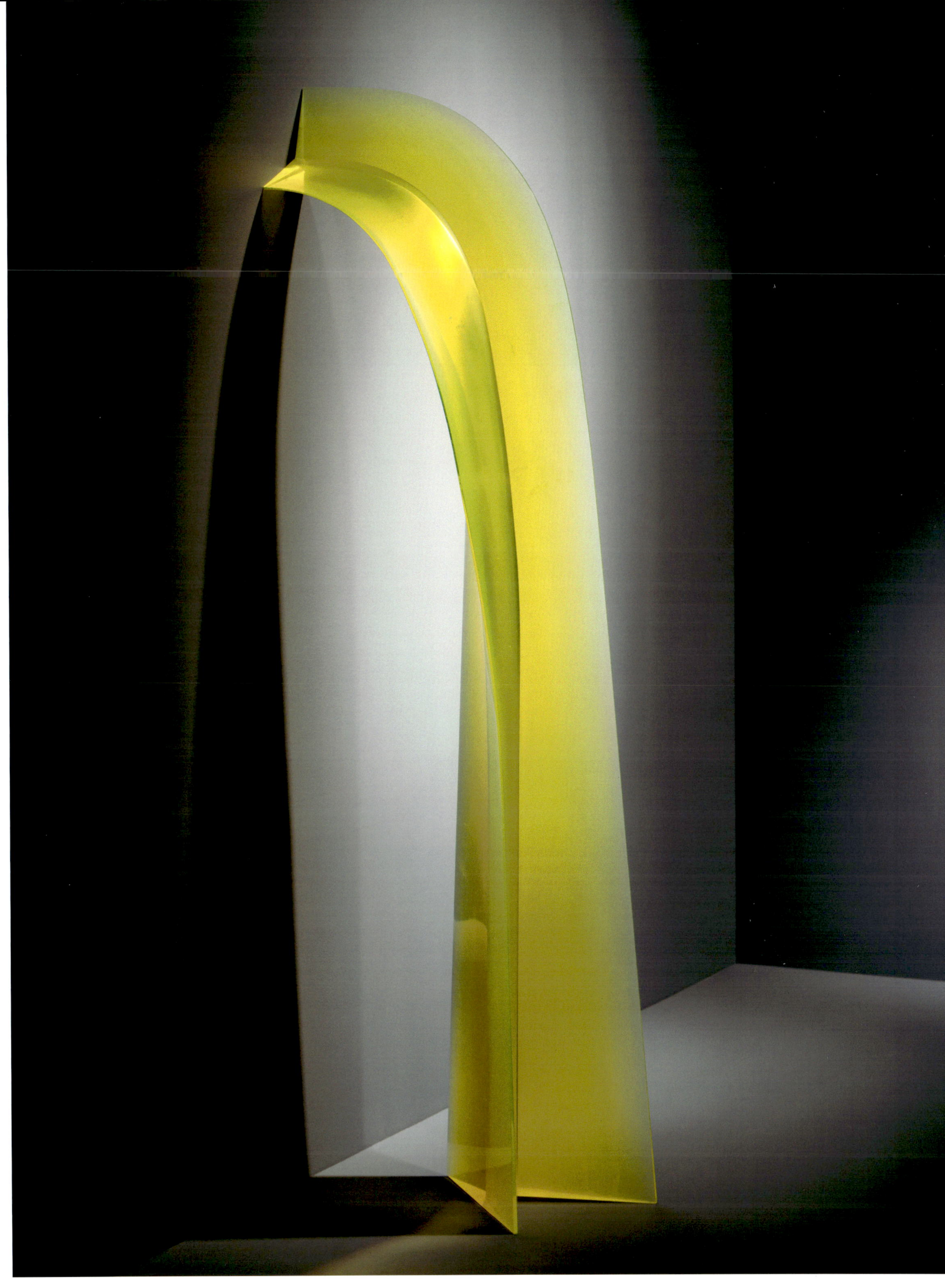

70   Vladimira Klumpar   CZECH, BORN 1954   *Reach*   2006
CAST GLASS   64¼ × 9½ × 22 INCHES   L2017.66

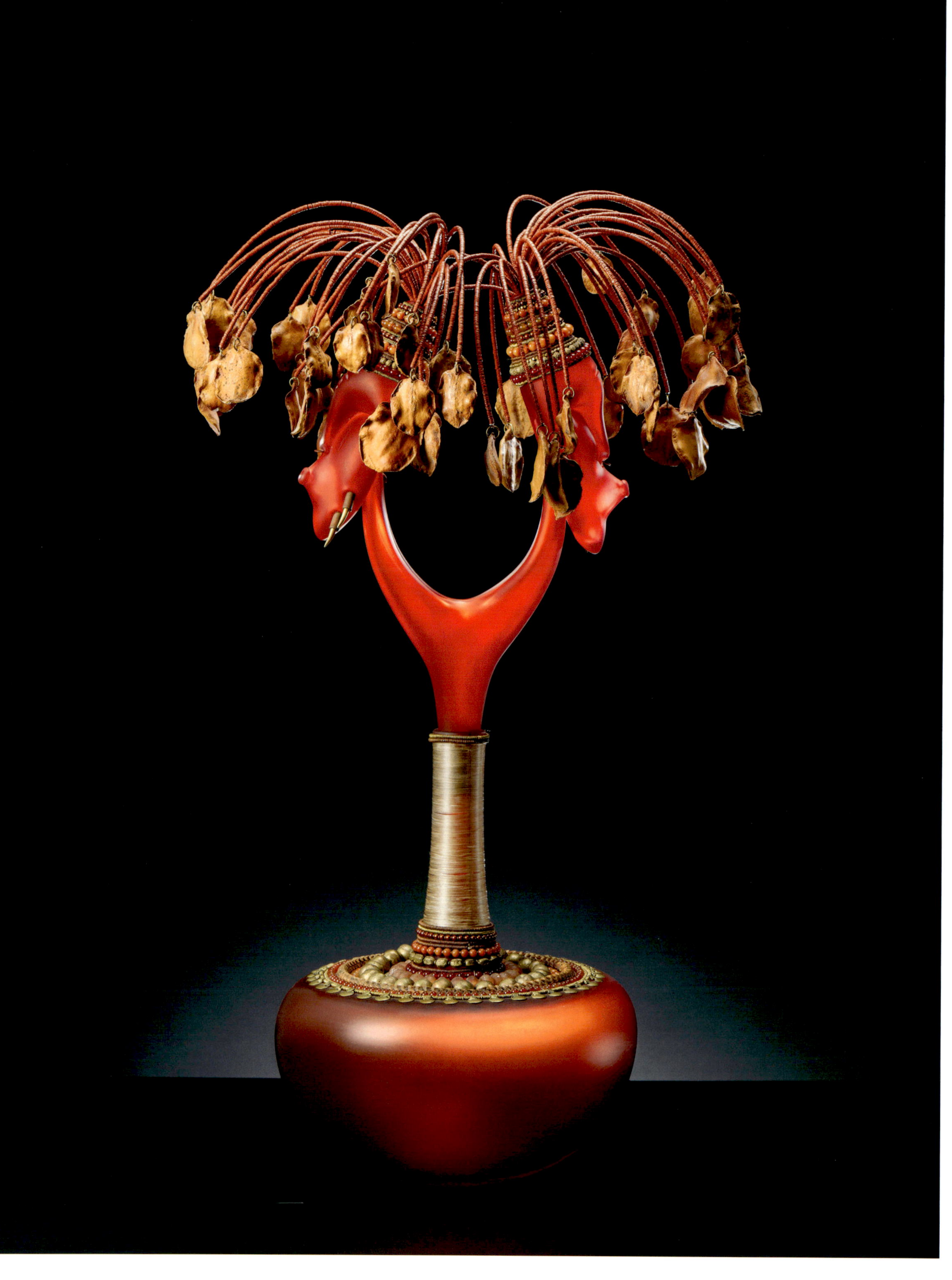

71   Sabrina Knowles AMERICAN, BORN 1955, Jenny Pohlman AMERICAN, BORN 1960   *Aryades: Split Neck Series*   2005
BLOWN AND SCULPTED GLASS, BEADS, STEEL, PODS   40 × 25 × 21 INCHES   L2017.99

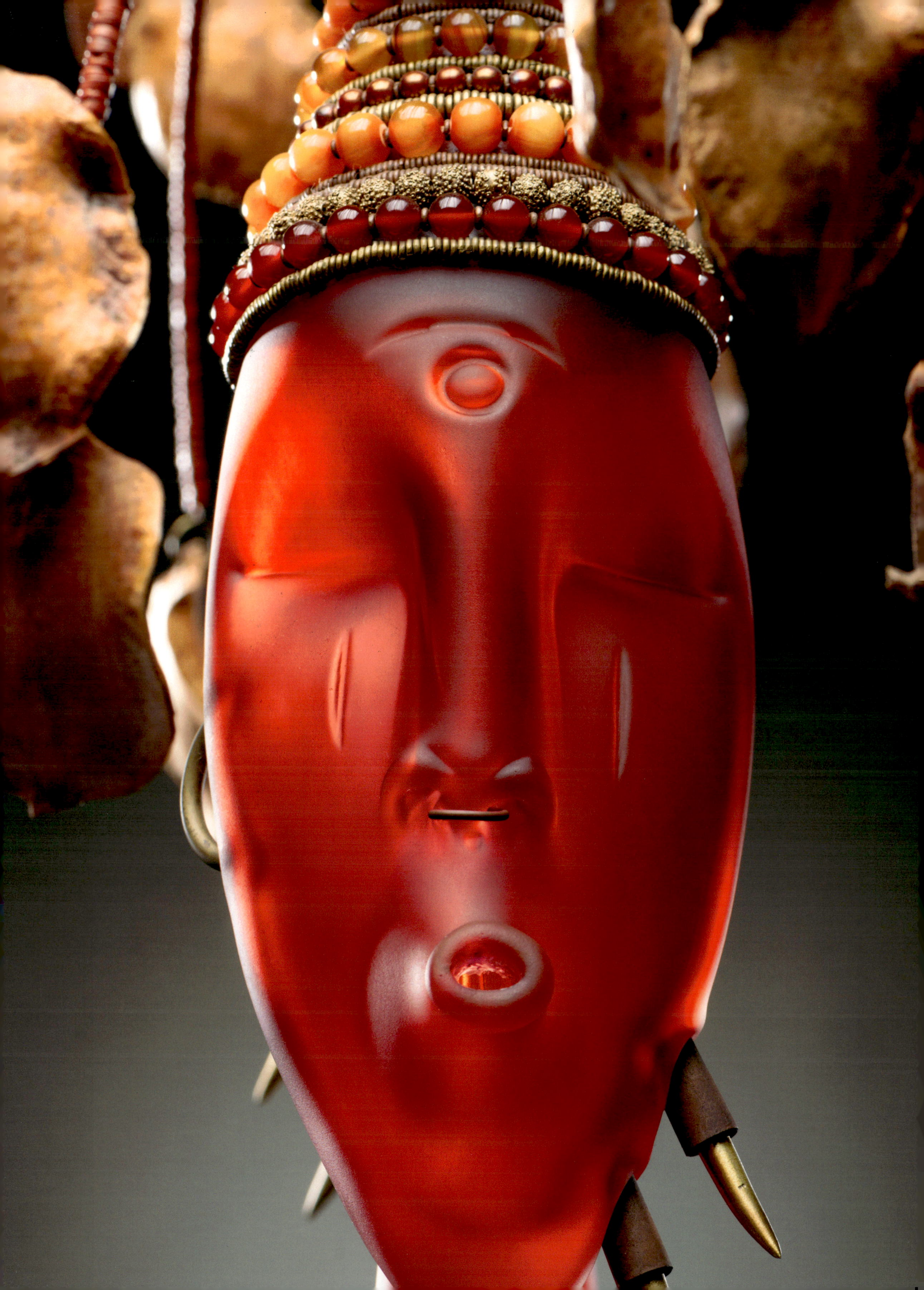

 Jon Kuhn   AMERICAN, BORN 1949   *Inspiration*   2003
CUT, POLISHED, LAMINATED OPTICAL GLASSES, INCLUDING LEAD-FLOURIDE, BOROSILICATE,
AND SODA-LIME GLASSES   43½ × 11 × 11 INCHES   L2017.68

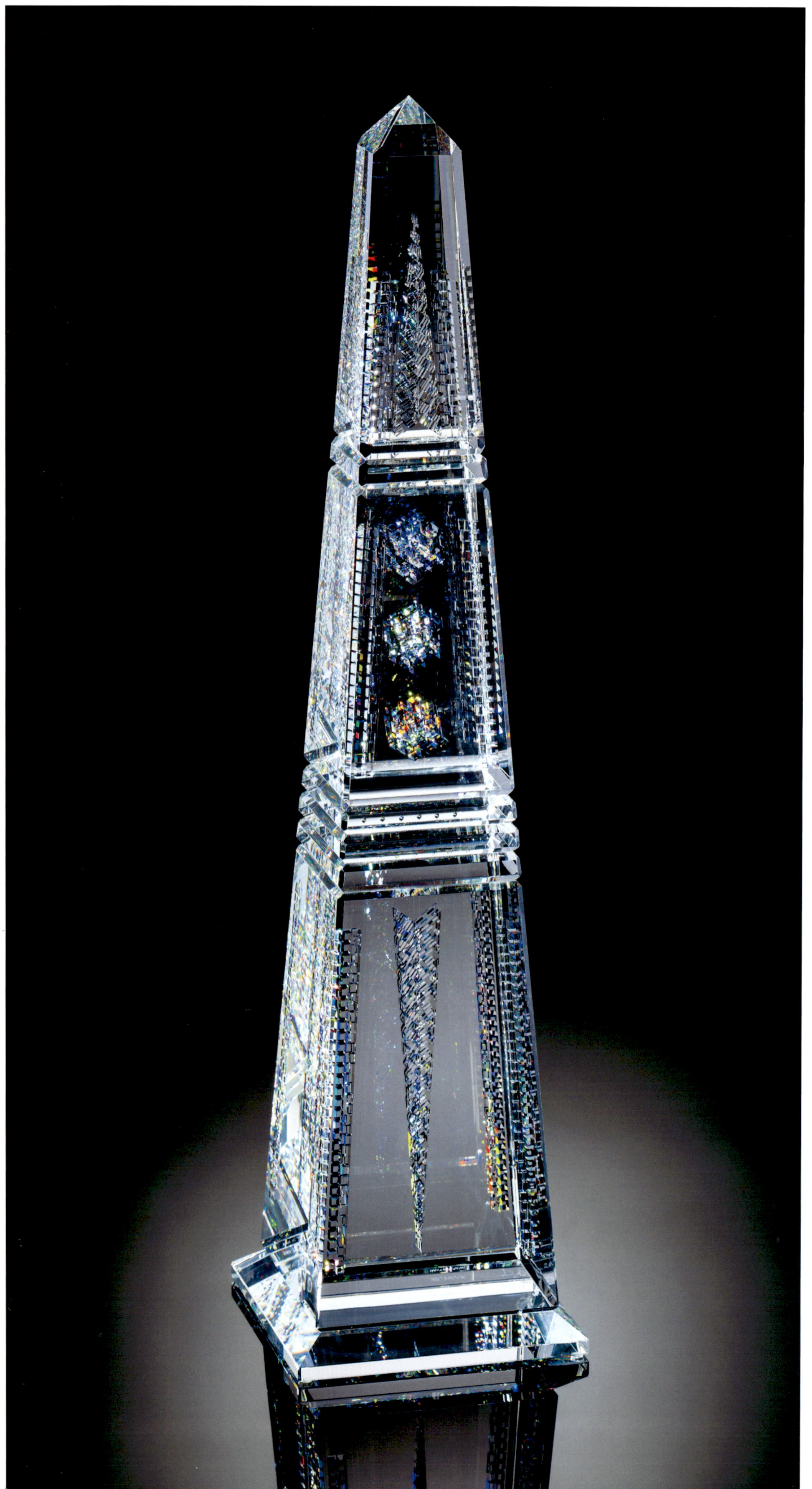

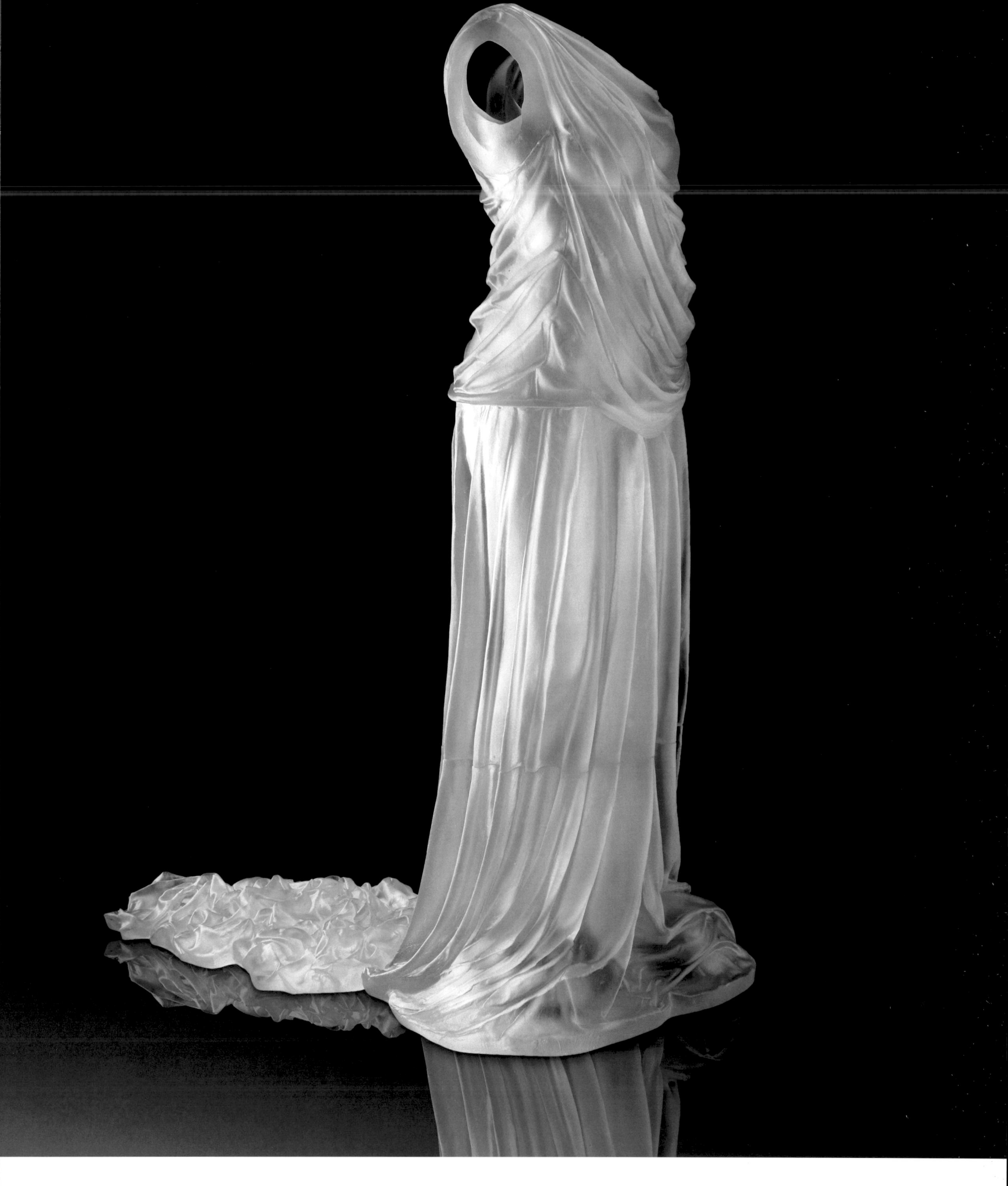

73   Karen LaMonte   AMERICAN, BORN 1967   *Dress Impression with Train*   2005
CAST GLASS   58⁵⁄₁₆ × 22½ × 43⁵⁄₁₆ INCHES   L2017.143

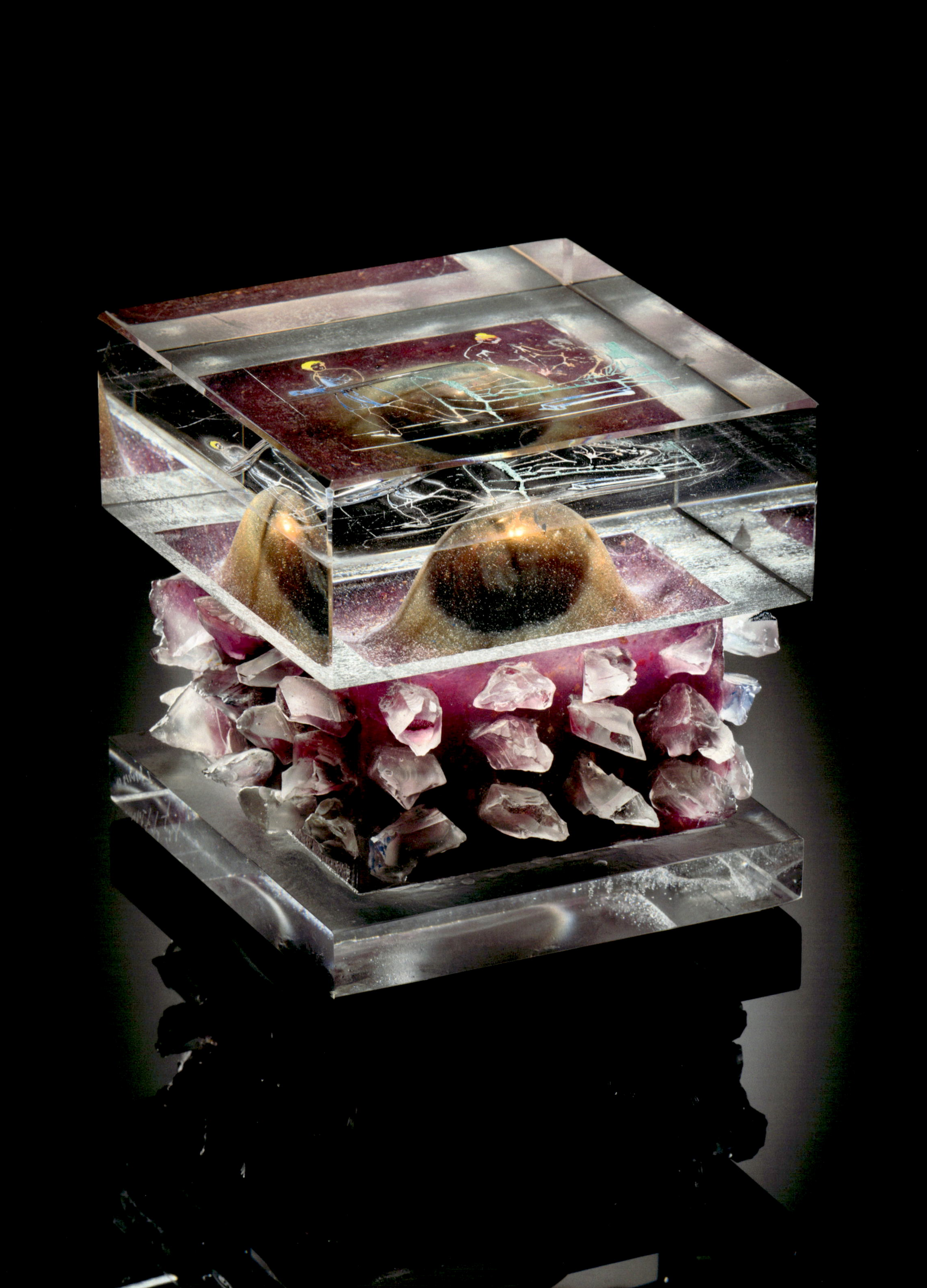

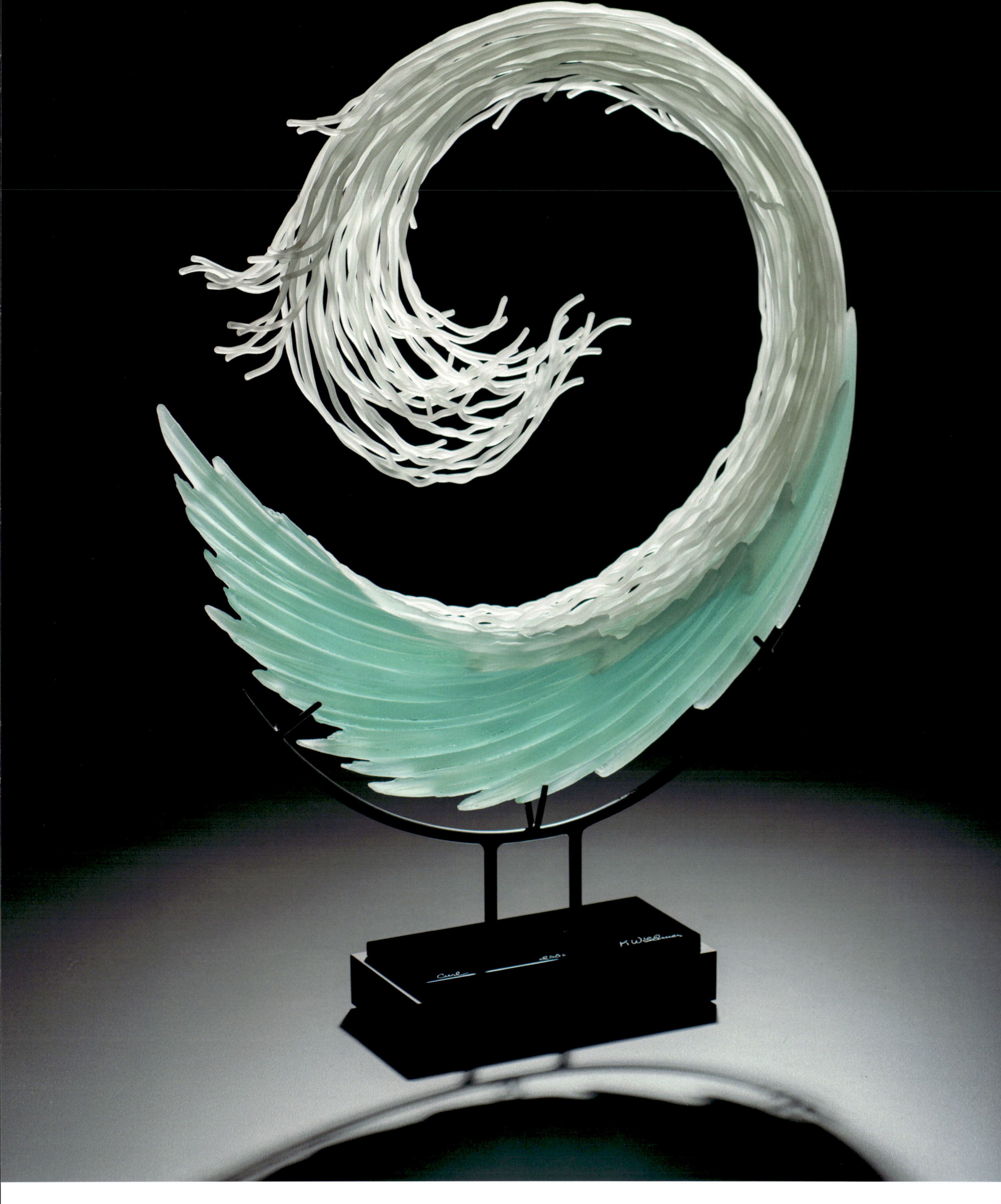

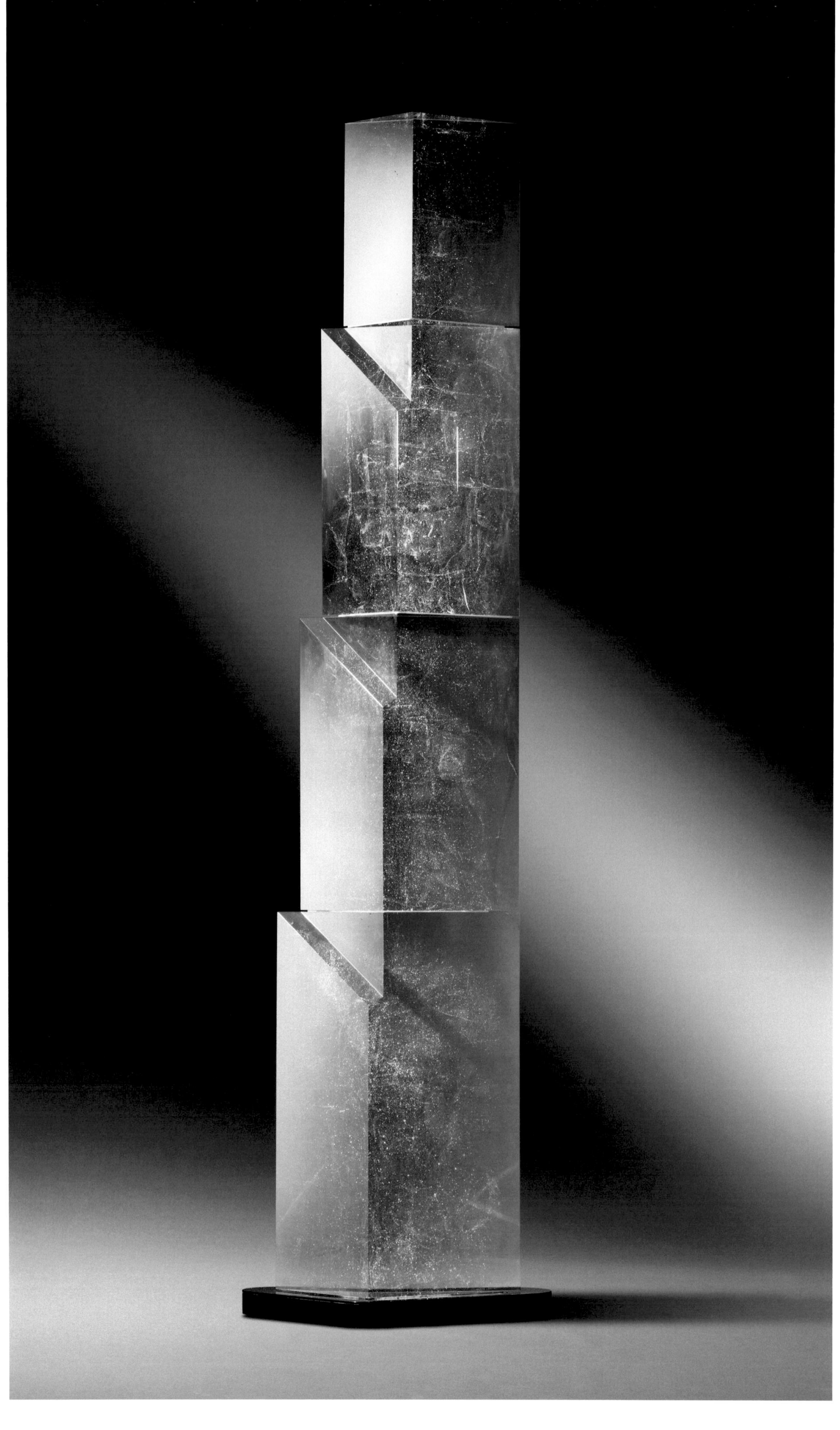

76   Stanislav Libenský CZECH, 1921–2002, Jaroslava Brychtová CZECH, BORN 1924   *3 V Column*   1989–2000
CAST GLASS   110 × 24 × 8 INCHES   L2017.144

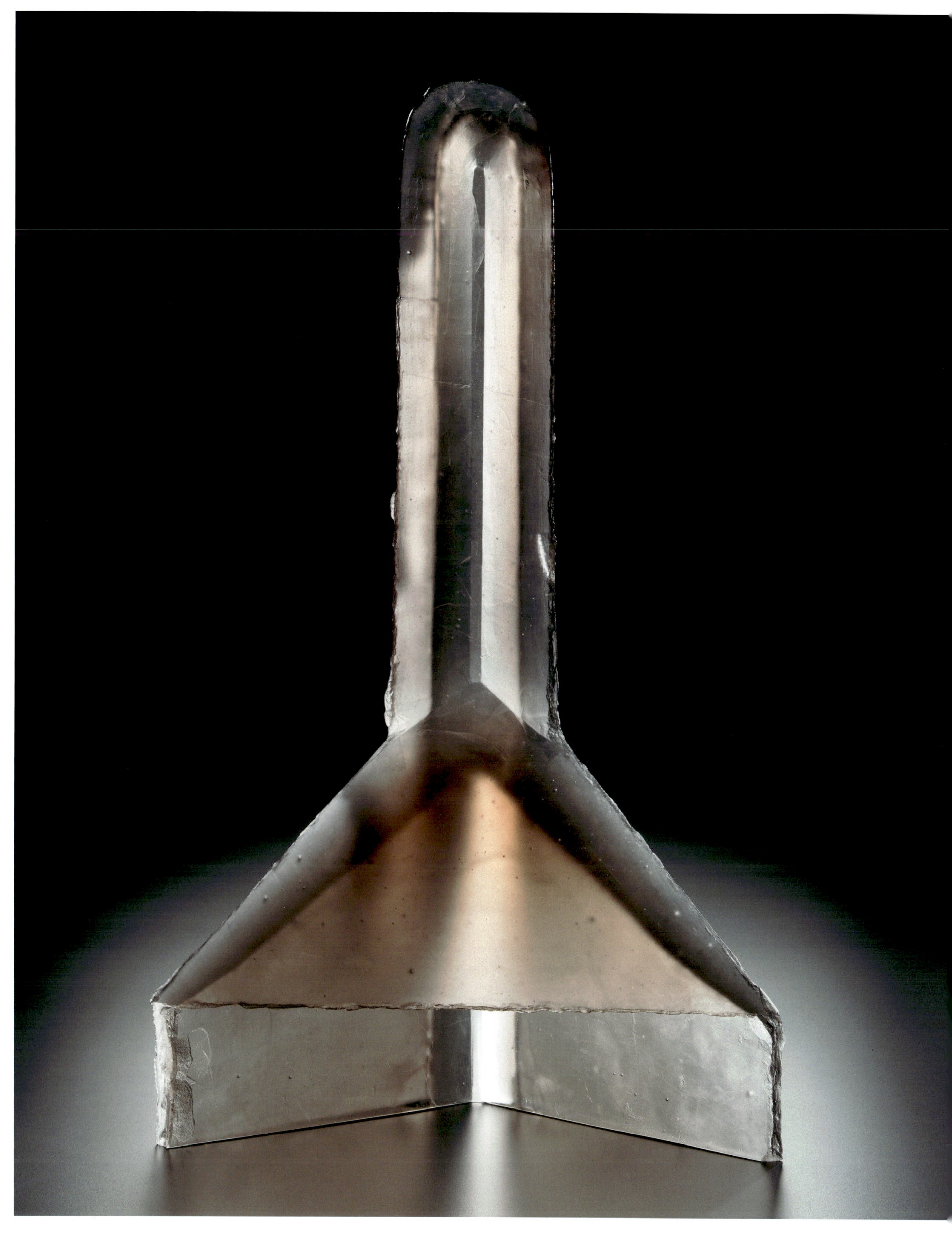

77   Stanislav Libenský CZECH, 1921–2002, Jaroslava Brychtová CZECH, BORN 1924   *Empty Throne II*   1989

CAST GLASS   39½ × 24½ × 11¼ INCHES   L2017.73

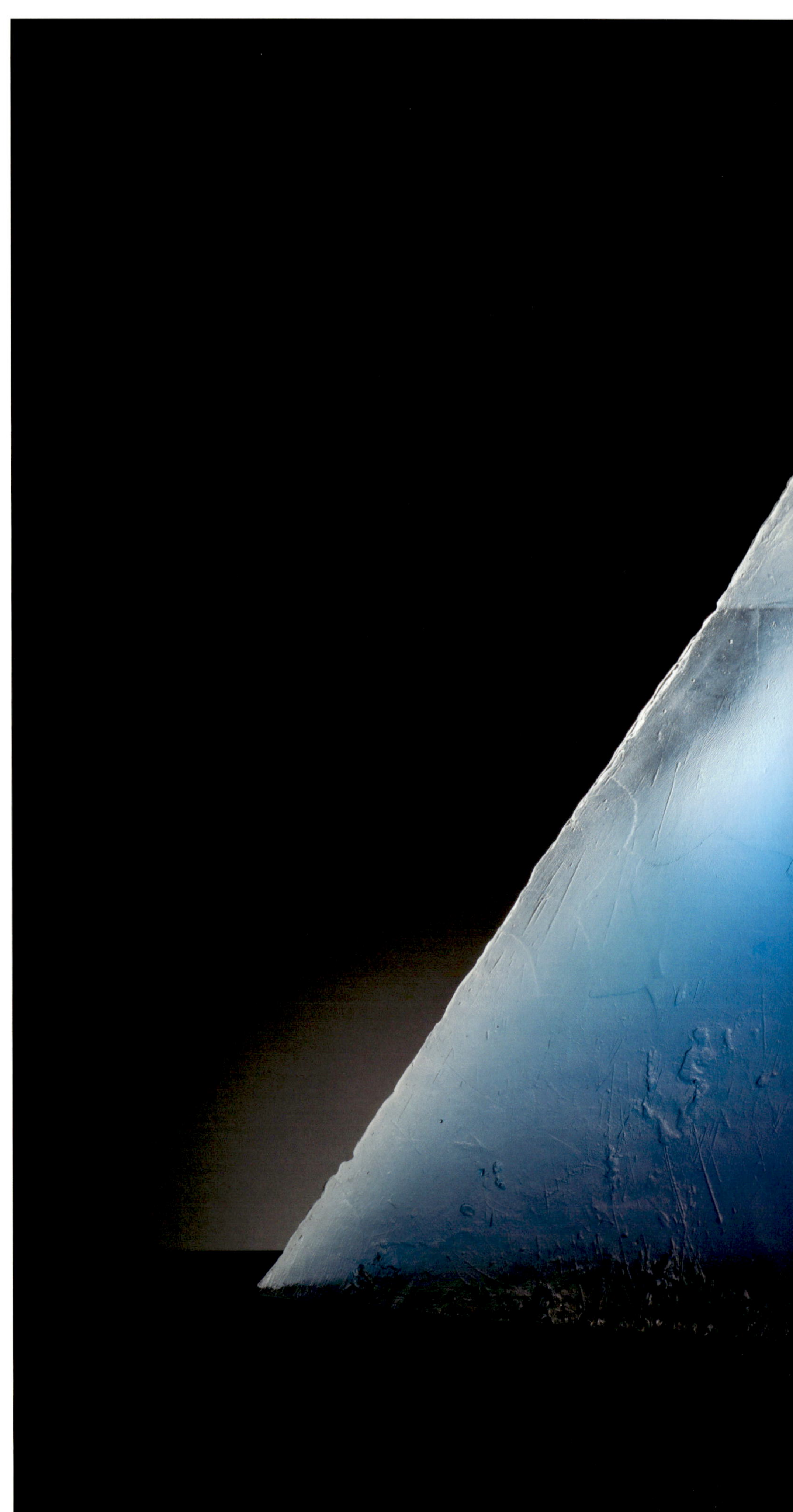

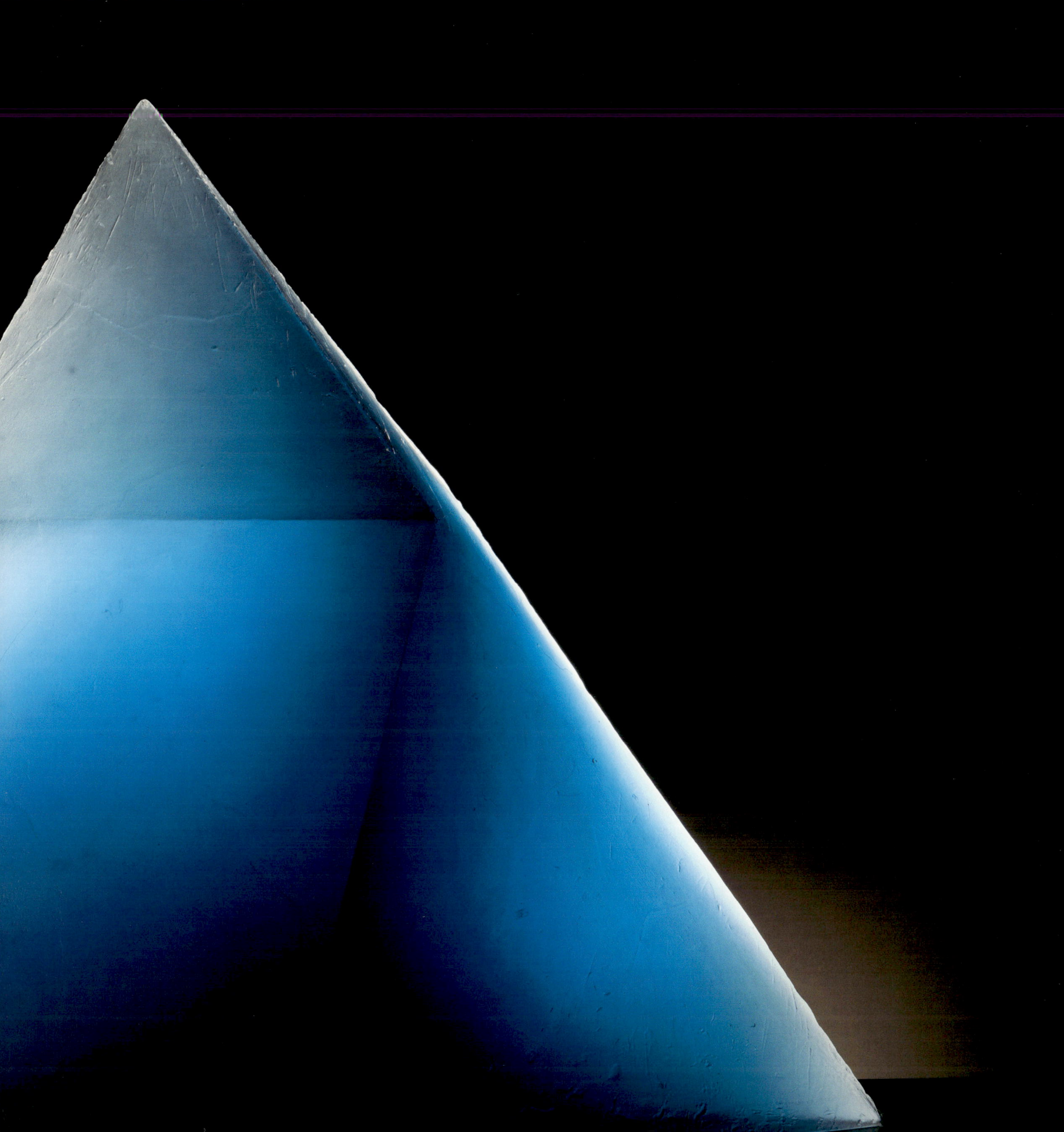

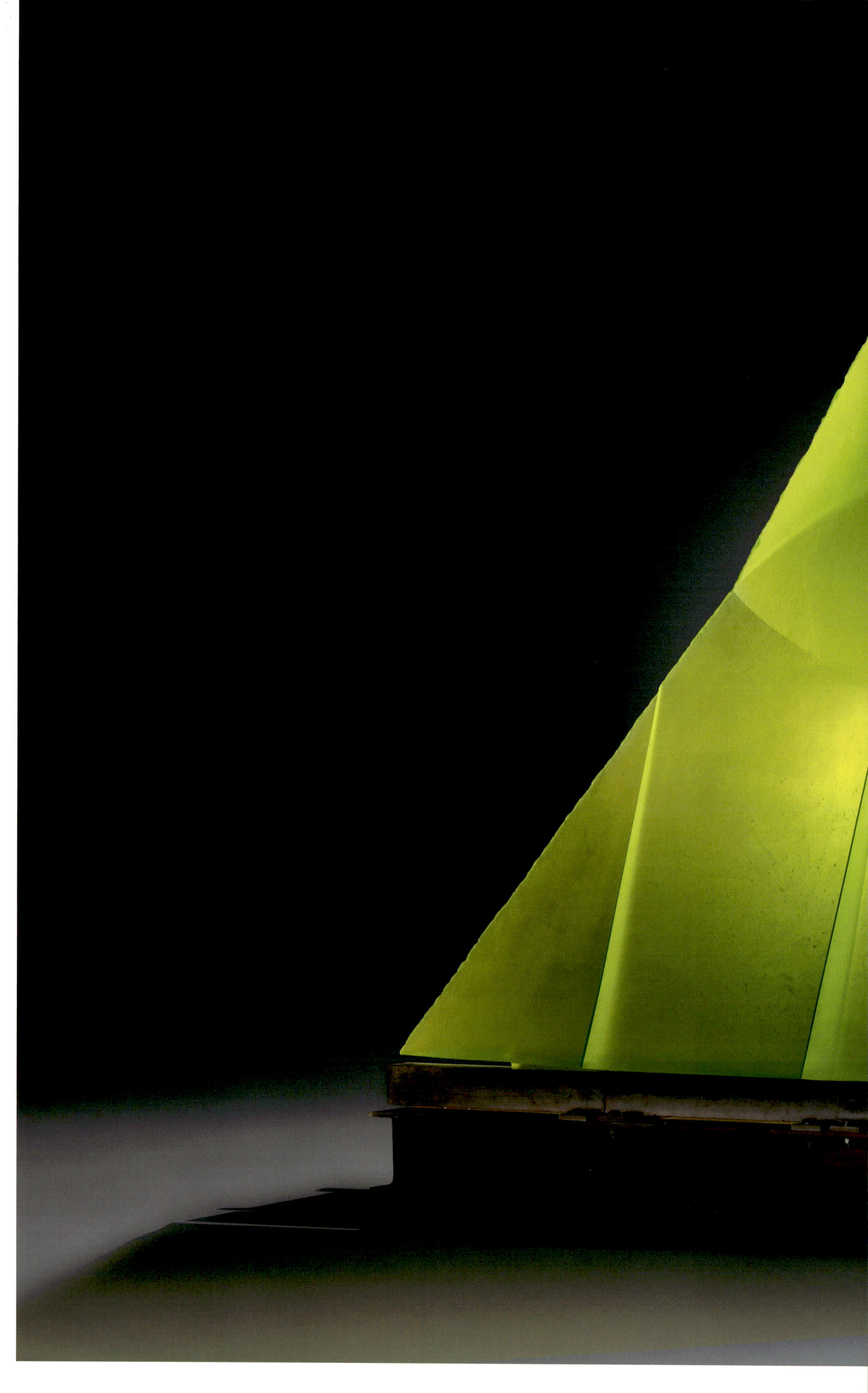

79 Stanislav Libenský CZECH, 1921–2002, Jaroslava Brychtová CZECH, BORN 1924
Green Eye of the Pyramid 1993–2004
CAST, CUT, AND POLISHED GLASS, I-BEAM PEDESTAL   82½ × 113 × 29¾ INCHES   L2017.72

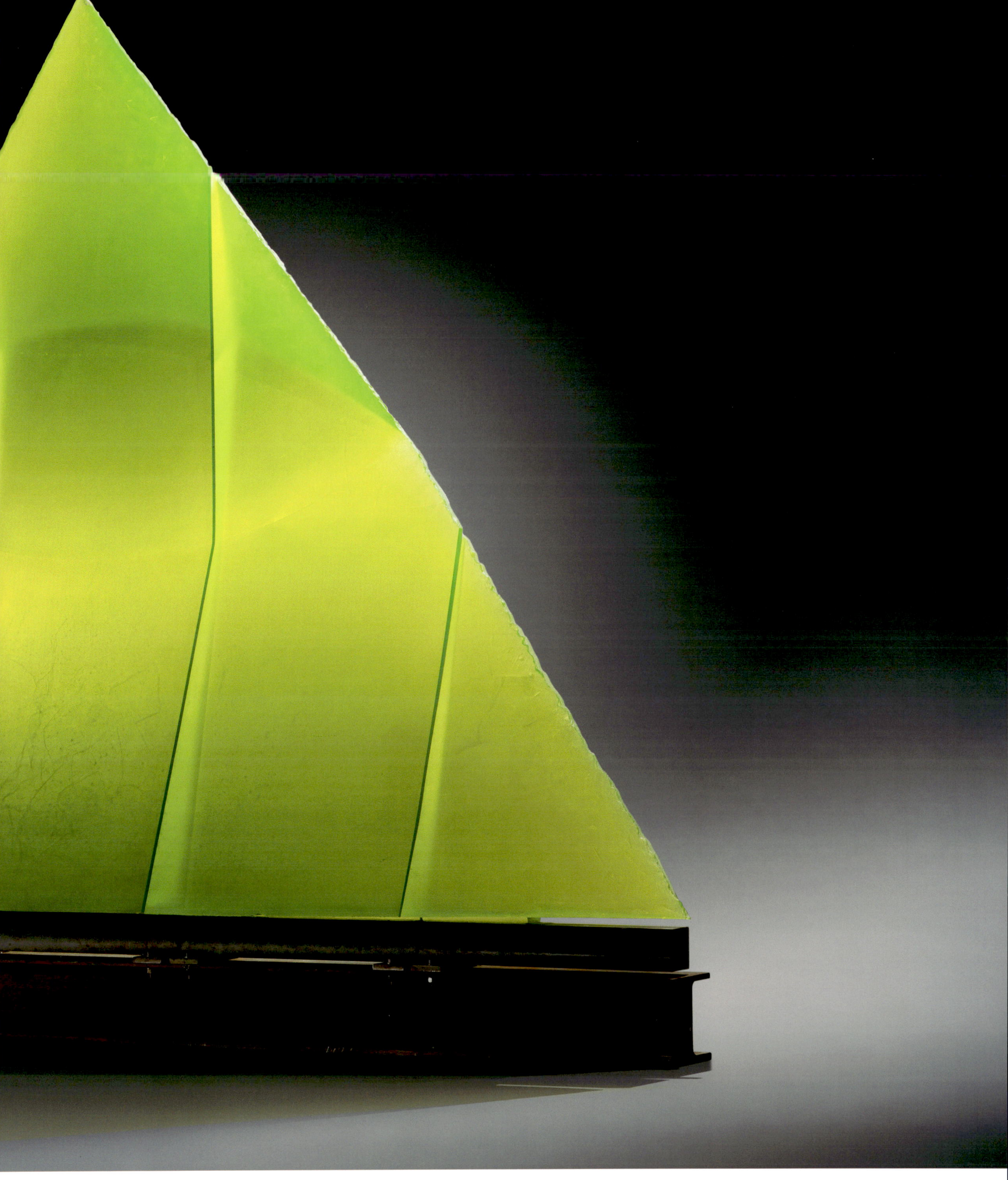

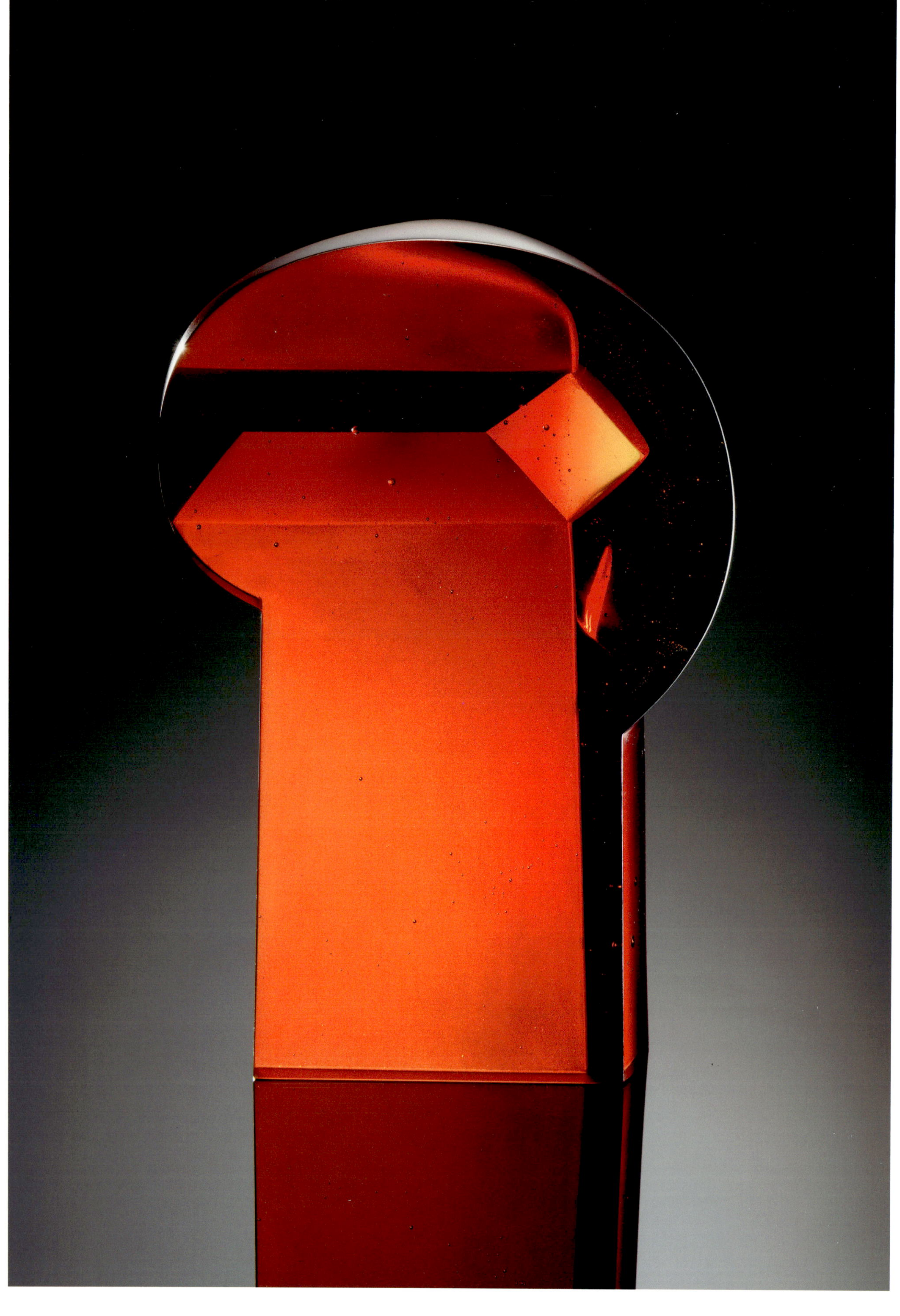

80 Stanislav Libenský CZECH, 1921–2002, Jaroslava Brychtová CZECH, BORN 1924 *Head with Square Eye* 1986–2002

CAST GLASS   11 × 7½ × 5 INCHES   L2017.71

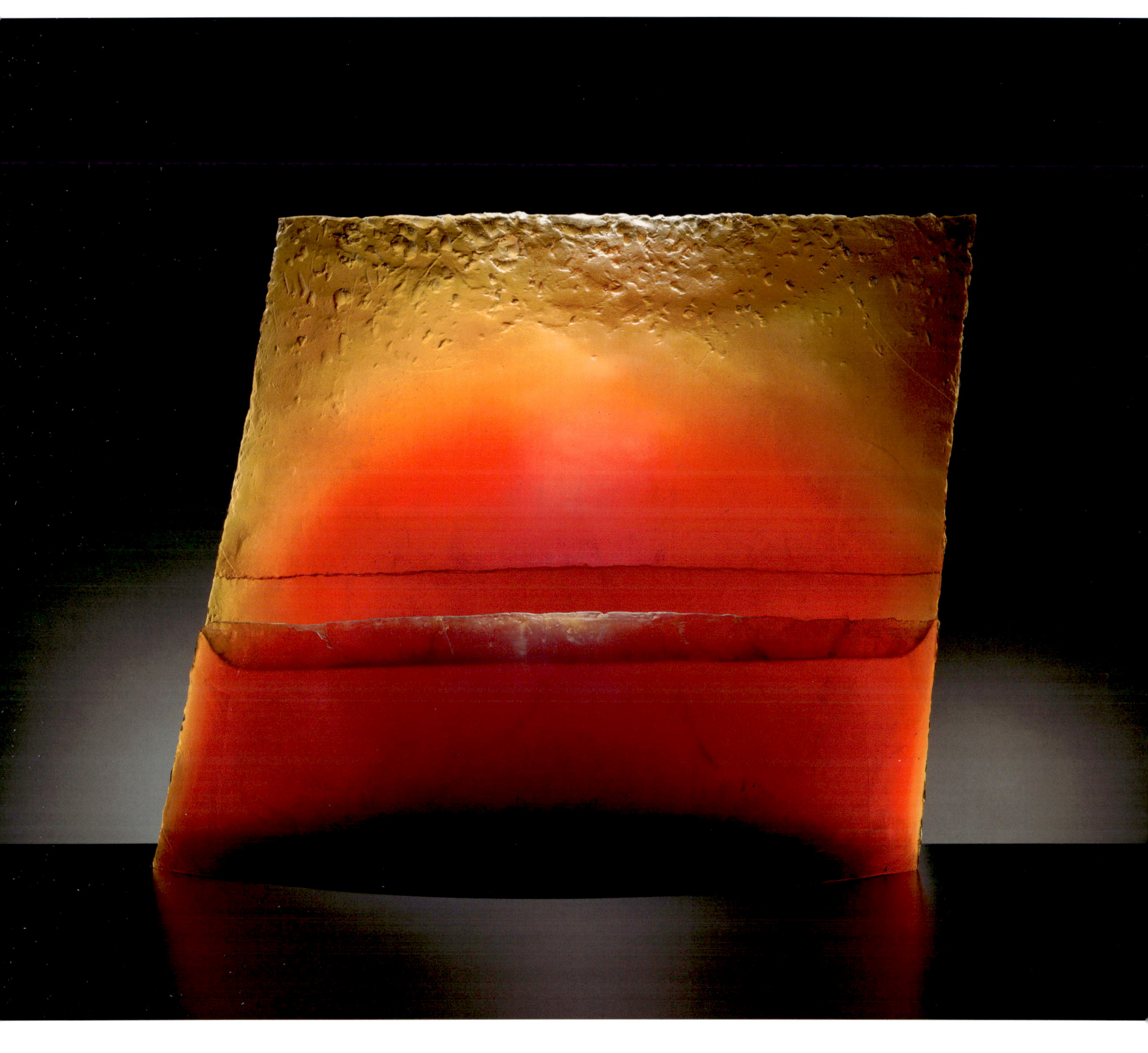

81 Stanislav Libenský CZECH, 1921–2002, Jaroslava Brychtová CZECH, BORN 1924 *Horizon* 1992–2005
CAST GLASS   33 × 43 × 11½ INCHES   L2017.74

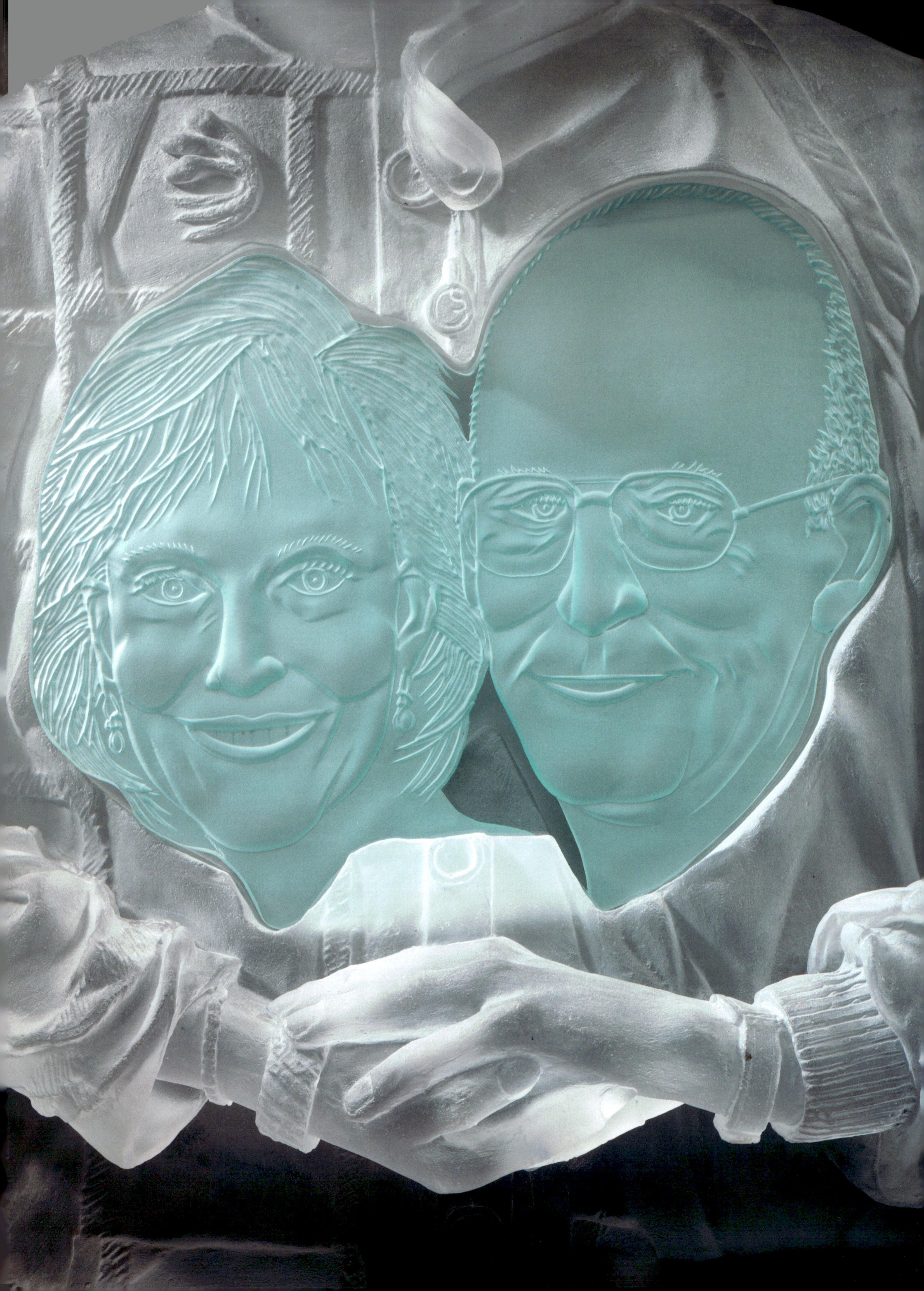

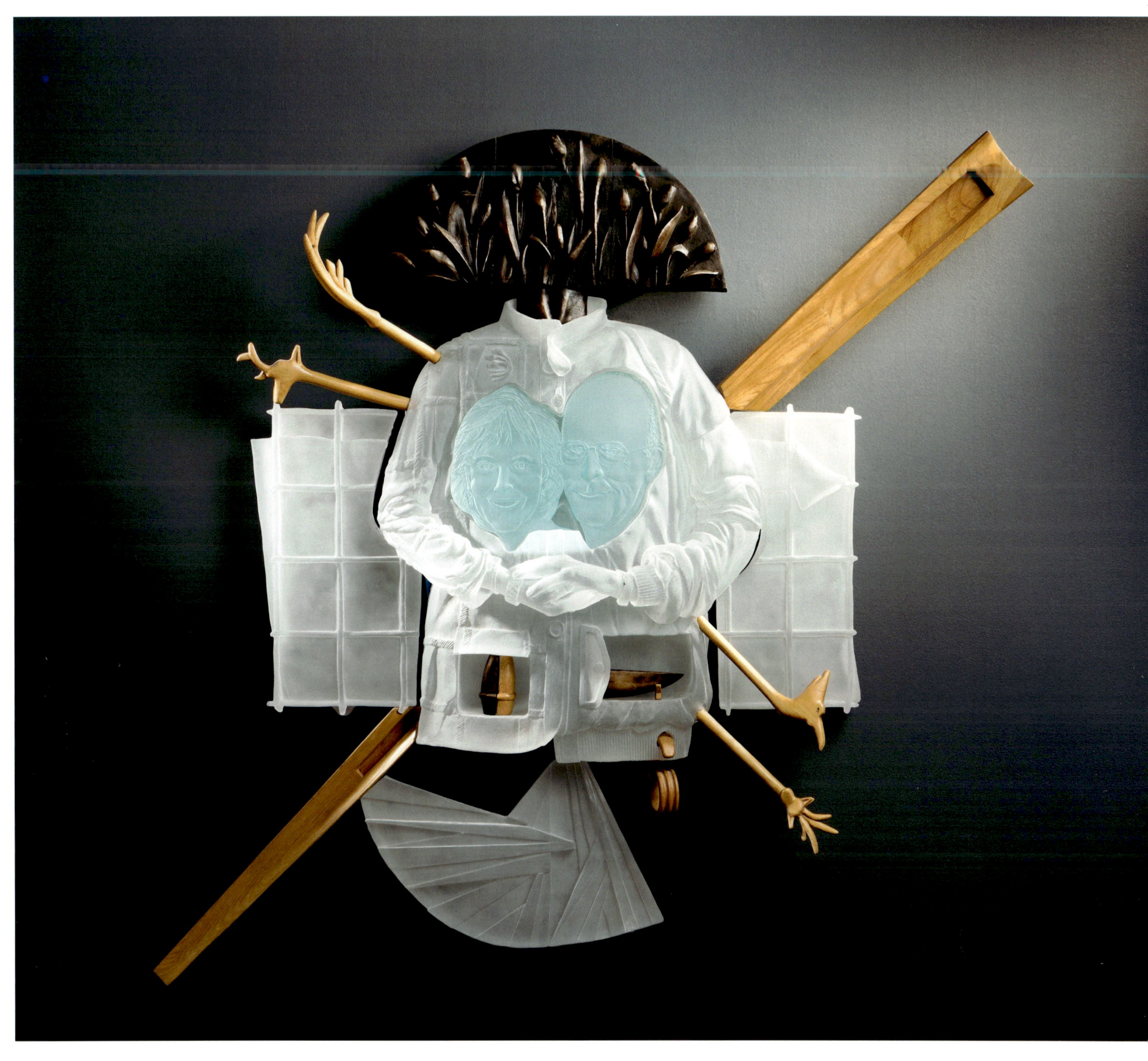

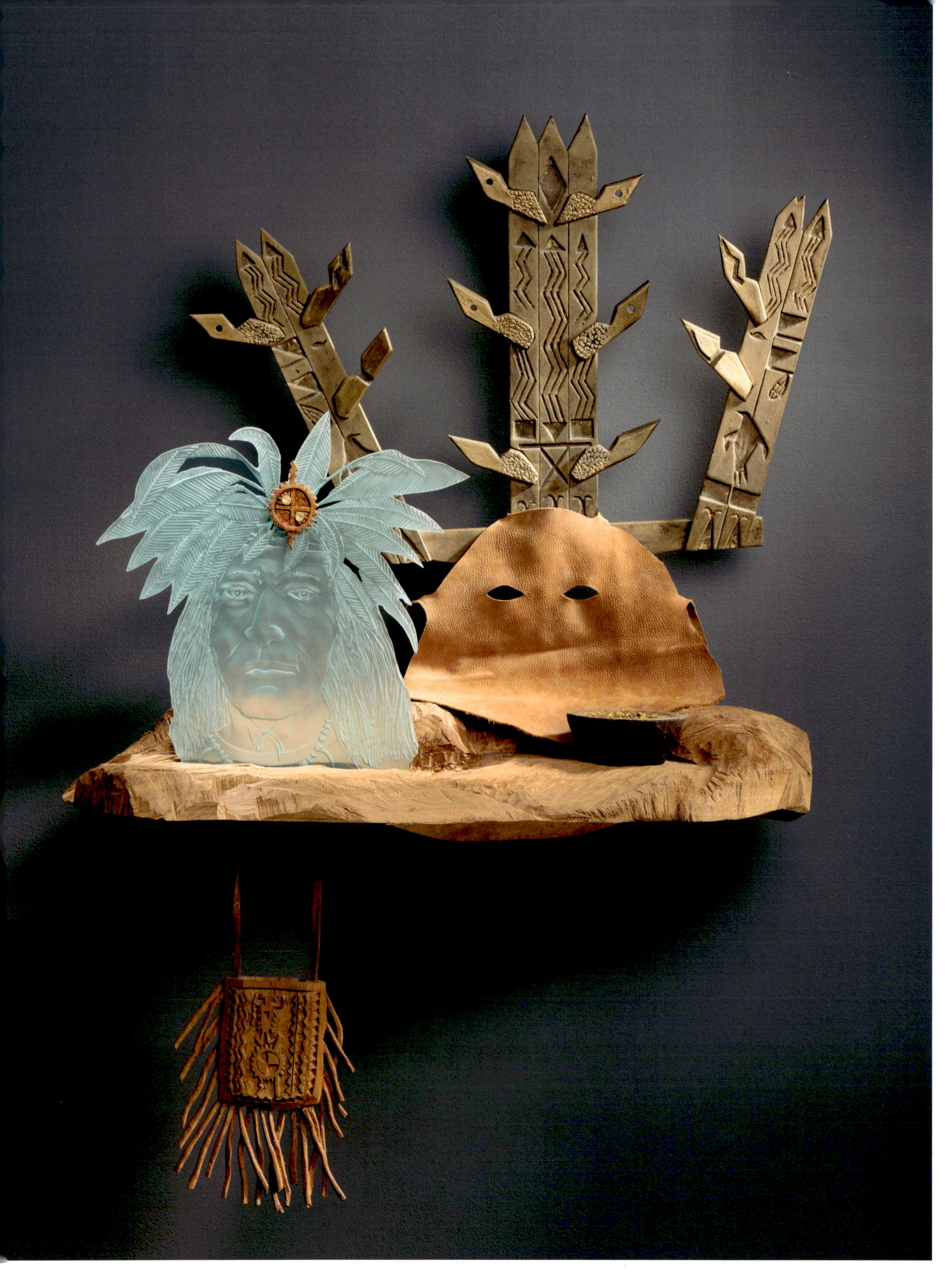

83   Steve Linn   AMERICAN/FRENCH, BORN 1943   *Chiricahua Spirits*   2004
MIXED MEDIA   48 × 34 × 18½ INCHES   L2017.75

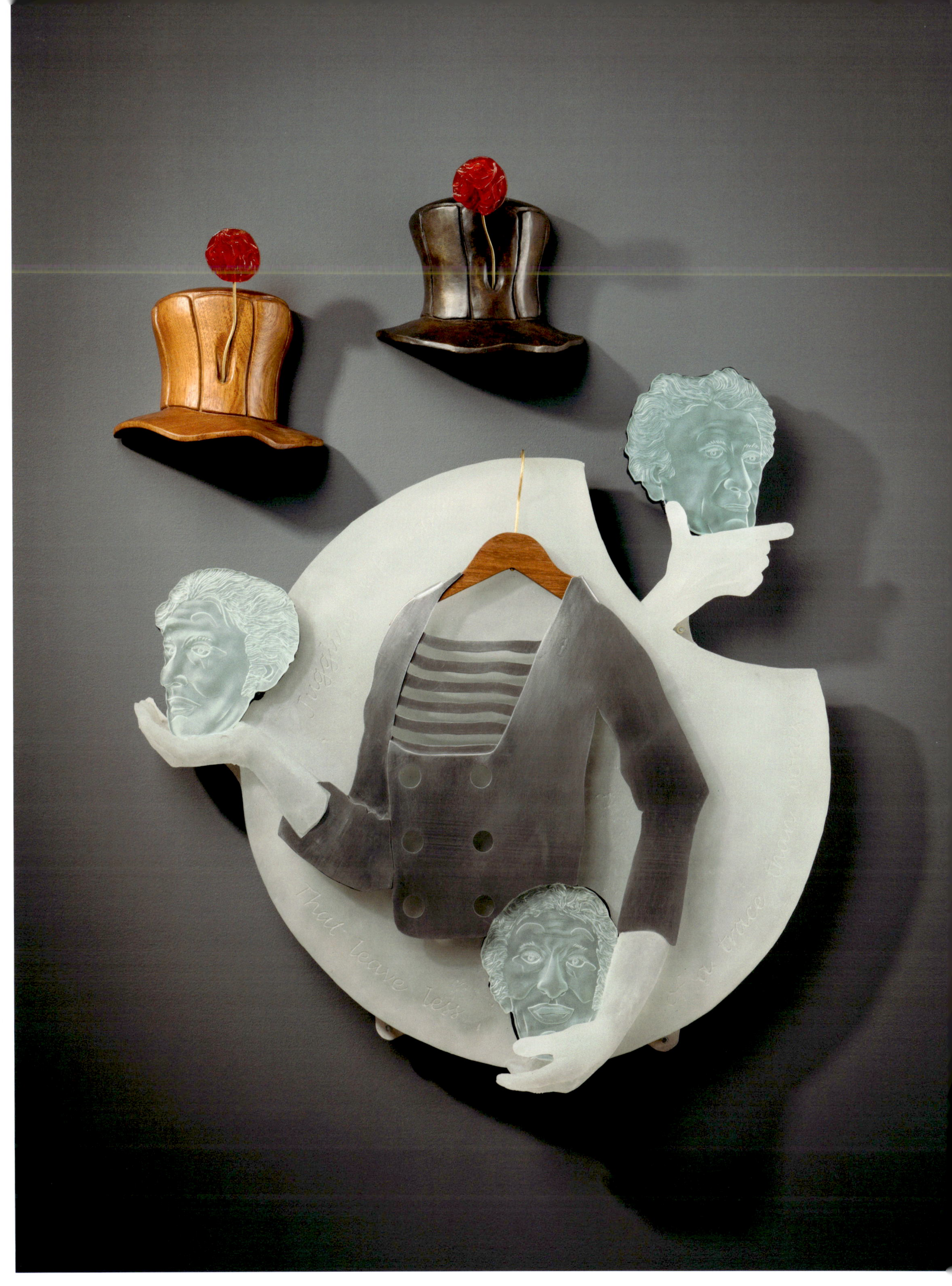

85 Marvin Lipofsky AMERICAN, 1938–2016 *IGS VI #8* 1997–98
ACID-POLISHED BLOWN GLASS 15 × 21¾ × 16½ INCHES L2017.78

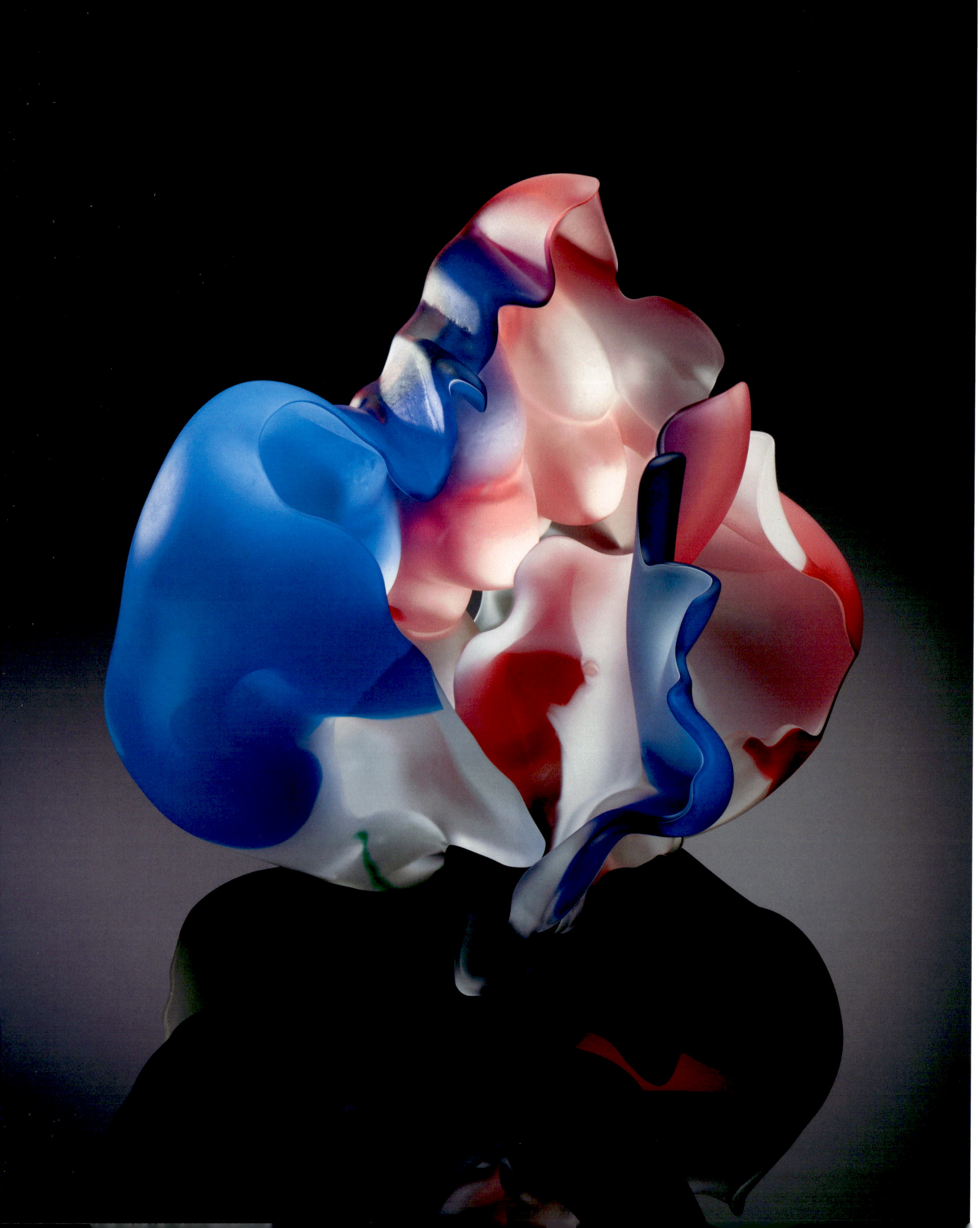

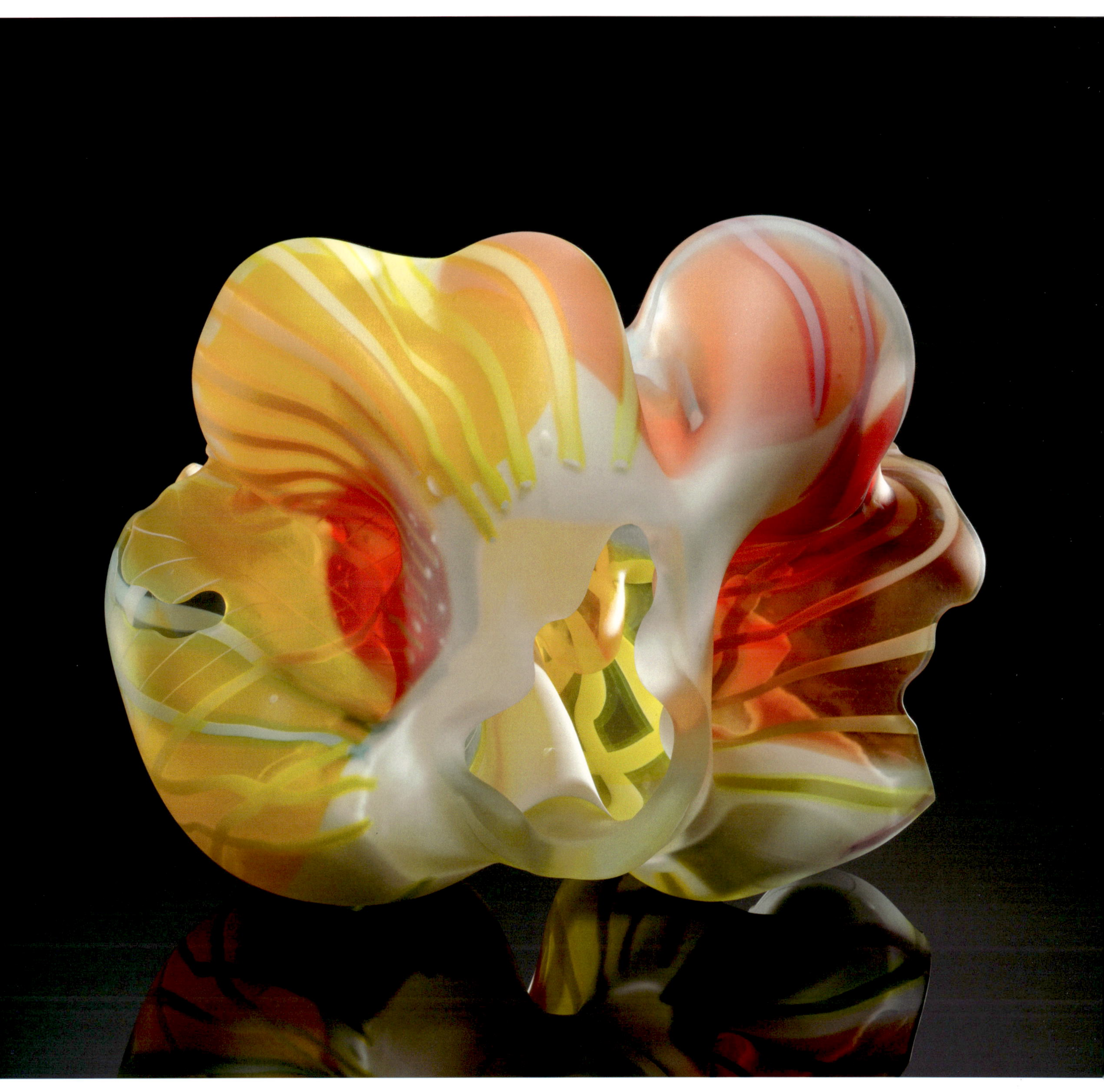

86 Marvin Lipofsky AMERICAN, 1938–2016 *Australian Landscape #8* 2004
ACID-POLISHED BLOWN GLASS   13¼ × 17½ × 12½ INCHES   L2017.79

Double Form   2004
LAMINATED, SANDBLASTED, GROUND, AND
POLISHED GLASS   19½ × 24 × 9½ INCHES
L2017.82

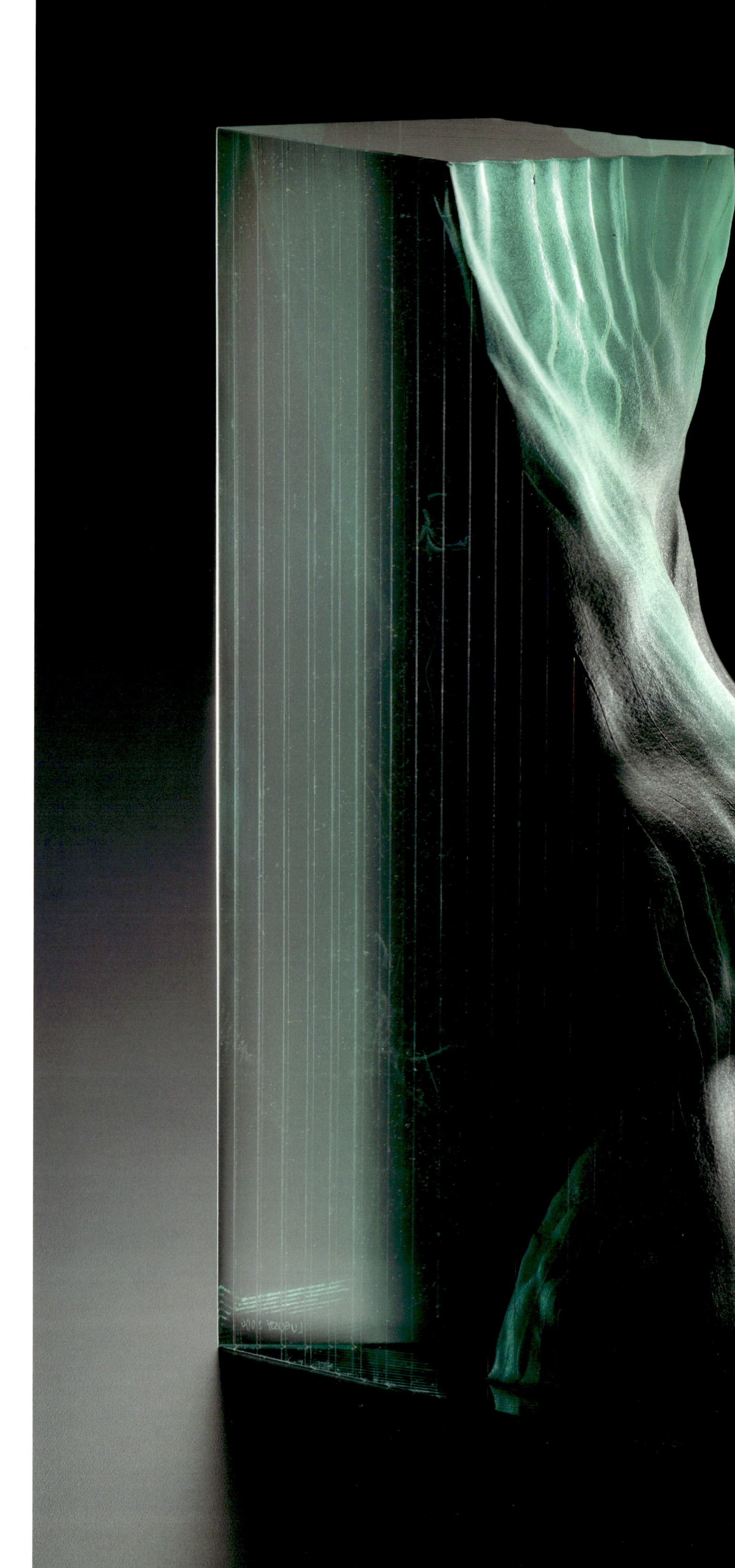

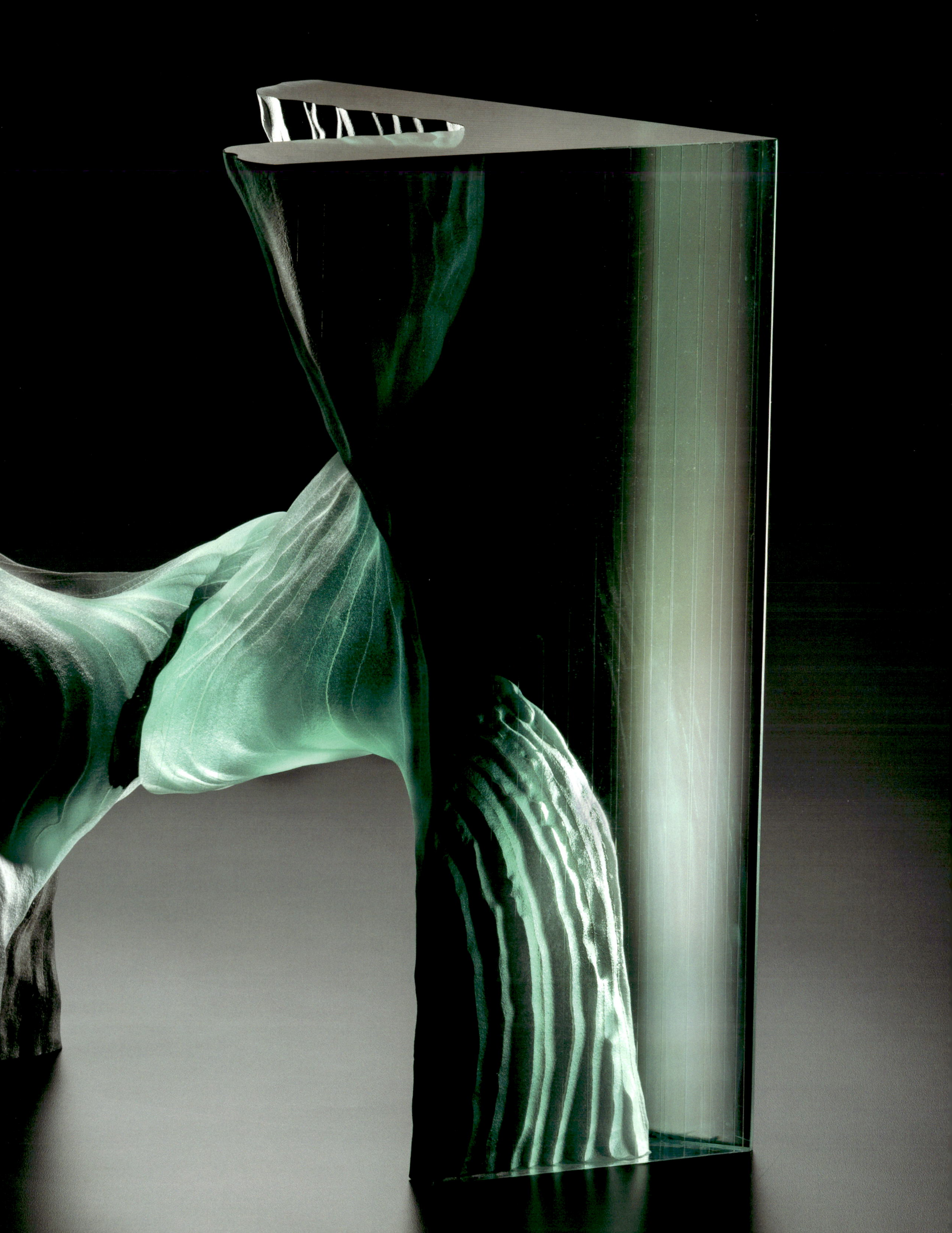

88   Maria Lugossy   HUNGARIAN, 1950–2012

Sefer Tanakh   2000

SHEET GLASS SANDBLASTED WITH CAST
BRONZE INCLUSIONS, GRANITE BASE
9½ × 33½ × 19¾ INCHES   L2017.145

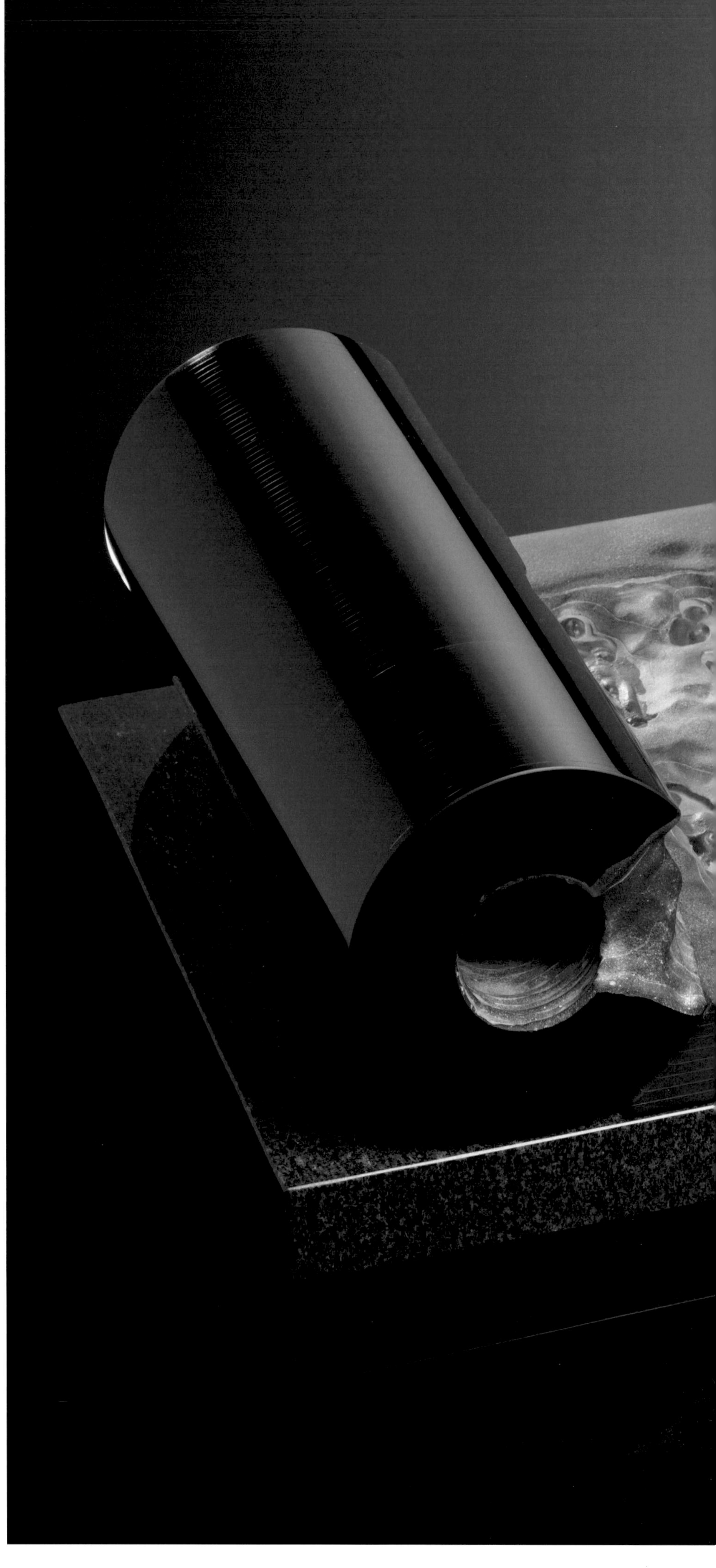

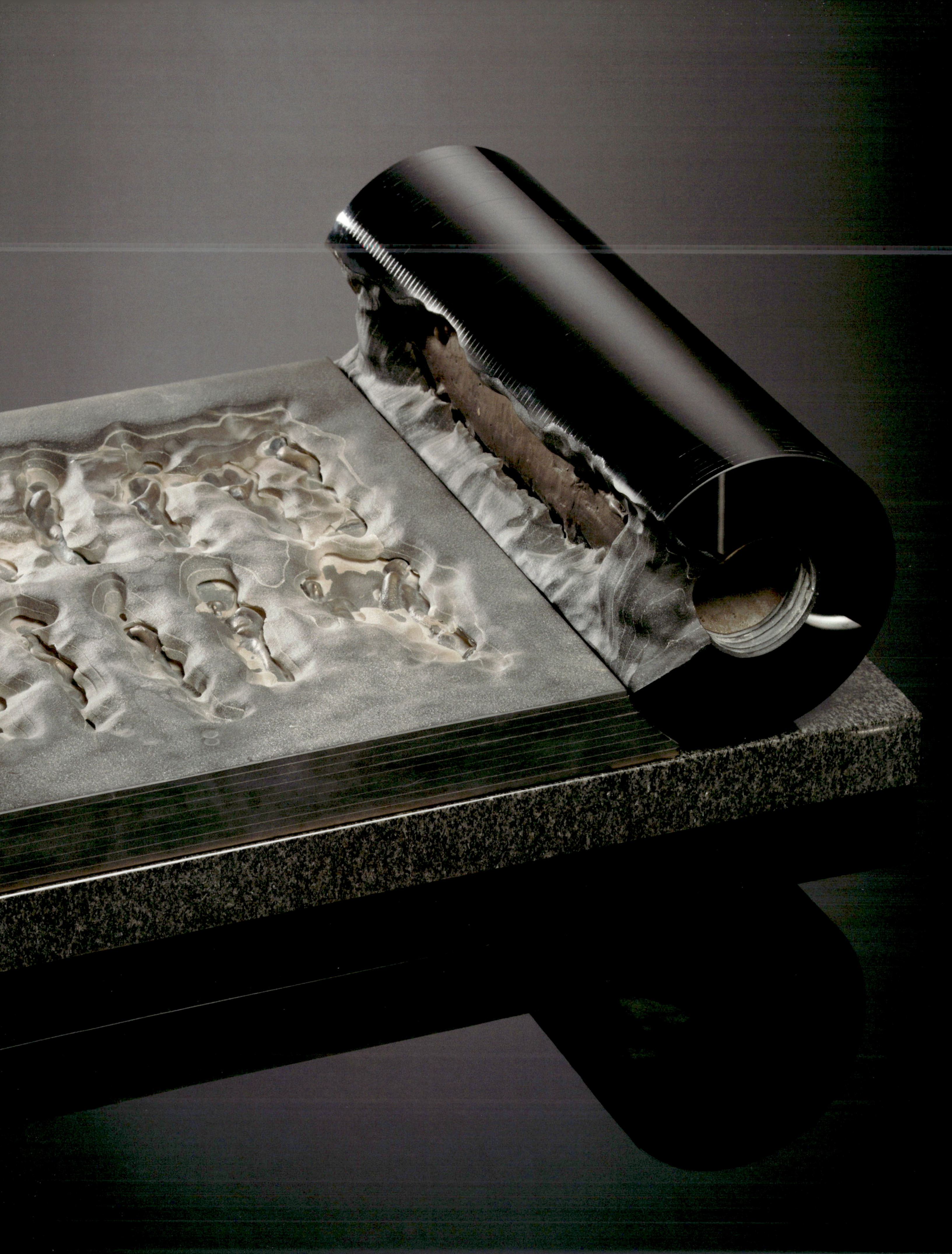

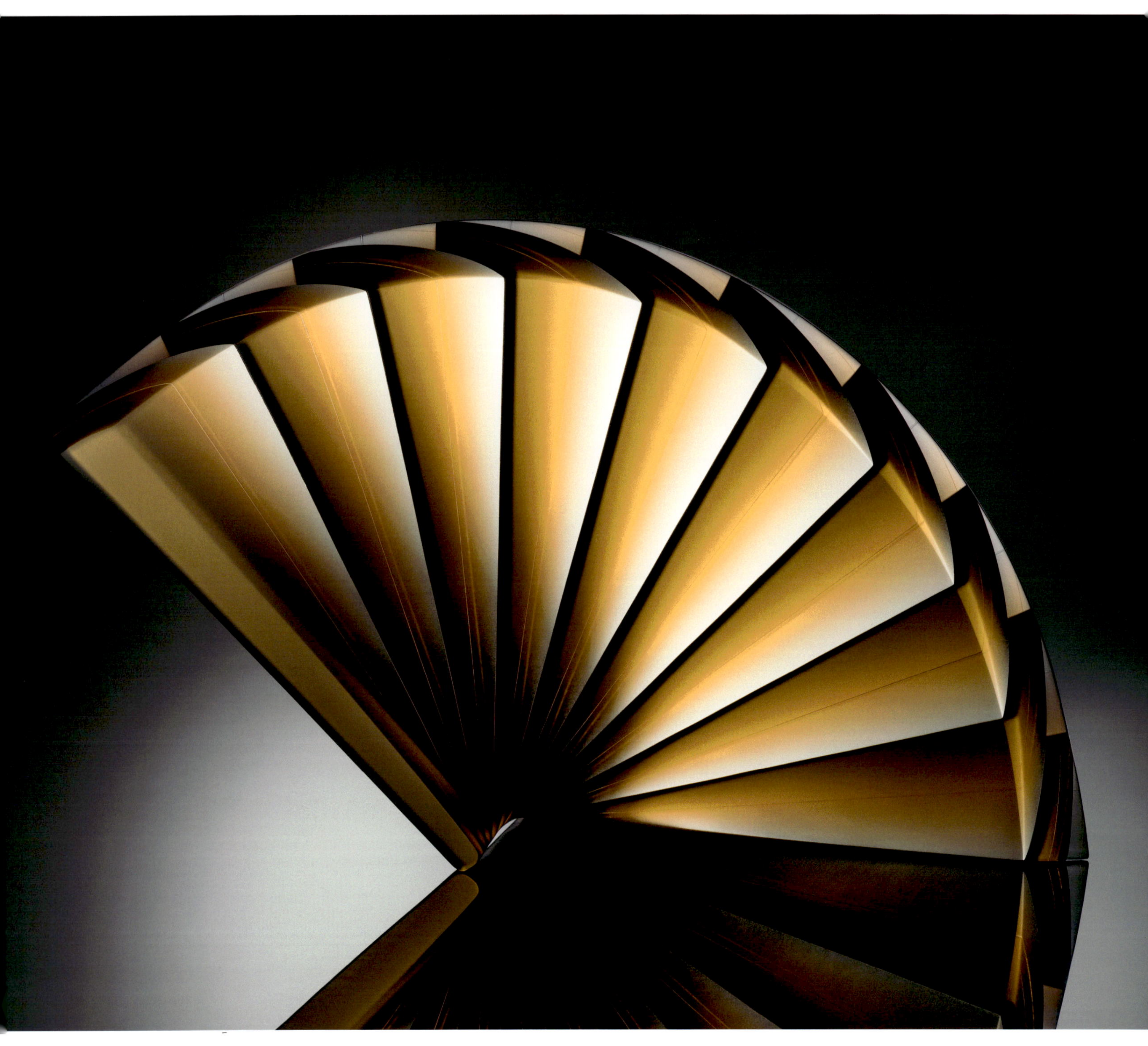

89   László Lukácsi   HUNGARIAN, BORN 1961   *Bronze Fan*   2005
LAMINATED PLATE GLASS   12¾ × 22¾ × 5¼ INCHES   L2017.83

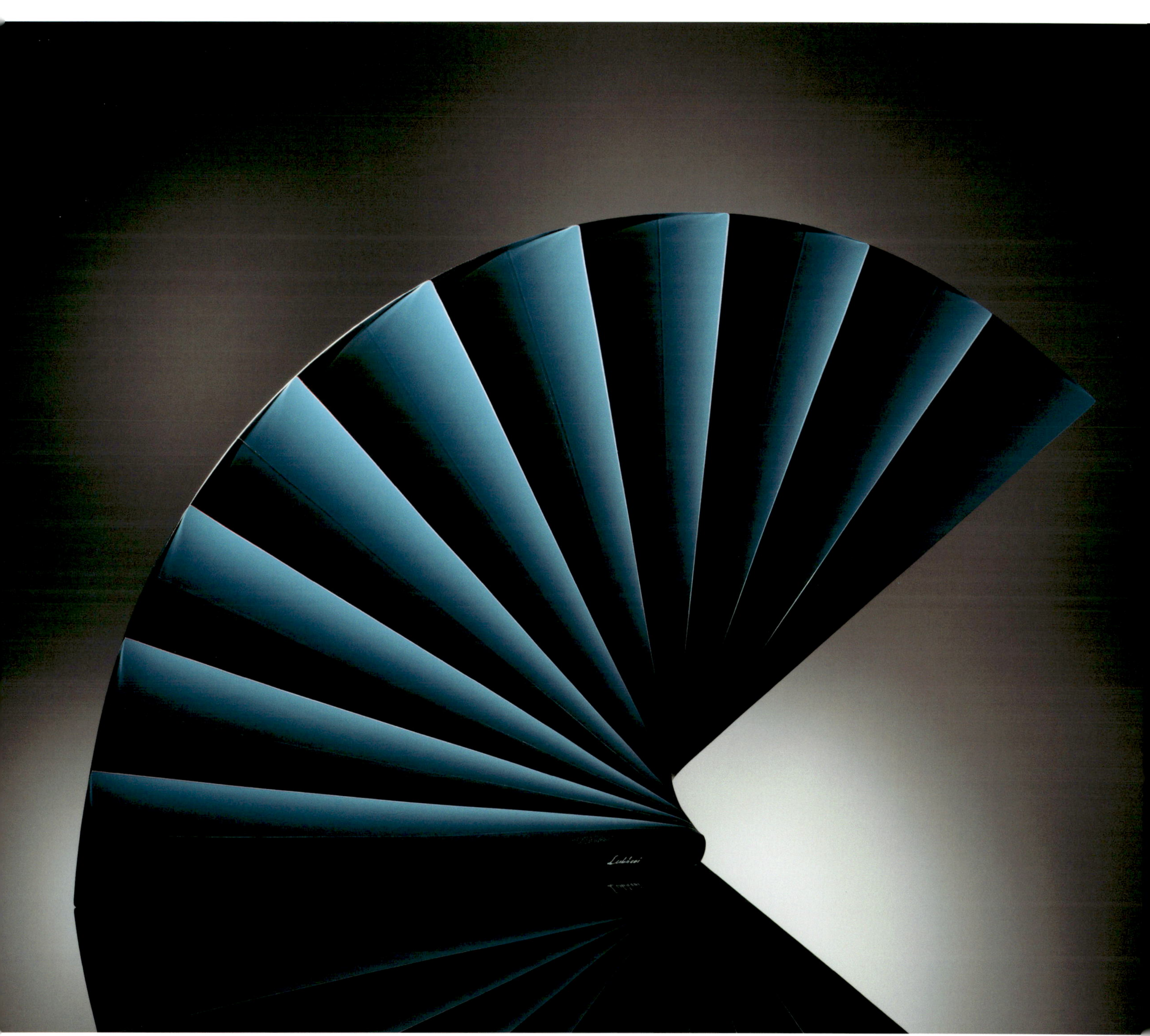

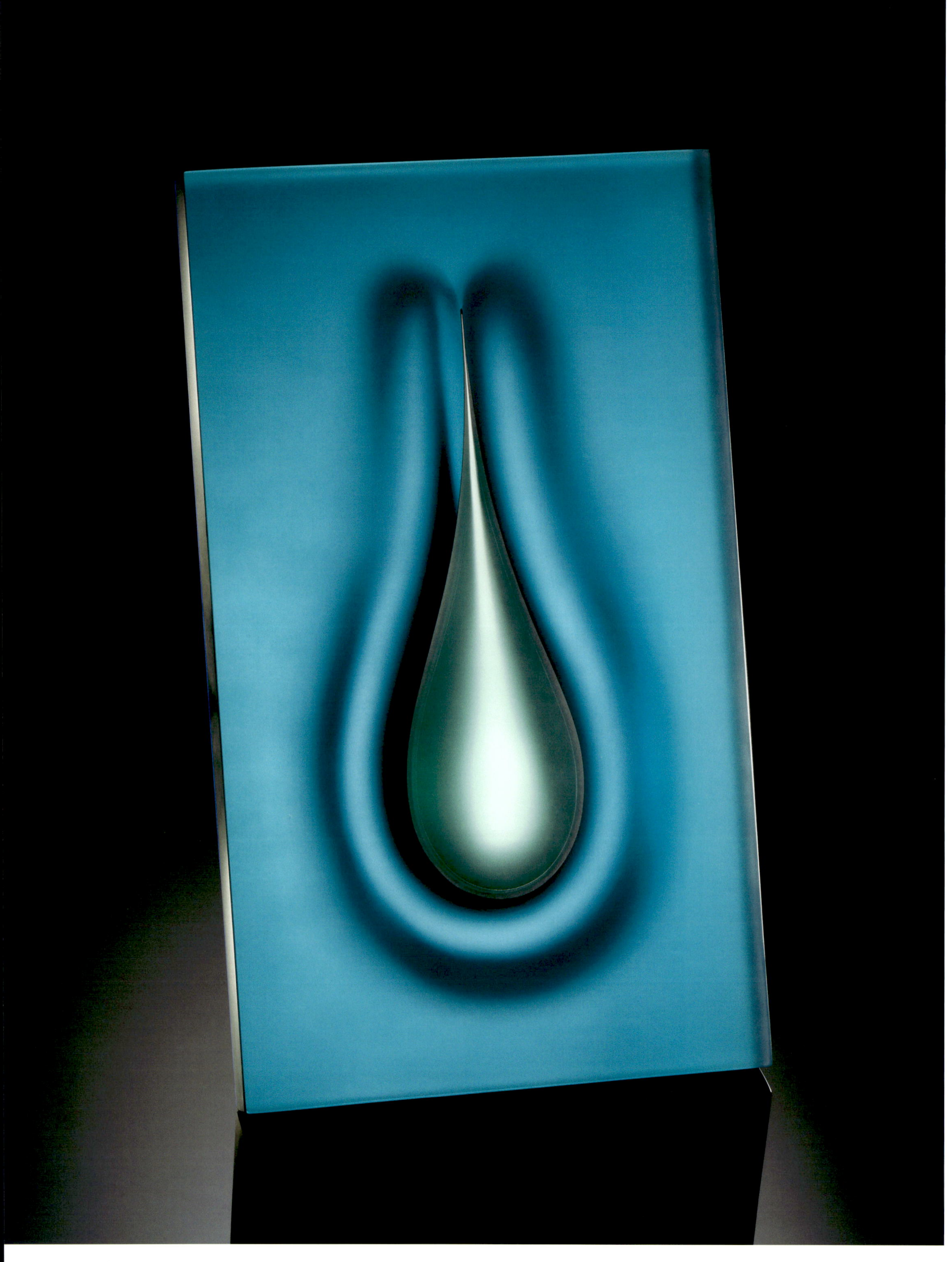

90   László Lukácsi   HUNGARIAN, BORN 1961   *Glass Drop*   2006
LAMINATED AND POLISHED PLATE GLASS, STEEL STAND   22¼ × 13½ × 2 INCHES   L2017.84

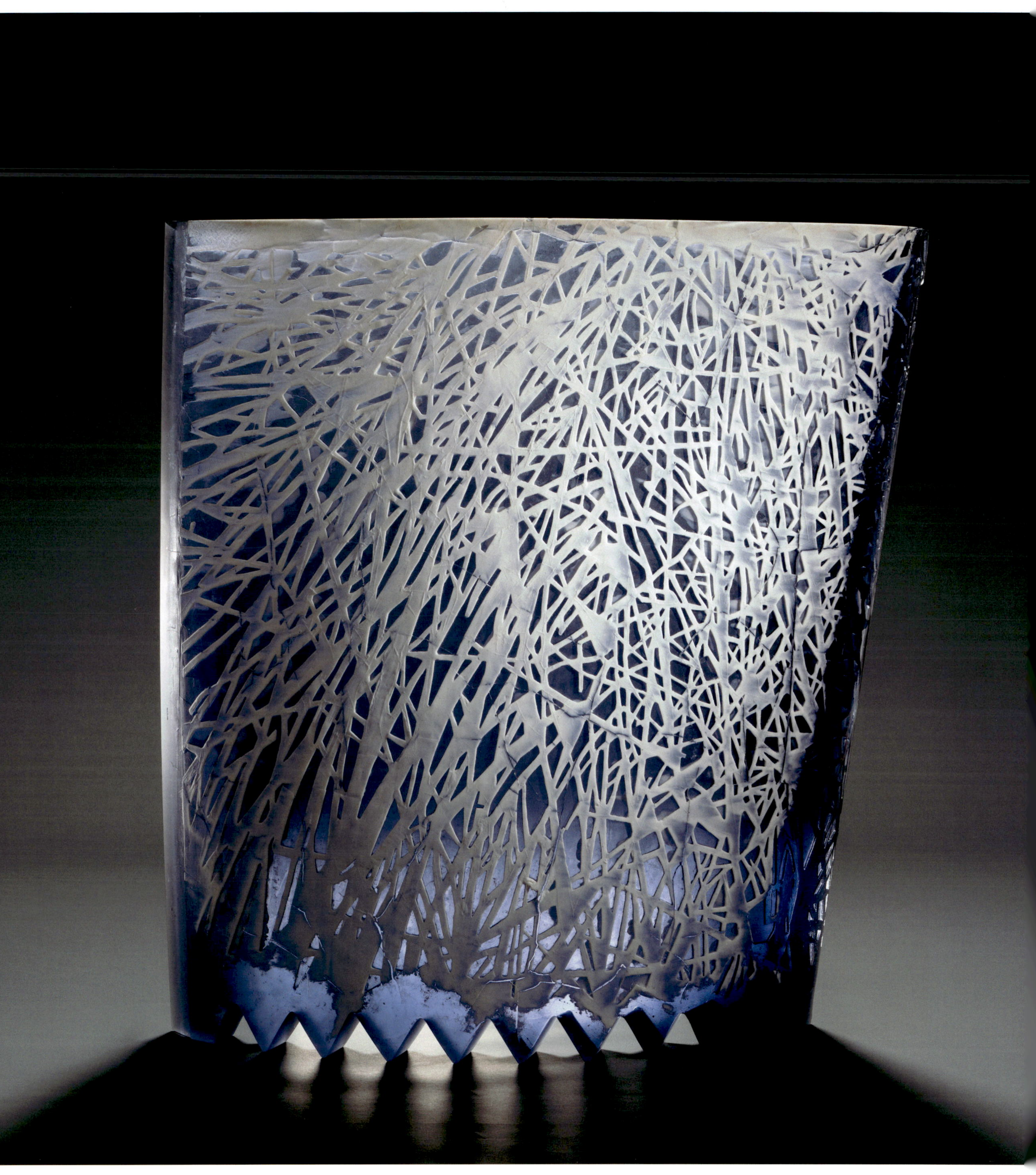

91 Ivan Mareš CZECH, BORN 1956 *Secret Garden III* 2007
KILN-CAST GLASS 42¼ × 40 × 8 INCHES L2017.138

92 Charlie Miner AMERICAN, BORN 1948
Shapeshifter 2007
PÂTE DE VERRE, STEEL AND WOOD STAND
15 × 27¾ × 6 INCHES L2017.88

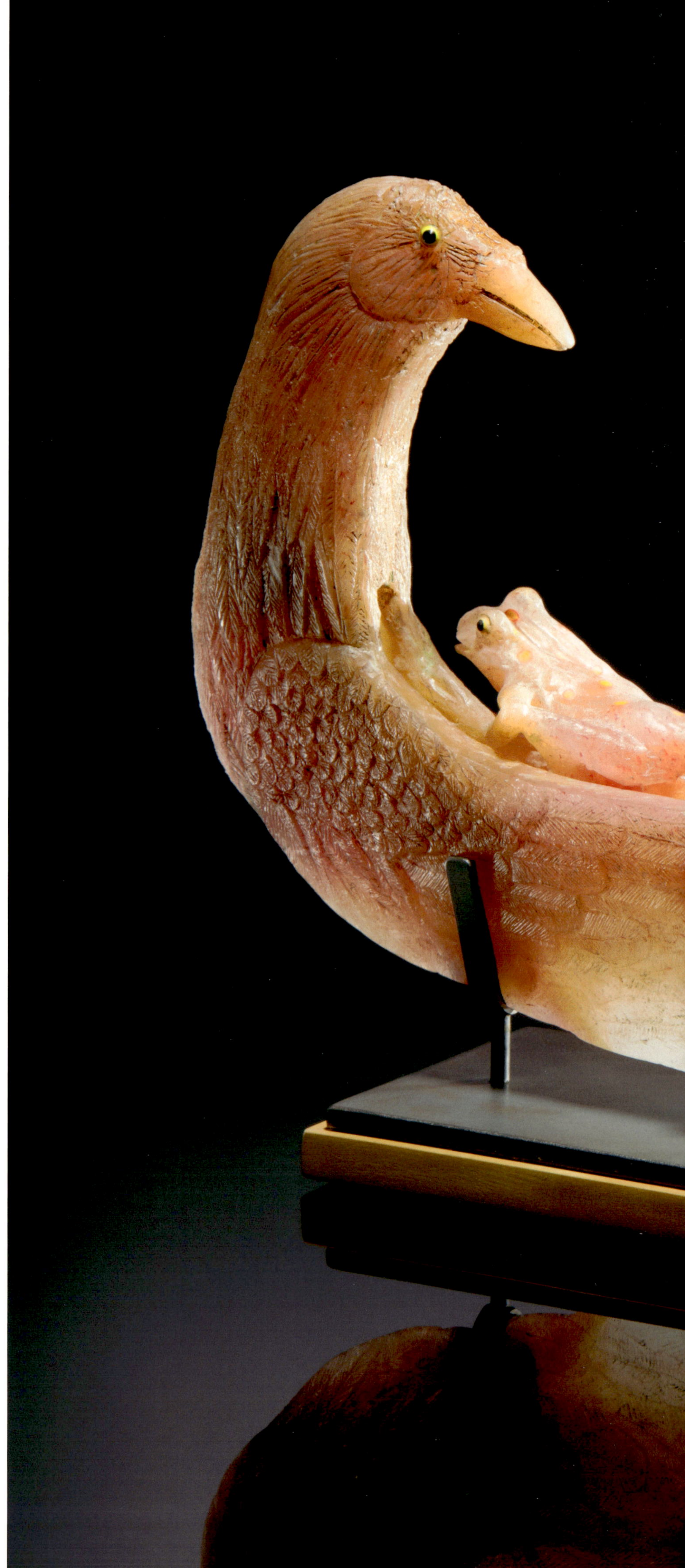

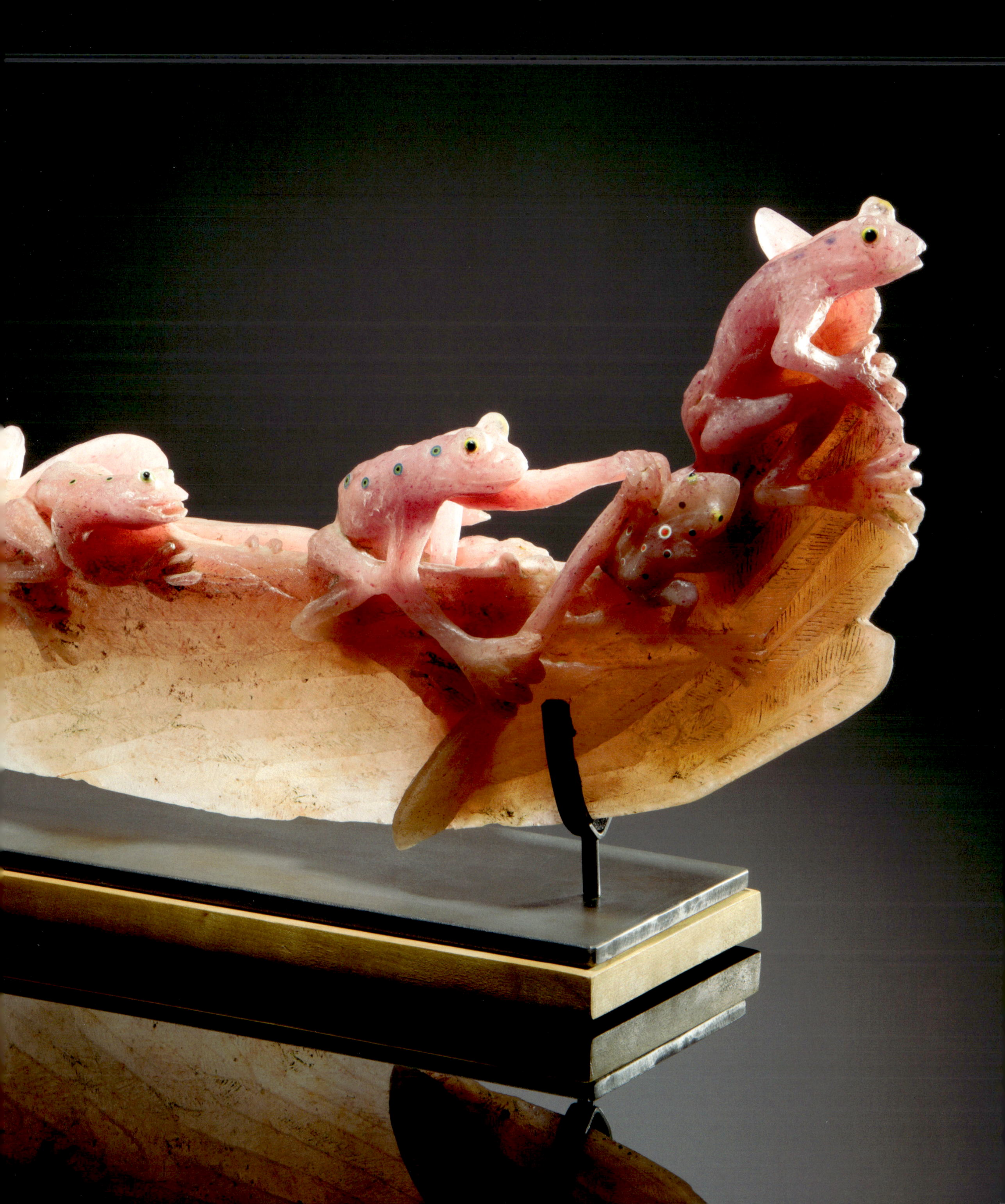

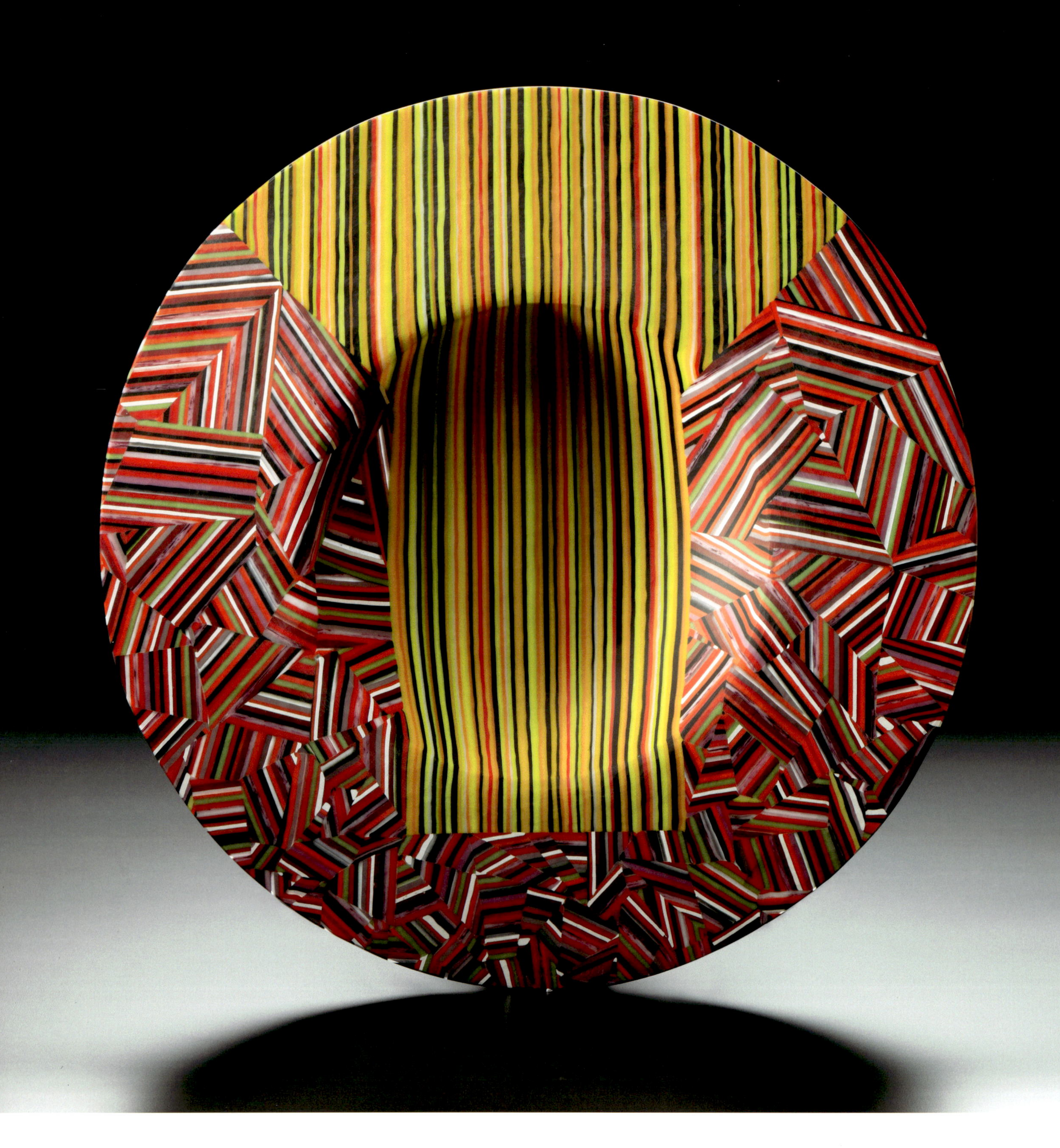

93 Klaus Moje AUSTRALIAN, BORN GERMANY, 1936–2016 *Penetration* 2004
FUSED AND WHEEL-CUT GLASS   21 × 21 × 2¾ INCHES   L2017.89

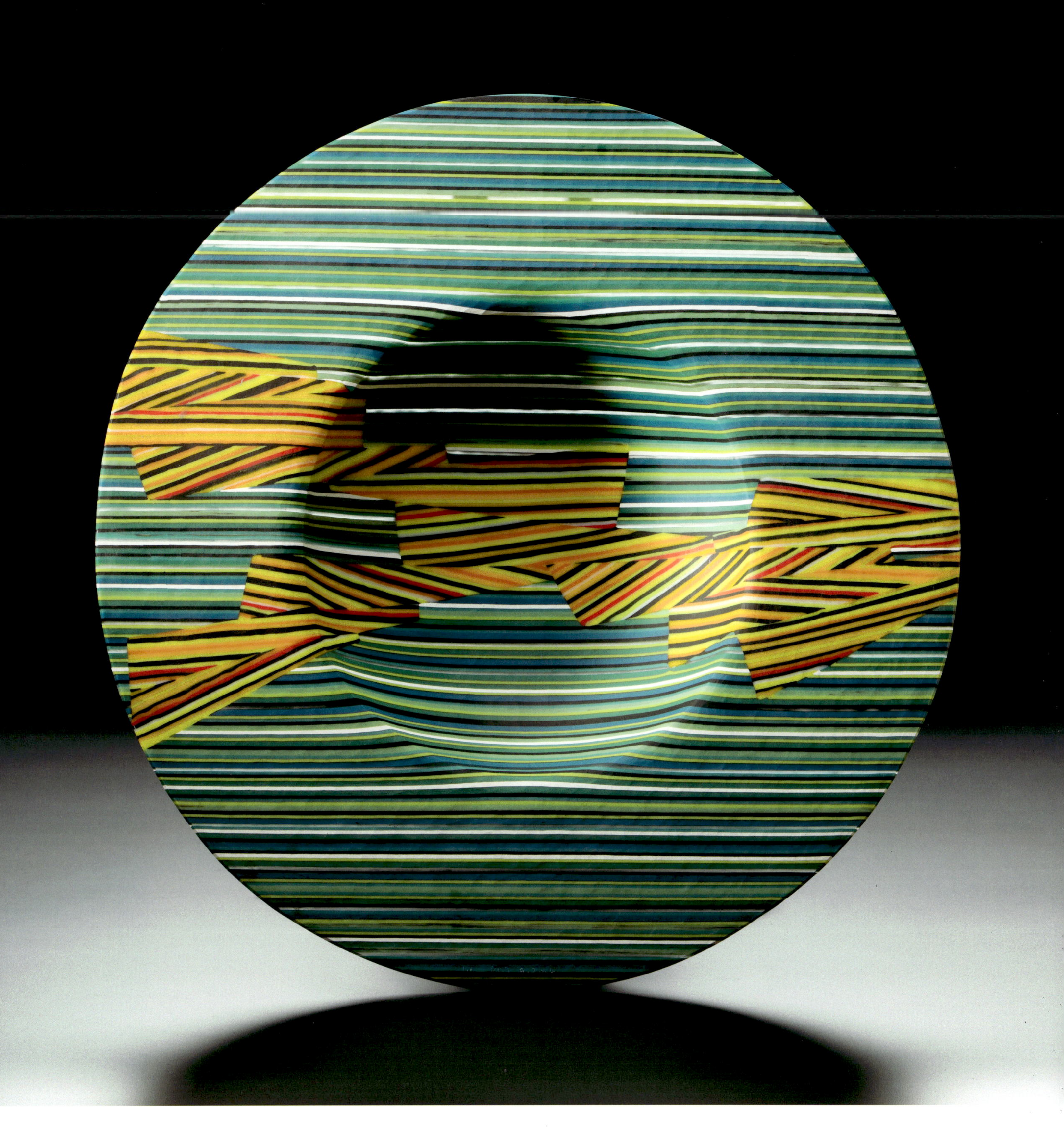

94   Klaus Moje   AUSTRALIAN, BORN GERMANY, 1936–2016   *Squeeze Impact Series*   2004

FUSED AND WHEEL-CUT GLASS   21 × 21 × 2¾ INCHES   L2017.90

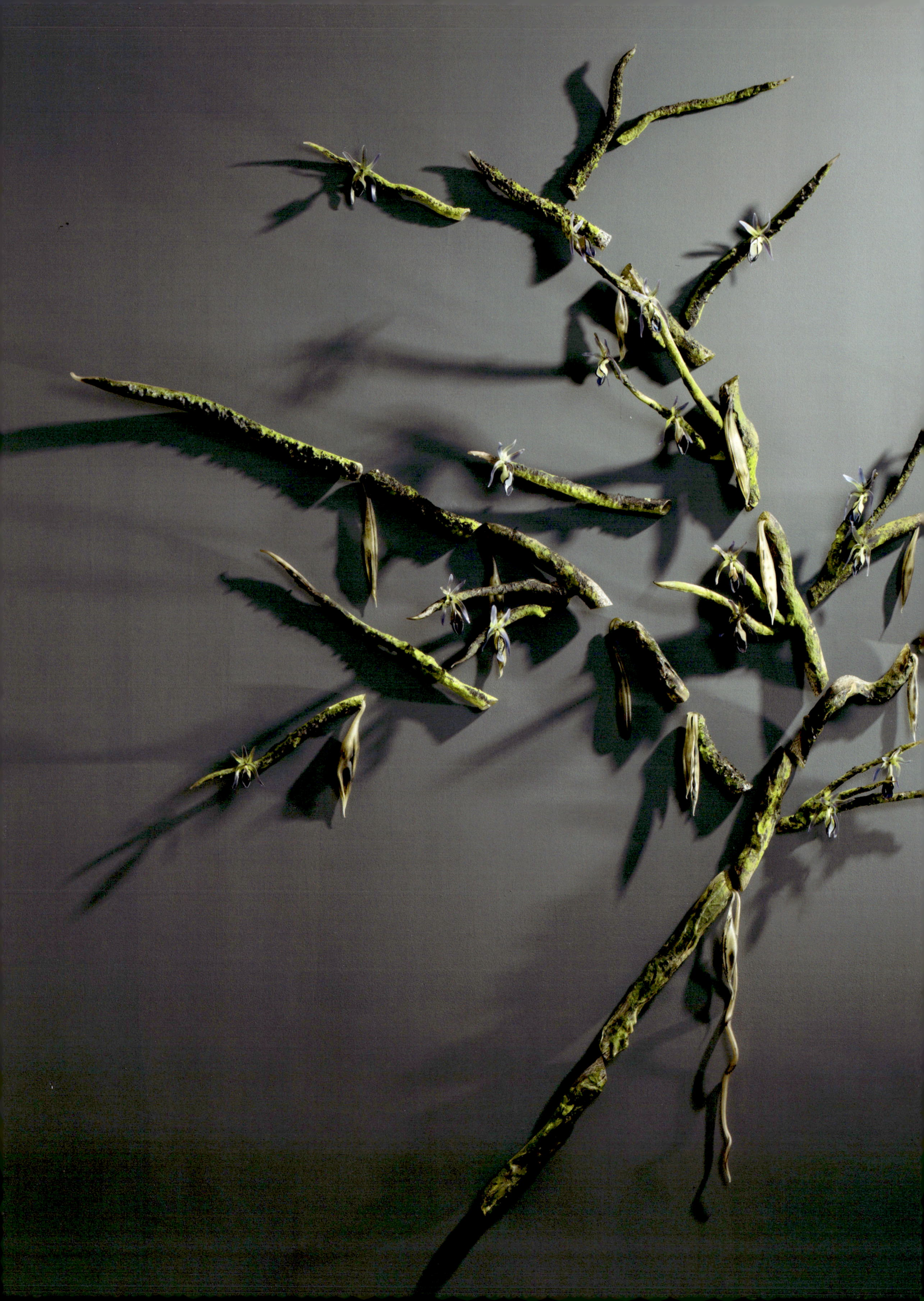

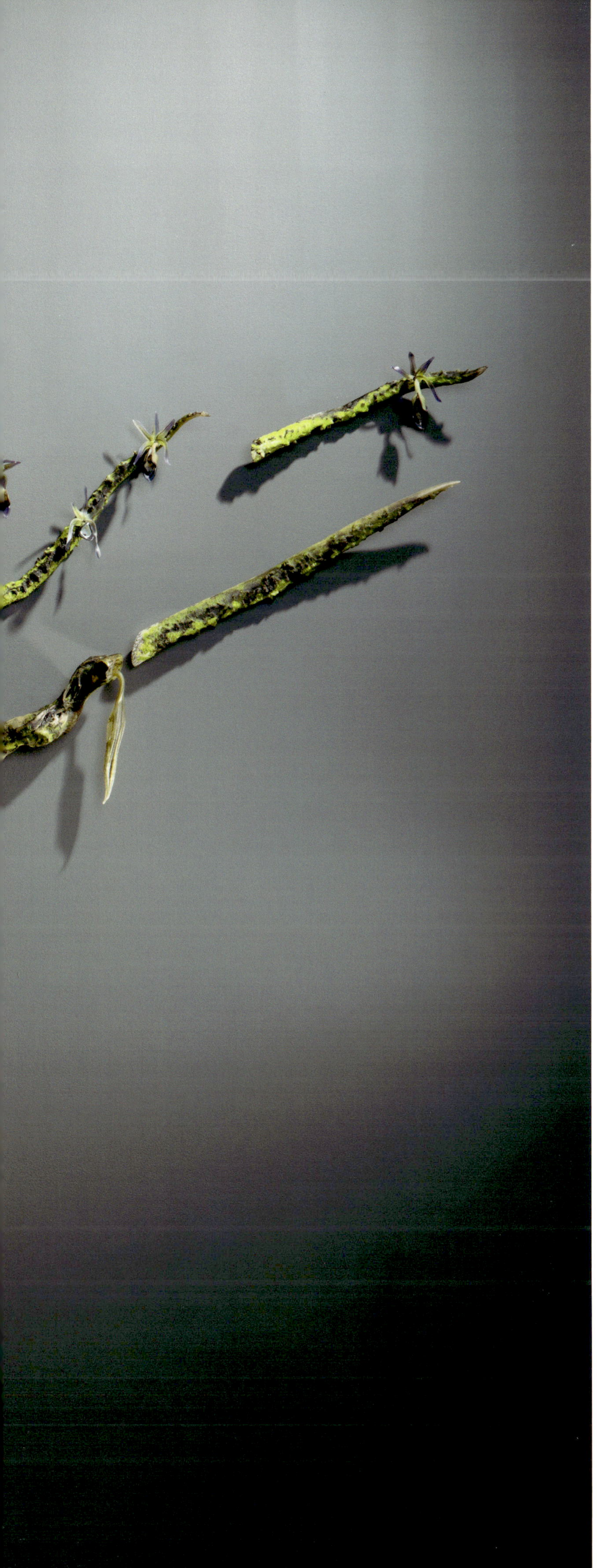

95 Debora Moore AMERICAN, BORN 1960
Orchid Tree 2005
BLOWN AND SCULPTED GLASS
110 × 114 × 9 INCHES (OVERALL)   L2017.26

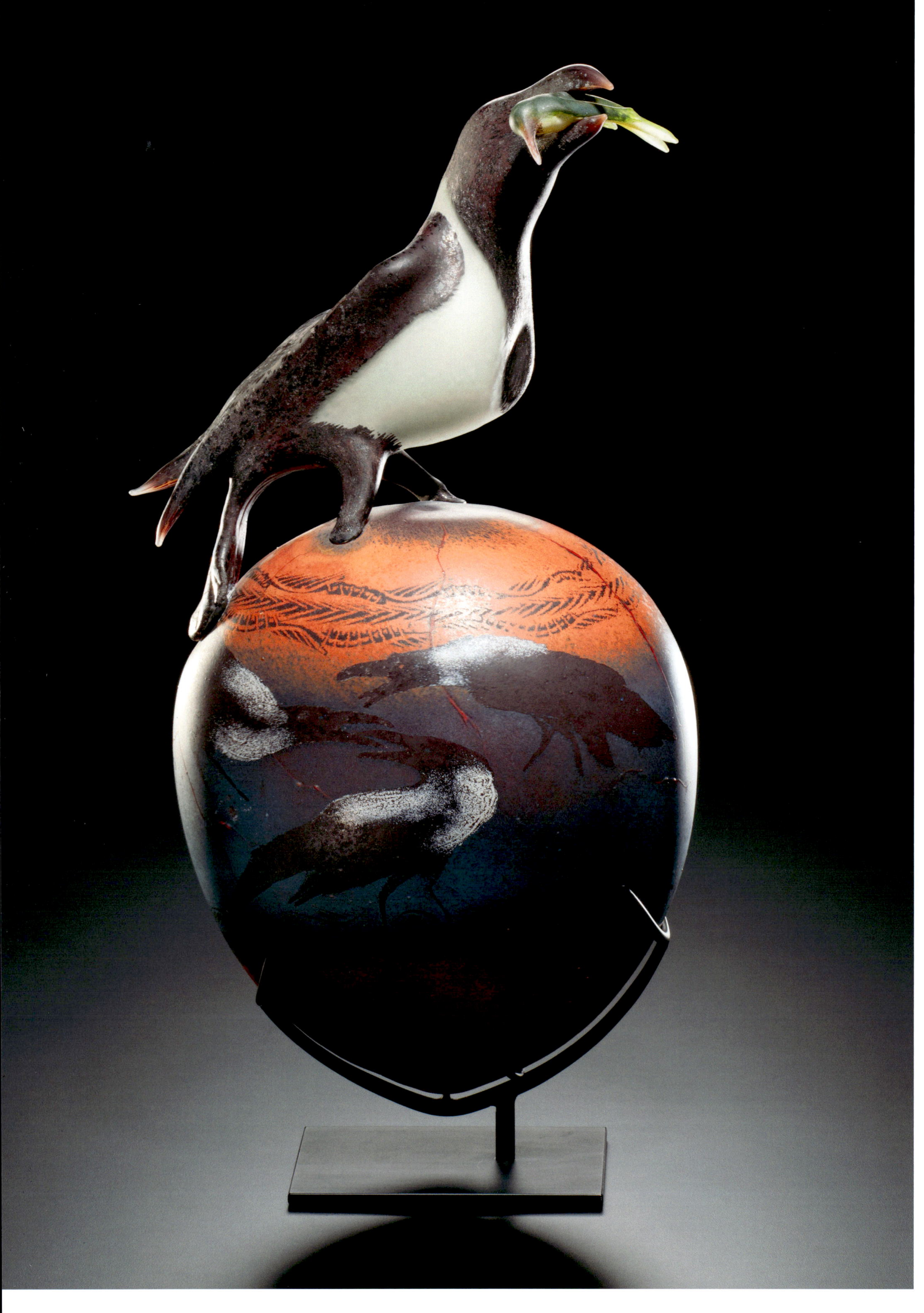

96   William Morris   AMERICAN, BORN 1957   *African Raven with Hummingbird*   1998
BLOWN GLASS, STEEL STAND   24¼ × 12½ × 8¼ INCHES   L2017.123

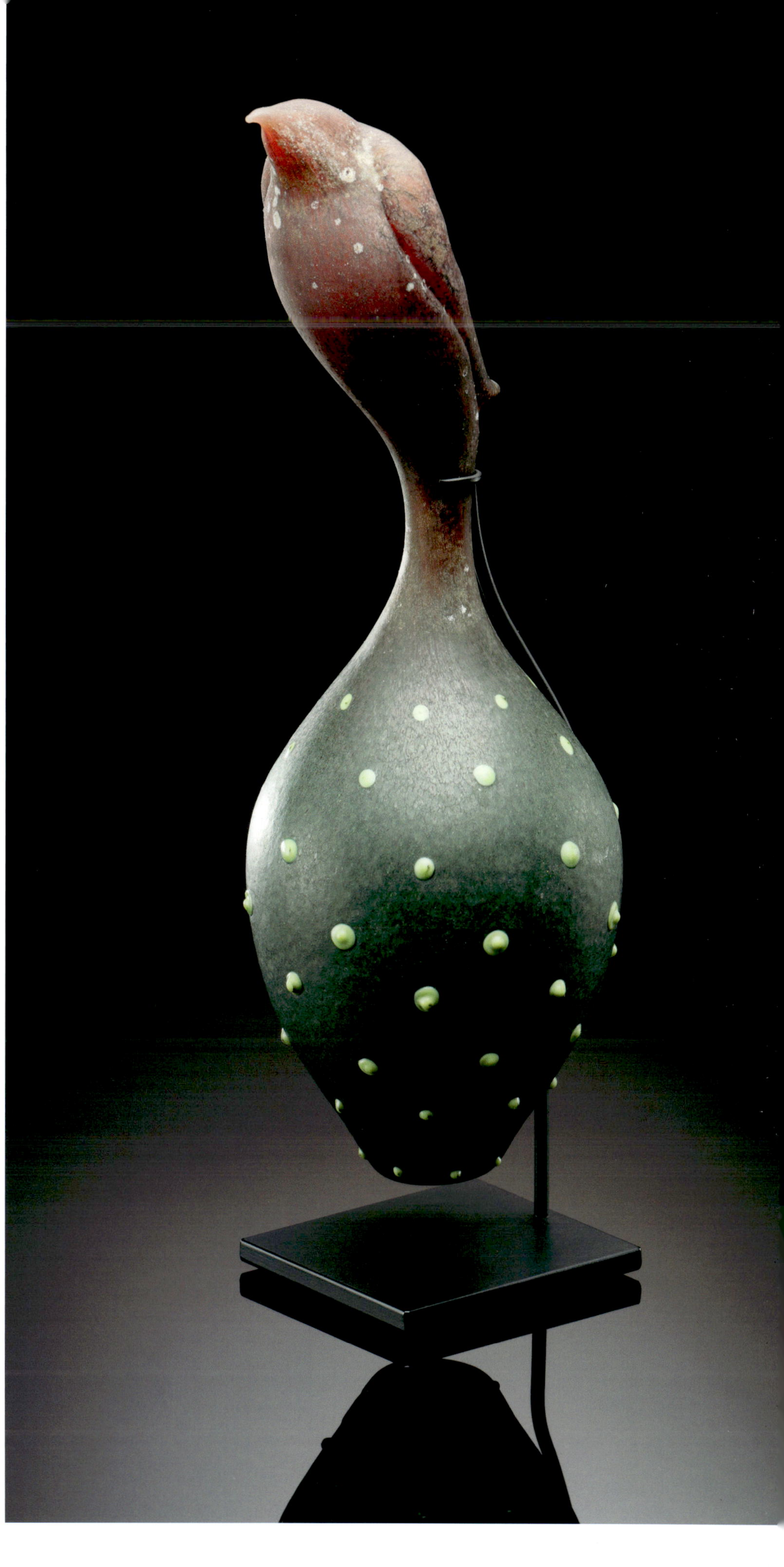

97   William Morris   AMERICAN, BORN 1957   *Bird Finial*   1999   **143**
BLOWN GLASS, STEEL STAND   13 × 4 × 4½ INCHES   L2017.121

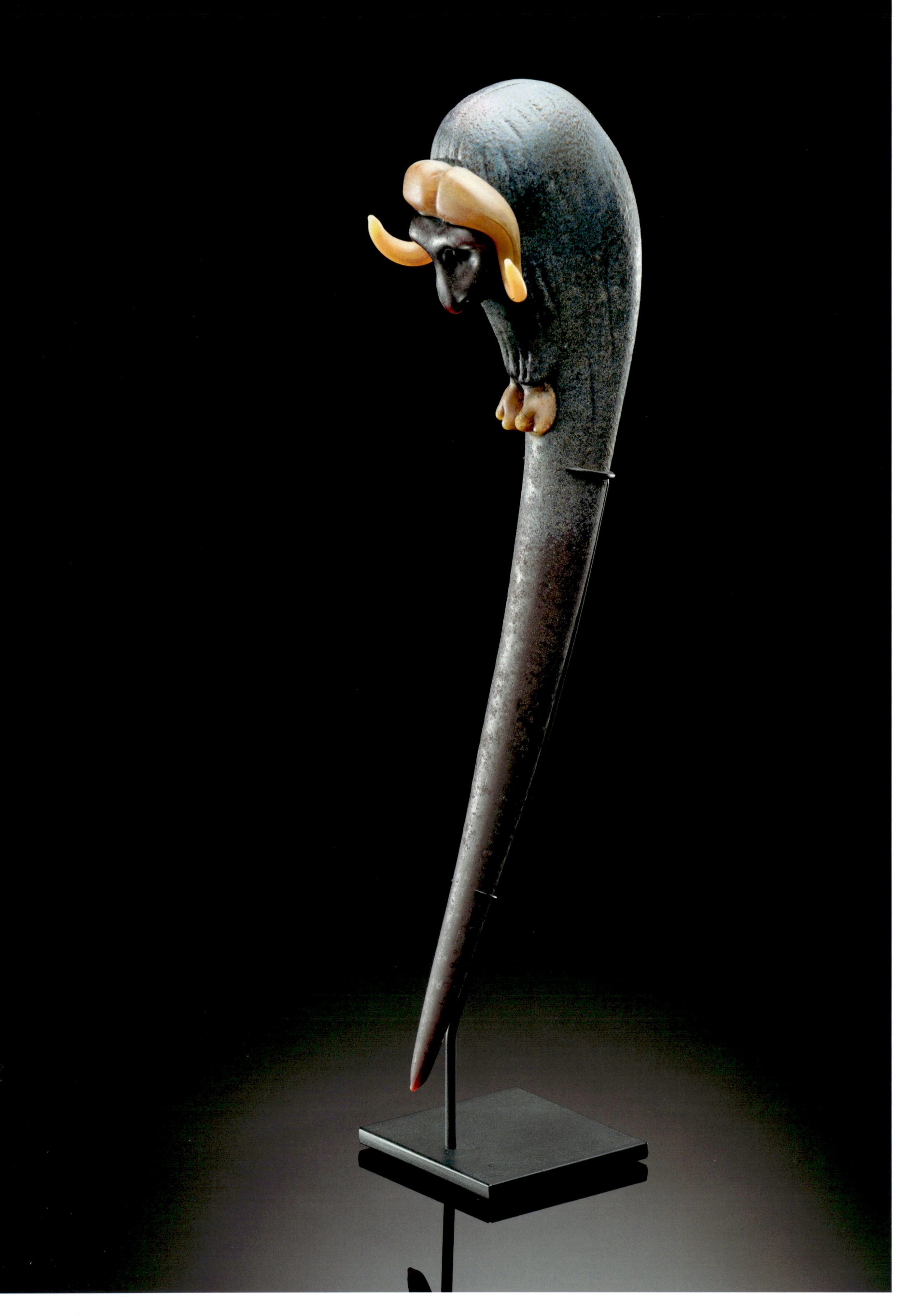

98　William Morris　AMERICAN, BORN 1957　*Musk Ox Pin*　2000
BLOWN GLASS, STEEL STAND　15 × 3 × 3¼ INCHES　L2017.122

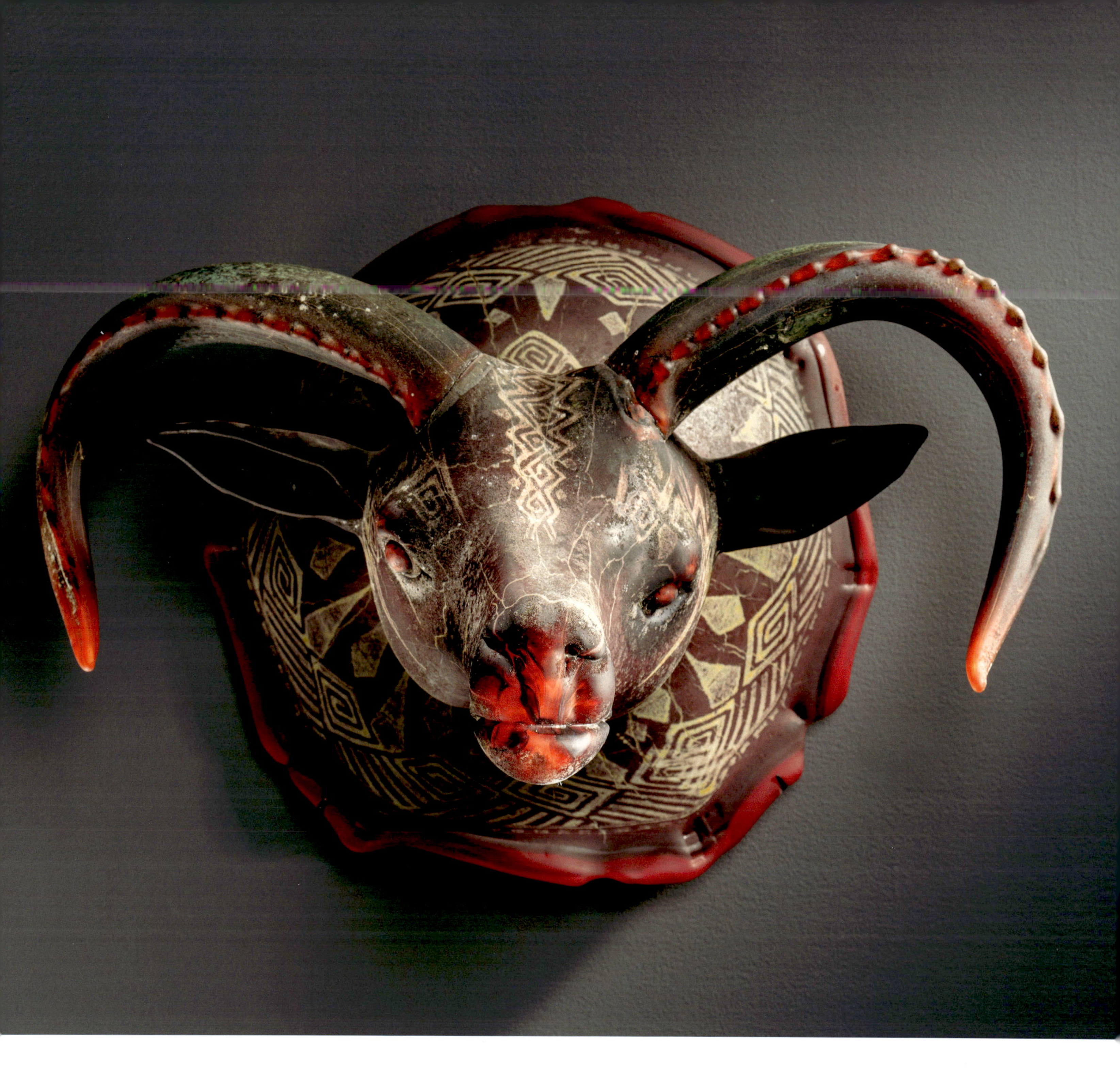

99 William Morris AMERICAN, BORN 1957 *Bull Trophy* 1999
BLOWN GLASS, STEEL BRACKET   16 × 23¾ × 16¾ INCHES   L2017.124

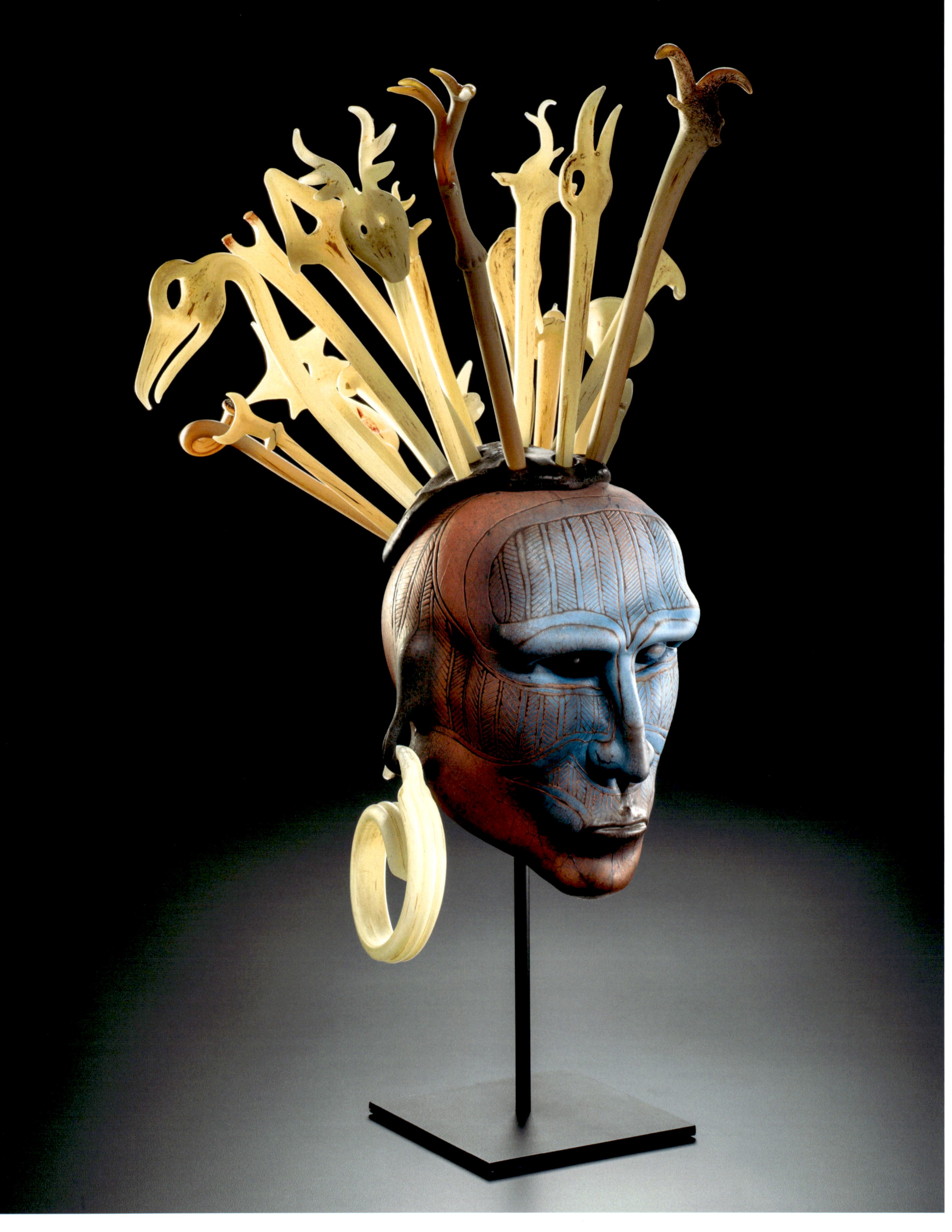

100   William Morris   AMERICAN, BORN 1957   *Zande Man*   2001

BLOWN GLASS, STEEL STAND   26 × 16 × 16 INCHES   L2017.120

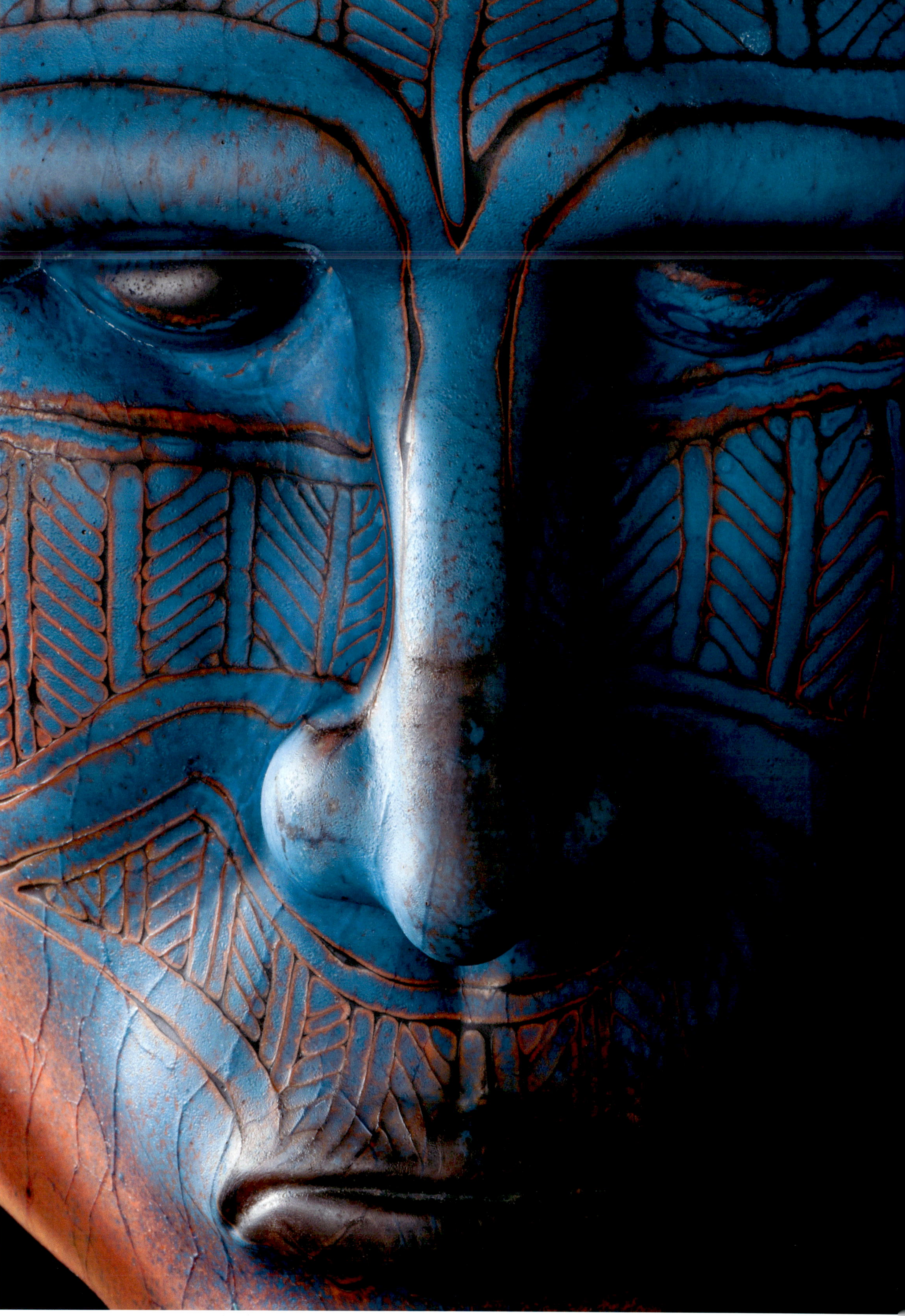

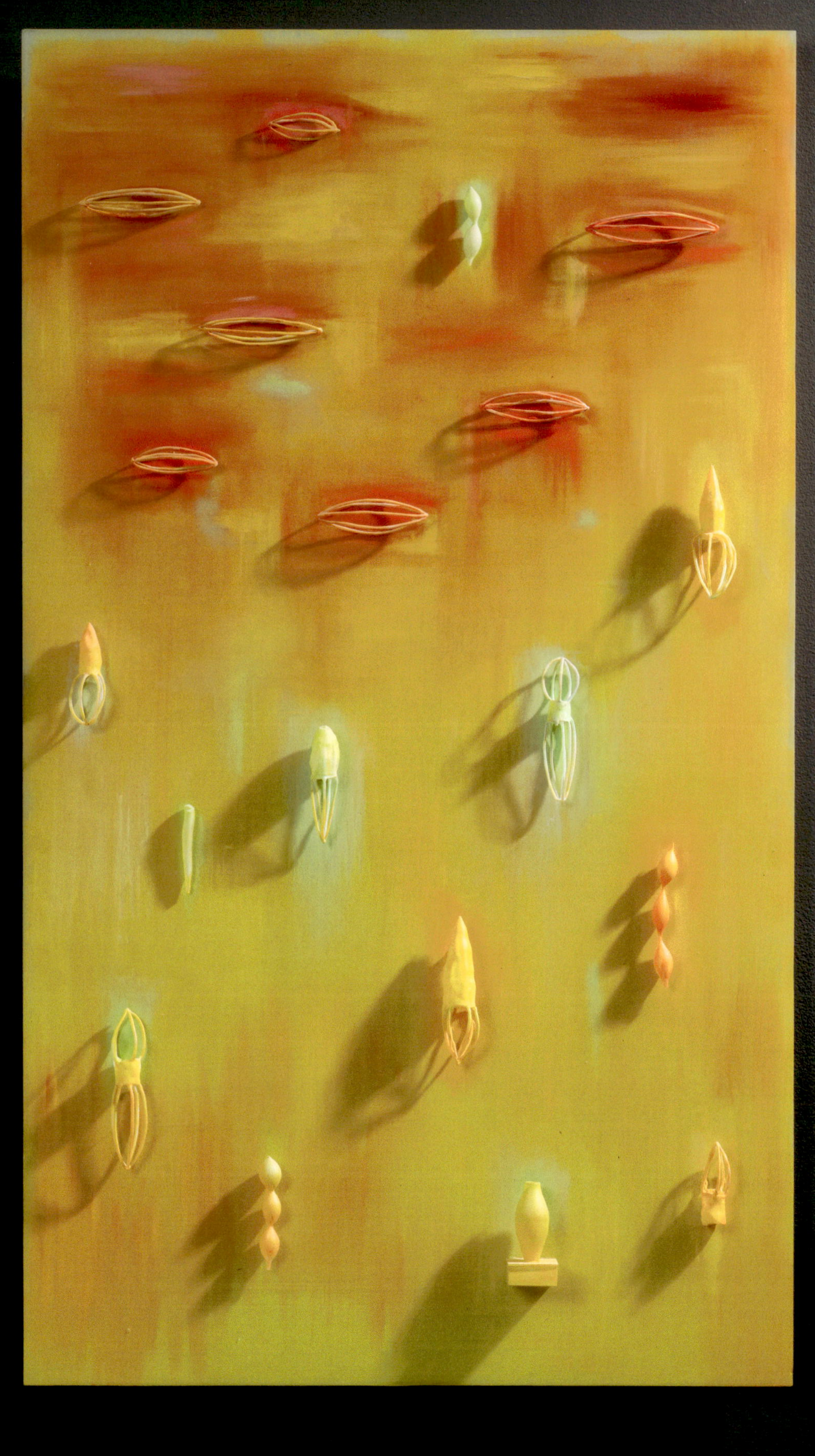

101   Jay Musler   AMERICAN, BORN 1949   *The Exotic Land of Forgiveness*   2008
GLASS, OIL PAINT   43½ × 25¾ × 2½ INCHES   L2017.92

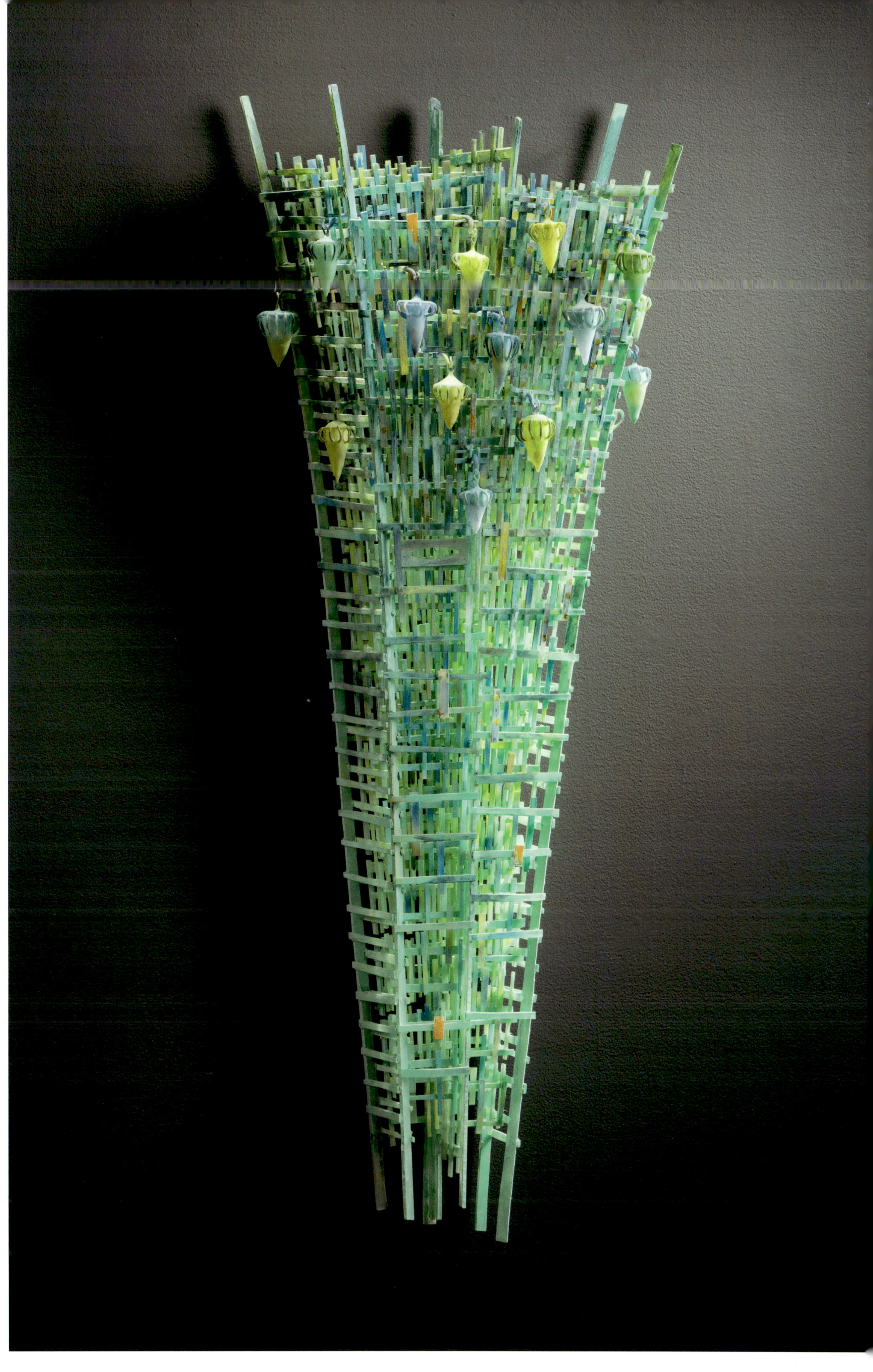

102   Jay Musler   AMERICAN, BORN 1949   *Visions of Space*   2001
LAMPWORKED, ASSEMBLED, AND PAINTED GLASS   48½ × 18¼ × 10½ INCHES   L2017.91

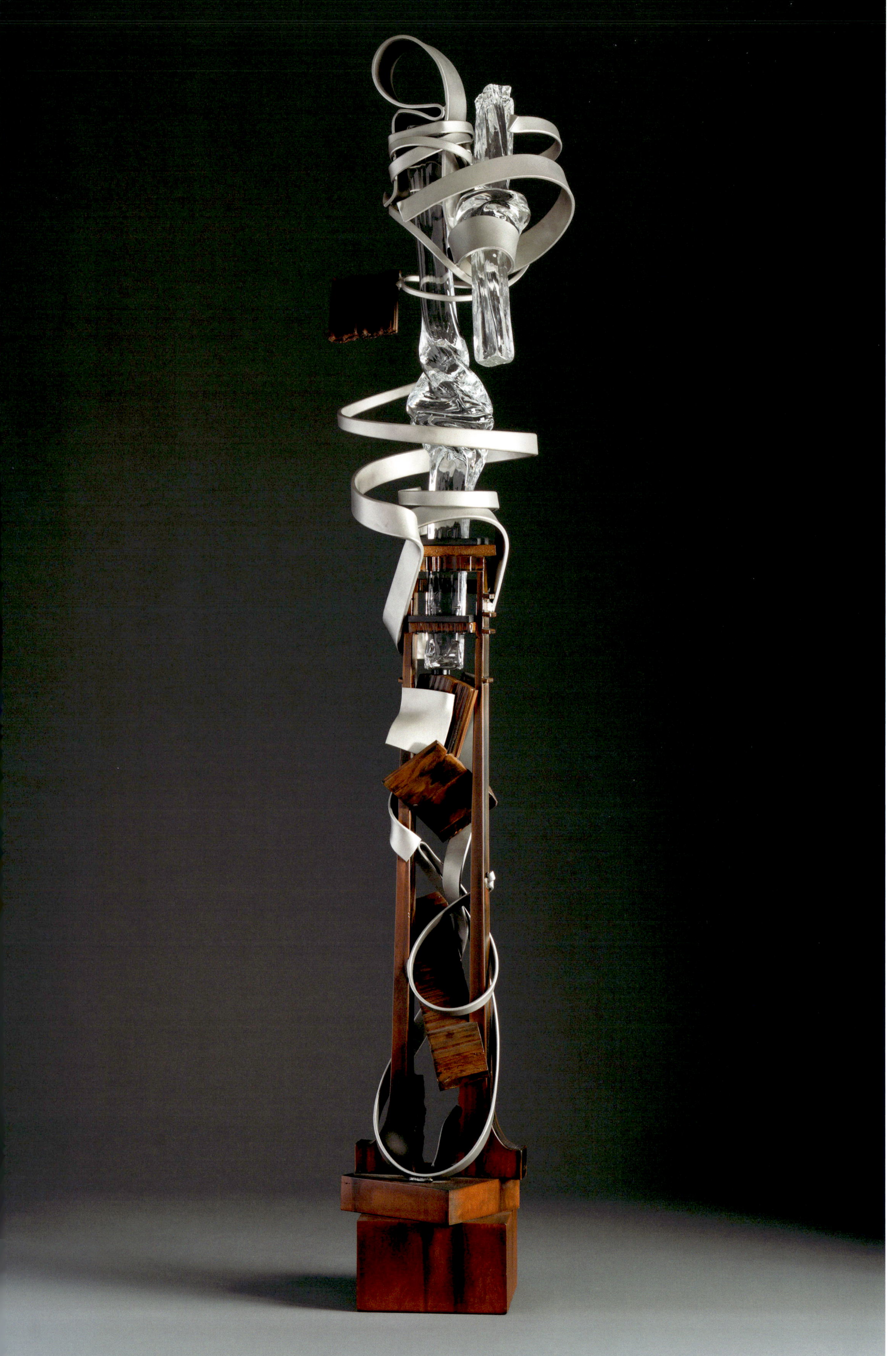

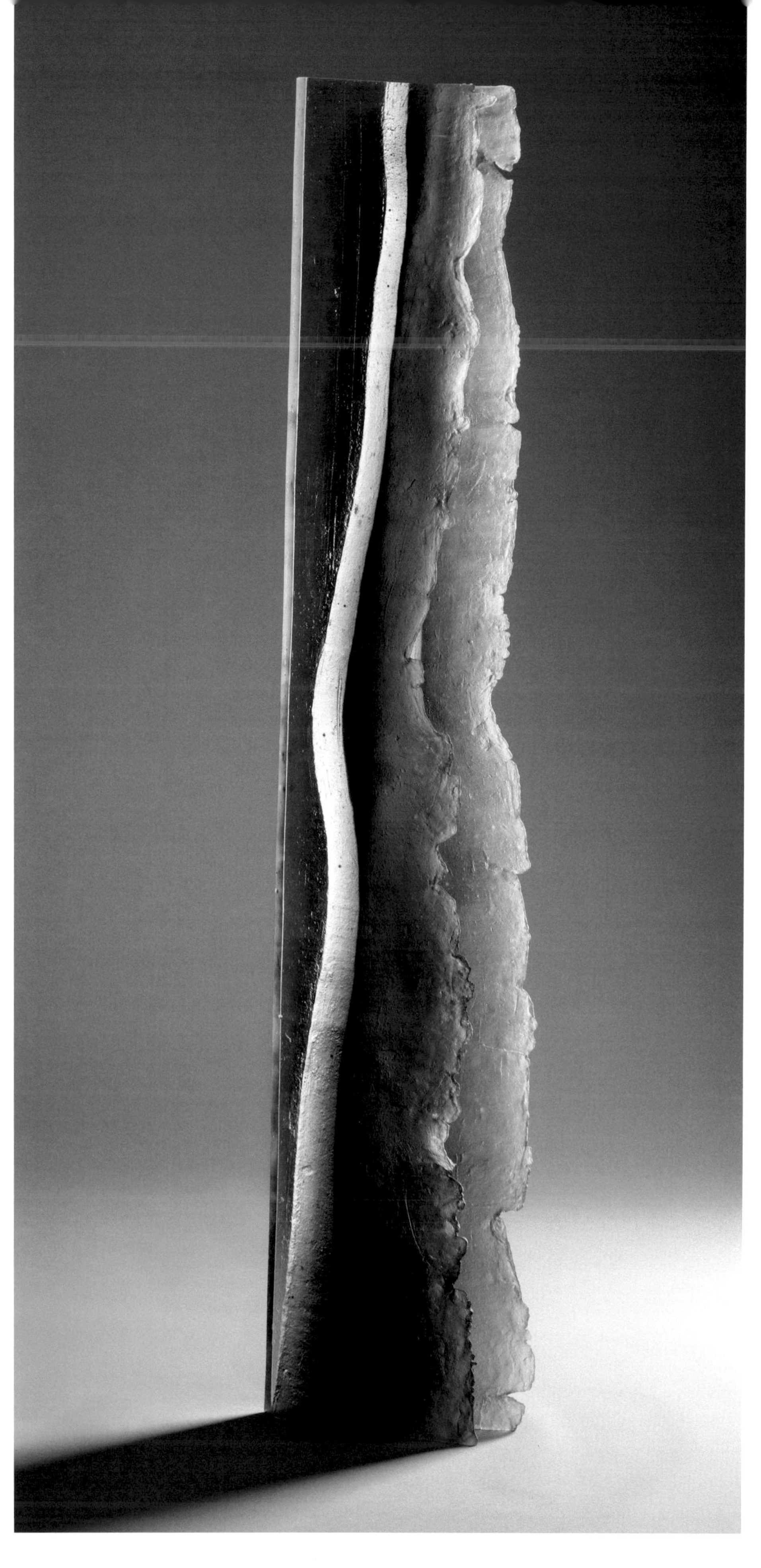

104   Zora Palová   SLOVAK, BORN 1947   *North Sea Waves*   2009
CAST GLASS   76¾ × 12½ × 13 INCHES   L2017.96

103   Albert Paley AMERICAN, BORN 1944, Martin Blank AMERICAN, BORN 1962   *Half Twist*   2001
STEEL, HOT-WORKED GLASS   89¾ × 19 × 14 INCHES   L2017.5

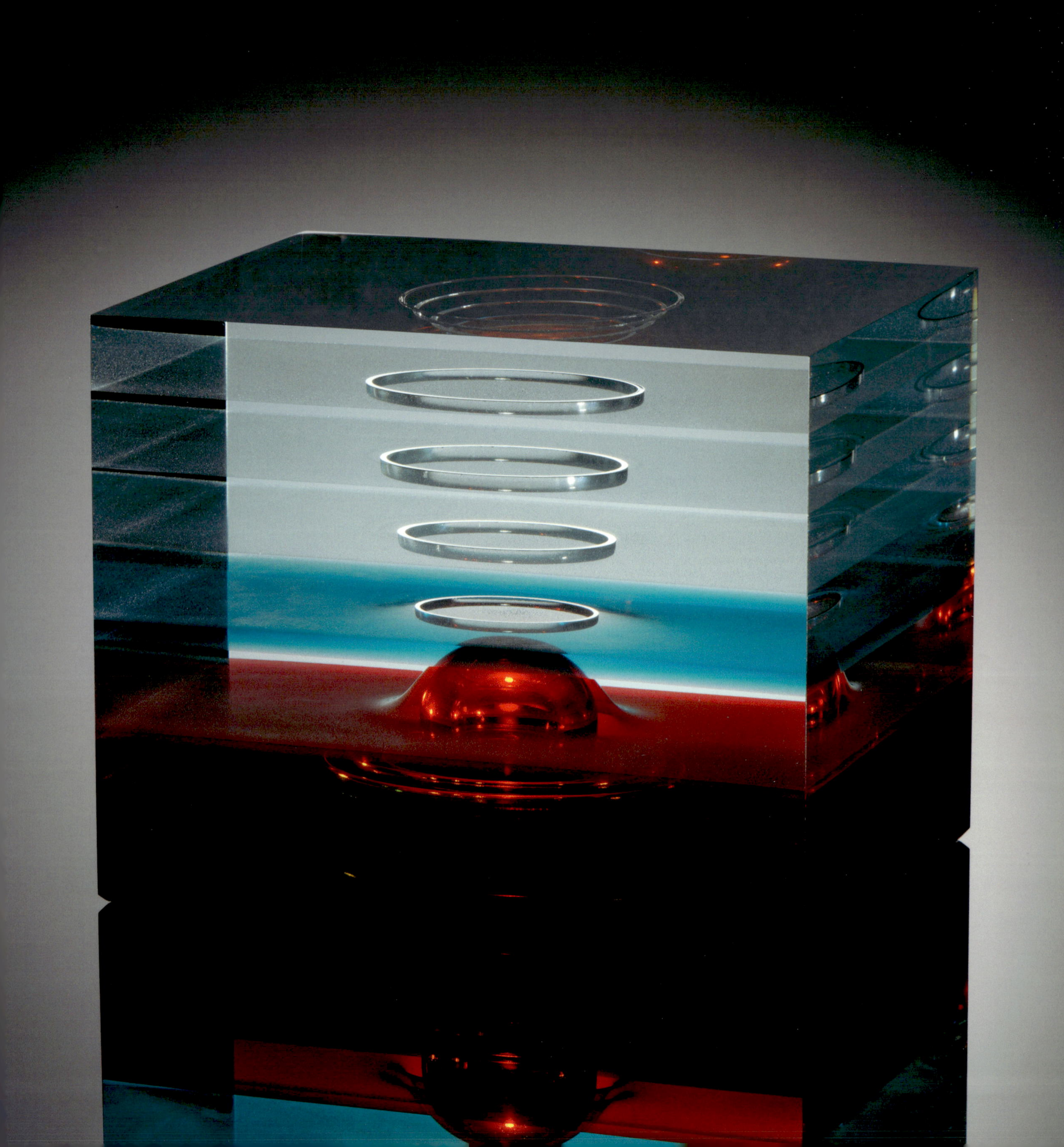

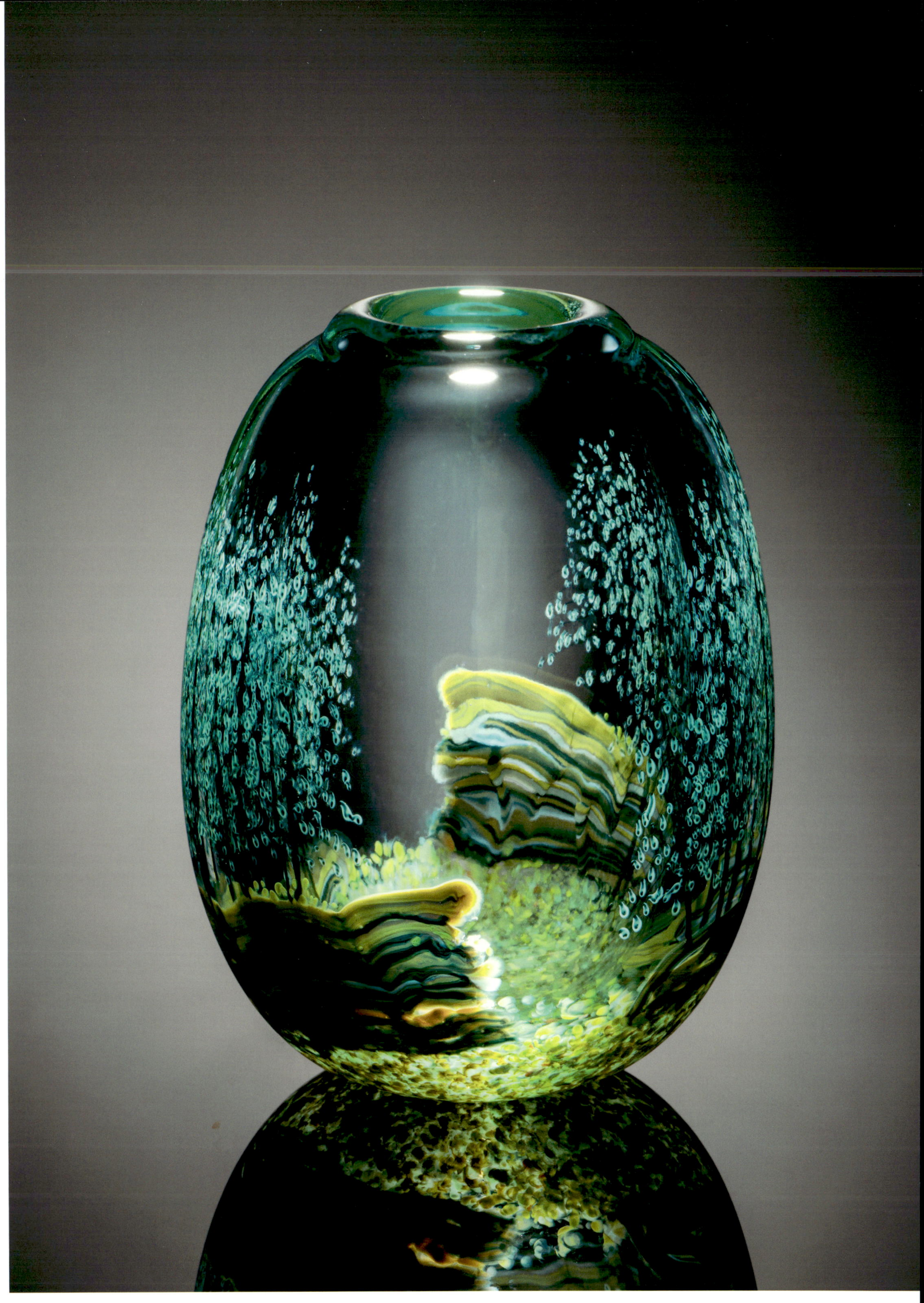

106　Mark Peiser　AMERICAN, BORN 1938　*Limestone Bluff*　1978
BLOWN GLASS　5⅝ × 4⅜ × 4⅜ INCHES　L2017.98

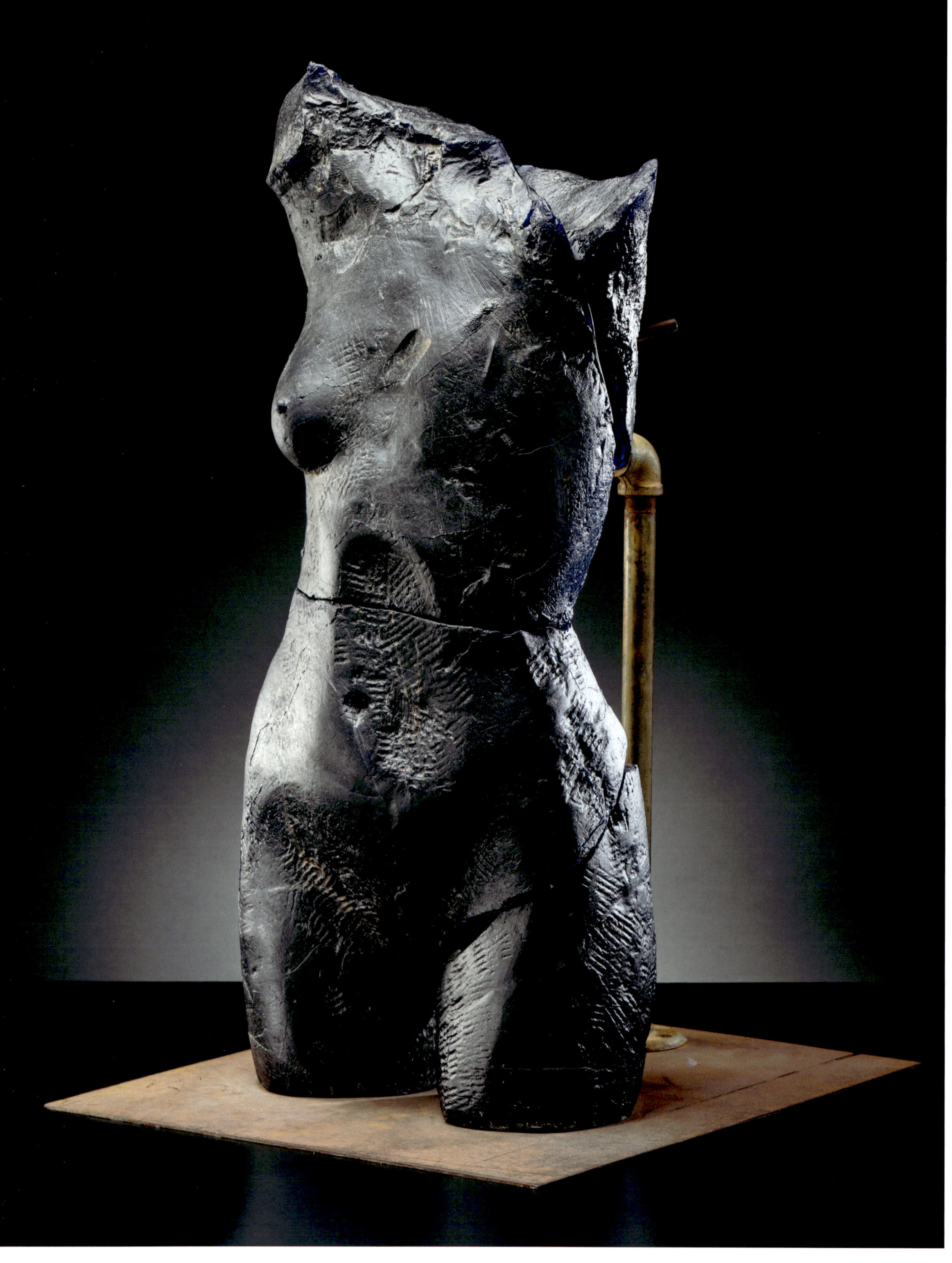

107   Clifford Rainey   BRITISH, BORN 1948   *Counting*   1999
CAST GLASS, METAL PIPE, STEEL BASE   32 × 19 × 22 INCHES   L2017.100

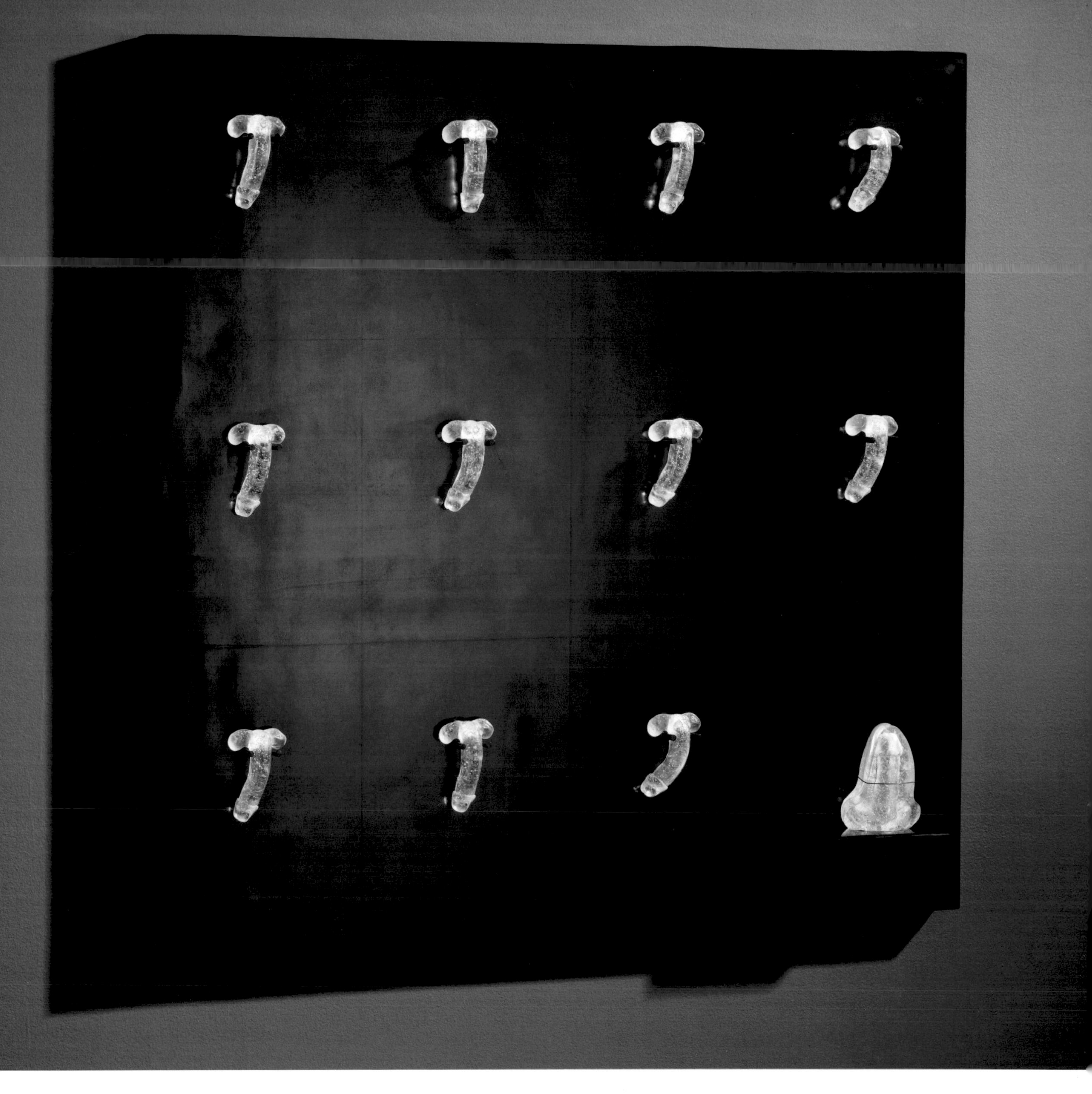

108   Clifford Rainey   BRITISH, BORN 1948   *The Art Committee*   2004
CAST GLASS, WOOD PANEL   36 × 36 × 4 INCHES   L2017.101

109   Richard Ritter   AMERICAN, BORN 1940   *Floral Core Series #53*   2003

GATHERED GLASS WITH MURRINE INCLUSIONS, CAST GLASS, COPPER ELECTROFORMING   15 × 17¾ × 10¾ INCHES   L2017.103

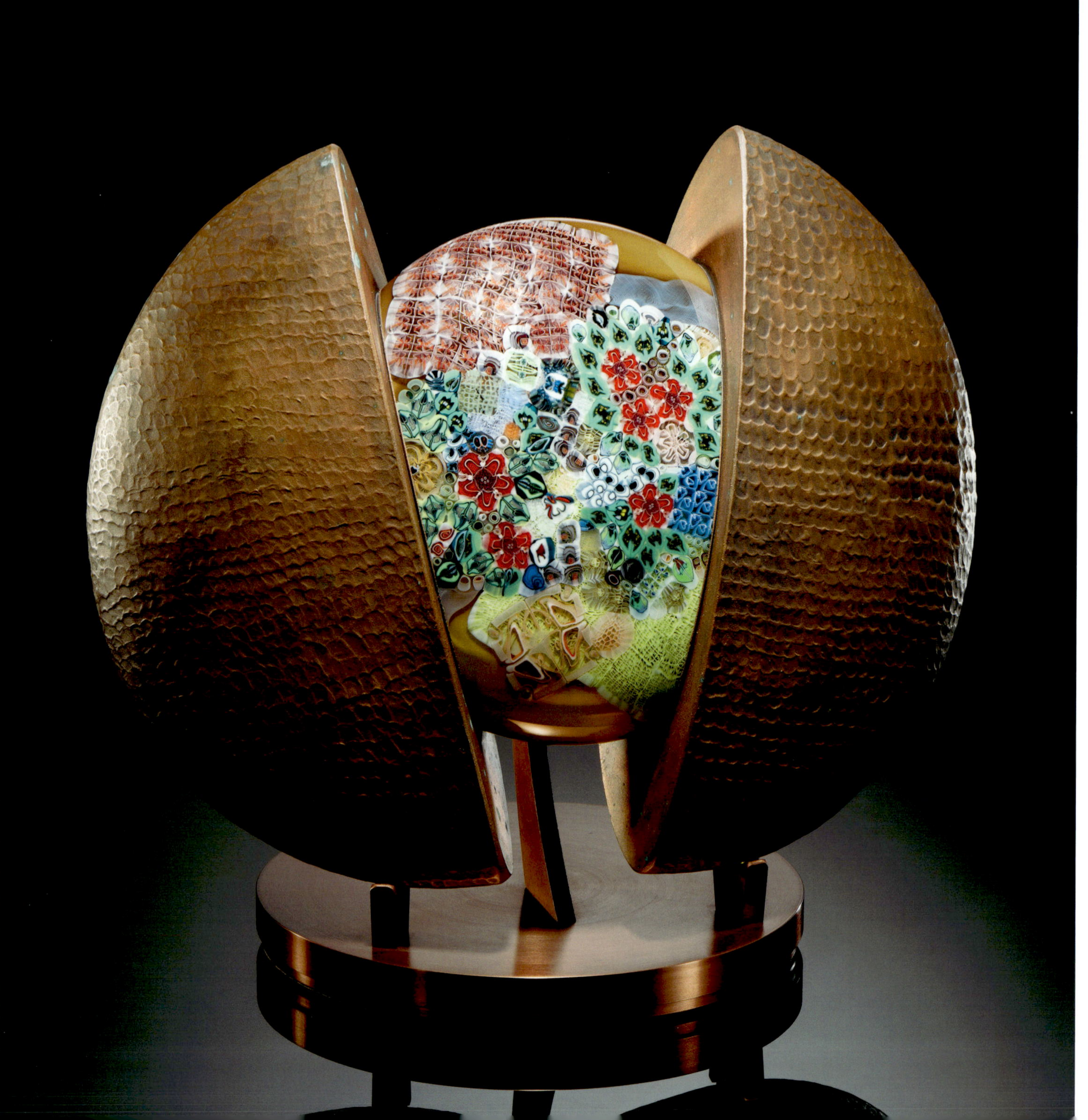

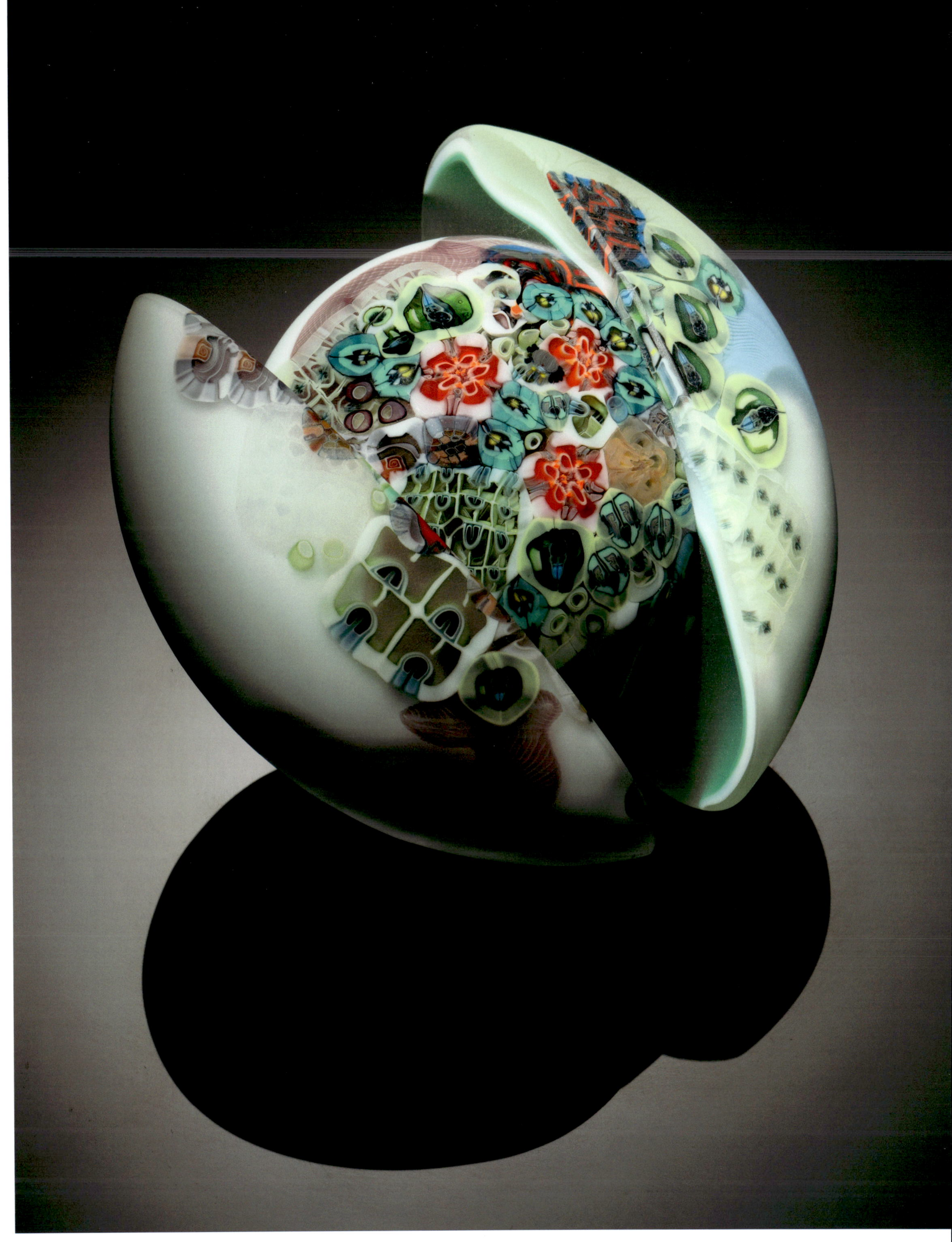

110   Richard Ritter   AMERICAN, BORN 1940   *Floral Core Series #80*   2007
GATHERED GLASS WITH MURRINE INCLUSIONS   5½ × 5½ × 3¼ INCHES   L2017.104

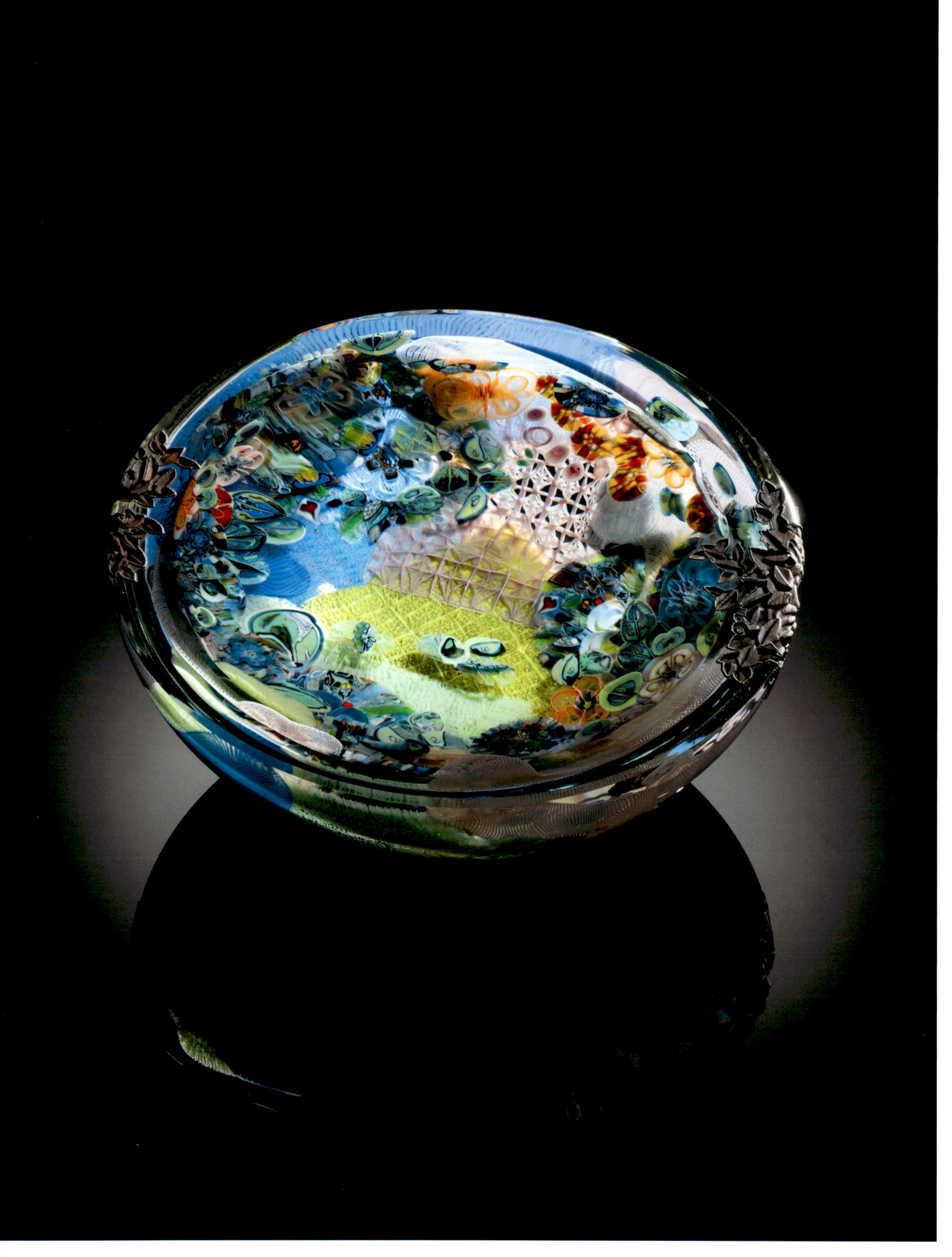

111   Richard Ritter   AMERICAN, BORN 1940   *Florescence Series #11*   2001
GATHERED GLASS WITH MURRINE INCLUSIONS, ETCHED AND COPPER ELECTROFORMED SURFACE   4¼ × 11½ × 11½ INCHES   L2017.102

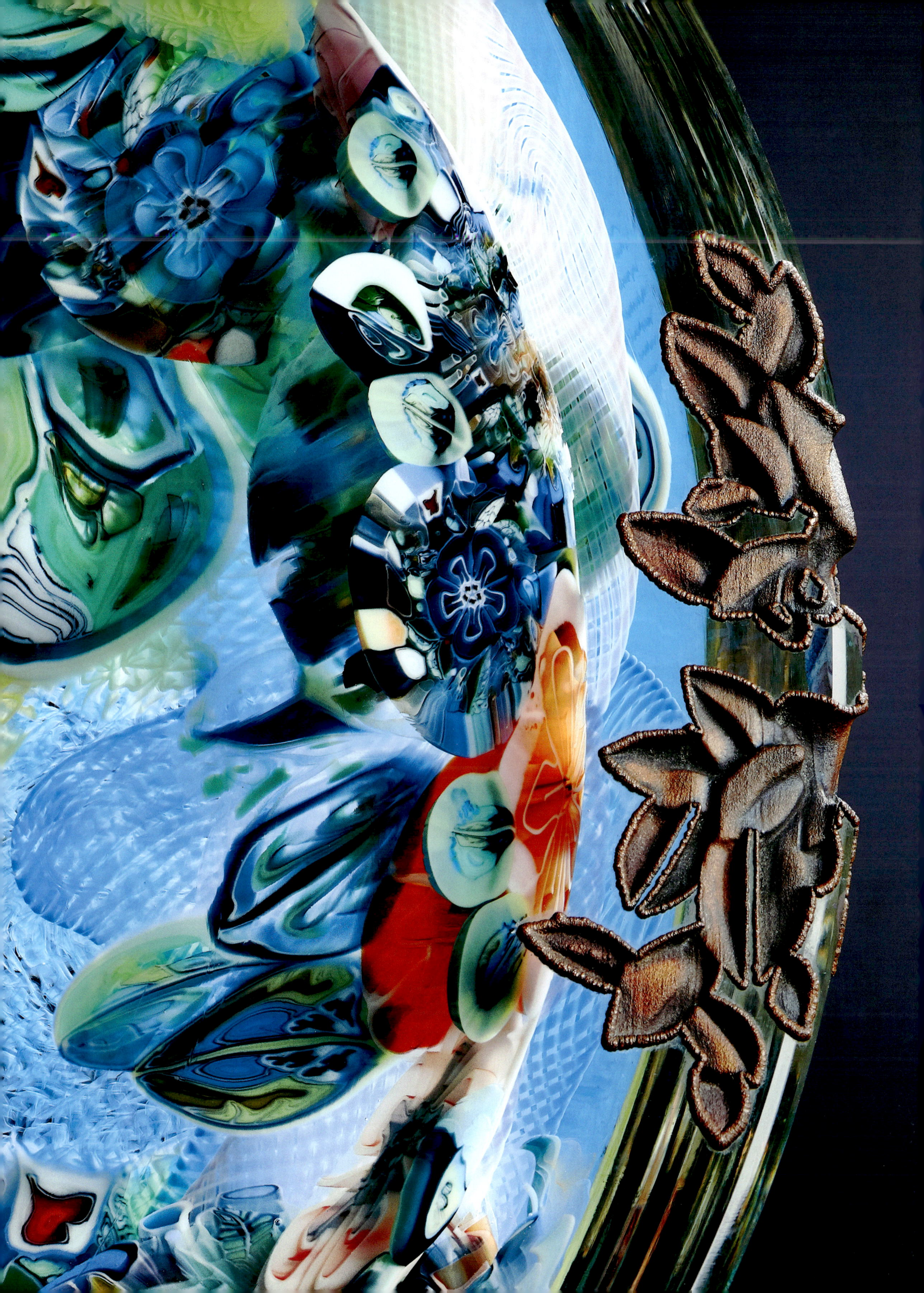

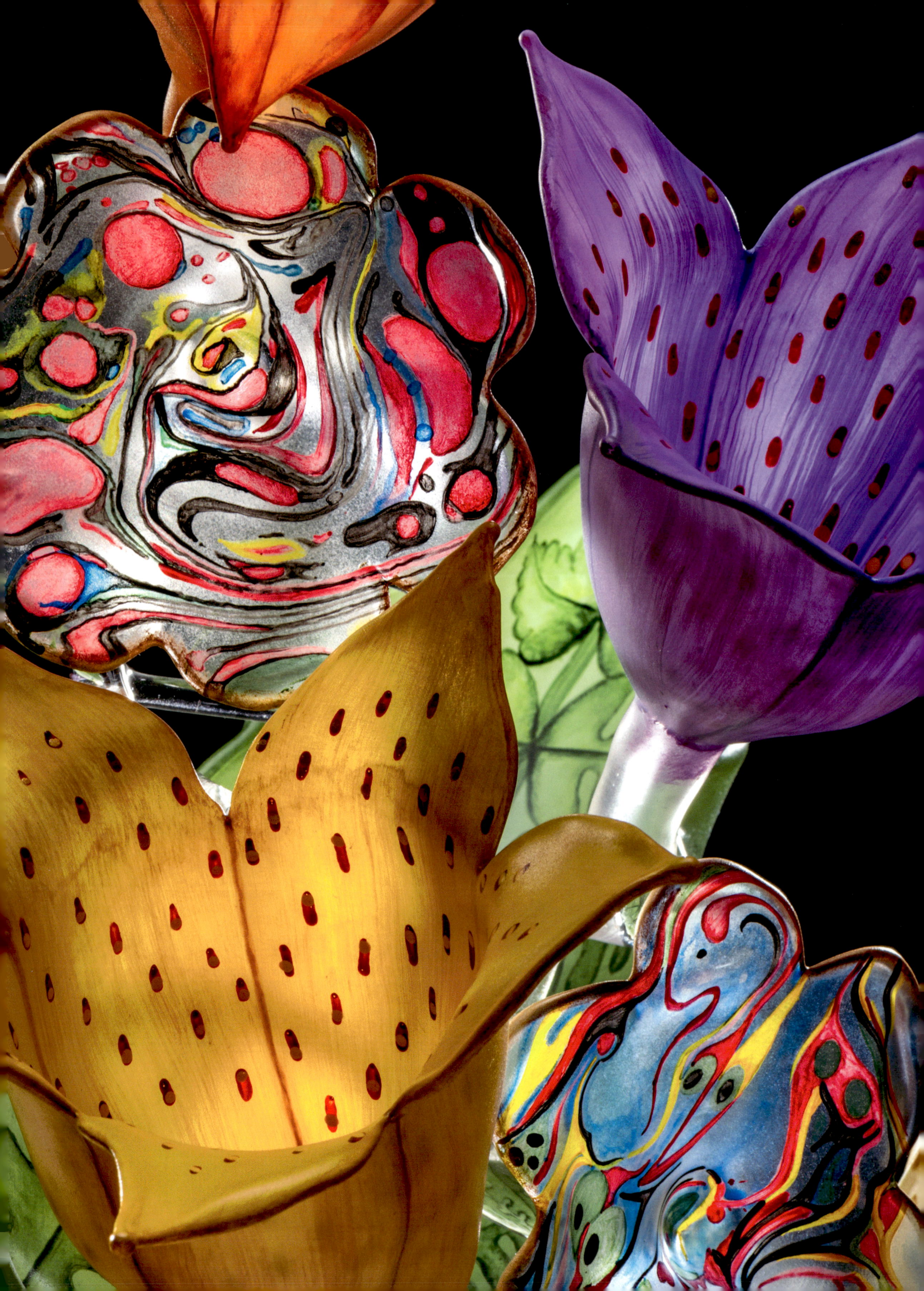

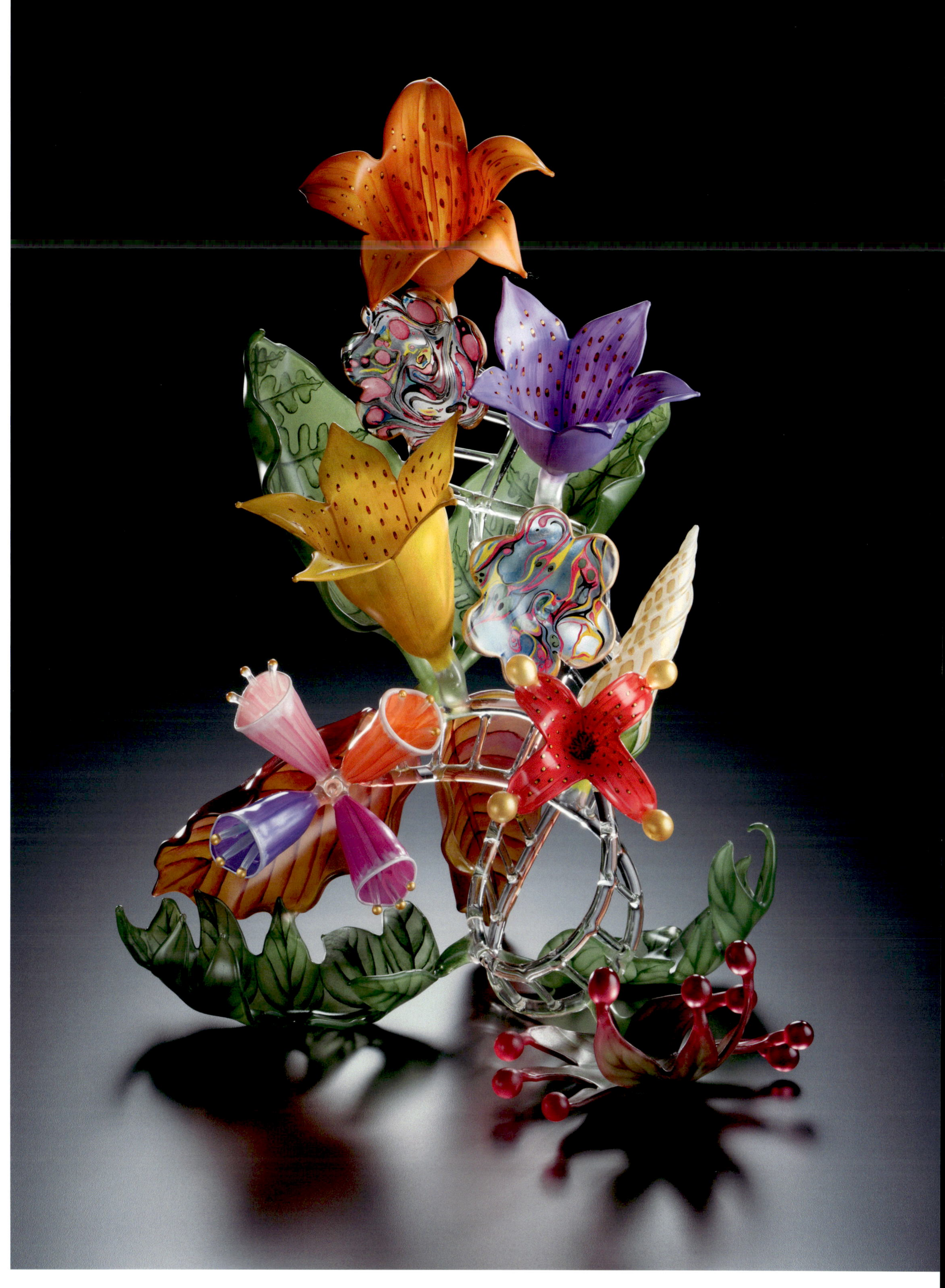

112   Ginny Ruffner   AMERICAN, BORN 1952   *Aesthetic Engineering Series: Inventing Flowers*   2005
LAMPWORKED, SANDBLASTED, AND PAINTED GLASS   24 × 18¾ × 17½ INCHES   L2017.106

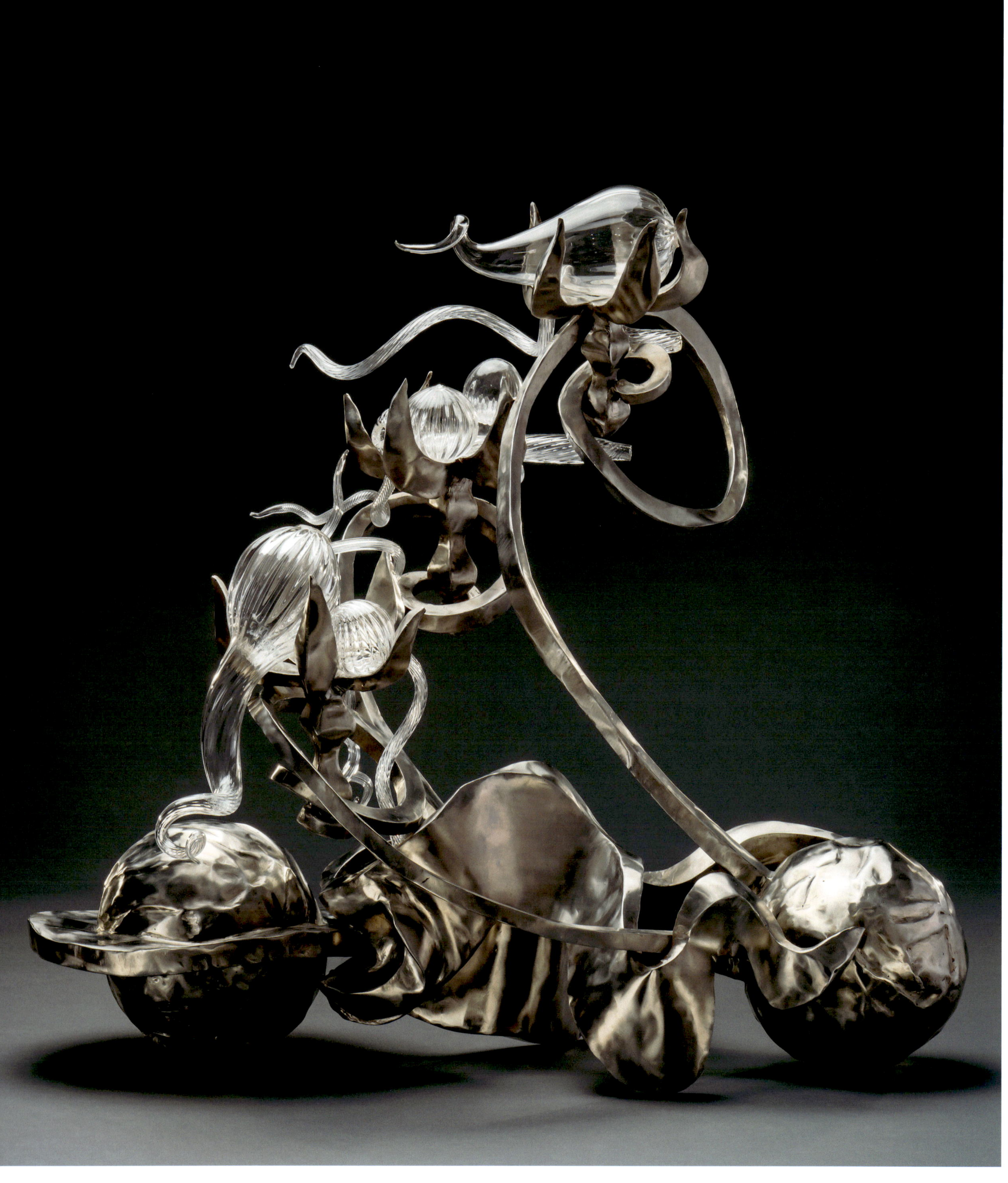

113   Ginny Ruffner   AMERICAN, BORN 1952   *The Phases of the Moon Flower*   2000
BLOWN GLASS, STAINLESS STEEL   48 × 42 × 32 INCHES   L2017.105

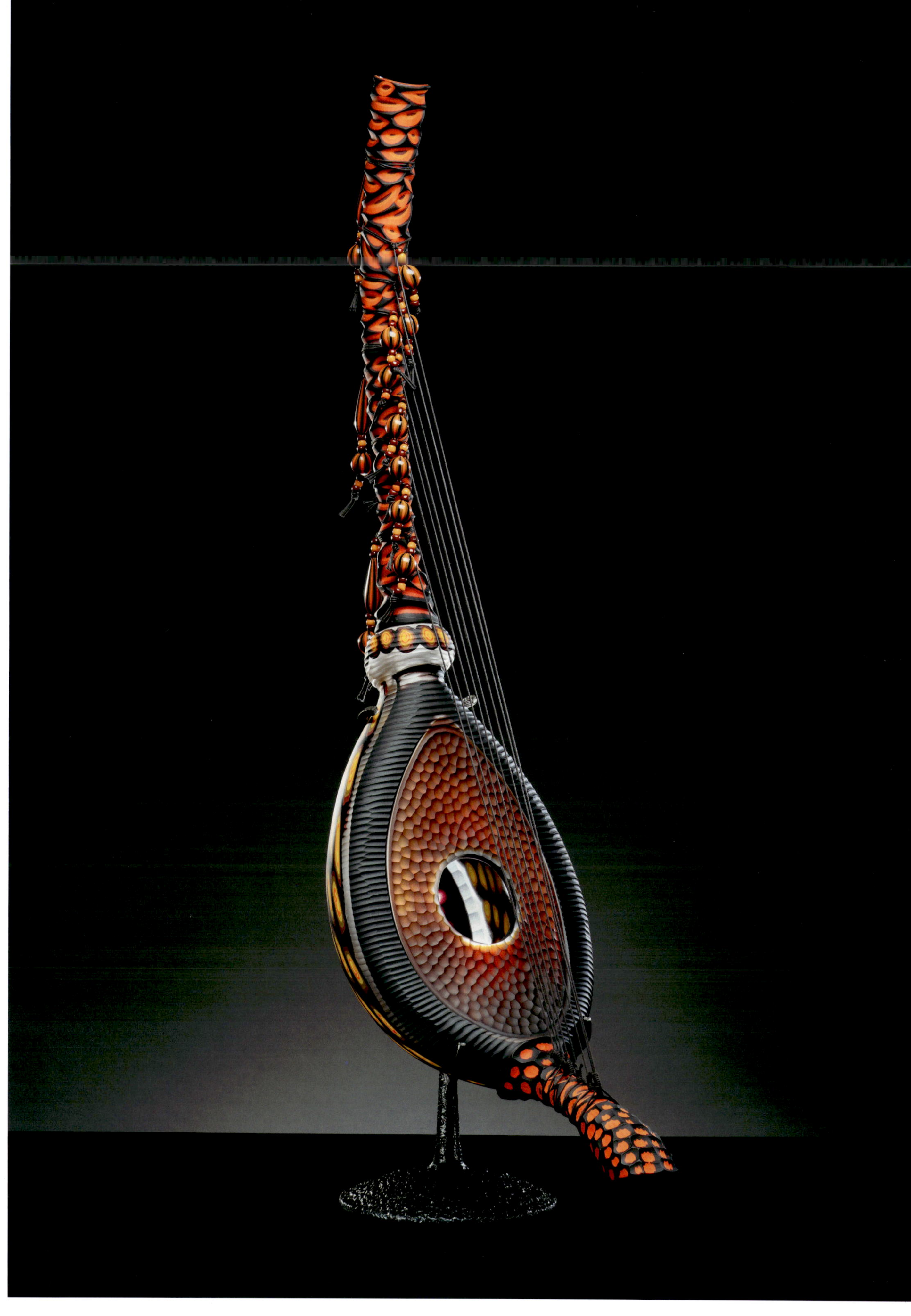

114   Davide Salvadore   ITALIAN, BORN 1953   *Springarpa 1*   2007

BLOWN, COLD-WORKED GLASS WITH MURRINE BEADS, STRING, STEEL BASE   47½ × 12¼ × 23 INCHES   L2017.110

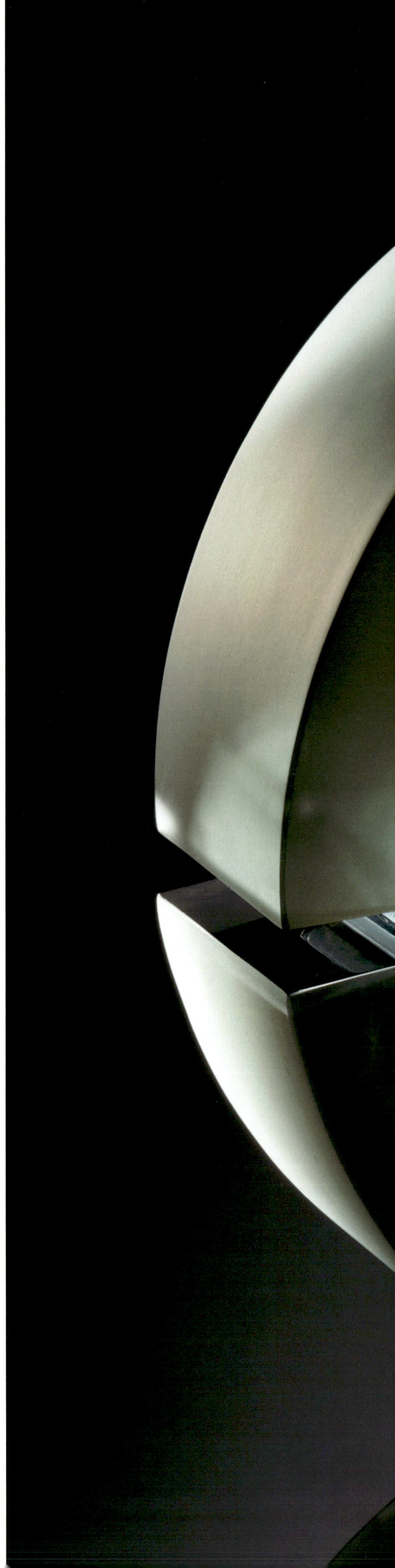

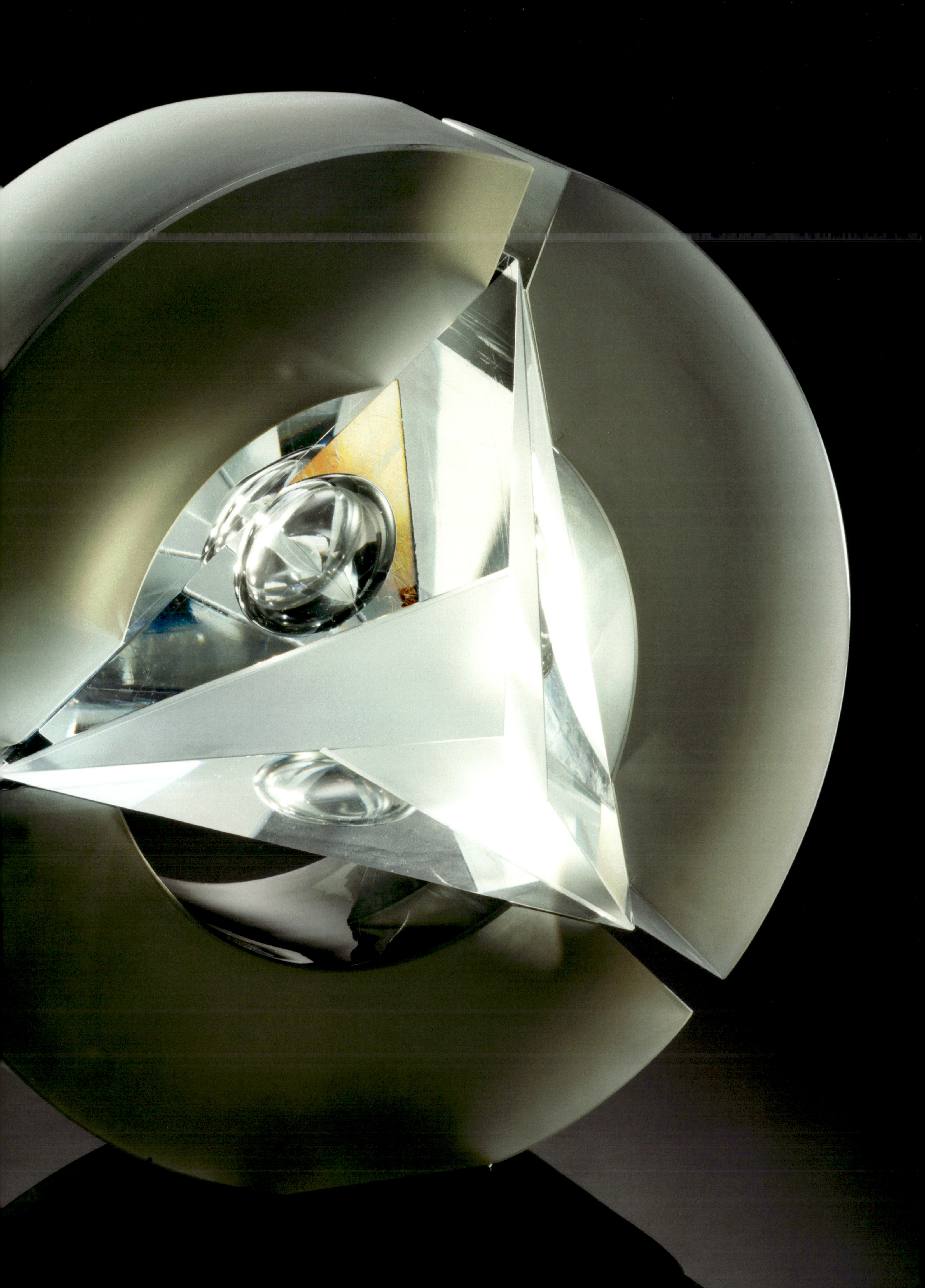

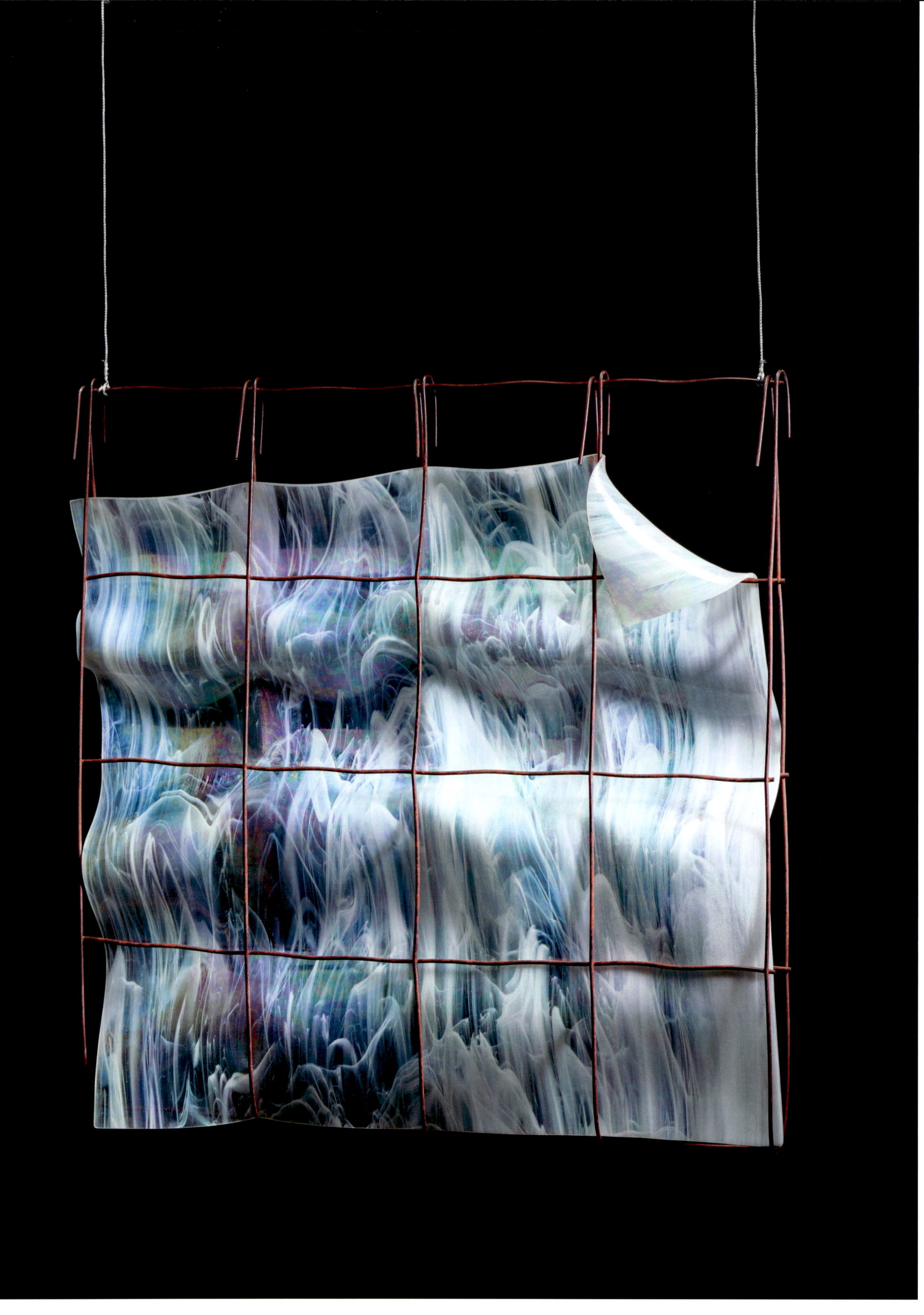

116 Mary Shaffer AMERICAN, BORN 1947 *Irish Clouds* 2003
SLUMPED GLASS, METAL   24 × 24½ × 2½ INCHES   L2017.112

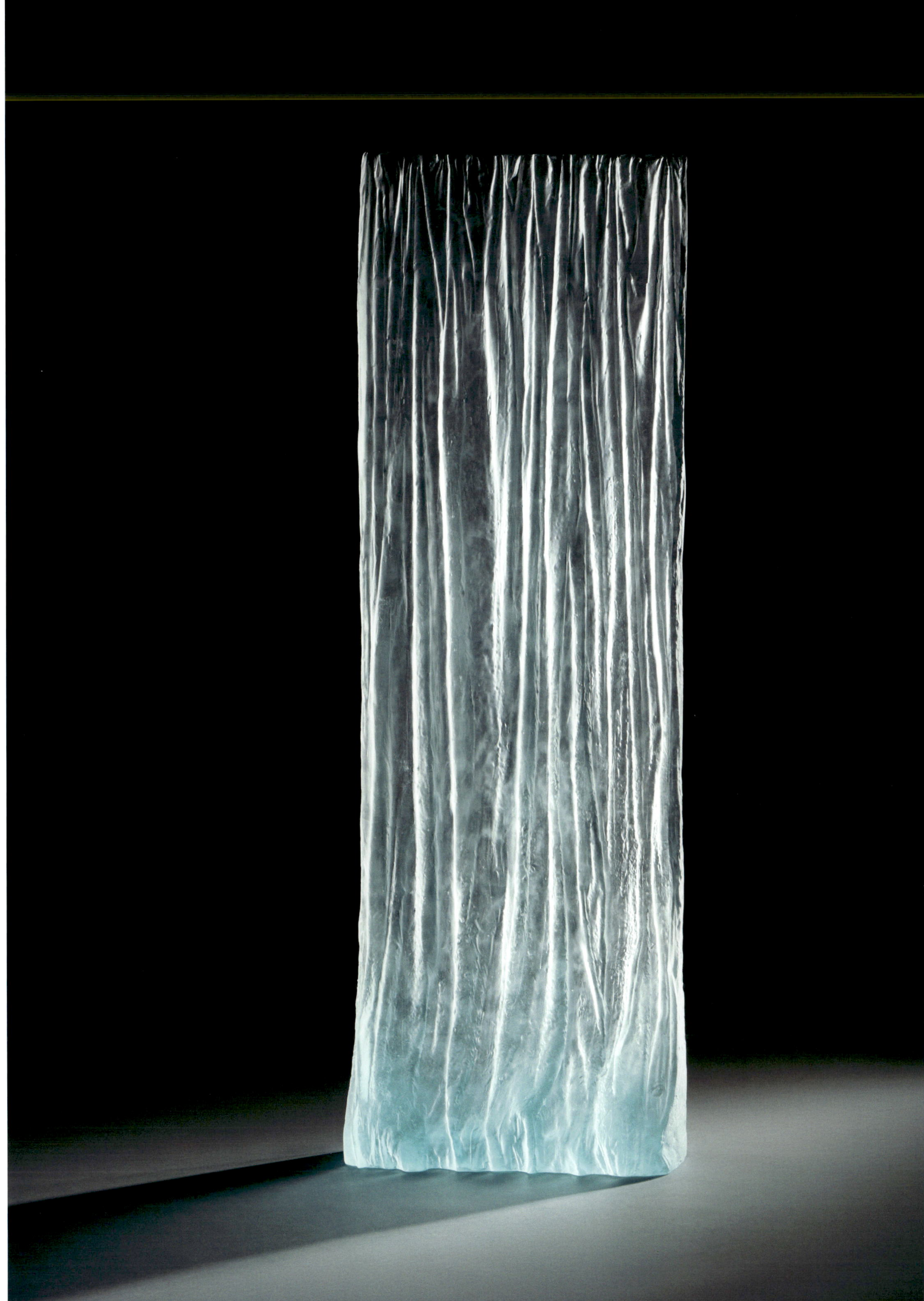

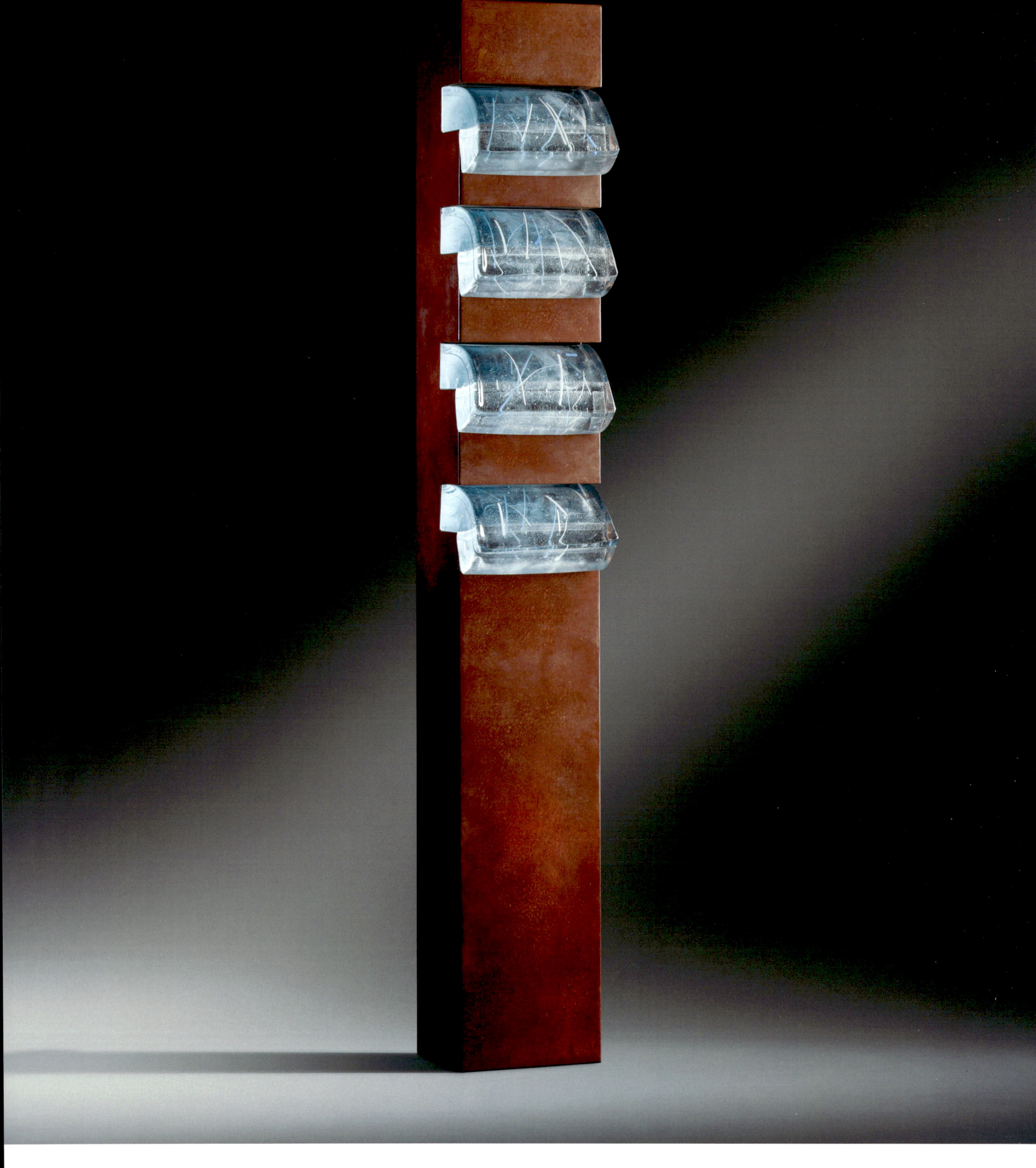

118   Mary Shaffer   AMERICAN, BORN 1947   *Ledge Mamoure Blue*   2001
STEEL, SLUMPED FUSED GLASS   79 × 11⅞ × 12⁷⁄₁₆ INCHES   L2017.113

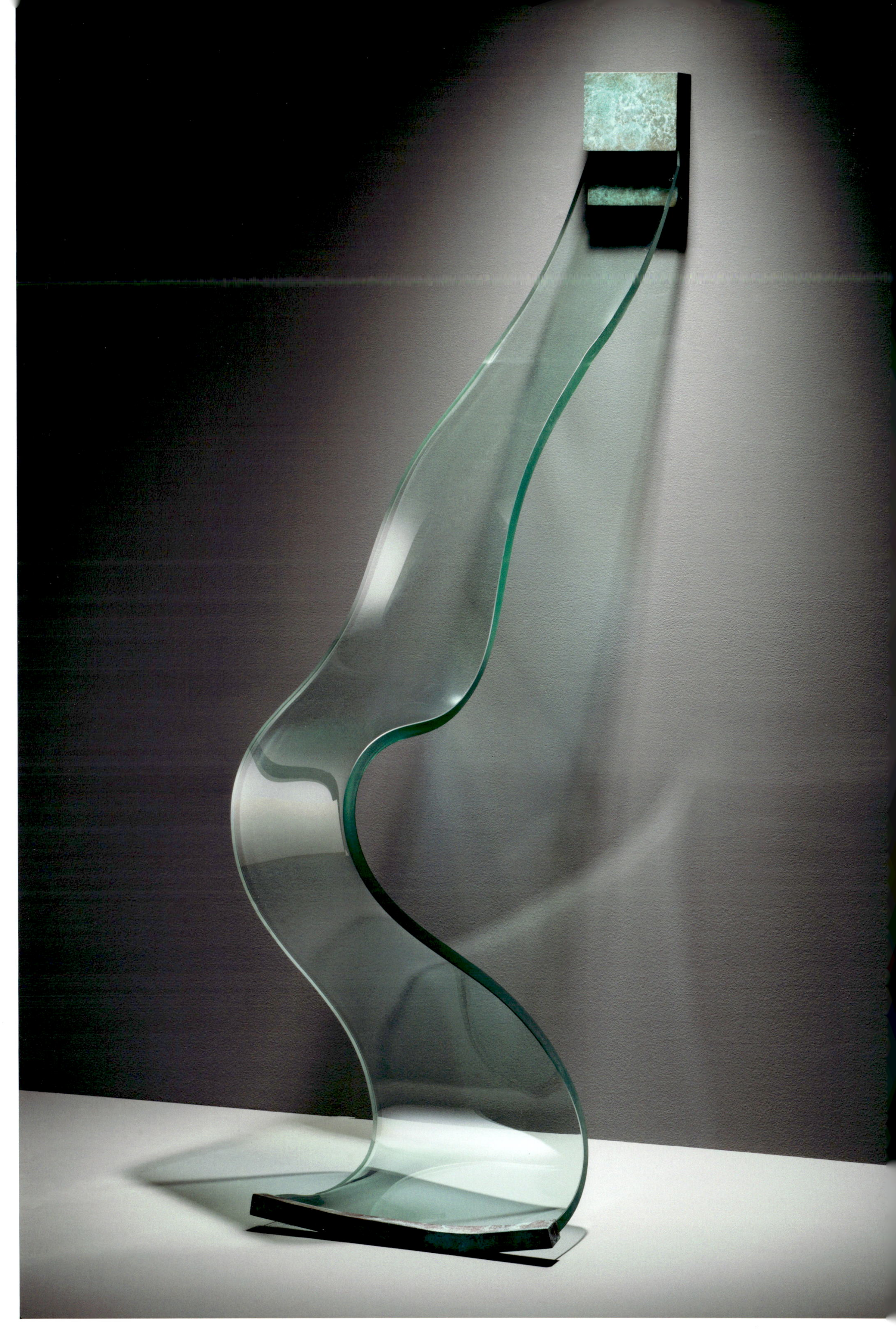

119   Mary Shaffer   AMERICAN, BORN 1947   *Wall Wave*   1997
SLUMPED GLASS, BRONZE, COPPER   66½ × 19½ × 15 INCHES   L2017.111

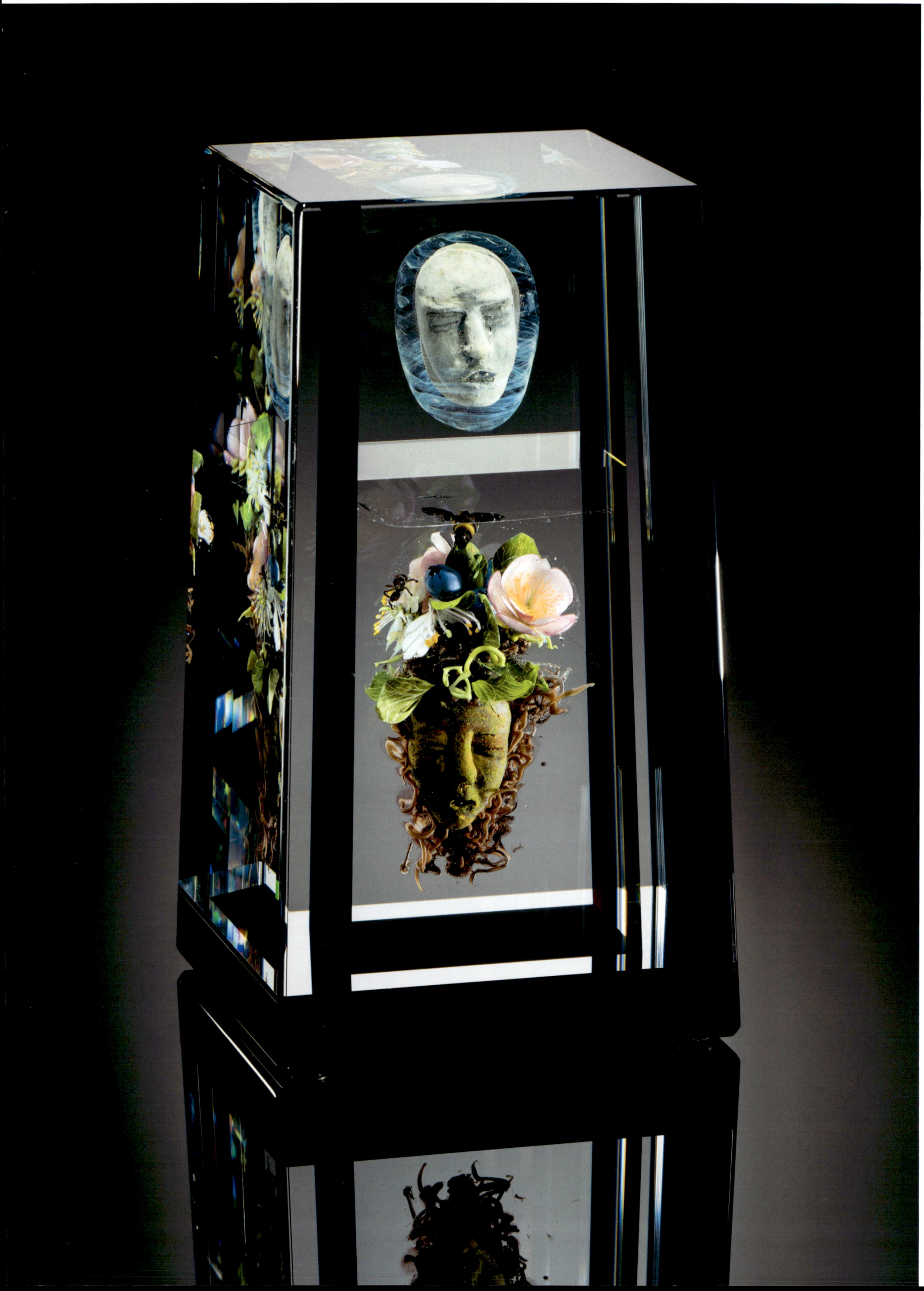

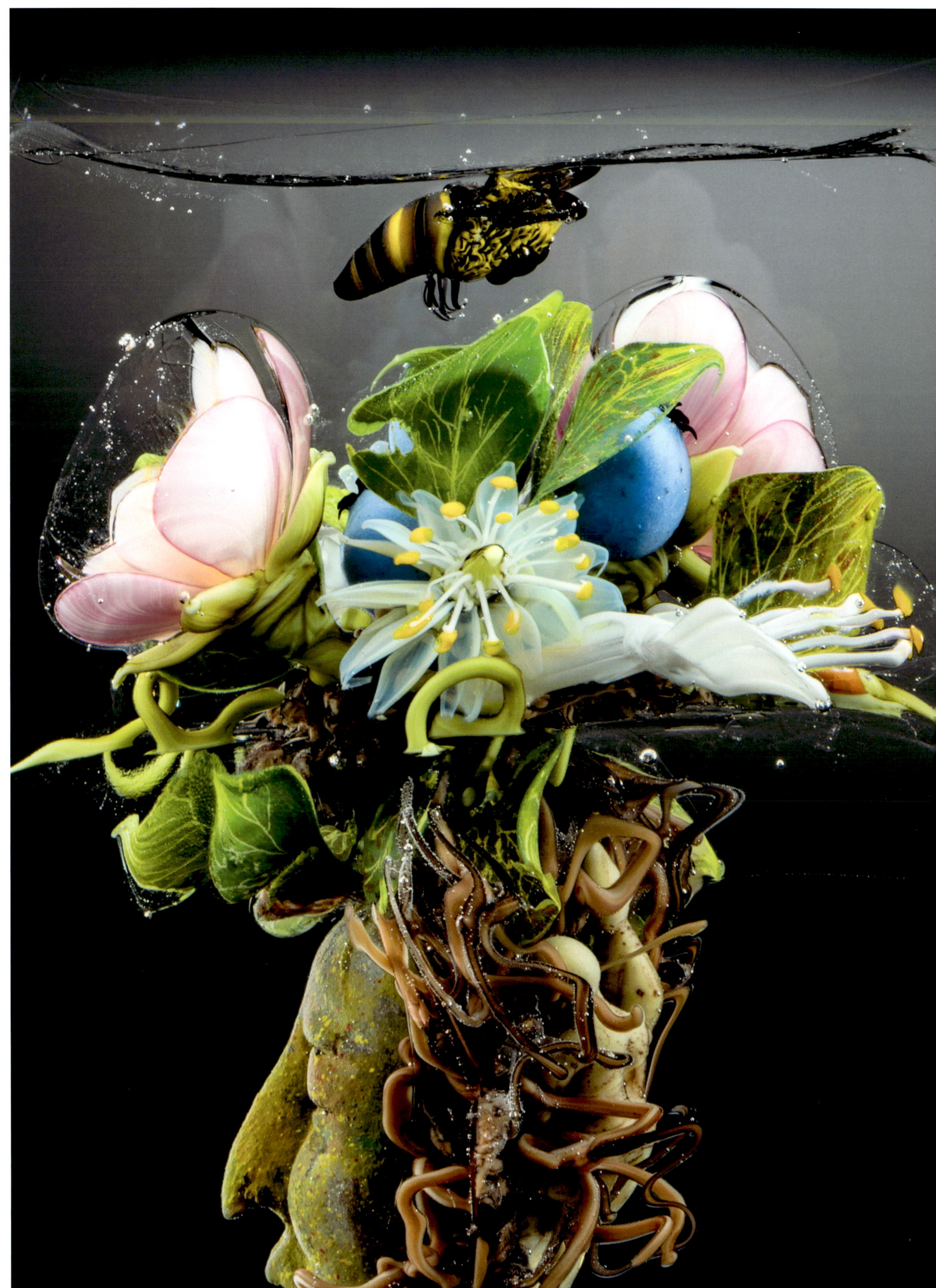

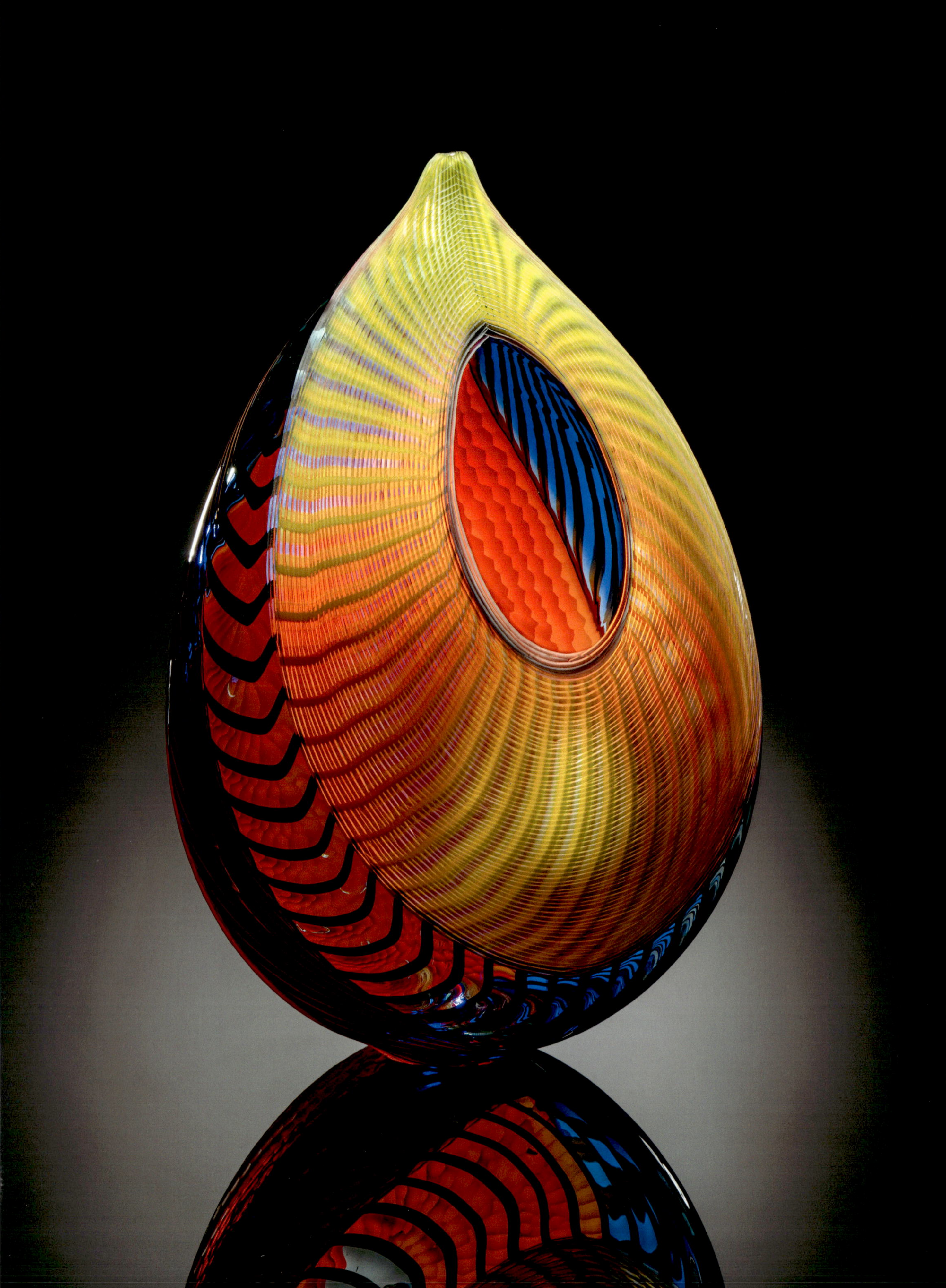

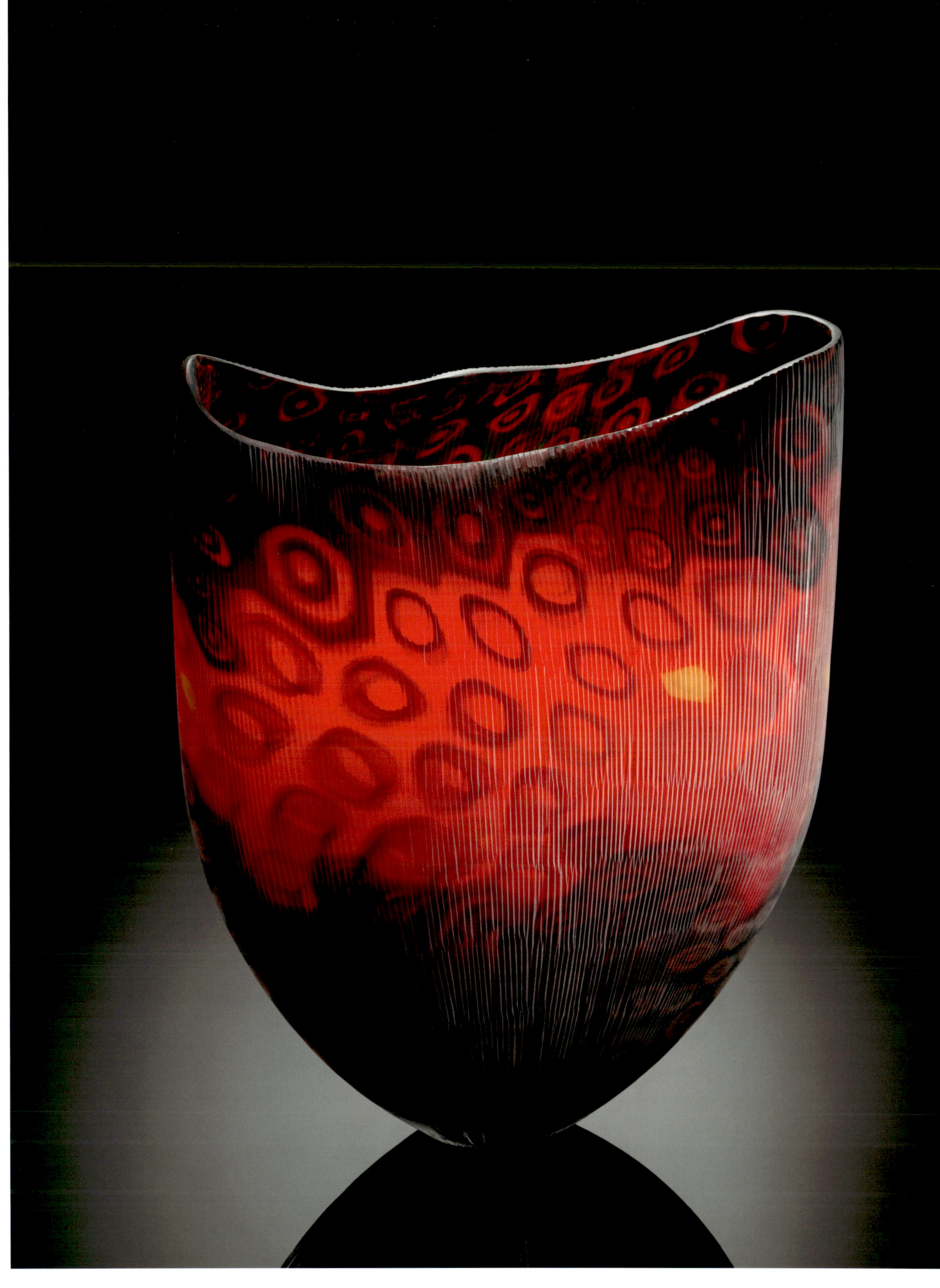

122   Lino Tagliapietra   ITALIAN, BORN 1934   *Stromboli*   2001
BLOWN AND COLD-WORKED GLASS   15 × 11½ × 7 INCHES   L2017.117

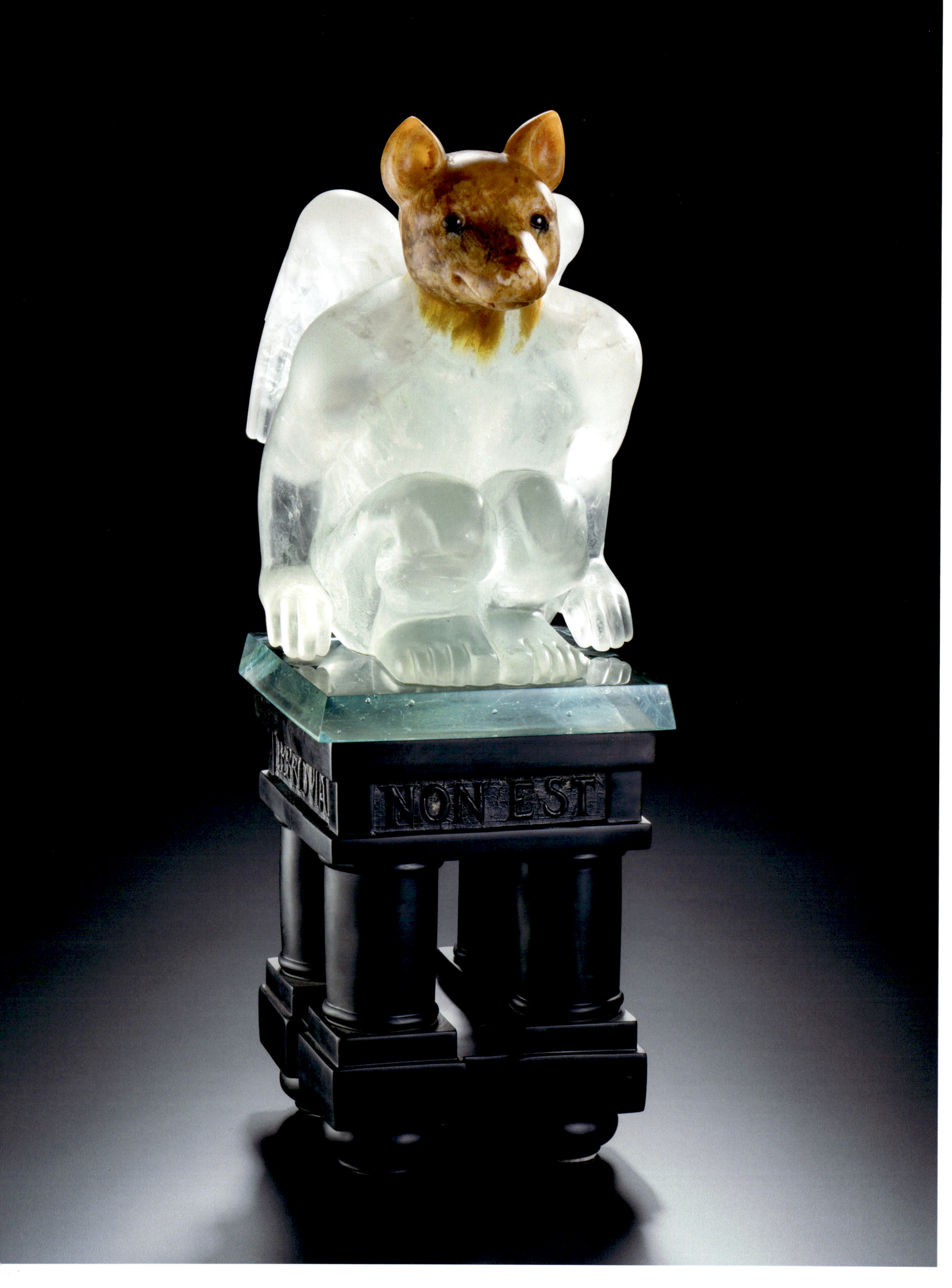

123   Margit M. Tóth   HUNGARIAN, BORN 1963   *Difficult to Reach the Heaven from the Earth*   2004
CAST GLASS   25 × 9¼ × 11¾ INCHES   L2017.118

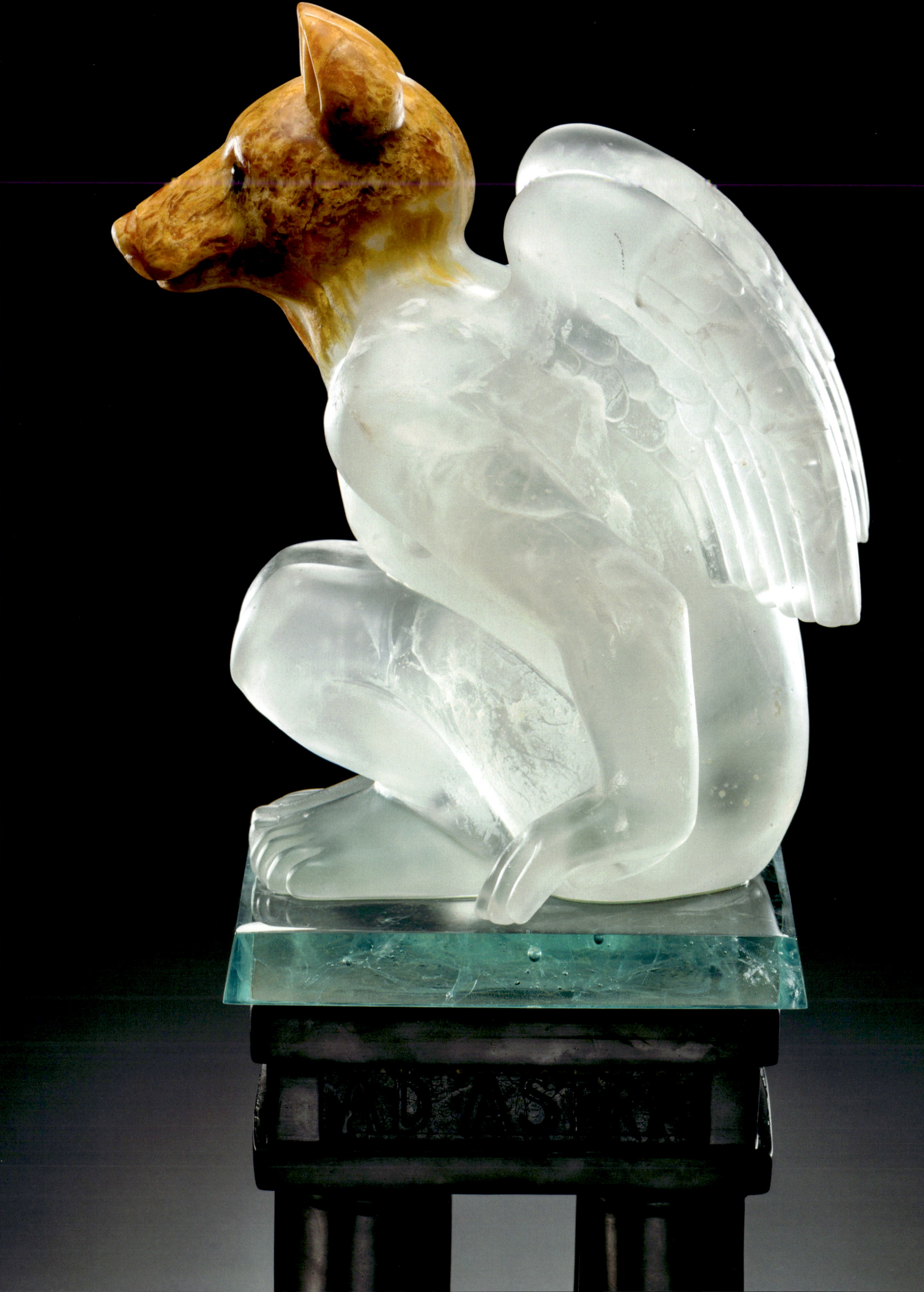

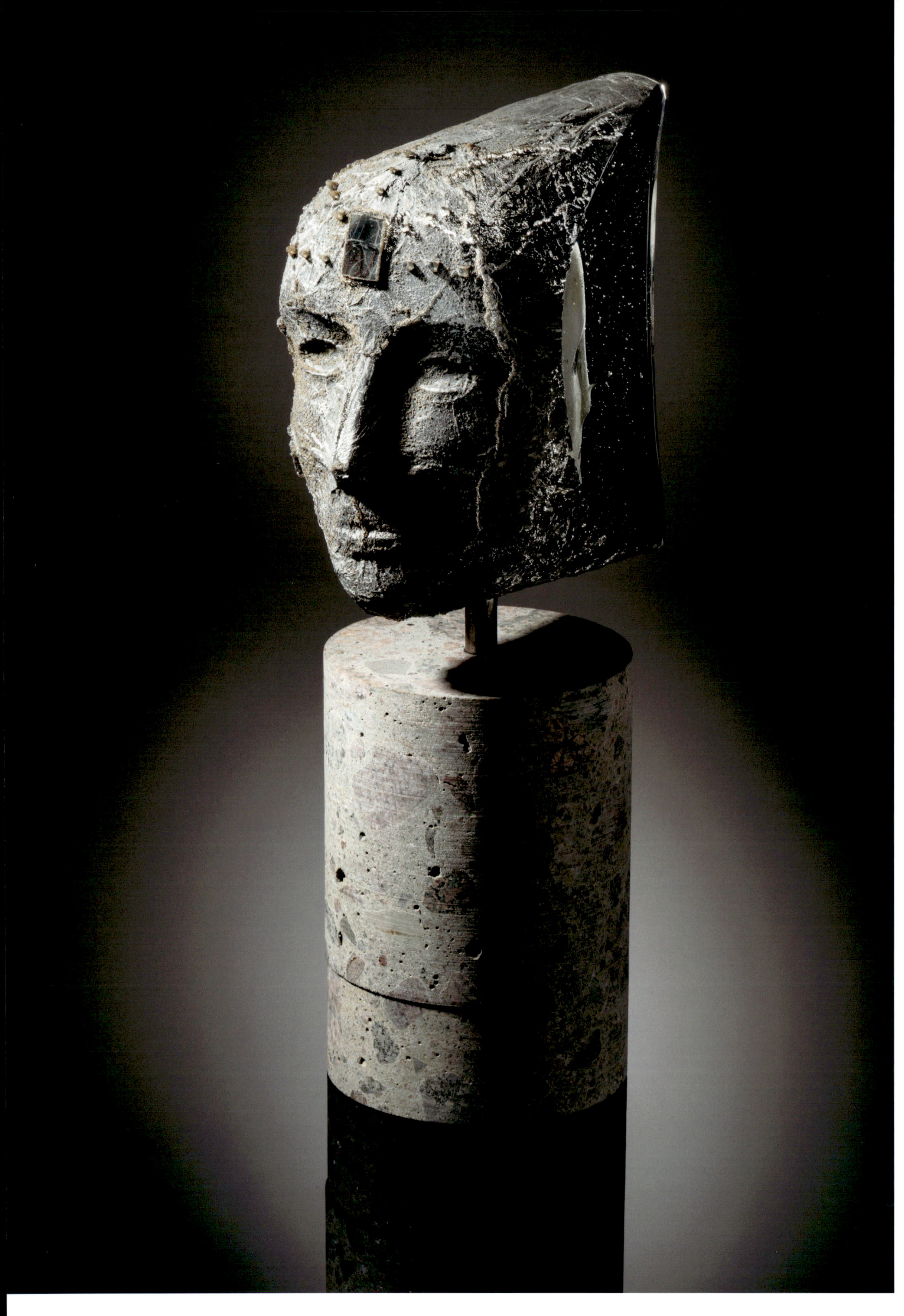

124   Bertil Vallien   SWEDISH, BORN 1938   *Janus*   1999
SANDCAST GLASS, MIXED MEDIA   17½ × 9 × 5¾ INCHES   L2017.10

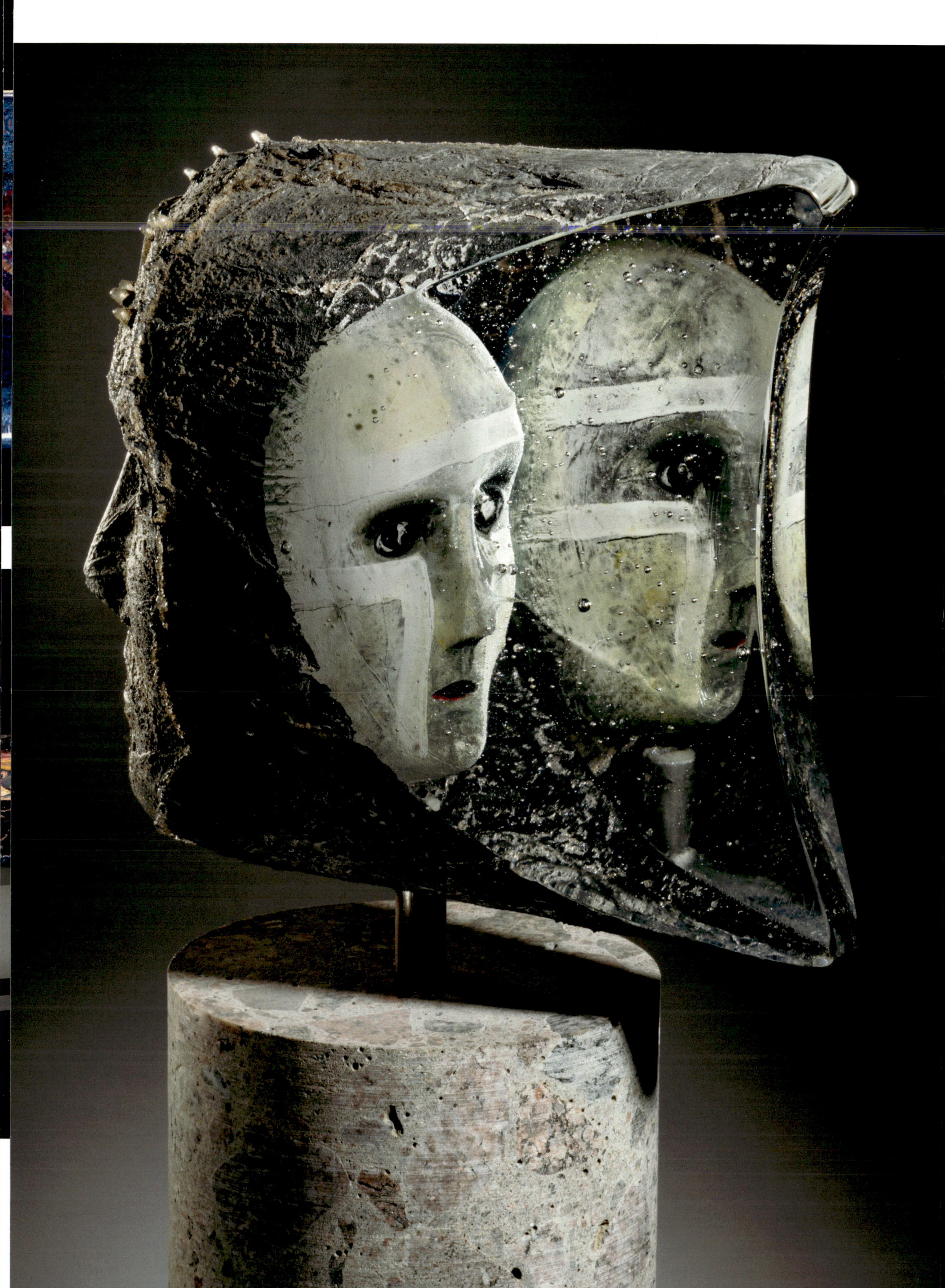

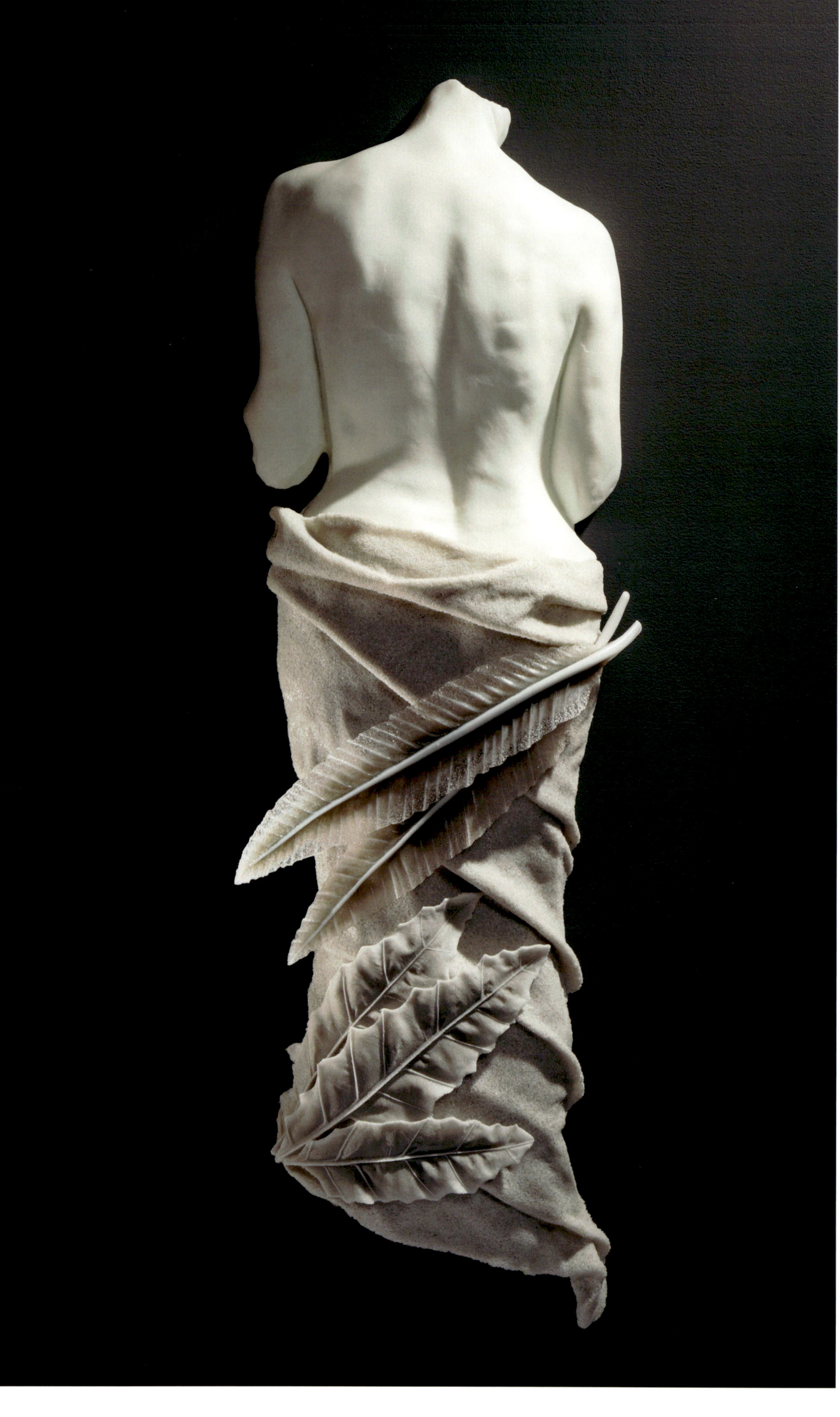

126 Mary Van Cline   AMERICAN, BORN 1954   *Ivory Figure* 2007
PÂTE DE VERRE   54½ × 19 × 9 INCHES   L2017.119

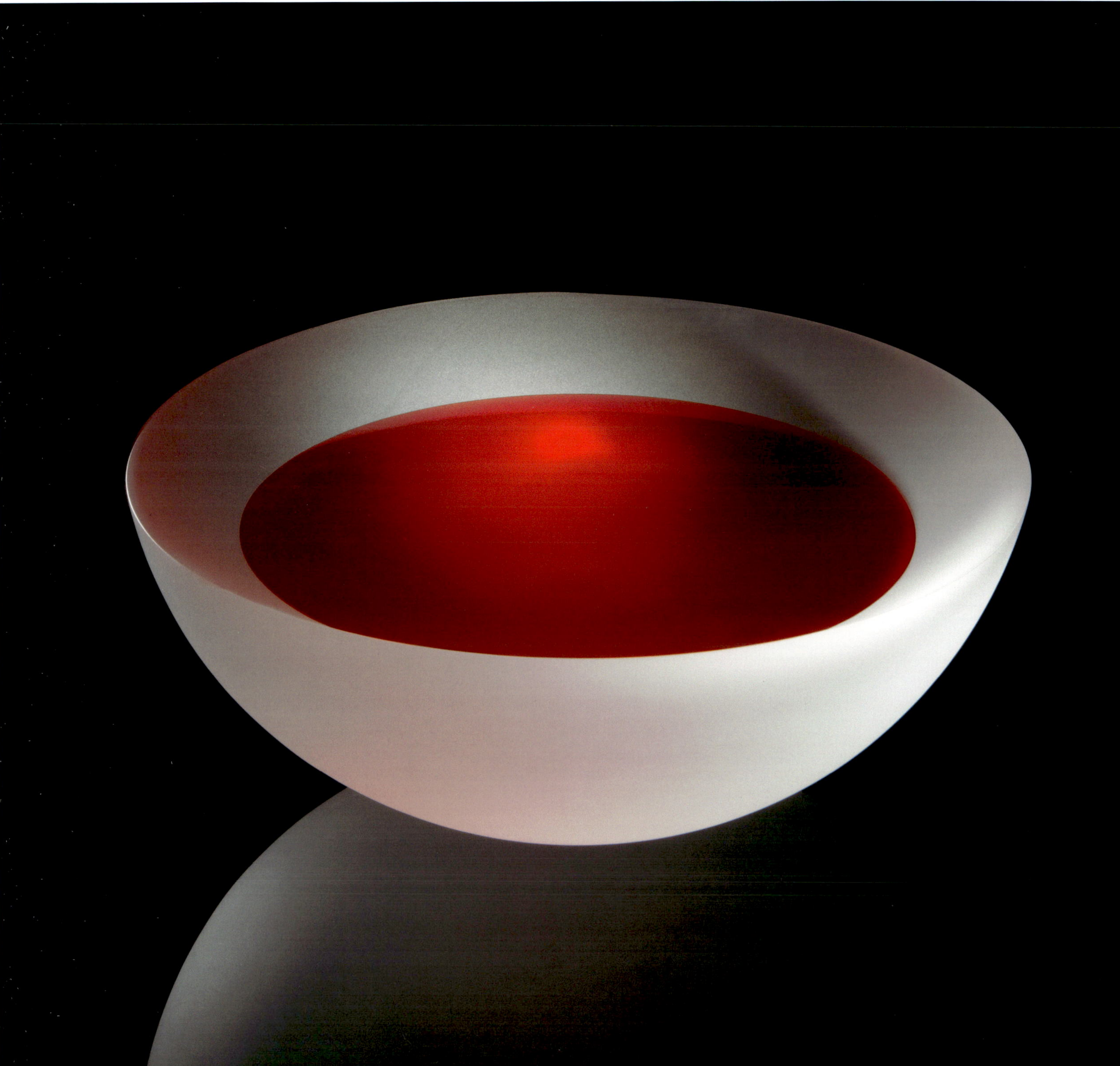

127   František Vízner   CZECH, 1936–2011   *Bowl with Circular Insert*   2007
CUT AND ACID-POLISHED GLASS   4¾ × 12¼ INCHES   L2017.41

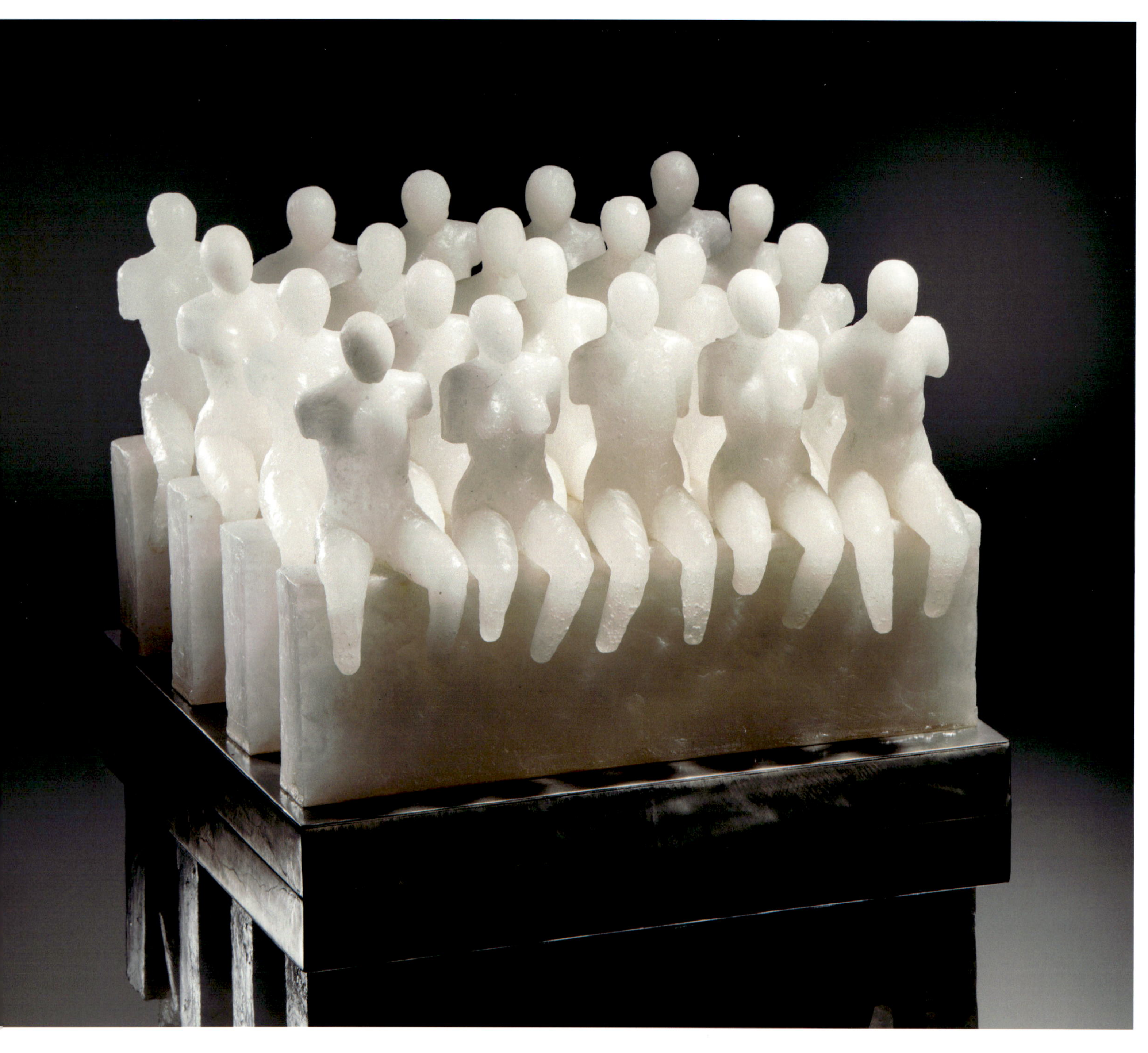

128 Janusz Walentynowicz POLISH, BORN 1956 *Next* 1999
CAST GLASS, MIXED MEDIA 16 × 22 × 21 INCHES L2017.127

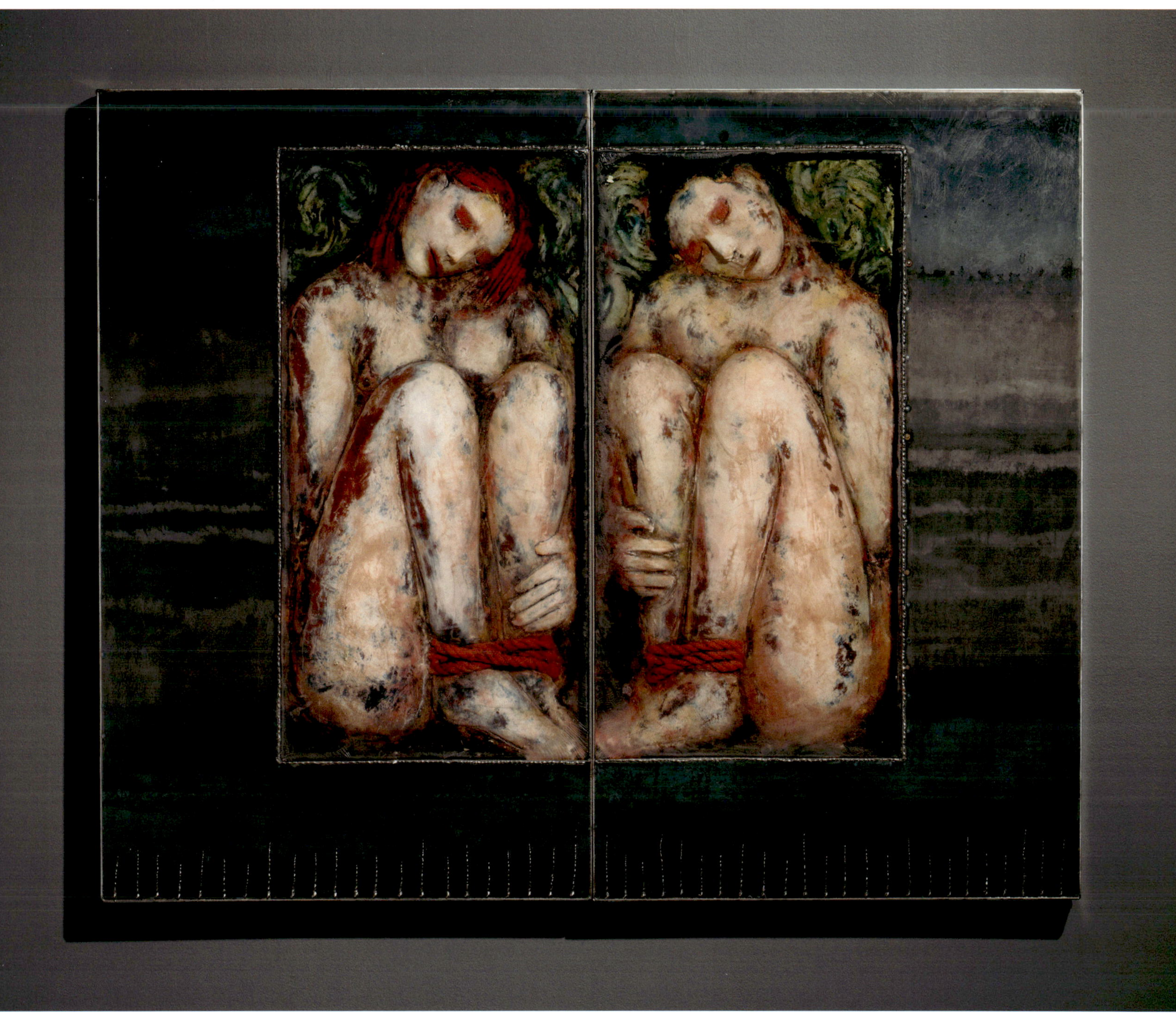

129   Janusz Walentynowicz   POLISH, BORN 1956   *Waiters*   2006
CAST AND REVERSE-PAINTED GLASS, STEEL   48¼ × 60½ × 2½ INCHES   L2017.128

   Steven Weinberg   AMERICAN, BORN 1954   *Fluted Concentrics*   1995
CAST AND CUT OPTICAL CRYSTAL $7\frac{3}{4} \times 7\frac{13}{16} \times 7\frac{13}{16}$ INCHES   L2017.129

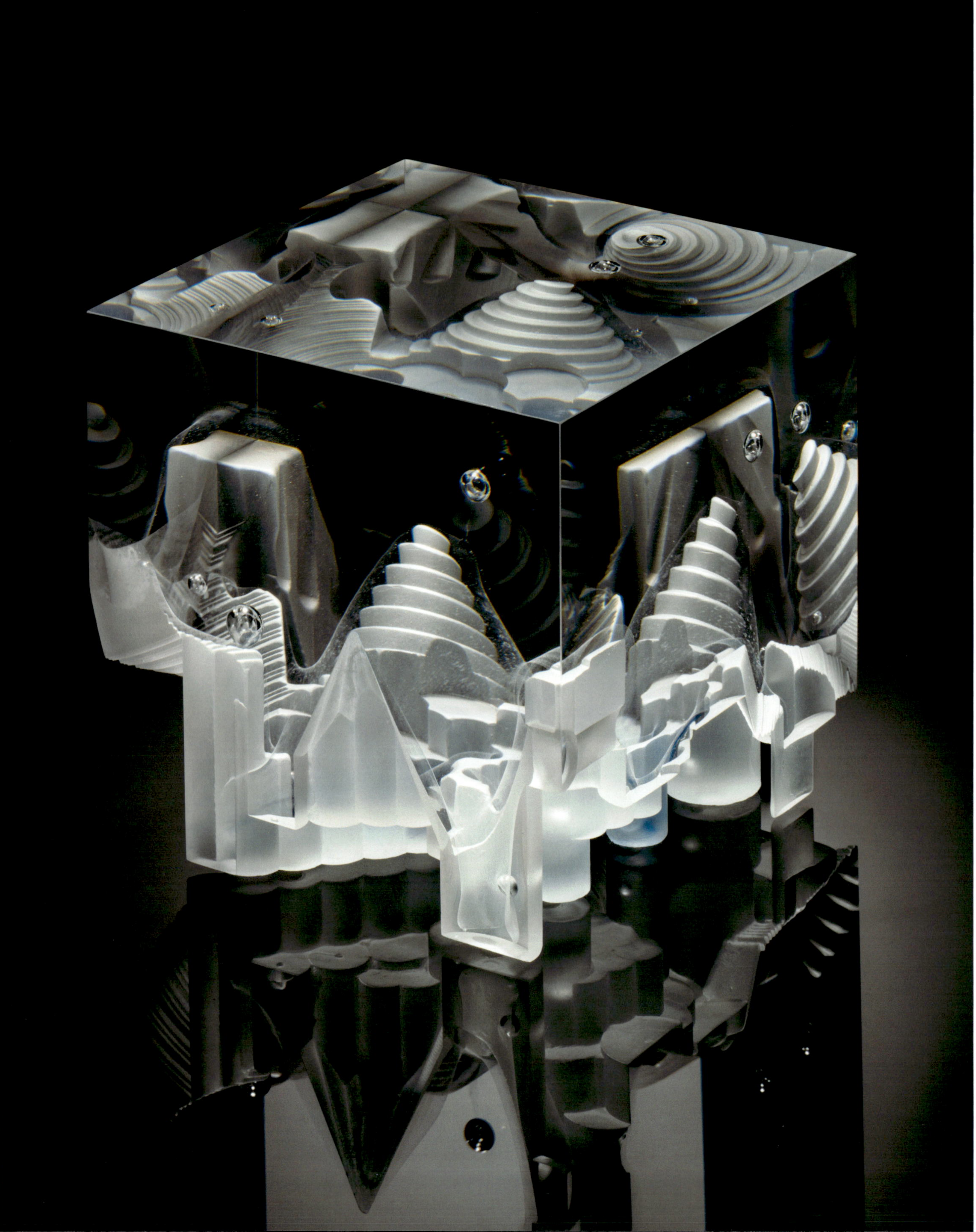

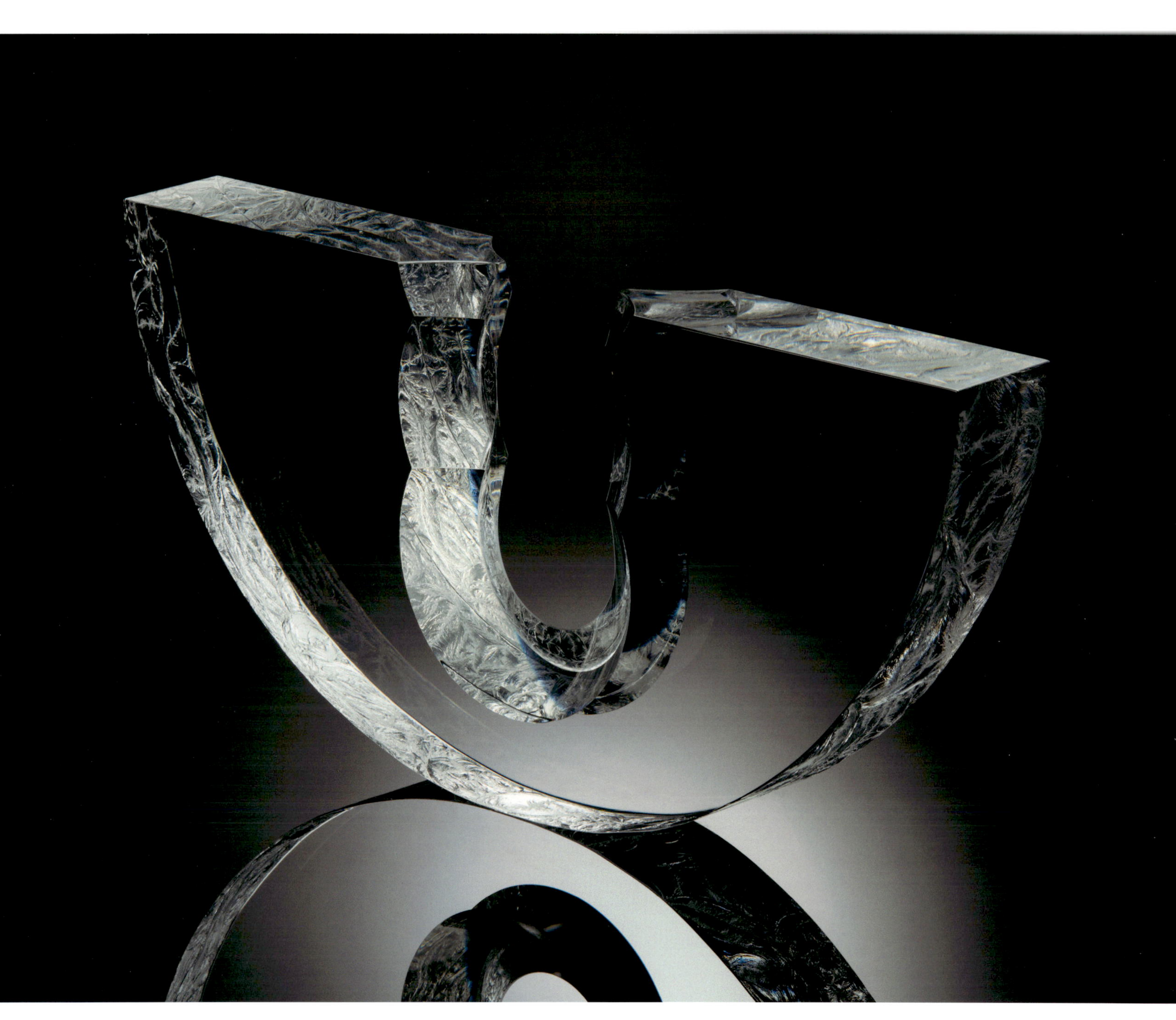

131　Steven Weinberg　AMERICAN, BORN 1954　*Moon Tide Boat*　2002
CAST, CUT, AND POLISHED CRYSTAL　11 × 22¾ × 3 INCHES　L2017.130

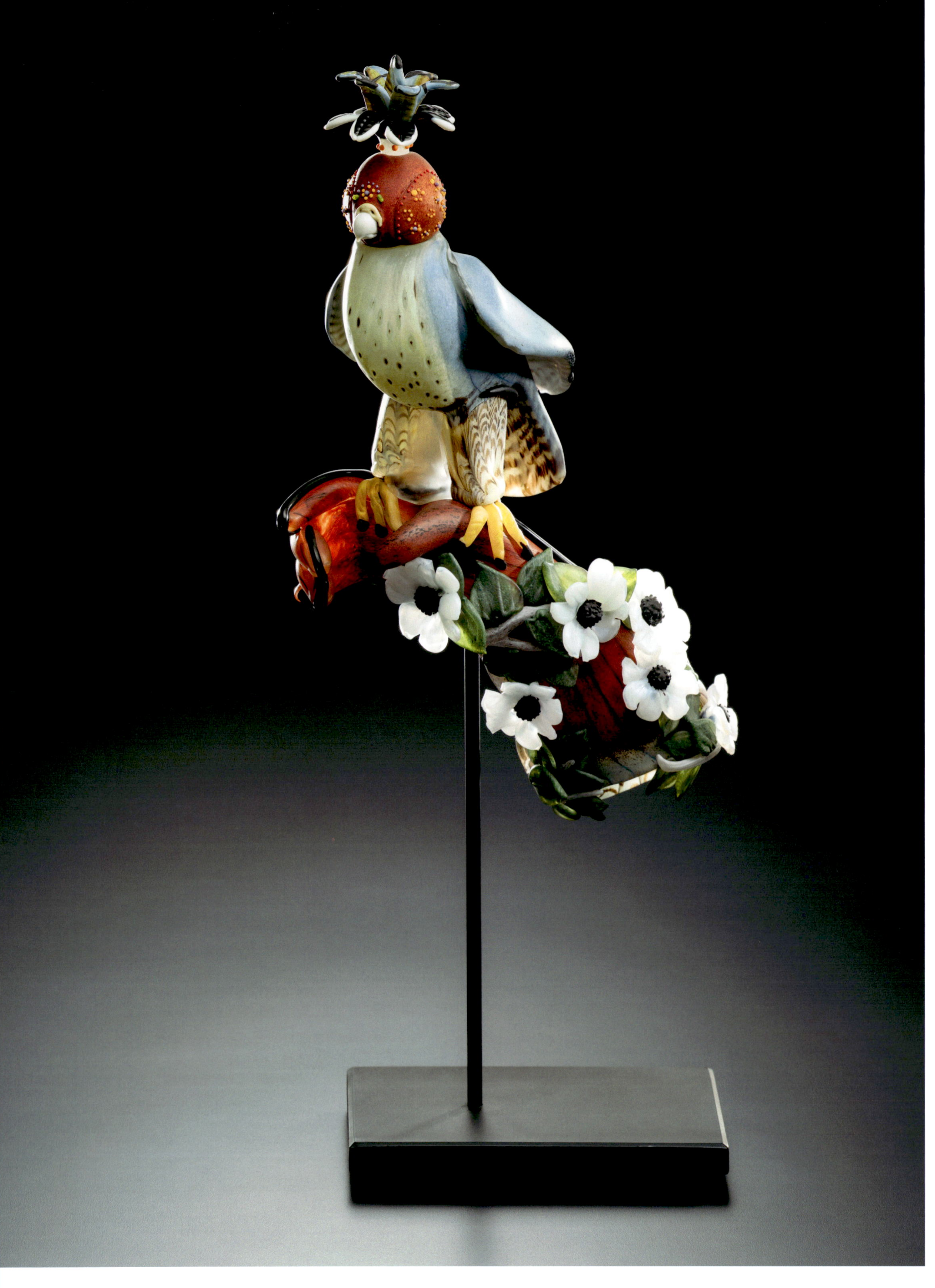

132   Karen Willenbrink-Johnsen   AMERICAN, BORN 1960   *Dogwood Falcon*   2004
BLOWN AND SCULPTED GLASS, STEEL STAND   23¼ × 10 × 7 INCHES   L2017.133

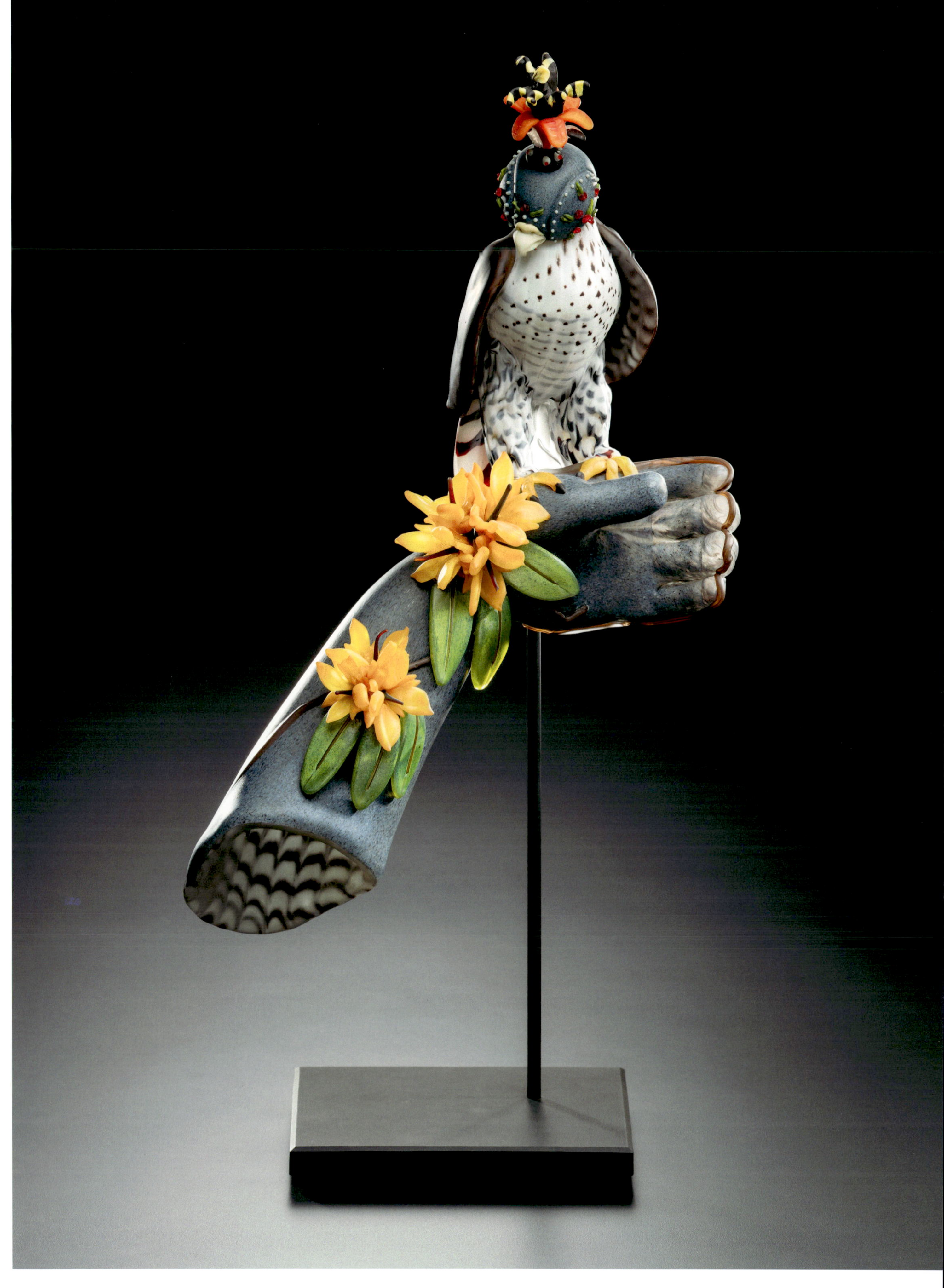

133   Karen Willenbrink-Johnsen   AMERICAN, BORN 1960   *Plum Falcon*   2004
BLOWN AND SCULPTED GLASS, STEEL STAND   25⅛ × 10⅜ × 9⅞ INCHES   L2017.131

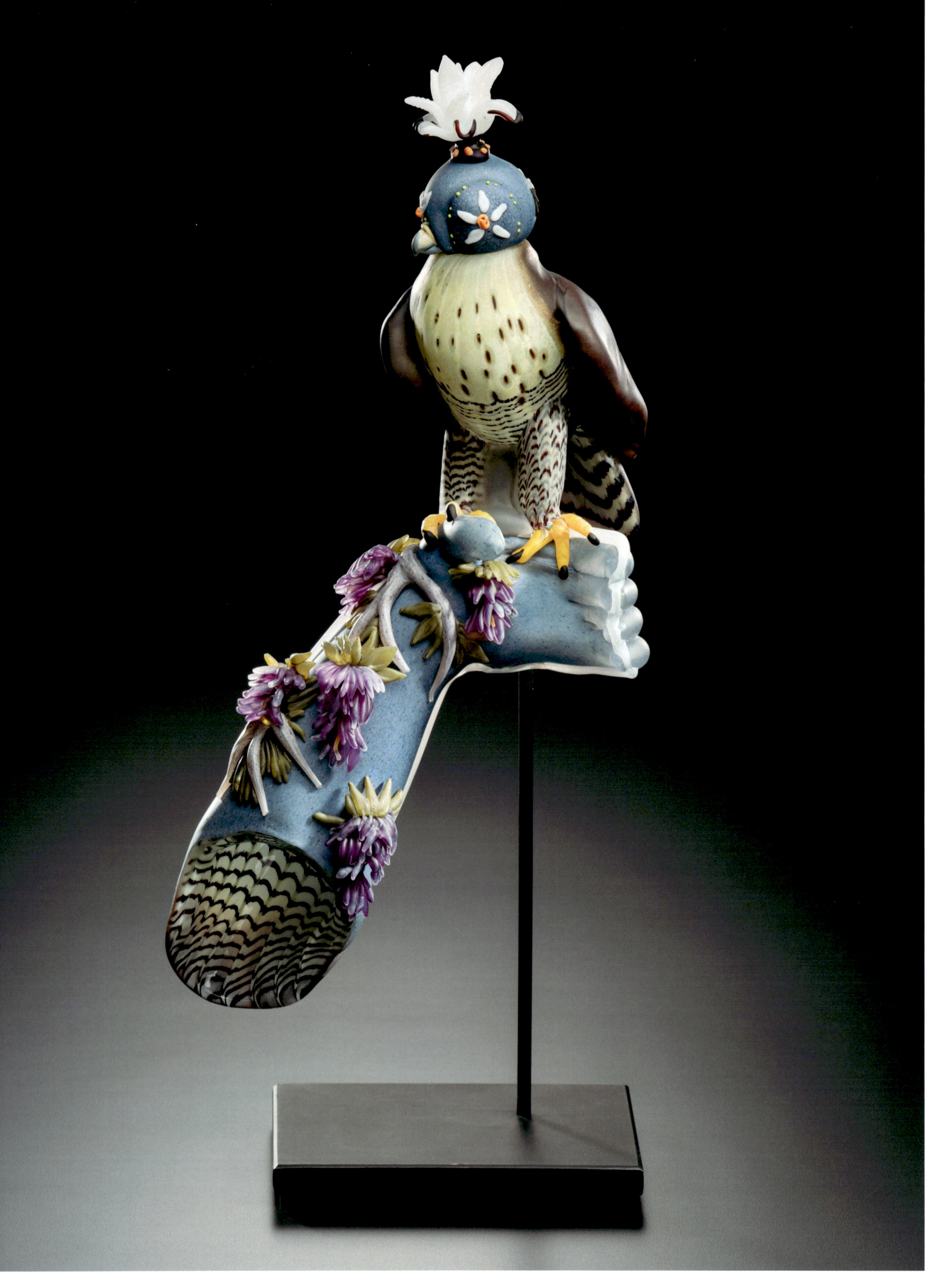

134 Karen Willenbrink-Johnsen AMERICAN, BORN 1960 *Rhododendron Falcon* 2004
BLOWN AND SCULPTED GLASS, STEEL STAND 24¼ × 10⁵⁄₁₆ × 8½ INCHES L2017.135

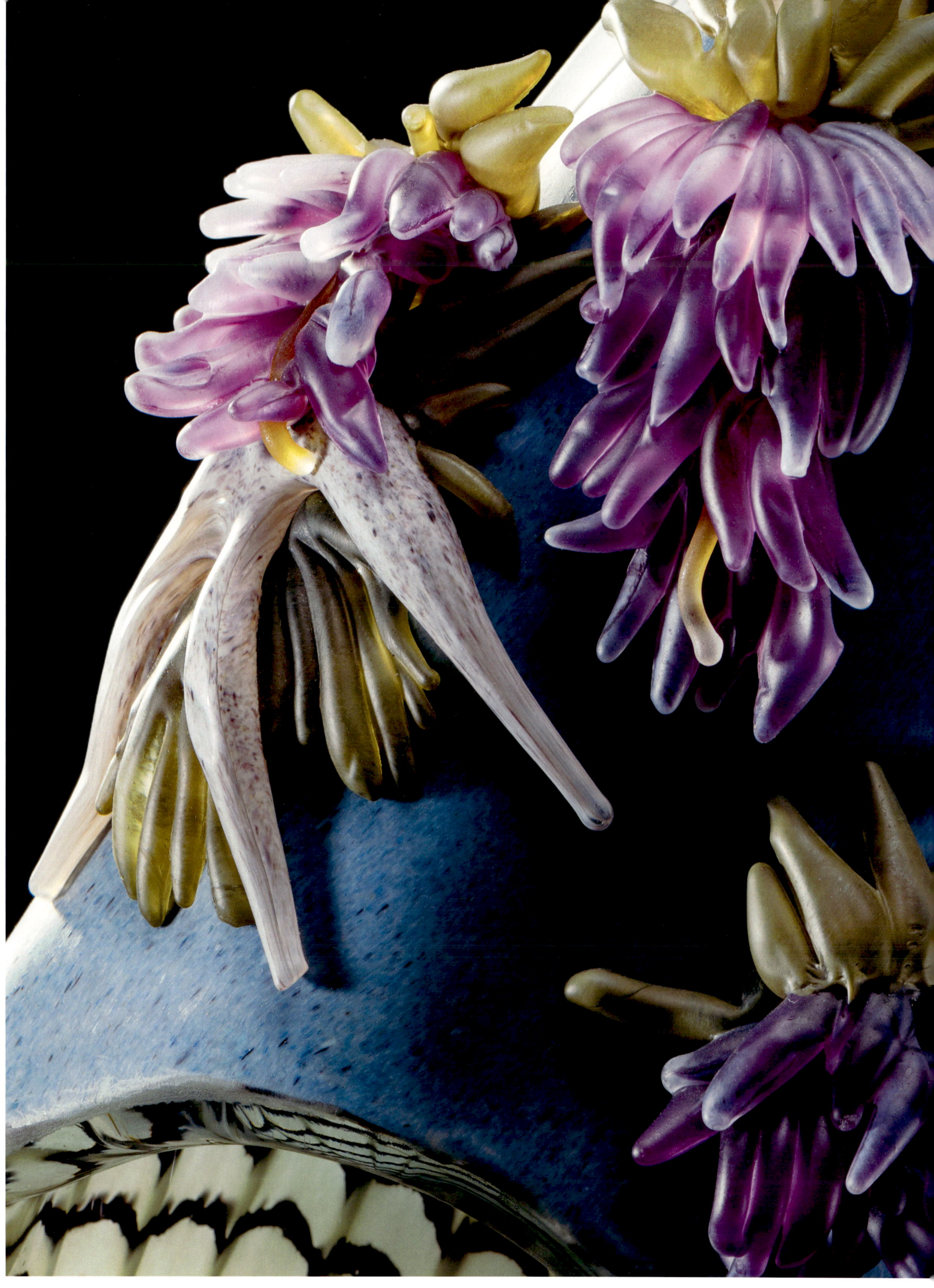

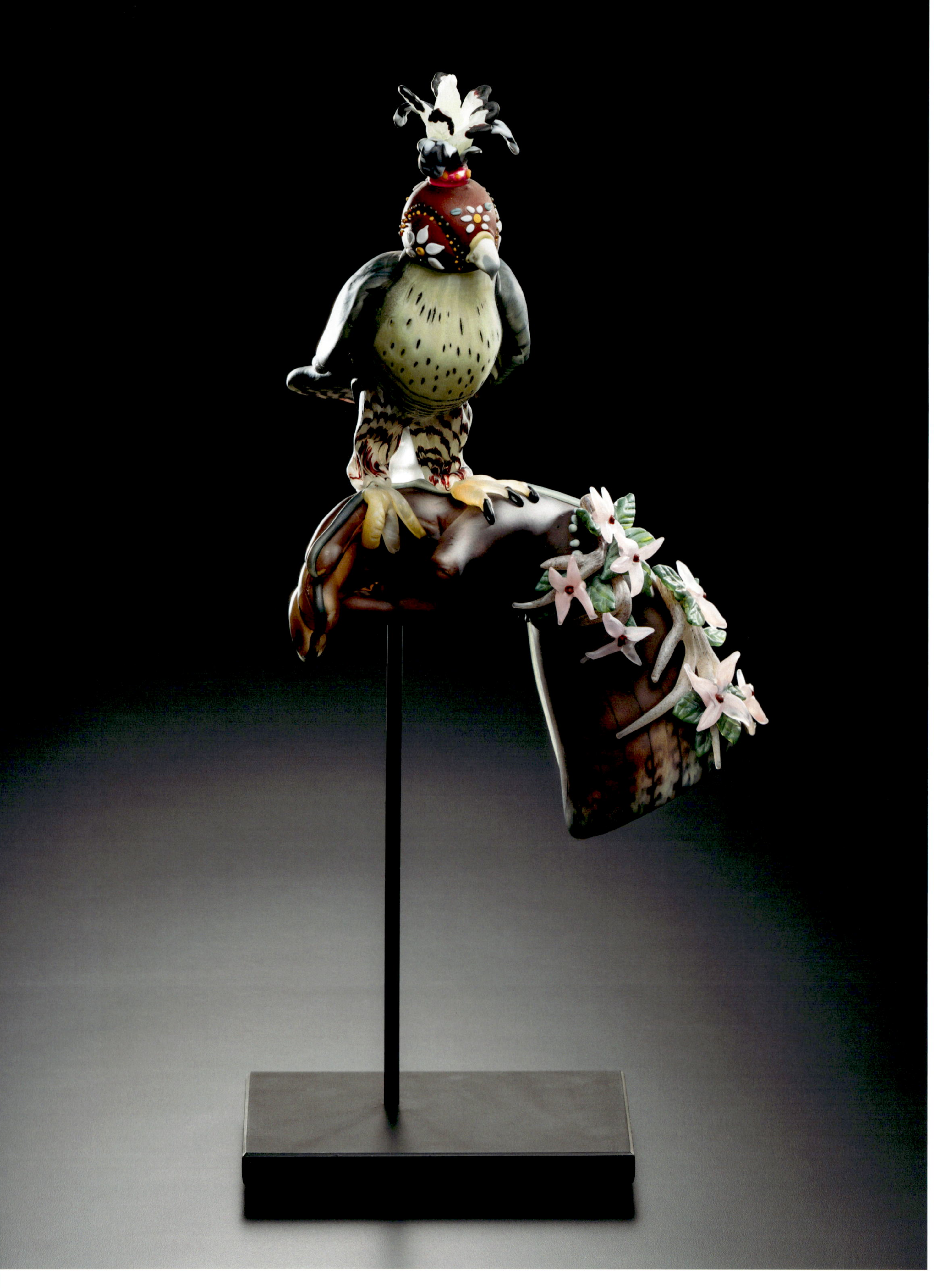

135   Karen Willenbrink-Johnsen   AMERICAN, BORN 1960   *Wisteria Falcon*   2004
BLOWN AND SCULPTED GLASS, STEEL STAND   22⅛ × 10¼ × 7 INCHES   L2017.134

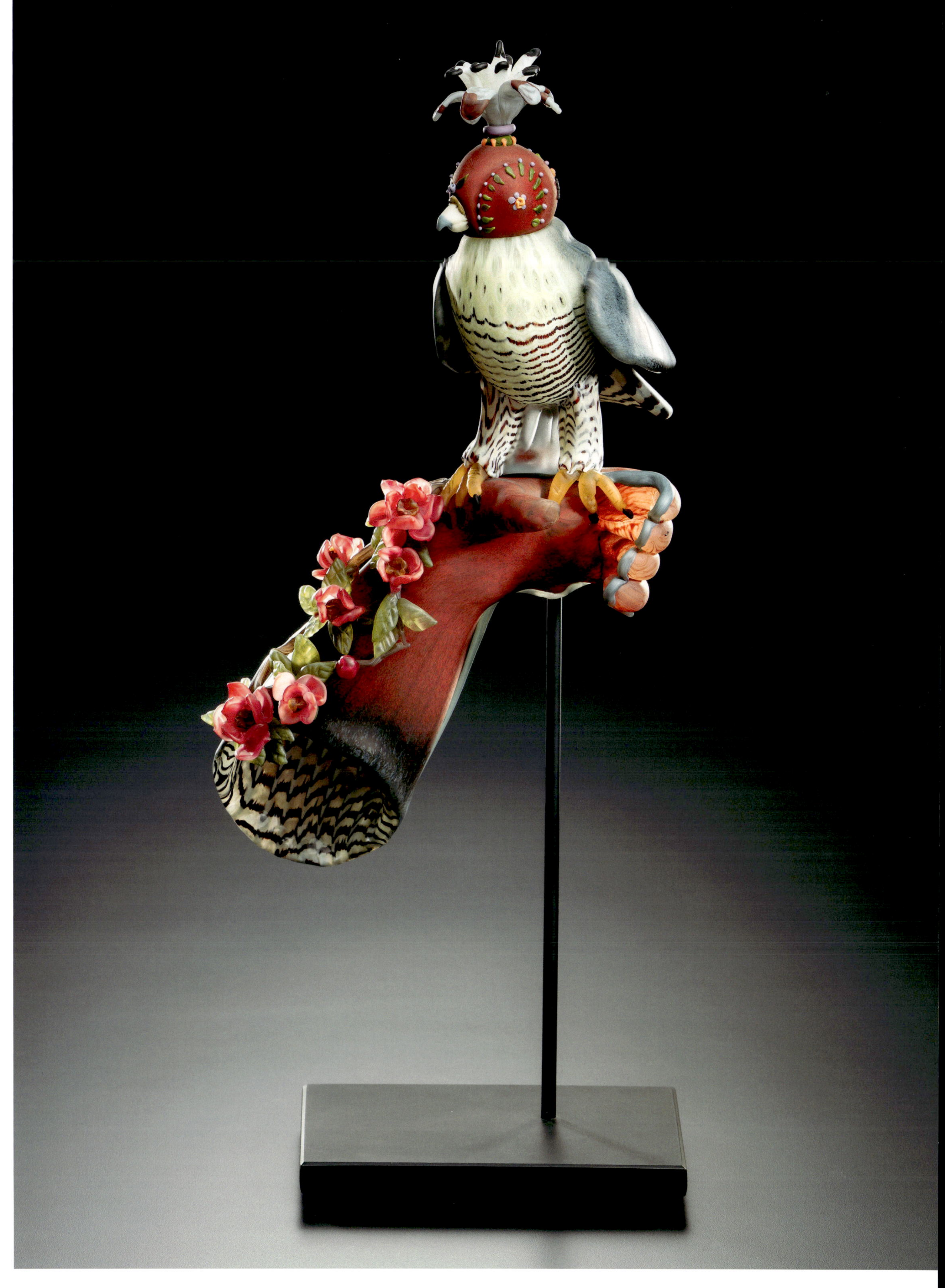

136   Karen Willenbrink-Johnsen   AMERICAN, BORN 1960   *Quince Falcon*   2004
BLOWN AND SCULPTED GLASS, STEEL STAND   23½ × 9⅞ × 7⅞ INCHES   L2017.132

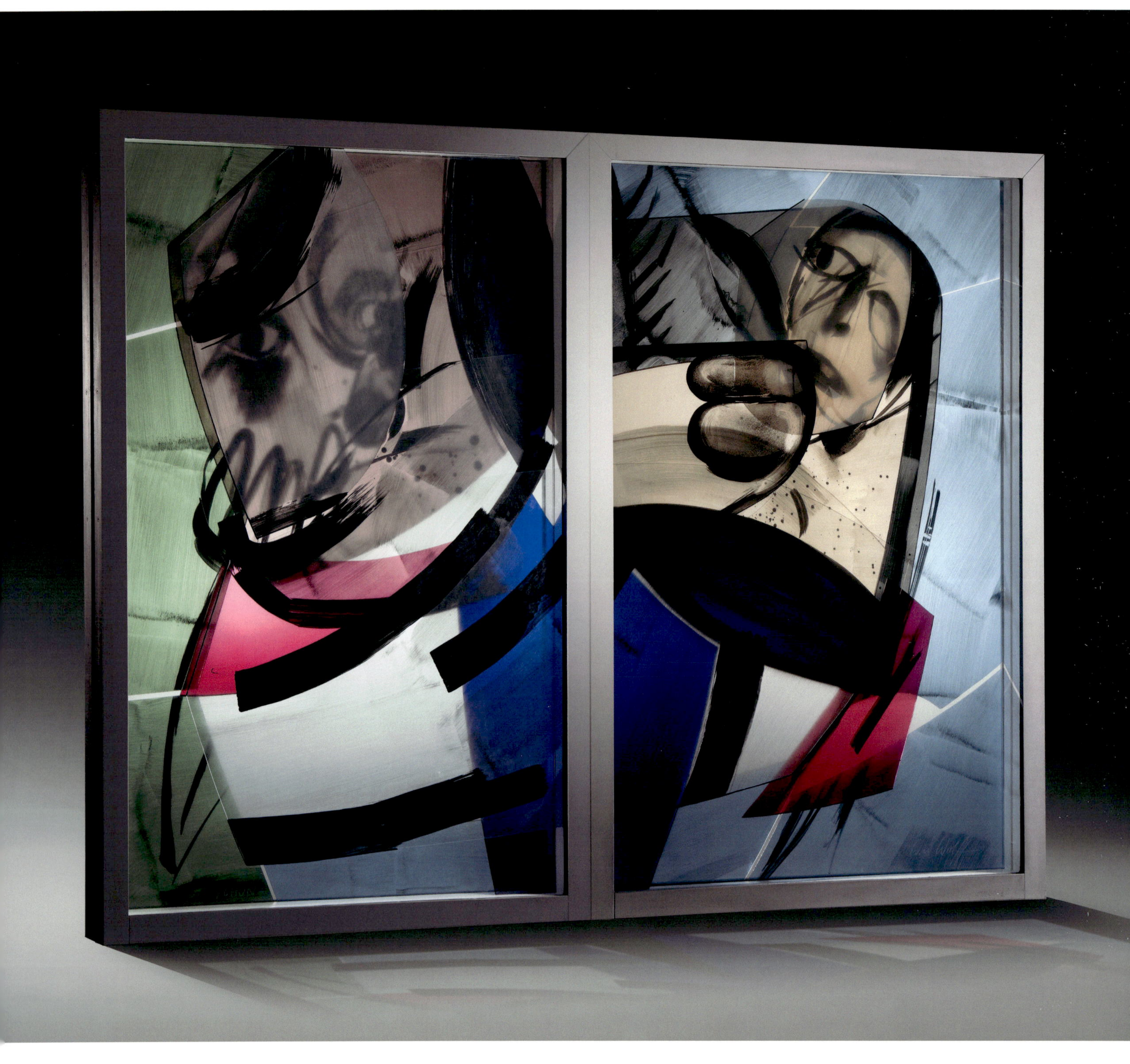

137   Ann Wolff   SWEDISH/GERMAN, BORN 1937   *Berlin Double*   2003
PAINTED AND ASSEMBLED PLATE GLASS, STEEL FRAME   70⅞ × 94½ × 5¾ INCHES   L2017.8

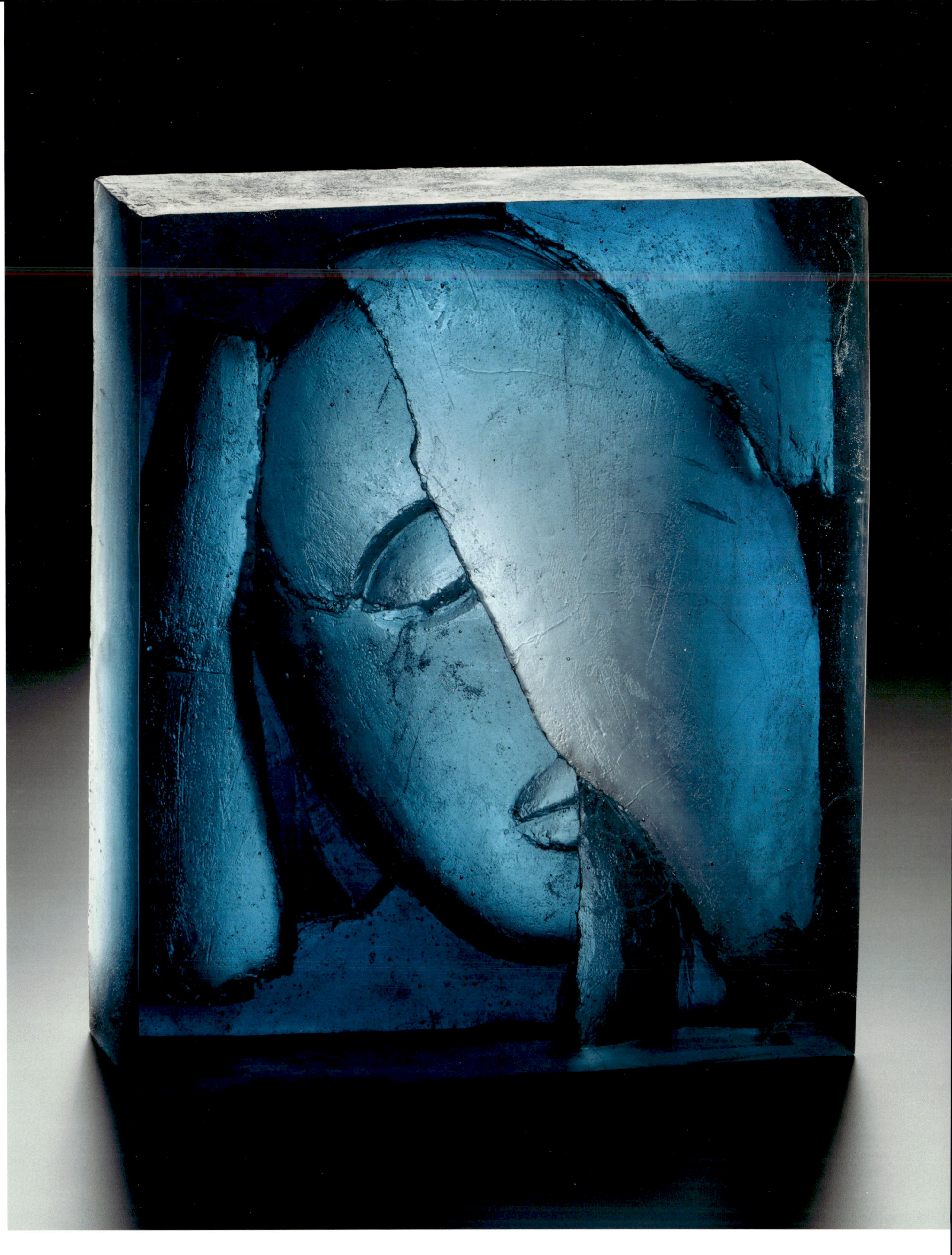

138   Ann Wolff   SWEDISH/GERMAN, BORN 1937   *Blues*   2005
CAST AND POLISHED GLASS   22¹³⁄₁₆ × 19¾ × 7¹¹⁄₁₆ INCHES   L2017.9

139   Loretta Hui-shan Yang   TAIWANESE, BORN 1952   *Proof of Awareness*   2009
PÂTE DE VERRE   13 × 26 × 30 INCHES   L2017.81

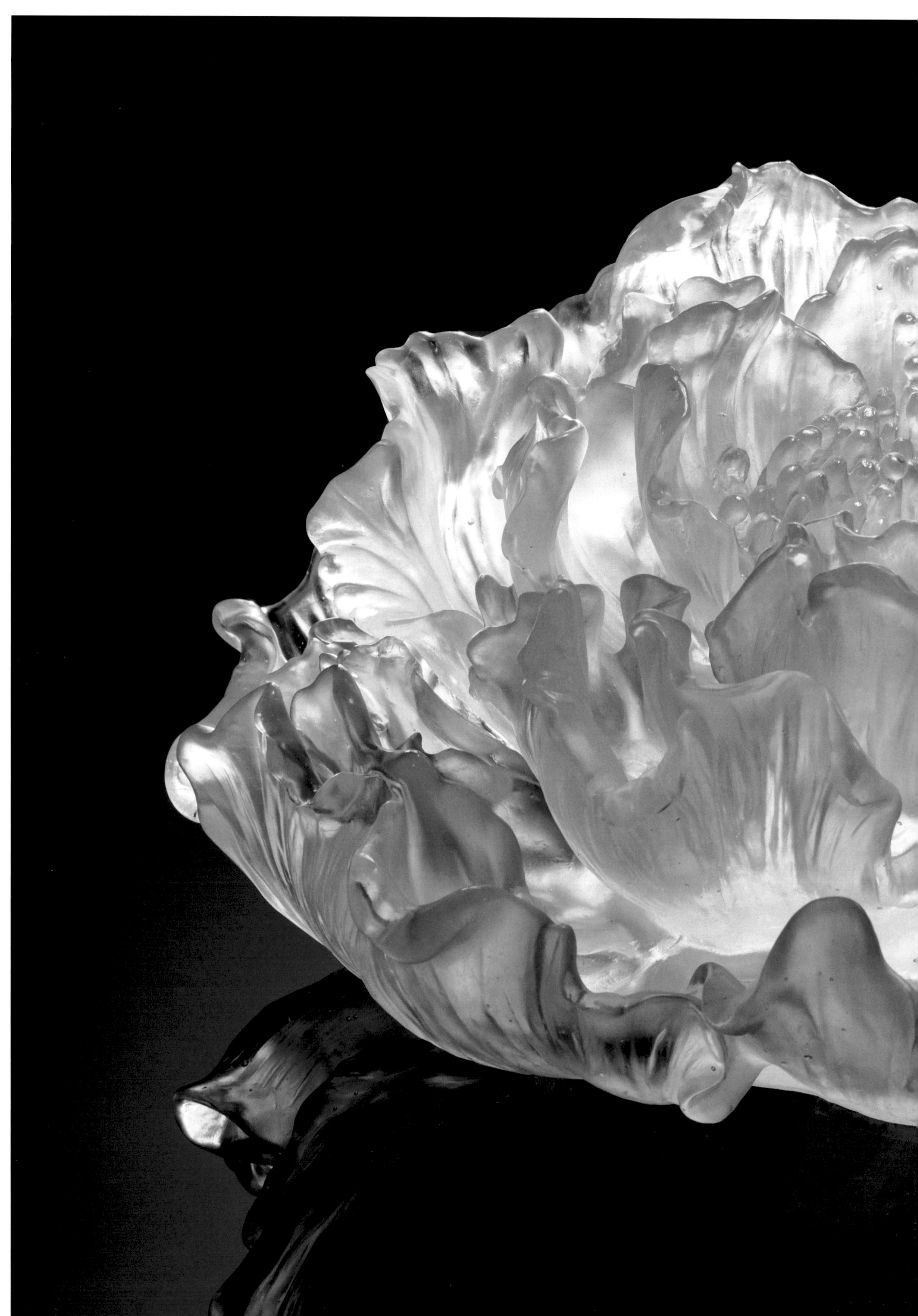

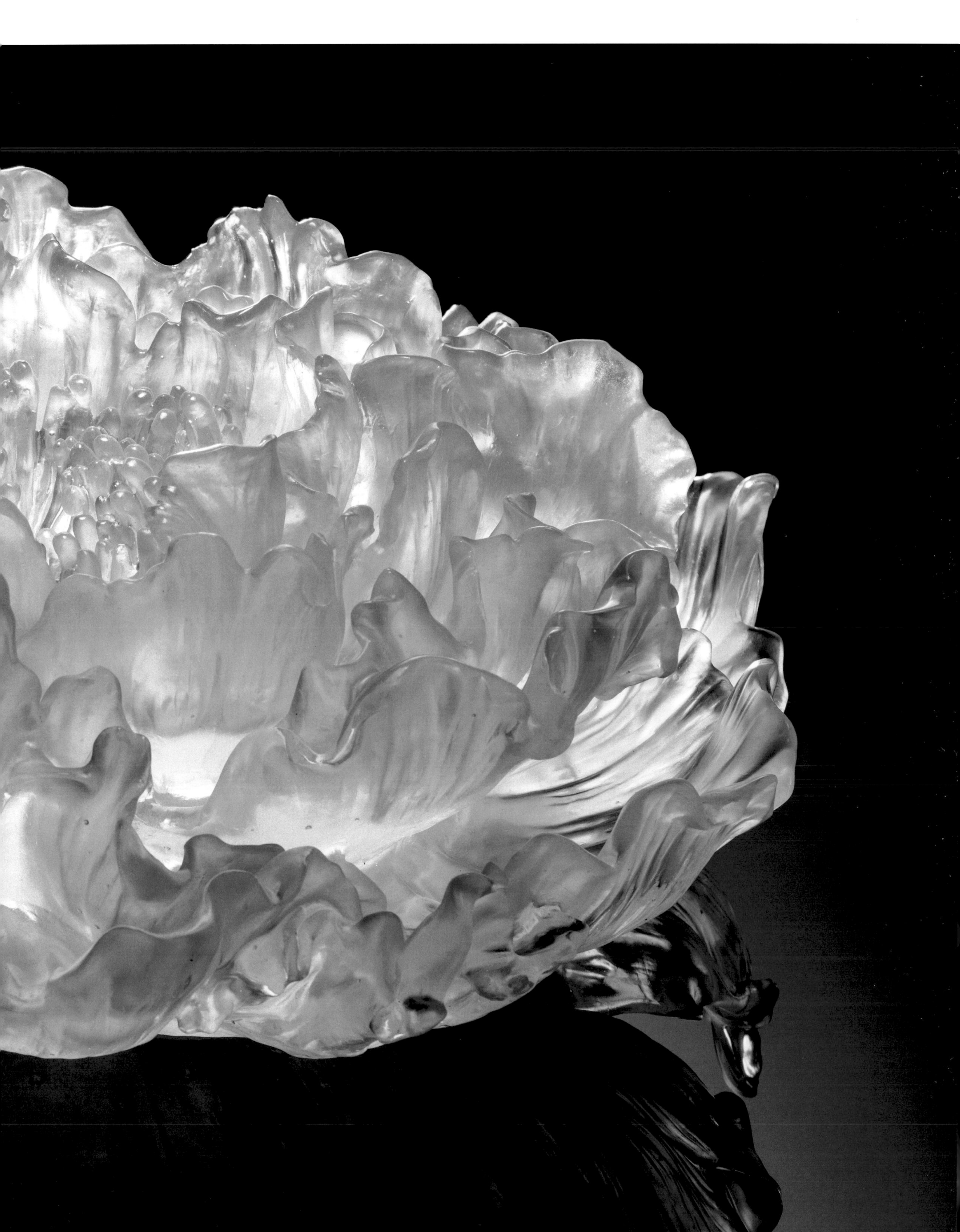

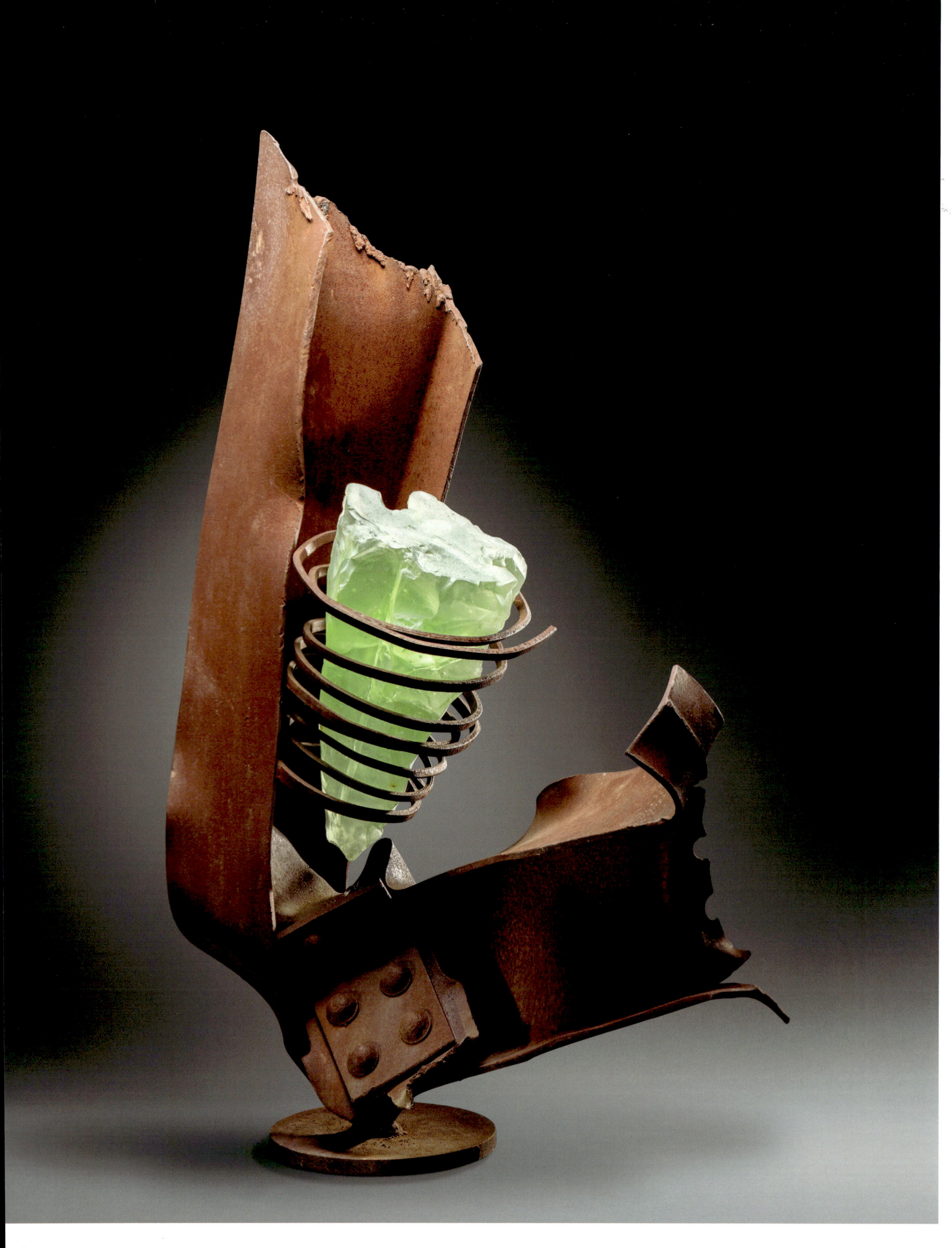

140   Albert Young   AMERICAN, BORN 1951   *Ulysses*   2000
CAST GLASS, WELDED STEEL   49¾ × 34½ × 18 INCHES   L2017.6

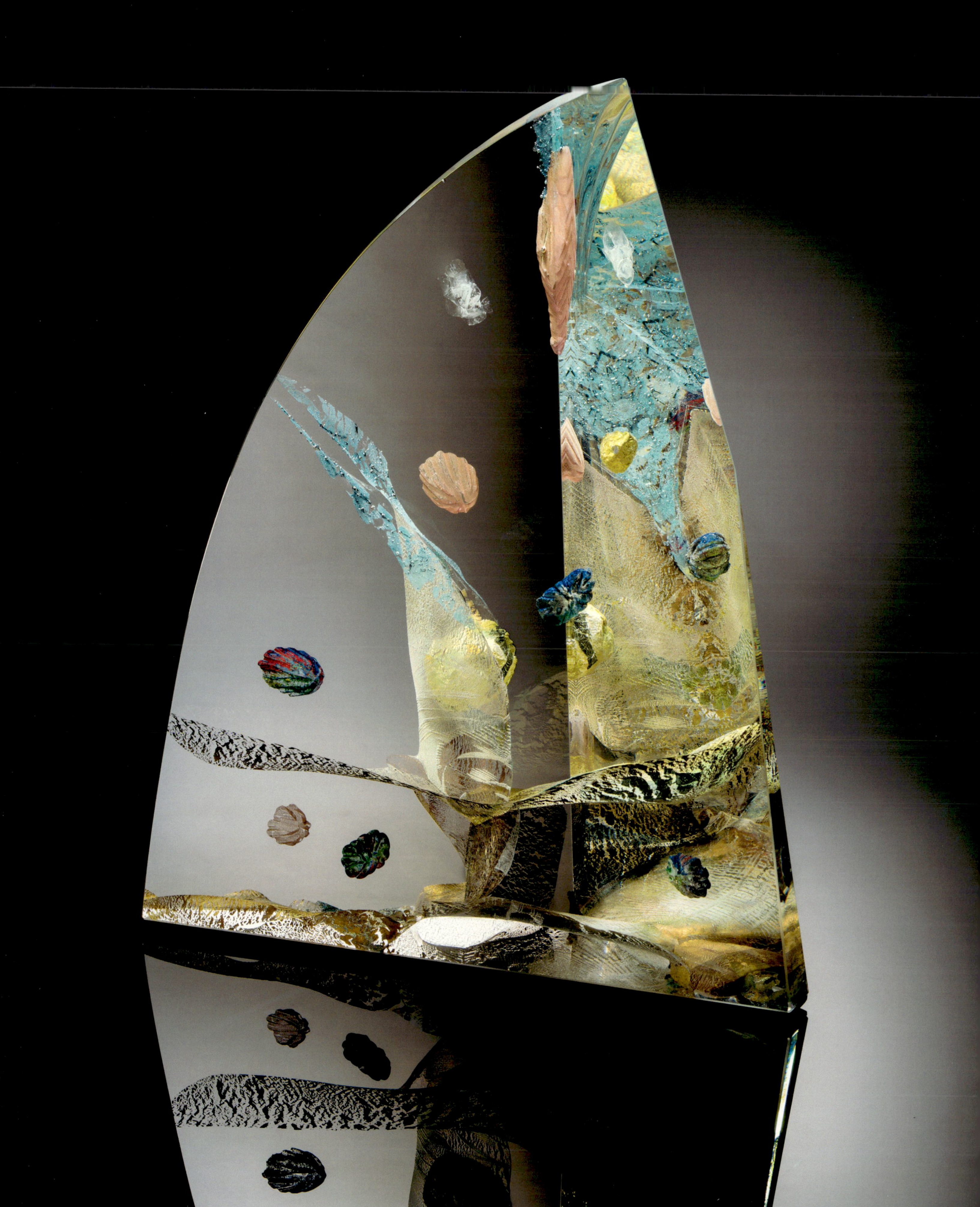

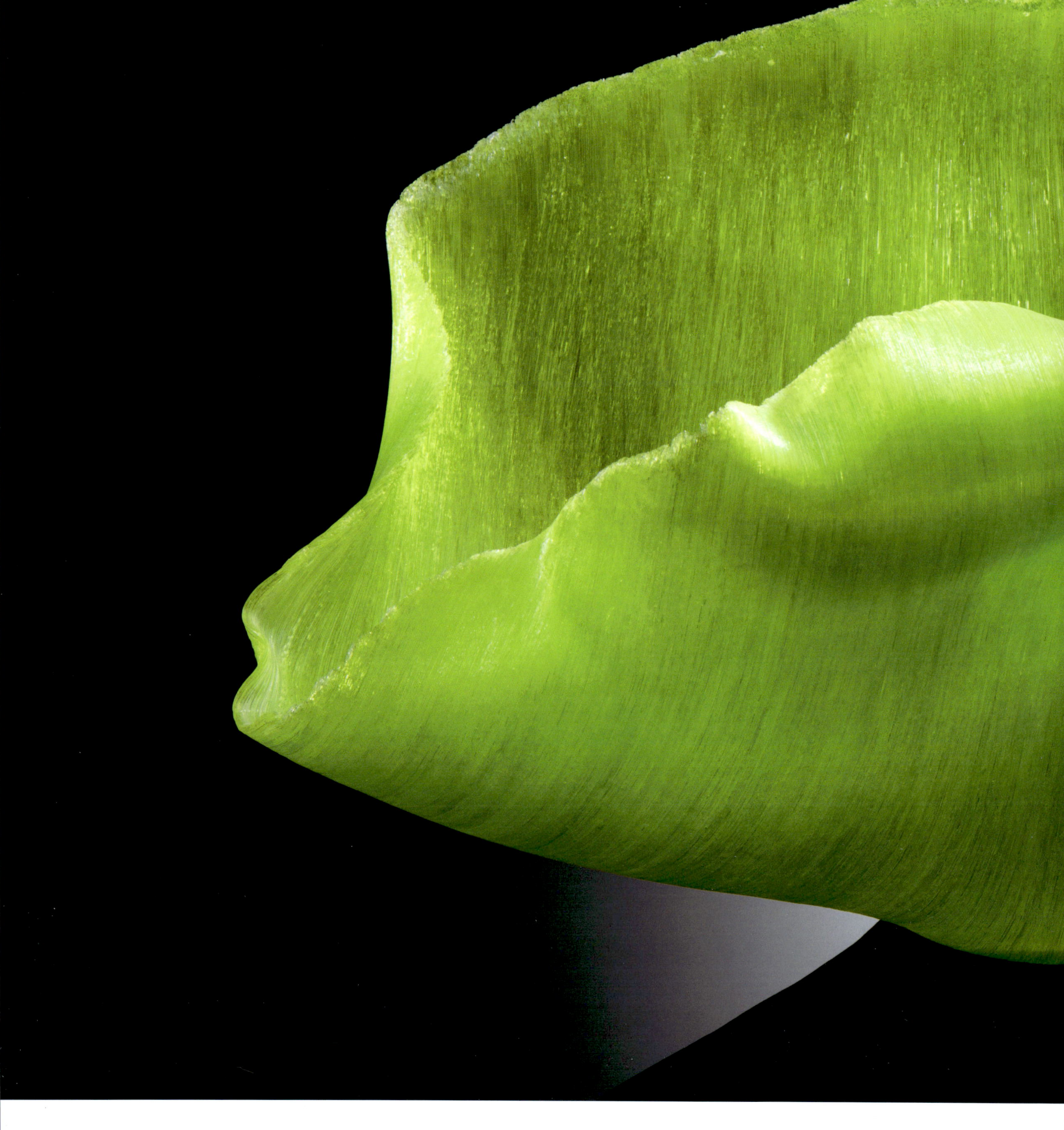

142   Toots Zynsky   AMERICAN, BORN 1951   *Libellula Mizimah*   2000
FUSED AND KILN-FORMED FILETS DE VERRE (GLASS THREADS)   11½ × 23⅜ × 10 INCHES   L2017.137

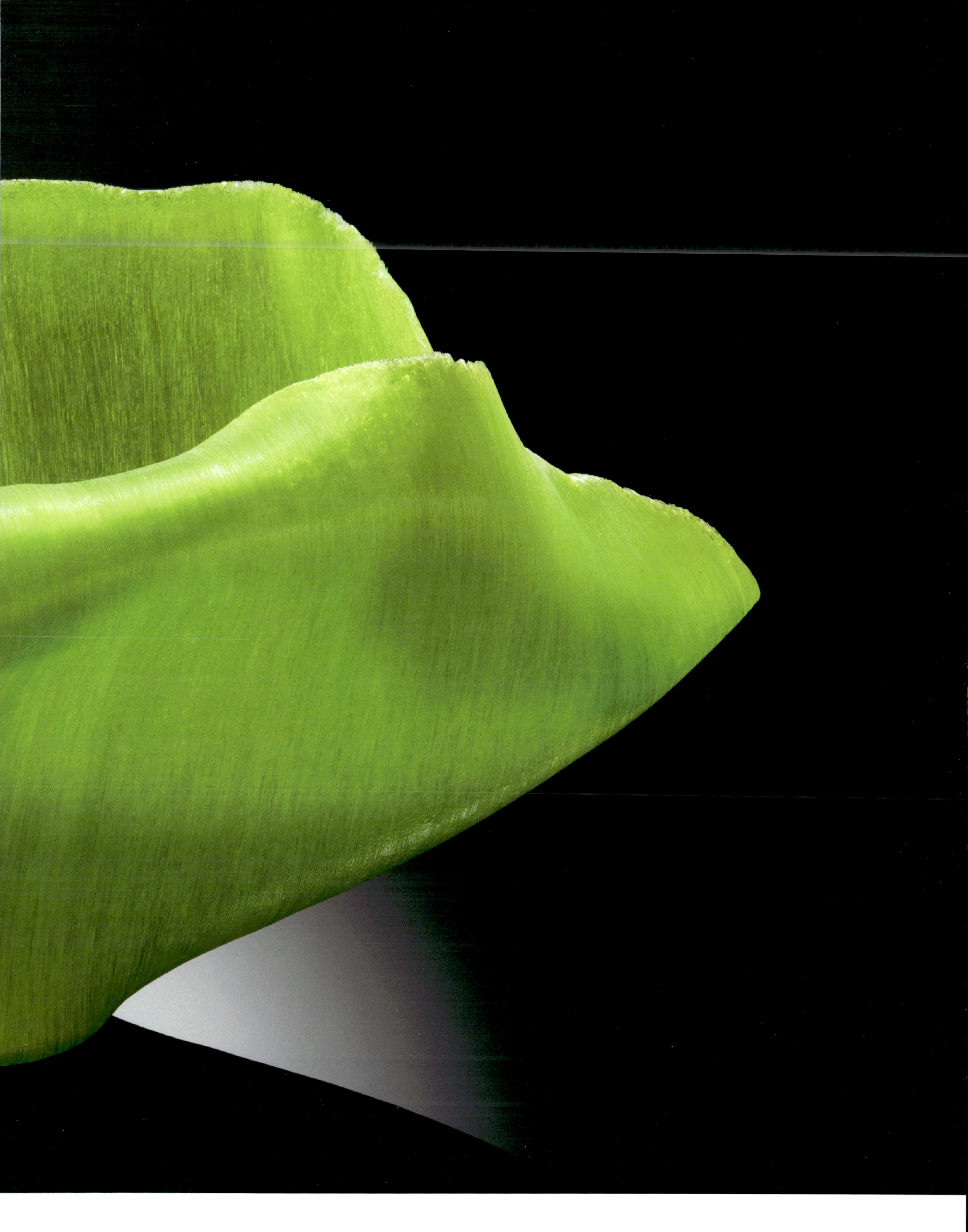